S0-DGG-761

**WITHDRAWN**
UTSA LIBRARIES

*China: Management of a Revolutionary Society*

*Studies in*
*Chinese Government and Politics*

1. CHINESE COMMUNIST POLITICS IN ACTION
Edited by A. Doak Barnett

2. CHINA: MANAGEMENT OF A REVOLUTIONARY SOCIETY
Edited by John M. H. Lindbeck

*Sponsored by the Subcommittee on*
*Chinese Government and Politics*
*of the Joint Committee*
*on Contemporary China of the*
*American Council of Learned Societies*
*and the Social Science Research Council*

MEMBERS OF THE SUBCOMMITTEE

Robert A. Scalapino, *Chairman*

A. Doak Barnett                  John M. H. Lindbeck
John W. Lewis                    George E. Taylor


MEMBERS OF THE JOINT COMMITTEE, 1969–70

John M. H. Lindbeck, *Chairman*

Albert Feuerwerker               Frederick W. Mote
Walter Galenson                  George E. Taylor
Chalmers Johnson                 Ezra F. Vogel
             Bryce Wood, *staff*

# China: Management of a Revolutionary Society

EDITED BY JOHN M. H. LINDBECK

## CONTRIBUTORS

LUCIAN W. PYE

CHALMERS JOHNSON

MICHEL C. OKSENBERG

FREDERICK C. TEIWES

PETER SCHRAN

VICTOR H. LI

DONALD J. MUNRO

DONALD W. KLEIN

ELLIS JOFFE

GABRIEL A. ALMOND

UNIVERSITY OF WASHINGTON PRESS

SEATTLE & LONDON

Copyright © 1971 by the University of Washington Press
Library of Congress Catalog Card Number 76-146540
Printed in the United States of America

# John M. H. Lindbeck

## July 8, 1915–January 9, 1971

*John Lindbeck was a rare man. All of us—and many of our readers—are indebted to him in very specific measure: for the lives we lead, the research we do, the many fine colleagues we have.*

*His sudden passing etches this on our minds, for John unselfishly devoted himself to serving the worldwide field of contemporary China studies. He unstintingly advanced a broad range of innovative scholarly projects which promised to increase our understanding of China or to improve Sino-American relations. He transformed many dreams into reality.*

*But no vita can possibly convey his special human qualities. His warmth, gentleness, and integrity brought forth the best in those with whom he worked. In this age of incivility, John always displayed patience, dignity, and propriety, and thereby achieved reconciliation and understanding among men. He was a unique man at a unique time, and his legacy is in those whom he touched.*

THE AUTHORS
ROBERT A. SCALAPINO
*Chairman of the Subcommittee on
Chinese Government and Politics*

*JOHN M. H. LINDBECK*

# Introduction

Contemporary China is the subject; the topic is government; the theme is change. Taken together, the nine studies in this volume present an overview of the political system fashioned by China's Communist leaders since 1949. Each addresses itself to questions, issues, or systems that are national rather than local in scope. They concern values, priorities, structures, developmental programs, and processes that have the attention and demand the decisions of the organizers and managers of power at the center. In so far as behavior and values are politically accessible, the realms of decision, organization, and action discussed in these papers affect, in large measure, all Chinese within the People's Republic. Each paper treats of political processes, structures, and trends in large aggregate or national terms.

This volume, however, is not a text on Chinese government, administration, and politics. Rather it is the product of the thought and current research of nine scholars working on related but separate aspects of the Chinese political system who participated during the summer of 1969 in a Conference on Government in China: The Management of a Revolutionary Society. This conference, like its predecessor on the Microsocietal Study of the Chinese Political System, held in the summer of 1967,[1] was organized to enable a growing but scattered group of social scientists studying topics related to the Chinese polit-

[1] Papers from this conference were published in A. Doak Barnett (ed.), *Chinese Communist Politics in Action* (Seattle: University of Washington Press, 1969).

vii

ical system to share and test their work with knowledgeable colleagues. The work presented at the conference, much of it based on new research and reflecting new analysis, clearly is of value to many others concerned with comparative politics and China. Some of the conference papers, therefore, are being made available here. Each paper was discussed at the conference, and many of the authors cut and revised extensively on the basis of suggestions and comments by discussants and participants.

The selection of papers drawn from this conference for publication is intended to highlight some but not all of the major features of Chinese political development during the past two decades. This volume, for example, contains no case studies on regional or local politics. Although the Communist Party in its organization, ideology, and behavior necessarily shadows and infuses the discussion and analysis presented in each paper, no paper was commissioned on the Party as such. This dimension of the Chinese political universe had already been directly probed at a conference on the Chinese Communist Party held at Ditchley Park in England in July of 1968.[2] Many other significant features of Chinese politics also are untouched, either for lack of space or because they have been largely neglected. The role of science and technology, social welfare programs and the institutions that have been created to service them, environmental and ecological problems, public health strategies, population policies, and many others were not or could not be included.

The Great Proletarian Cultural Revolution was in full tilt at the time the papers were being written and the conference held. The fate of the political structures and processes crafted and evolved over two decades of Communist control appeared uncertain. To some of the conference participants it seemed that a new revolutionary upheaval in China was forcing them to be political historians, looking back at a vanishing system. Another constitution and a political order apparently were being added to the growing heap of China's abortive efforts to create a modern system of government. Each author, in the end, decided for himself how he wished to handle the impact of the Cultural Revolution on his topic.

Should some of these papers prove to be history, the volume of data they cover and the quality of interpretation they present nonetheless

---

[2] For papers presented at Ditchley Park see John Wilson Lewis (ed.), *Party Leadership and Revolutionary Power in China* (Cambridge, Eng.: Cambridge University Press, 1970).

provide a basis for understanding the future and stand as a record of essential features of the political cartography, basic issues, and cultural predilections that mark this era in China's development. Even more, the Chinese creation of a system of management that terminated the chaos of the pre-1949 period and mobilized and directed one-fifth of the world's people in productive and cooperative activities for a significant segment of time within a new framework of social, economic, and political behavior and control is in itself an achievement on the order monumentally displayed by some dynastic systems in pre-modern China. Because the Chinese experience is now part of world experience, this stage, should it prove to be that in her political development, has more than sinological implications.

This volume is divided into five parts. Part V presents an essay on China and comparative politics that provides additional testimony to the collapse of the parochial American and European illusion that "the history of the world is the history of Europe and its cultural offshoots; that Western experience is the sum total of human experience; that Western interpretations of that experience are sufficient, if not exhaustive; and that the resulting value systems embrace everything that matters." [3] The concluding essay was written after the conference by Gabriel Almond of Stanford University, who deftly raised questions and pushed topics beyond their intended limits in the role of an external, non-China-specialist critic. He points to the need, on every scientific count, of pressing ahead to understand the formal and informal ways in which values, power, developmental processes, and varieties of institutions in China and elsewhere create the political environments in which we now work out our national and international destinies. China's experience, behavior, and prospects already shape ours—directly and indirectly, perceived and unperceived.

The nine specialist papers are divided into four parts. Part I deals with problems of authority, the relation of the polity to society. Both Lucian W. Pye and Chalmers Johnson see the interplay of changing factors that relate Mao to the people. To win power and to accommodate to the shifting political culture of post-dynastic and revolutionary Chinese, China's political leaders have had to play on old and new feelings and expectations. It is clear that a society in transition presents a combination of opportunities and hazards to those who must

[3] *Non-Western Studies in the Liberal Arts College: A Report of the Commission on International Understanding* (Washington, D.C.: Association of American Colleges, 1964), p. 11.

at once both lead and manage. In this situation, real lines of influence and power are masked, but the people see and feel the imperative drive of the power holders to create a new order in the use of symbols and political and coercive assets that often are crude and harsh in their uncertain search for legitimacy.

In Part II, dealing with the two upper tiers of national and provincial management, Michel Oksenberg provides an interpretive and analytical overview of policy making under Mao from 1949 to 1968 at the highest levels of political concern. His portrayal of the style and instrumentation of national politics reflects the intersecting of personalities, Chinese environment, and organizational structures. Frederick Teiwes in his study of provincial politics brings together more data than has appeared elsewhere in order to locate some of the basic issues and political habits of those who work under Peking to manage, in defined territories, the people of China. Teiwes provides us with another large step forward in the still neglected study of provincial government and politics in China.

In Part III the focus is on the strategies and problems of China's leaders in trying to restructure Chinese society. Peter Schran deals with the economy by delineating Peking's basic goals and the broad approaches the center has taken at different times to achieve them. Victor H. Li relates the development of the legal system to shifts in perspective and pressures that changing conditions brought into play. Finally, Donald J. Munro perceptively explores the educational system through which the next generation is processed. The promises it holds are blunted by poverty of resources and disagreement or uncertainty about final ends and intermediate strategies, by the impossibility of converting everyone into both "reds" and "experts" at once.

The management of foreign affairs by Donald Klein and the role of the Chinese Army in the pre-Cultural Revolution period by Ellis Joffe are covered in Part IV, which relates to China and the outside world. In both these spheres, China's leaders appear to have given domestic politics primacy. Lin Piao refashioned the army not to deal with foreign threats but to provide Mao and himself with a secure instrument to dominate China's political processes. The army's role was first to foil and then to achieve the destruction of his and Mao's enemies. The reinfusion of politics in the army was at the expense of professionalism, but to what extent is not certain. In any case, no foreign enemy has been tempted to test the professionalism of Lin's politicized army. At the same time Mao and Lin have avoided provocations that might put the army's military, rather than political, capabilities to a test. Klein's paper gives us the broad spectrum of channels and mechanisms that China uses in handling international transactions, official and quasi-official. Once again, the pressing problems of domestic politics rather than the maximal use of the nation's assets to influence other countries or to exploit outside resources for domestic development have turned a high proportion of China's energies inward rather than outward.

Political science has now begun to accommodate the Chinese experience. In the course of ten years a new generation of specialists on China has emerged, scholars who are as deeply involved with the revolution in political science as with the Chinese revolution. Happily, the new political science is not viewed as a self-contained field, but is open to methods, concepts, and data drawn from many other academic disciplines. Several of these studies are as interesting for their use of political science concepts, methods, and data as for their analysis of China.

On the other hand, the contribution of political science to the understanding of China is demonstrated, even at this early stage, in the papers presented here. The new perspectives and questions the authors raise about China set an exciting agenda for further thought and research.

# Contents

## PART IV. CHINA AND THE WORLD: THE SUBORDINATION OF FOREIGN AFFAIRS TO DOMESTIC POLITICS

## PART V. CHINA AND COMPARATIVE POLITICS

# ABBREVIATIONS USED IN NOTES

| | |
|---|---|
| *CB* | *Current Background* |
| *CFJP* | *Chieh-fang jih-pao* (Liberation Daily) |
| *CKCN* | *Chung-kuo ch'ing-nien* (Chinese Youth) |
| *CKCNP* | *Chung-kuo ch'ing-nien pao* (Chinese Youth News) |
| *CQ* | *The China Quarterly* |
| *ECMM* | *Extracts from China Mainland Magazines* |
| *JMJP* | *Jen-min jih-pao* (People's Daily) |
| *JPRS* | *Joint Publications Research Service* |
| *KJJP* | *Kung-jen jih-pao* (Workers' Daily) |
| *NFJP* | *Nan-fang jih-pao* (Southern Daily) |
| NCNA | New China News Agency |
| *SCMM* | *Selections from China Mainland Magazines* |
| *SCMP* | *Survey of the China Mainland Press* |
| *TKP* | *Ta kung pao* (Impartial Daily) |
| URI | Union Research Institute |

# PART I

*Authority and the Masses*

🏵🏵🏵🏵🏵🏵🏵🏵🏵🏵🏵🏵🏵🏵🏵🏵🏵🏵🏵🏵🏵🏵🏵🏵🏵🏵

### LUCIAN W. PYE

# Mass Participation in Communist China: Its Limitations and the Continuity of Culture

Of all the ways of characterizing the first decade and a half of the Chinese Communist regime the one that may be most likely to elicit consensus among the widest range of observers is to stress Peking's efforts at mobilizing mass activities and participation. From the beginning of their rule the Communists have had a constant ambition to reach the people and to mobilize their energies. From massive parades and demonstrations down the great avenue of Chang An Ta Chieh to the nationwide proliferation of mass organizations and the pronouncement of the doctrine of the mass line, the Chinese apparently have placed an absolute value on mass participation. And in the estimation of some observers, Mao's goal in the Cultural Revolution has been to establish an even more sublime form of popular participation in revolution and national development.

Yet, the accumulative consequences of these years of exhausting mobilization and frantic activity may be a significant decline in popular participation and an increase in the isolation of the leadership in the years ahead. The conclusion of this analysis, at least, is that the Chinese Communists, building on some fundamental characterological and structural traits of the Chinese people and their society, rode a tide of popular need for collective involvement which is now receding, and that possibly the regime has lost its institutional capabilities for mobilizing the Chinese people.

During the first decade of Communist rule many observers saw the ultimate genius of Peking's leaders to be their startling ability to organize all manner of mass groups.[1] Instead of concentrating only on their Leninist-elitist party organization, the Chinese vigorously deployed their basic "organizational weapon" to create a variety of other organizations for mobilizing the great multitudes of China. Impressive as the Chinese organizing abilities have been, with the Great Leap and the Cultural Revolution, the Maoist faith in the potency of participation finally exceeded the bounds of effective mass organization.

At present, there is little new that can be added to our collective understanding of the institutions for participation in Communist China. In the work of James R. Townsend on the doctrine and practices of political participation,[2] of A. Doak Barnett on control and bureaucratic organizations,[3] and of Ezra Vogel on local urban practices,[4] we have a fairly complete picture of the institutions of participation. In addition, there is a formidable array of scholars—including Chalmers Johnson, John W. Lewis, Franz Schurmann, and many others—who have enriched our understanding of the relationship of theory and practice with respect to leadership and organization.[5]

There are, however, three areas of inquiry which might now be appropriately examined. First, there is still a need to ask questions about the relationships between traditional forms of social participation and the state of Chinese society just before the arrival of communism, and about the relationship between these conditions and the remarkable successes of the Communists in mobilizing mass participation. Second, in the light of the Cultural Revolution, it may be useful now to speculate on the value for Chinese development of Maoist forms of mass participation and the likely future of such forms once their institu-

[1] For a description of the early successes of the Communists in building mass organizations see: A. Doak Barnett, "Mass Political Organizations in Communist China," *Annals of the American Academy of Political and Social Science,* 277 (September, 1951), 76–88; Franz Schurmann, "Organization and Response in Communist China," *Annals of the American Academy of Political and Social Science,* 321 (January, 1959), 51–61; Richard L. Walker, *China under Communism: The First Five Years* (New Haven, Conn.: Yale University Press, 1955).

[2] James R. Townsend, *Political Participation in Communist China* (Berkeley and Los Angeles: University of California Press, 1967).

[3] A. Doak Barnett, *Cadres, Bureaucracy, and Political Power in Communist China* (New York: Columbia University Press, 1967).

[4] Ezra Vogel, *Canton under Communism, 1944–1968* (Cambridge, Mass.: Harvard University Press, 1969).

[5] Chalmers A. Johnson, *Peasant Nationalism and Communist Power* (Stanford, Calif.: Stanford University Press, 1962); John W. Lewis, *Leadership in Communist China* (Ithaca, N.Y.: Cornell University Press, 1963); Franz Schurmann, *Ideology and Organization in Communist China* (Berkeley and Los Angeles: University of California Press, 1966).

tional bases have been eliminated with the destruction of the mass organizations which were once so important. Third, with respect to both of these first two question areas our speculations may be enriched by trying to understand better the subjective meaning and the emotional significance of social and political participation in Chinese culture.

These, at least, are the directions in which I feel somewhat less intimidated in suggesting the possibility of useful added work being done on a topic which has already been so well covered by so much talent. In so indicating at the outset some of the ground to be covered in this chapter, we should probably also state here that, as a result of looking in these directions, our conclusion is a hypothesis which holds that although there have been revolutionary but still uninstitutionalized changes in the structures of participation, the basic style and emotional content of individual behavior in a group context has remained remarkably constant in Chinese culture in spite of communism. Consequently, there may be surprisingly few enduring effects from all the years of mass participation in Communist China if the organizational basis for such participation is eliminated in the current phase of Maoism.[6]

In part, what we shall be saying is that the Chinese have always had a significantly high level of social participation, that the identity and behavior of the individual Chinese have always been shaped above all by his sense of belonging to and having a participatory role in some social grouping, and that the basic style of Chinese interpersonal relationships has always supported a pervasive concept of participation and a denial of the legitimacy of autonomy or isolation. With communism, the foci of participation have shifted from more immediate, localized, and ascriptive groupings to larger and slightly more impersonal ones. It is, however, difficult to say that with communism participation has become more "political" than were the earlier forms. The mere fact that government determines the arena for participation and introduces apparently "political" slogans does not make the "participation" either political or so different from the past situation. Indeed, this is why this form of mobilization, which leaves the individual

---

[6] Although it is still too early to say what the post-Cultural Revolution period will be like, we have assumed for this analysis that the Maoists will succeed in more or less permanently destroying the organizational or administrative linkages between the leaders and the masses, and that they will continue to emphasize the need for a form of spiritual and revolutionary communion between leaders and followers even as they rely more heavily upon the army for administration.

still merely a subject and not a citizen, seems in the last analysis to be inadequate as a means of making a truly integrated modern polity for Chinese society.

## COMMUNITY AND GOVERNMENT IN CONFUCIAN CHINA

Descriptions of traditional China generally tend to reinforce each other and to accentuate many of the same themes. Some interpretations stress the formal characteristics of Confucianism and the ideals of mandarin rule, while others emphasize the role of the gentry and the pervasive powers of family control and informal associations. Specialists have argued intensely about marginal differences in such matters as the degree to which the examination system provided social mobility and honest recognition of talent, and the extent to which China was or was not susceptible to centralized rule.[7]

In characterizing Chinese society, scholars have frequently noted the strange lack of explicit linkages between society and government in a system that was otherwise elaborately structured. This fundamental quality of traditional China has been noted in a variety of ways. Many authors have written of the authoritarian bases of traditional China, others have stressed its more benevolent but still despotic qualities, still others have made harsher judgments, and some have spoken of "oriental despotism." For our purposes, the vital point is that even though the Chinese recognized a great array of legal, quasi-illegal, and illegal groups and associations to which citizens might belong, there was a fundamental denial that any such group should engage in open political competition in order to make claims on the

[7] Indeed, near unanimity of general interpretation might be possible if it were not for differences along a continuum between those who constantly strive to make the Chinese essentially similar to Westerners and those who appreciate differences. At the one extreme are the China specialists who, after years of exploring Chinese society, feel compelled to deny its exotic dimensions by insisting that many Chinese practices, both traditional and Communist, have their equivalence in the West, and, therefore, nothing is really all that different. On the other hand, scholars such as John K. Fairbank and the late Joseph Levenson have shown no sign of shame or guilt in stating unequivocally that Chinese civilization is not Western civilization, and that no matter how much the West may fail to live up to its ideals this does not make Chinese into Westerners. (Among those who would minimize all suggestions of differences there is a strange belief that whatever differences may seem to exist at the level of professed ideals, or "rhetoric," as they like to say, they tend to be less significant at the level of actual practices; while on the other hand it is noteworthy that those who have had long experiences living with the Chinese tend to see differences as greater at the level of behavior.)

These remarks and the reminder that no true Confucian scholars would have taken offense at the suggestion that Chinese society was elitist in orientation and that in Chinese politics there should be no confusion over the roles of rulers and subjects, are necessary preambles to any observations about the distinctive characteristics of traditional China.

governmental system. The striking fact is that the Chinese possessed a great variety of groups and institutions that resembled what we might today call voluntary and involuntary associations; but they never developed processes that resembled interest group politics in any form, and they never accepted the notion that government should be responsive to the interplay of social, economic, and political forces.

Traditionally, Chinese of any degree of status belonged at a minimum to a family or clan association. These were not just formal groups in which one's role and status were determined entirely by birth, age, and sex; for in the clan associations, in particular, there were mechanisms for decision making, some competition for leadership, and a constant play of politics as conflicts were mediated, influence sought, and discipline maintained.[8] Thus, membership in even an involuntary association generated a sense of participation and an awareness of roles and of qualities of performance.

In addition, there were well-established voluntary associations which represented trades and professions, geographic locations, and particularly provincial ties and interests, and, finally, the religious, fraternal, and ideological groups that made up the world of the secret societies.[9] In times of peace and normal economic activities the various trade guilds were active in all the urban commercial centers, and all the middle-sized and large cities had *hui-kuan* or *"Landsmann* halls" where people originally from the same provinces and regions could meet and gain a sense of collective security. Also strong in normal times—but even stronger during periods of civil disorders—were the secret societies which protected the interests and personal security of many at all levels of the social order.

The mere existence of these private, nongovernmental organizations of both a voluntary and nonvoluntary nature would suggest that politics in traditional China should have followed the principles elaborated in various contemporary theories about group interactions and opinion

[8] For discussions of the traditional family and clan associations see: Marion J. Levy, *The Family Revolution in Modern China* (Cambridge, Mass.: Harvard University Press, 1949); Martin C. Yang, *A Chinese Village* (New York: Columbia University Press, 1945); Olga Lang, *Chinese Family and Society* (New Haven, Conn.: Yale University Press, 1946); Francis L. K. Hsu, *Under the Ancestors' Shadow* (New York: Columbia University Press, 1948); C. K. Yang, *The Chinese Family in the Communist Revolution* (Cambridge, Mass.: The M.I.T. Press, 1959); Yueh-hwa Lin, *The Golden Wing* (New York: Oxford University Press, 1947).

[9] These associations have not been well studied for the obvious reason that it has not been easy to obtain accurate information. See: Hosea Ballou Morse, *The Guilds of China* (London: Longmans Green, 1909); Sidney D. Gamble and John Stewart Burgess, *Peking: A Social Survey* (New York: Doran, 1921); John S. Burgess, *The Guilds of Peking* (New York: Columbia University Press, 1928).

formation. There are, for example, three rather sophisticated theories —pressure group politics, mass politics, and cross-pressure politics— which appear to be applicable to the conditions of traditional China, but are not. First, according to the pressure group theorists, all the various groups and associations in traditional China should have been vigorously competing over the allocation of scarce resources and values as they battled over who should get what, when, and how.[10] Yet, in spite of the fact that on objective grounds it would appear that the various associations did represent conflicting economic interests, they did not in fact behave like pressure groups. Their objectives were not to make demands or to assert their claims on the political or governmental system. Even though they represented substantial potential political power, they always behaved like aggregates of subjects and never like organizations of citizens.

Second, according to the theories of mass politics, the organizations of traditional China should have been active mediators between rulers and ruled.[11] To some degree the organizations did perform such a function, but they served mainly as communicators of government messages to their membership and rarely acted as the voice of their constituencies. Yet, to the extent that such organizations did serve as mediating agents between the mandarin bureaucracy and the general population, they were acting illegitimately according to Chinese standards of politics. The emperor, his court, and his officials were presumably adequate for the tasks of government, and in neither formal doctrine nor informal practice did officials feel that they should rely upon private associations or mediators to back their rule. It is true that in giving order and structure to the social participation of significant segments of the population, these associations did ease the problem of government. But as a means of providing informal support for the maintenance of the political system, the traditional Chinese family and the Confucian-pattern social life were far more fundamental than were the various associations. And in any case, this essentially supportive spirit is not the pattern of relationship between informal groups and ruling elites described in "mass politics" theories that reflect the realities of Western societies.

[10] For a discussion of group theory see: Arthur Bentley, *The Process of Government* (San Antonio, Tex.: Principia Press of Trinity University, 1949); E. Pendleton Herring, *Group Representation Before Congress* (Baltimore: Johns Hopkins University Press, 1929); David Truman, *The Governmental Process* (New York: Alfred A. Knopf, 1951).

[11] For a discussion of mass politics theory see: William Kornhauser, *The Politics of Mass Society* (Glencoe, Ill.: The Free Press, 1959); Robert A. Nisbet, *The Quest for Community* (New York: Oxford University Press, 1953).

Third, the theories of cross-pressure politics, which were developed to explain the relationship of organizational membership and political stability in modern industrial societies, also fail to account for traditional Chinese practices. According to this approach, multiple, overlapping memberships in organizations prevent the polarization of political conflict; conversely, when people belong to only a single organization, each representing a way of life or a general belief system, conflicts tend to become more acute. The logic of the theory is that when people belong to many organizations, as in the United States, they are constantly exposed in different contexts to people with opposing political views, and hence they feel the need to reduce their sense of political competitiveness. On the other hand, when there is little overlapping of memberships and when people are exposed to others of like views in the organizations to which they belong, the tendency is for attitudes and views to be constantly reinforced within each organization and for political competitiveness between groups to be intensified.[12]

The theory makes sense logically, but it falls apart when applied to traditional China. In the Chinese situation there was little multiple or overlapping membership; people belonged to groups that gave them total orientations. Thus, according to the theory, competition should have been intense and politics highly polarized. Instead, the Chinese had a high level of consensus, little competition, and little tension among associations or between the associations and government.

Our purpose in juxtaposing these contemporary theories with the evidence from traditional China is to dramatize the degree to which the imperial governmental system dominated the socially and economically based associations with the result that a highly participant society had a subject, and not a citizen, political culture. The power of the bureaucratic tradition, the pervasiveness of the Confucian ethic, the mystique of the divinity of the emperor, and the assumption that politics should be left to the spiritual and intellectual worthies of the empire all conspired to make a socially vigorous people politically docile. For any of the various groups and associations to have openly asserted claims on the system would have been tantamount to initiating a revolt against all the powers of entrenched tradition. Leaders of voluntary associations were hesitant to appear, in any manner what-

[12] For an excellent analysis of cross-pressure theories see: Sidney Verba, "Organizational Membership and Democratic Consensus," *The Journal of Politics,* XXVII (August, 1965), 467–97. See also, Bernard C. Hennessy, *Public Opinion* (Belmont, Calif.: Wadsworth Publishing Co., 1965).

soever, to be challenging authority, and to the extent that they did make any claims on governmental powers, they were always careful to suggest that they were seeking personal and limited favors that could only illuminate the power of the officials who might grant them; they never suggested that as subjects they had any rights whatsoever.

It was not, however, just the structural and ideological qualities of traditional China that prevented social and economic participation from producing political demands. There were also the attitudes and the expectations of the individual Chinese as they became members of such associations. As we have already suggested, participation in social groupings was vital to the Chinese sense of individual identity. Ping-ti Ho has noted the deep social importance for the Chinese of their

. . . neighborhood and village organizations, guilds, and various *Landsmann* groups, which first appeared in early Ming and became increasingly common in all parts of China in Ch'ing times. While all these organizations transcend biological ties, they have nevertheless offered their members a face-to-face intimacy that usually characterizes primary social associations. Supplementing the family and the clan, they have provided the Chinese with a much-needed sense of belonging, helped them to settle disputes between individuals, families, and occupations, and performed an important function of educating them on the art of getting along with their fellowmen and of understanding and satisfying each other's emotional and psychological needs.[13]

In short, belonging to an organization and experiencing interactions with the other members were the prime purposes of membership for the individual. People identified with particular groups, not because they were concerned with the ultimate policies or programs of the group or because they saw the group as having power in relationship to other groups, but because it was in some fashion meaningful for their identities to be associated with a group.

It might not be quite proper to call such groups "voluntary" associations because the Chinese probably did not feel that they could casually choose which one to join. An individual's social identity, his general status, the place his family occupied in the community, and his occupation were powerful factors that determined the particular group to which he belonged. The very importance of these associations in shaping the individual's social identity mitigated against

[13] Ping-ti Ho, "Salient Aspects of China's Heritage," in Ping-ti Ho and Tang Tsou (eds.), *China's Heritage and the Communist Political System* (Chicago: University of Chicago Press, 1968), I, 32.

multiple membership. If an individual truly took seriously the meaning that went with belonging to an association, he would have compromised his integrity by seeking identification with more than one group. This intensity of commitment meant that identification with an otherwise voluntary association took on the psychological and behavioral characteristics connected in other cultures with involuntary associations. Membership in secret societies or guilds, neighborhood associations, and *Landsmann* groups was essentially similar to membership in clan and family groups. They were lifelong commitments that became integral to the individual's life pattern.

At the same time it was the very depth and intensity of such identifications that apparently inhibited competition among the associations. With voluntary associations hardly distinguishable from involuntary ones, groups tended to react toward each other as families or clans react—each looked after its own and was prepared to tolerate the existence of the others. Or if a clash were unavoidable, it generally took the form of a direct feud between the two parties involved and not the form of open competition for influencing governmental policies associated with interest group politics. Thus, the intensity with which individuals focused inward and concentrated on intra-group relations reduced their sensitivity to potential issues of inter-group relations.

The ideological emphasis in both Confucianism and Taoism on the importance of face-to-face relationships and the discounting of more distant and abstract matters also contributed to the intensity of intra-group competition. In building his own sense of identity out of his social relationships, the individual began from his own ego and then followed the web of his direct personal relationships with those about him with whom he had any recognizable connections. He did not, therefore, identify himself with others on the basis of highly abstract or ideological definitions of mutual interest or purpose, and, thus, he did not put himself in conflict with others merely because they held to different abstract principles.

On the basis of this distinctive mixture of authoritarian institutions, a humanistic but also elitist ideology, and a powerful socializing process that stresses group identity, it was possible for the Chinese to be intensely active participants in some collective activities, to be extremely sensitive to the manner of interpersonal power relationships, and to be very conscious of issues of self-interest, personal security, and a sense of belonging, without, however, developing in the larger context a sense of political efficacy. In terms of the struc-

turing of the basic institutions of the society, the content of the dominant ideologies, and the dynamics of individual identification with
social and economic associations, the traditional Chinese pattern contributed to the dual (and to the Western mind rather contradictory)
objectives of expanding social participation while encouraging a passive attitude toward government.

These were the traditions and cultural attitudes that provided the
historic background for a similiar pattern of high level participation
in, but little public demand on, policies under the Communists in
China. Before we can turn to the contemporary scene we must, however, first examine the conditions that affected political and social
participation in modern China just prior to the advent of communism.

## THE DISRUPTIONS OF MODERNIZATION

If this in general terms was the pattern of social participation in
traditional China, then the question arises as to why China did not
develop along the lines of a more competitive political system when
the restraining influences of the imperial-bureaucratic order were removed. Why did the various informal associations not come into their
own and become the bases for competing power groups, each seeking
to make its claims on Chinese society? Why, given the high level of
social participation in traditional China, did the process of erosion
of higher and more repressive authorities not result in the Chinese
social activists readily becoming citizens and not merely subjects? To
some degree such a process did take place as students and intellectuals
made demands on government after the May 4 movement began.[14]
Also, the pattern of warlord struggles did introduce a clumsy form of
political competition. In the main, however, the Chinese citizens
turned inward toward their basic associations in the face of rising general insecurity, and the result was a more conservative and undemand-
ing approach to politics. Confusion about the state of national political
development made people concentrate more than ever upon their immediate concerns.

Structurally, the elimination of the imperial system was soon followed by even more repressive patterns of localized military rule.
Thus, the end of bureaucratic and mandarin domination did not really
open the way to more competitive group politics. Individuals, no
matter how they were banded together, could scarcely hope to in-

[14] Chow Tse-tsung, *The May Fourth Movement: Intellectual Revolution in Modern
China* (Cambridge, Mass.: Harvard University Press, 1960).

fluence the course of national development by pressing forward their particular interests. For one thing, there was no national arena or national political system toward which groups could make their claims in the hope of receiving policy benefits. China lacked a basic system of national political communications and thus lacked national integration. The model of input demands and output policies simply did not apply to the China of the warlord period.

On the other hand, the period did see a steady increase in various forms of "participation" and political awareness. Historically, the array of voluntary associations of traditional China, while passive toward formal government, did serve a fundamental political purpose in support of that system in that they provided a solid basis of disciplined and ordered social participation which relieved strains and stresses on the formal government. The mass of the Chinese were caught up in family, village, neighborhood groupings, and other associations which gave order to their lives, scope for social interactions, and a basic sense of social belonging, so that they did not have to make social and psychological demands on the formal structure of government. So long as people could find their social security and their basic sense of identification in the context of these more immediate sets of relationships they did not have to expect much of government itself.[15]

By the 1920's, however, there were increasing numbers of Chinese who were dissatisfied with the old patterns of social arrangements and voluntary associations. They still had a compelling need to find their sense of security in a social context, but they also saw their national politics as hopeless. Dissatisfaction was particularly acute with the small class of emerging intelligentsia who had a broader sense of social and political awareness but who did not analytically understand the nature of transitional China. They could, therefore, only articulate their frustrations over the degree to which China failed to meet their aspirations for a modern society and a modern nation. At the same time, increasing numbers of young Chinese, in particular, began to speak the language of a responsive, integrated form of politics in which government should seek to meet the articulated demands of the citizenry.

In the realities of Chinese politics, however, the age-old gap remained between society and government. Even the more fragmented

[15] For the orderliness of traditional Chinese social life and its divorcement from government, see: Francis L. K. Hsu, *Clan, Caste and Club* (Princeton, N.J.: D. Van Nostrand, 1963); H. T. Fei, *Peasant Life in China* (London: Routledge and Kegan Paul, 1939).

and localized structures of government proved remarkably insensitive
to forces in the society at large. It is true that local warlords needed
funds and made local bargains; accommodations were struck with
those in command of resources; but those who commanded the formal
structures of government always had the upper hand, and nobody
was confused as to where power lay. This was possible because what
passed for formal government was based on the overwhelming advantages of military force. The warlord period revealed the extent to
which all Chinese governments have rested upon a peculiarly intimate
tie between military power and civil authority. In spite of its ideological dressing, the Confucian imperial system that went before was ultimately dependent upon military power. As Ho has pointed out:

> . . . the prevailing of the civilian ideal in traditional Chinese government ad-
> ministration should not blind us to the hard fact that every dynasty was founded
> on military strength or by the transference of military power. . . . From the
> dawning of the first empire in 221 B.C. to the founding of the People's Republic
> of China in 1949 there has not been a single exception. . . . In contrast to the
> weakness of European monarchies which aided the rise of democracy, the persistent
> historical fact is that the Chinese state has always derived its ultimate power
> from the army, and this has largely predetermined its authoritarian character.[16]

And, of course, both the Nationalists and the Communists have
continued the tradition of combining the military with domestic rule
in a way that provides an ultimate check upon the influence of popular
participation upon government. But to speak of this takes us ahead
of our story. Returning to the warlord era, we note that the pattern
of modernization of China maintained the basic division between government and society, but with considerably increased tensions. Although government's authority was eroded, the government did not
become more responsive to domestic pressures. As for the people
themselves, many clung more strongly than ever to their traditional
associations, while others sought new groupings or became free float-
ing. Everyone sensed a decline in efficacy and a rise in insecurity. At
the same time, political events became even more disruptive of personal lives, so that everyone had to become more concerned with
trying to understand the course of public affairs.

Thus, for rulers and population alike the changes that came with
modernization increased the feelings of insecurity, which intensified

---

[16] Ho, "Salient Aspects of China's Heritage," pp. 15–16.

frustration and caused almost universal awareness of the individual's inability to be efficacious. At the same time a new mood emerged with a craving for a unity of government and society that could produce national power, the restoration of authority, and the comforts of order and predictability in public affairs.

## WAR AND PARTICIPATION

The great trauma of the Japanese War taught the Chinese that political events could shatter their private lives and that neither government nor their historic associations could offer them security. Millions of Chinese were completely uprooted and forced to replan their lives because of political events beyond their control. It has been estimated that during the years of fighting nearly twenty million Chinese left their homes and became essentially political refugees; in many cases their flight involved all members of the family, but for the majority the shock involved more or less permanent separations. For those who stayed behind to accept the Japanese occupation there were equally fundamental adjustments to be made.

The sociopolitical consequences of the Japanese War and occupation for the vast majority of the Chinese people have been little studied. Studies of the period that do exist have concentrated almost entirely upon the political fortunes and competing appeals of the Nationalists and the Communists; they have not dealt with the experiences of the people themselves as they had to adjust to public events without a deep identification with either of the contending parties. Yet, political behavior in Communist China must be assessed against this background, which was one of the most profoundly traumatic periods in the history of any country in modern times.

The depth of the trauma for millions of Chinese cannot be measured merely by the extent of physical dislocation. In West China the impact of refugees from the coastal areas and the extractive demands of a government at war challenged and disrupted the most traditional and provincially oriented populations of China. The political socialization of entire communities of old and young took place in a context in which nationalism and foreign occupation were the initiating forces, but these were soon followed by unrelenting pressures for change that came from fellow Chinese who insisted that old authorities and old patterns of life would have to be replaced by new and fundamentally threatening ones. As the Kuomintang armies and the coastal peoples that accompanied them were driven into West China, the people of the interior found their old patterns of life challenged as never before.

As someone who was personally on the scene, I have long felt that most analyses of postwar China fail to appreciate the profound divisions that war and occupation produced in Chinese society. One part of Chinese society, which had been deeply committed to resisting Japanese conquests, paid a high price in personal sacrifice and disillusionment. Another part of Chinese society had quite frankly accommodated itself to the realities of Japanese occupation; in a very fundamental sense these people had found niches for themselves that were not entirely consistent with the values of nationalism. In the months following the Japanese surrender, I observed in Peking what seemed to me to be the initial sounds of an irreconcilable clash between east coast Chinese, who were vulnerable to the charge of accommodation with the hated enemy, and West China returnees, who were consumed with the arrogance of righteousness as they sought to put behind themselves the pains of sacrifice and the need for cynicism.

First of all, there were the entire university and high school populations of Peking, Tientsin, Shanghai, and the other east coast cities who had made their adjustments to a Japanese educational system; these people now were profoundly anxious for their education to be recognized and accepted in the postwar period as being equal to that received by the students who had lived in "Free China." The East China students justifiedly feared that the Nationalists would feel compelled to discriminate in favor of those who had gone west; those who came back from the ordeal of the war years in West China felt that they did indeed deserve favorable treatment from the government.

In this situation it is not surprising that among the east coast students there was an urge to have the slate wiped clean; thus, there was a responsiveness to the Communists' appeal that "bygones should be bygones" and a growing belief that only with a new regime could there be a re-establishment of national unity. And among those who had gone out to West China the prevailing mood was that they had already suffered as much as was just for any generation, and therefore they were basically unwilling to take on new sacrifices for political reasons.[17]

[17] In the immediate postwar months I was made aware of these student sentiments and of the deep division in Chinese society that made more than one-half of one generation feel that it might indeed be a "lost generation"; delegations of students in their desperation sought out American officials in Peking in the hope of learning what the

What happened with the students was repeated in various ways among other groups, so that when the war ended China was deeply divided between those who had been in "Free China" and those who had lived under the Japanese-sponsored regimes. The second most critical group was the nearly one million Chinese who served as puppet troops and as members of the Peace Preservation Corps sponsored by the Japanese. At the time of the Japanese surrender these puppet troops were ordered to stand fast, and the plan was that they were to be gradually incorporated into the Nationalist armies. It soon became apparent to the officers in these units, however, that they could expect little in the way of careers and advancement if they were placed in common competition with the Nationalist officers who had fought against the Japanese. They too, like the students, would have been a "lost generation" if there had not been a significant change in China's political order.

A third important group which felt the divisions of China between occupied and free areas were the technicians and routine bureaucrats of government. These included railroad and customs officials, the telegraph and postal workers, teachers and administrators in the elementary and secondary schools, the judges and magistrates in the entire range of court systems, the collectors of land revenue and the supervisors of public health, the mayors, and all the specialists in the various bureaus and departments of the city governments. Would those who had stayed at these posts or who had advanced to them during the Japanese occupation be allowed to continue in their offices into the post-war period, or would they be replaced by those who had served with the Chungking regime?

The fact that China was longer and more completely divided by war and occupation than any other country in World War II has been generally overlooked. More important, it was never reunited by the movement of war and the dynamic processes of liberation in which temporary forms of military government could provide a phased process of adjustment and of reuniting the people. Instead, once the war was over the Chinese experienced profound uncertainty, and there were no mechanisms for change or for seeking justice.[18]

future policy would be as far as recognizing the relative credits and degrees of those who had stayed in the east coast universities and of those who had gone to West China.

[18] Most accounts of the five years from the end of World War II to the victory of the Communists have dealt almost exclusively with the weaknesses if not the sins of the Kuomintang. One of the rare reports that captures some of the moods of those years is A. Doak Barnett, *China on the Eve of Communist Takeover* (New York: Frederick A. Praeger, 1963).

## FROM CHAOS TO CONFORMITY

In the light of all the uncertainty facing many Chinese after the war and the occupation, it is surprising that the enthusiasm for the arrival of the Communist forces was not greater. The private anxieties which had done so much to reduce all commitments to the previous order also seemed to work to make people somewhat cautious and wary of the new rulers who were so extraordinarily anxious to create the impression of popular enthusiasm for their act of "liberation." [19]

All that had preceded does, however, go far to explain why, once the new regime was clearly in control, so many Chinese were willing and anxious to conform to the demand for participation in the new order. Historically, of course, Chinese have always responded to the end of chaos and to the establishment of a new dynasty with a great commitment to order and industry; and given the truly monumental confusion of the preceding years and the general disorder of earlier decades, their craving for order and national power is easily understood.

Thus, the stage was set, both psychologically and politically, for an era of conformity and for widespread acceptance of the dictates of an acknowledged superior authority. The search for security and the need to escape from uncertainty, confusion, and disorder provided strong reinforcements for the natural acceptance of a honeymoon period for the new regime.

The Chinese people were ready to rediscover their sense of social belonging by committing themselves to social and political participation. And the Chinese Communist leaders were ready to provide them with a rich variety of socially and politically acceptable vehicles for this form of mass, but essentially limited and controlled, participation. During the next few years the Chinese Communists displayed a genius for creating organizations that reached every segment of the population and every area of the country.[20] At the same time, the Chinese people displayed their equally impressive genius for quickly learning the style and the vocabulary of proper participation in all manner of new organizational contexts. Leaders and followers both seemed to

[19] Some of the feelings that accompanied the Communist advance into the major cities of China in 1949 are recaptured in such reminiscences as: Eric Chou, *A Man Must Choose* (New York: Alfred A. Knopf, 1964); Shaw-tong Liu, *Out of Red China* (New York: Duell, Sloan and Pearce, 1953).

[20] These institutions of participation are best described and analyzed in Townsend, *Political Participation*, chaps. v and vi.

have compulsive cravings for the tidiness of obligatory participation.

Although the style and the emotional context of participation were radically new, the situation in the early 1950's did share many basic similarities with the patterns of traditional China. Individuals were compelled once again to find their social identities in the context of associational relationships; much of society was organized into distinct groups which limited multiple membership and which were not truly voluntary in recruitment; and above all, government again was untouched by anything resembling pressures from private groups and organizations. An amazingly high level of participation produced, paradoxically, as of old, a docile population. Political sensitivity and awareness produced conformity and discipline, not autonomy and initiative.

What we are suggesting is that during the first few years of the Communist regime the Chinese population needed to engage in the conforming and reassuring practices of public participation. It is true that as people were swept up into their various groups for ideological training they found at times that the experiences of "self-criticism" and "mutual criticism" were threatening and even traumatic. In no small measure, however, the fear associated with these sessions came from the danger that one would feel "isolated" and no longer a part of a conforming community.[21] In the larger social context people felt it was important to be identified with the new dominant forces in China. Consequently, those who might have had some associations with the previous regime were anxious to display publicly their acceptance of the new, and those who were unattached in the past were anxious to show that they could be accepted now as loyal members of the new order.

Thus, the more the new regime called for revolutionary changes, the more anxious the Chinese people were for the opportunity to demonstrate in public their readiness to identify with the new order. In this fundamental sense it can be said that by the time the Communists came to power the Chinese public had an almost compulsive need to "participate." It seems likely that they would have responded in a spirit of conformity to any regime that came after the previous period of disorder and tensions.

---

[21] The fear of finding oneself cut off from the group was one of the most powerful disciplinary factors among the Chinese in the Malayian Communist Party. See: Lucian W. Pye, *Guerrilla Communism in Malaya* (Princeton, N.J.: Princeton University Press, 1956).

## THE POWERS AND LIMITATIONS OF PARTICIPATION

It is in many respects more difficult to explain why the Chinese Communist leaders were so intensely committed to the idea of mass mobilization and participation. In some ways they seem to have been caught up in the same mood as the public, and they seem not to have asked the hard question as to whether progress and power were indeed likely to come through mass participation. Why were the leaders so unthinkingly committed to mass mobilization, and why were they so blind to the danger, revealed in the Great Leap and the Cultural Revolution, that unlimited "participation" could threaten national development? A complete answer to these questions would require a detailed analysis of the essential qualities of Chinese communism in general and Mao Tse-tung's personal qualities of leadership and thought in particular. For our purposes we can only outline briefly some of the more general considerations and then advance some more speculative hypotheses about aspects of modern Chinese culture.

The case can certainly be made that out of a combination of commitment to Marxism and extensive experiences with guerrilla warfare, Mao developed his deep faith in the powers of mass participation. Both ideological considerations and the example of the rising powers of Russia after the October Revolution suggested to Mao that "when the masses of the people were united they constituted a great historic force." And, of course, Mao's doctrines about the critical role of a supporting population in creating the necessary environment for success in guerrilla campaigns provide a further rationale for the importance of "participation" for any revolutionary leadership.

Furthermore, during the first years in power the leaders must have received their greatest sense of accomplishment from their successes in building mass organizations and in generating apparent enthusiasm for participation. In part, the concern for stimulating active participation was related to the Party's desire to identify itself as the wave of the future and to set in motion a bandwagon psychology that would win over the support of doubtful and hesitant elements. It was tactically appropriate for the Party to seek to convey to the entire population a feeling that all right-thinking and intelligent individuals in all walks of life were enthusiastically committed to the new revolutionary forces that had just succeeded in capturing the commanding heights of political power. Conversely, however, the responsiveness of the public which came out of its deep craving for order and participation must have reassured the leaders and must have made them believe that they were able to accomplish anything they set out to do. To some degree the leaders may have mistakenly identified the people's desire for participation as an indication of their own powers of manipulation.

In seeking to evaluate the significance of the Communist participation practices for China's progress, the first point that must be made, thus, is that the regime probably had little choice, for the Chinese people were by 1949 anxiously seeking an "escape from freedom." There was a widespread desire to regain a sense of order and unity after the years of disruption. Their profound search for security, which also meant dependency, made the Chinese people anxious to comply with the dictates of any apparently strong leadership. They were ready to put aside uncertainty and the frustration of ambiguity in order to gain, once again, the comforts of conformity and unanimity. The traditional Chinese reverence for form and ritual made it easy for them to learn the new sacred words and rituals. These widespread tendencies must have been most gratifying to the cadres who were responsible for seeing that the ideological level of each group was raised through self-criticism and mutual-criticism sessions, but what did they mean for the system as a whole?

Tactically, of course, the ideal of mass participation was also useful as a device for separating friend from foe, and for psychologically isolating remnants of the old order. For example, during the process of land reform the Party cadres who organized the "People's courts" strove to create disgust with the evil ways of the landlords, and "participation" often took the form of popular demands for executions.[22] The climate of opinion created by the Party was certainly one in which an individual who might have had reservations about the new policies would feel that he stood alone. Anyone who had been bothered by feelings of insecurity as a result of the social disorders of the earlier periods must have welcomed the possibility for easy participation or, at least, must have been extra sensitive to the dangers of social isola-

[22] Note the following description: "A landlord is to be liquidated. The party member launches into a harangue concerning the landlord's crimes against the people and demands to know what the people's judgment is. Agitators in the crowd shout for liquidation of the criminal. The malcontents pick up the theme and some of the timid go along from fear. Soon the whole crowd is swept by a frenzy of mob feeling and expressed hate, leading to the unanimous decision to execute the victim. Such demonstrations no doubt serve many functions. The one we wish to point to here is that the party member, though he knows he staged the whole thing, is nevertheless reassured and absolved by the final unanimous people's decision. Self-fulfilling prophecies are no less reassuring than other kinds, and in some sense perhaps more so." Edgar H. Schein, *Coercive Persuasion* (New York: W. W. Norton & Co., 1961), p. 97.

tion as the new forces of history appeared to be taking over control of the country.

This psychological climate also provided an effective backdrop for the more intimate processes of mutual criticism, self-criticism, and general ideological and thought remolding. It is questionable whether the Chinese Communist techniques of "thought reform" and "coercive persuasion" could have worked as well as they apparently did in the first decade of the regime's history if they had not taken place in the context of apparently unlimited mass participation.[23]

## QUESTIONS ABOUT THE VALUE OF PARTICIPATION

According to almost any known form of political calculus it is possible to evaluate the stress on participation which took place in those early years of the regime as having some utility for the leaders in strengthening not only their position but also the national power of China. Indeed, the rest of the world did react to the appearances of monolithic solidarity of the new China by assuming that the Communists had in fact found a way to make China into an Asian, if not a world, power. The capacity of the government to control its widespread forms of participation seemed to suggest that China could quickly rise above its state of underdevelopment, and that it would soon be able to mobilize resources for purposeful development at a rate far exceeding that of any of the other newly emerging states of Asia and Africa.

Now that there has been a second decade of experience, it is possible to question whether the political advantages of controlled participation can in fact be so readily transformed into effective modernization and development. It is true that the totalitarian model has always suggested that when mass participation is effectively directed the results are greater freedom for the policymakers and, hence, opportunity for more rational or efficient allocation of resources.

These apparent advantages, however, have to be weighed against the "costs" of maintaining controlled participation. Was the course of action followed by the leadership particularly wise? Could the

[23] The psychologists who have worked on the Chinese methods of mutual criticism and thought reform have, understandably from the point of view of their discipline, tended to focus on the powerful effects of face-to-face confrontation and on the dynamics of the small group. Yet the general political environment in which these sessions took place gave them an added dimension unknown to group situations in any other society. See: Robert Jay Lifton, *Thought Reform and the Psychology of Totalism: A Study of "Brainwashing" in China* (New York: W. W. Norton & Co., 1961); Schein, *Coercive Persuasion.*

pattern of participation encouraged by the Party have significantly increased China's national power? Is the mobilization of human energies, as envisaged and practiced by the Chinese Communists, relevant for the modernization process? Or have the Chinese become prisoners of their own necessities, and have they had to fall back upon controlled participation as a substitute for actual development and modernization?

As we have just noted, the one critically important advantage that flowed from the popular mood and behavior of the Chinese was that their capacity for disciplined participation did provide legitimacy to the new order. The readiness of the population to adhere to the new practices and to follow the leadership of the mass organizations meant that the new order was quickly accepted. The stress on popular participation helped to isolate selective "enemies" and to define the ways of the good citizen. Thus, the Chinese craving for order facilitated the process of governing and made it easier to rule. Indeed, if it were not for these sets of cultural attitudes that were well implanted before communism, it would be impossible to rule such a huge population. When Chinese are anxious about security, they tend to become a public that is relatively easy to govern.

While it may be true that the Chinese desired to have manifest ways of displaying their search for order, the question remains as to whether the practices of participation designed by the Communists have been of positive value in facilitating the modernization of China. Before the Great Leap it was possible to speculate that there might be a connection between the successes that the regime was having in building up mass organizations and the growth of the economy. At one time there seemed to be a relevant issue as to whether the regime's capacity for controlling popular participation and establishing mass organization was a valid indicator of its capacity for controlling the economy—that is, could ability or effectiveness in one area be taken as suggesting comparable potentialities in another? Similarly, it once seemed reasonable to ask the slightly different question as to whether the capacity for mobilizing the population might not in itself be a direct means or technique for producing economic development. Ever since the Great Leap, however, neither assumption seems quite so reasonable. It has become apparent that the regime's capacity for popular mobilization may not be so directly related to its capacity for producing economic development, and it does not seem so easy to utilize a capacity for controlled participation as a means for advancing economic policies. Indeed, Peking's strengths in controlling mass participation might seem, if anything, to be an actual liability in producing economic growth.

We may still ask, however, whether even though mass participation in recent practice has not helped economic growth, it might still be possible in theory to do so and, hence, whether at some future time the Chinese Communists might be able to turn their skills at mass mobilization in highly productive directions. This question is important for those who expect that with the passing of Mao the Chinese government will become a more "rational" center of policy. Could not the successors of Mao possibly use Peking's capacity for controlled mass participation to bring about the constructive development of the country? Once the question is posed in this manner, it still appears to be a rather hypothetical one because the capacity of the Chinese for controlled mass participation is closely associated with a Maoist style of politics, and, thus, any successors might show less interest in expending resources and talents in maintaining mass organizations as they seek more "rational" approaches. Although it is impossible to foresee history, it may still be of value to examine the best case that can be made for the Chinese Communist system of mass participation as a means for achieving modernization and development.

Such a case might begin by noting that the enthusiasm generated by mass participation practices may make it possible to discount material incentives and to provide essentially symbolic rewards for increased outputs of energy on the part of the population. Closely related to this argument is the one that holds that in a transitional society such as China it is essential to bring about a change in attitudes in order to reduce feelings of fatalism and lack of initiative, and to increase the spirit of self-reliance and all the other attitudes associated with the productive and enterprising personality basic to a modern industrial society.

A plausible case can indeed be made that Mao's objective both before and during the Cultural Revolution was to change the basic values and attitudes of the people in order to make them more virtuous according to nineteenth-century Victorian standards of self-reliance and moral commitment. Certainly, much of the preaching in the "red book" is in the style of the old-fashioned Protestant Sunday school teacher. The values are those associated with the modern achievement spirit, and the stress on physical labor does represent a radical departure from the older Confucian and mandarin values.

While it is impossible to fault the values that have been extolled in the participation campaigns—since they are the old virtues of hard work, loyalty, truthfulness, enterprise, and the like which are basic to all societies that have successfully industrialized—it is possible to ask whether the Maoists have correctly diagnosed what have been the obstacles to Chinese development in modern times. In the Western literature on China of the nineteenth and early twentieth centuries there was a tendency, particularly among the missionaries, to argue that China's backwardness in modernization stemmed from a deficiency in Victorian virtues. More recent studies of Chinese society suggest that the Chinese personality is strongly achievement oriented and that like the Japanese they have a potential for success in a modern environment. In many respects it almost seems as though the Communist leaders, and particularly Mao, have taken as gospel the criticism of Chinese national character and morality made by the early Western missionaries, and as though Mao were now basing his campaigns to change the Chinese version of human nature on the criticisms and observations of Arthur H. Smith.[24]

In spite of this apparent agreement between a Communist and an early missionary, it is questionable whether China's problems in modernization and development lie mainly in a deficiency in Victorian values. The overwhelming evidence is that the Chinese people are more than adequately trained to be industrious and hard working. It is true that most of her elites have not looked with enthusiasm on working with their hands, but then neither have the elites of any other society that has successfully modernized.

The real weaknesses of the Chinese would seem to be less those of motivation and individual determination, and more a tendency toward rigidity and, particularly, a lack of an adequately imaginative and flexible leadership. China's problem in modernization has not been the absence of a willing labor force; it has been mainly the narrow-mindedness and lack of perspective of its decision makers. Thus, much of the preaching of new values has been largely beside the point, and in so far as the process has stressed the need for determination and steadfastness, it has been detrimental since it has made Chinese leaders, planners, and entrepreneurs more rigid than ever.

Therefore, in terms of economic development the Maoist stress on participation as a means to new attitudes may not be particularly

[24] Arthur H. Smith, *Chinese Characteristics* (2nd ed.; New York: Fleming H. Revell, 1894).

useful or relevant, and at times it may even be a severe liability. And, of course, during the extreme periods of this participation, such as during the Great Leap and the Cultural Revolution, the economy was severely damaged. At other periods the opportunity costs of such policies would seem to have been extremely high, for tremendous numbers of intelligent, dedicated, and energetic people have been employed as the cadres for developing and maintaining the mass organizations and for controlling and changing opinions, and thus this prize talent has not been available for tasks of much more economic importance.

Indeed, in a strange way the Chinese Communist emphasis upon participation and mobilization seems to result in a discounting rather than a heightening of the importance of the human factor in development. In spite of all the talk about the human element being superior to machines and technology, the Maoist approach does blur human differences, and hence, it minimizes the importance of the most critical scarce resource in China, the talented human resources.

## THE LOW ROAD BACK TO CAPITALISM

Before turning to the future political implications of mass participation practices let us pause a moment to reflect on some possible effects that the Maoist approach after the Cultural Revolution may have on Chinese economic development. At this point in time it is premature to make any firm forecasts about what may happen to the Chinese economy if the Maoist approach dominates many more years, but we can engage in some reasoned speculations and in particular can note that, paradoxically, the Maoist views could, for quite unintended reasons, result in some positive trends in the economy; most surprising of all they might, if they are carried to extreme lengths, even open the way to a modest revival of some forms of capitalism.

Economically, the central theme of the Cultural Revolution was that the bureaucratic tendencies of the Party could set the stage for "revisionism" and for the establishment of state capitalism. The very capacity for centralized economic planning was thus a potential source of danger for the development of communism. The consequence of Mao's attack upon "those in positions of authority" has been to shift power to the revolutionary committees and, hence, to more local authorities. This may mean that the Chinese will weaken their capacity for tightly coordinated central economic planning and for strict control of the entire economy. A likely result, if this were to happen, might be a greater degree of flexibility and accommodation to local and regional conditions, which in turn might produce more "rational" policies. Any such tendency toward more decentralized controls and planning would, however, have to be accompanied by innovations which would permit interregional coordination; this in turn might result in new forms of "trade" among raw material producers, the factories, and the distributors. To carry out such forms of "trade" would require the establishment of "prices" that would reflect the actual terms of trade and the realities of the bargains that would have to be made in order to maintain the process.

The Maoist arguments against "bureaucratism," the attacks on the technicians and economic planners, and the destruction of the linkage mechanism between the ministries at the center and the activities in the factories and communes, mean that China has weakened its potential for socialist planning. In the post-Cultural Revolution period authorities at the center may continue to pretend that they are in command of all economic activities, but if they lack the organizational means for engaging in continuous and subtle controls, the most likely result will be a trend toward ever increasing autonomy in decision making. People on the spot with responsibilities will have to carry on as best they can, and this will mean that they will have to assume initiative and display enterprise.

Hence, in a paradoxical fashion, Mao's attack upon "revisionism" and the bureaucratic dangers of reviving capitalism may in fact be opening the way to a much more fundamental form of revived "capitalism." In their drive to liquidate the "capitalist roaders in places of high authority" and the "anti-Party and anti-socialist freaks and monsters," the Maoists may have put China on a new low road back to a form of the market system. Thus, ironically, the only way that Mao can build a dynamic economy while eliminating the central bureaucracy is to encourage local decision making; for this approach to be successful, China will have to move quite far in the direction of restoring a market economy.

Needless to say, the possibility for the restoration of some such form of "capitalism" only follows logically from certain consequences of the Cultural Revolution and the Maoist approach to government, and it may not necessarily happen. First and foremost, the Maoists are not likely to be consistent, and they may soon be adopting some of the policies and emphases of those whom they have just been attacking. Yet it does seem likely that the general trend in China will be away from the high-water mark of mobilization of the recent past. In theory it is much easier to make the case that a decline in the capacity for political mobilization and the organization of mass participation will result in a decline in capacity for central economic management, than to make the case that such political capabilities can be translated into effective economic development.

## THE POLITICAL VALUES OF PARTICIPATION

On the face of it there should be fewer questions about the value of mass participation for political development than for economic development. As we have already observed the practices of mass mobilization in China have given a degree of legitimacy to the regime, trained people to avoid unacceptable practices, and strengthened the spirit of national unity. And beyond the case of Communist China, nearly all general theories of political development stress the basic importance of expanding participation for political modernization and nation building.[25]

During the early years of the regime, Peking's emphasis upon mass organization did seem to mean that China was solving many aspects of the basic crisis of participation inherent in the modernization process. Through these organizations and out of the close relationship between cadres and followers, it did appear that the gap between the orientations of elites and masses was being reduced. Increasing numbers of Chinese appeared to be learning about the problems of government, and more and more the people were able to find in their political orientations the attitudes and disciplines essential for achieving a coherent social order. This is a fundamental development in the modernization process, for as societies change the older primary institutions, such as family, community, and church or religion, lose their powers of giving form and structure to social life, and it becomes the task of formal government to make the necessary inputs to give order and coherence to society. Once a people become responsive to this socializing and structuring role of government, the process of modernization becomes smoother and the government can perform more effectively.

During the 1950's the systematic creation of mass organizations, in which nearly every citizen had a place, greatly increased the sup-

---

[25] For a discussion of the "participation crises," see: Myron Weiner's chapter in Leonard Binder et al., The Crises of Political Development (Princeton, N.J.: Princeton University Press, 1970).

√ portive inputs to the Chinese political system, and the consequence was an increase in the capacity of the system.[26] The blending of personal security and national pride provided a strong basis of commitment to the government. This spirit possibly reached its highest point during the Great Leap period when millions made sacrifices without asking for personal benefits. All of these supportive activities depended, however, upon the mass organizations which provided the context within which the individual felt secure to "participate."

Thus, the organizations were essential for the Chinese version of "participation" which in turn was significant in providing necessary supports to the government. However, many observers, apparently including Mao himself, began to question whether such organizationally structured and controlled forms of "participation" could fully meet the function of genuine participation in the modernization process. The need for spontaneity in participation is not just a matter of democratic value preference, for if a system is to derive the full returns from "participation," there must be an "input" of supportive sentiments that exceeds the "output" of the government in building commitments. If the Chinese government and the Party were expending more energy, talent, and resources in controlling "participation" than they were obtaining in support sentiments, the net effect would be a "drain" on the system.

For rather different reasons Mao was, by the time of the Cultural Revolution, led to believe that the organization structures, essential for the earlier forms of mass participation, should be eliminated, and that "participation" should take a more direct and spontaneous revolutionary quality. Thus, ideologically the Cultural Revolution and the Red Guard represented an effort by the Maoists to expand participation and to reduce the gap between the leaders and the masses. In actual practice, however, the effect of the Cultural Revolution has been to destroy the mass organizations which had been so important in giving order and security to the Chinese and in making them feel that they could cope with the problem of identification with the new order. The dismantling of the Party has possibly destroyed the capacity of the system to organize and direct many forms of mass participation. If the new patterns of "participation" had been fully internalized by the Chinese people and if they were now capable of reflecting

[26] For a discussion of the concepts of "supports" and "capacity" as related to political systems, see: Gabriel A. Almond and G. Bingham Powell, Jr., *Comparative Politics: A Developmental Approach* (Boston: Little, Brown and Co., 1966).

all the spontaneous qualities Mao would like them to have, then the elimination of the props of the mass organizations would not make any difference as far as gaining support from the public; in fact, it would reduce a fundamental "drain" on the system.

It is still too early to say what the consequences will indeed be, but there are already certain signs which suggest that the reaction of the Chinese public is not going to be a continuation of "spontaneous revolutionary" behavior. Instead, the reaction to the weakening of the Party and of the organizational framework for participation seems to be a tendency to pull back and to seek security in more private activities. If this is indeed the case, then one of the main aftereffects of the Cultural Revolution will be a lower rather than a higher level of participation in the future.

Thus, politically as well as economically, the extraordinary paradox appears to be that Maoists will have produced out of the Cultural Revolution the very results that they have been denouncing. Rule through revolutionary committees may mean that the top leaders in Peking will be psychologically, if not physically, further removed from the masses than were the leaders who had the mass organizations and the communication channels of the Party. Indeed, it would seem that with the destruction of most of the institutions of mass participation, Chinese politics after the Cultural Revolution will have to become more elitist than ever. Thus, in spite of the extolling of an ideology of intimacy between the leaders and the masses, the Chinese may be moving steadily in the direction of a system of government composed of court politics at the top, with the splendid isolation of the topmost ruler, and with localized authorities in command throughout the region with little in the way of day-to-day controls through a centralized bureaucracy.

In short, China may be moving toward a system that is in many ways reminiscent of that of imperial China. And the basis for such a system seems to be well prepared as the Chinese people appear to be again ready to take on their social identities by joining groups that do not make any demands on government.

## THE RETURN OF OLD PATTERNS OF PARTICIPATION

If, as seems not too unlikely, the aftereffects of the Cultural Revolution will be a decline in the levels of mass participation, an increasing sense of isolation of the top leaders who will lack the organizational means to communicate with all segments of society, and the revival of more autonomous enterprise in the economy, then there will be a greater gap than ever before between the rhetoric of Mao and Chinese realities. How are the Chinese people likely to react to such a prospect? Twenty years ago the collective need was for unity, a sense of belonging, and guidance for mass behavior; but what remains of these needs after the Cultural Revolution, and where are the Chinese likely to turn next in their endless quest for personal security in a modernizing world?

In the authoritarian traditions of Confucian China the promise of personal security for those below lay in accepting the moral precepts of those above and in making no explicit demands on authority. Yet historically, whenever the Chinese system confronted social and economic change, the result was an increase in insecurity that led to a need to make more explicit demands on the political system; in turn, authority felt threatened and instinctively sought to restore order, and hence, it had to resist change. This linkage between change and challenge to authority has continued to plague a culture which still emphasizes dependency upon authority and the expectation that those above should be able to solve all problems.

The strength of the Confucian system resided in a socialization process that enforced filial piety and taught the need to separate emotions from behavior, to adhere to form and etiquette, and to reduce social tensions by valuing ritual and group identity over content and self-interest.

Mao, in seeking to make change acceptable without undermining governmental authority, tried to tap the emotions of the Chinese people and to link them to collective actions. He assumed that the spirit of revolution and the mass demonstration of anger and enthusiasm would provide China with a new historic force. During the early years, however, mass mobilization often led to the expression of emotions without significant actions. In time emotions became ritualized, and mass participation became a new form of public pretense. Mao's efforts to reverse the traditional Chinese stress of form over content did for a brief period result in a freeing of forms so long as the content was appropriately revolutionary; but in time content became formalized, and new forms of ritualized struggle and criticism restored essentially the old Chinese pattern. For the Maoist the display of emotions is valued above the actual effectiveness of behavior, and thus performance is once again more related to ritual than to substance.

In the early years of the regime, practices of mass mobilization

were designed to expand the individual's commitment and identification in order to reach beyond family and class and to incorporate
the nation and the forces of world revolution. For the Maoist, participation was supposed to submerge the individual into historically significant groups and classes and to bring an end to private interest and
individual concern. Yet, after the extreme experiences of the last years
in which emotions seem to have got out of hand, the Chinese people
have apparently become more self-conscious and self-calculating, and
the masses have become more aware of their private, individual identities. Since the mass organizations which provided their social identities
have been destroyed by the Cultural Revolution, they have had no
alternative but to look to their individual identities.

Thus, after twenty years of Maoist rule the general trend seems
to be that mass mobilization has produced a growing sense of privati-
zation: Mao is more isolated and alone as a god figure, the rest of
the top leaders have had to struggle separately for their positions
instead of being members of a solid leadership group, and the masses
of the people have increasingly had to look to their own interests.
The end of the mass organizations and the confusion about the state
of the Party have left the Chinese people with few reliable cues to
guide their public and collective behavior.

Presumably they will have to look to more immediate leaders in the
future as the revolutionary committees and the People's Liberation
Army assume more and more the responsibilities for the day-to-day
administration of public affairs. In the meantime, the Maoist leadership at the center will continue to proclaim ideological visions and
to set vague general goals for society. The likely result will be an increased gap between pretensions and reality—between Chinese revolutionary rhetoric and the hard Chinese struggle for economic and
social betterment. In a sense, Mao will have to seek to restore the
authority of his highest offices, not through the efficacy of actual rule,
but by reigning as the emperors did. Through the expedient of not
trying to administer everything from the center, the regime can avoid
openly demonstrating its limited authority.

The era of controlled mass participation may thus have ended—
at least until the Chinese have again a central, bureaucratic authority.
The Chinese people have gone through much in the last few years,
and they are certainly wiser if not more cynical about the manipula-
tions of their national leaders. At present they appear to be turning
inward to their more private concerns. Indeed, in spite of Mao's pro-

fessed drive to eliminate entirely any gap between the Chinese public and their leaders, the masses seem to be going along with the pretenses of Mao's revolutionary rhetoric so long as they can be spared the need to belong to organizations that reflect the interests of their leaders.

Thus, it seems that the most likely consequence of the Cultural Revolution is a gradual drift back toward the traditional equilibrium of the Chinese political system. What is extraordinary is that a people who have been mobilized into mass participation like no other people in history and who have also experienced many currents of modernization, should show at present so little inclination to turn their acceptable ideological doctrine of "participation" into more spontaneous demands upon the political system. In a strange way elements of the old political culture seem to continue to hold sway as, contrary to all normal expectations, "participation" in China has not led to competition and open politics. And, again it seems to be that the role of a semidivine figure at the top and the dependence upon military authority throughout the land have been major factors in inhibiting the spread of the expected dynamic consequences of participation.

## CHALMERS JOHNSON

# The Changing Nature and Locus of Authority in Communist China

In this article I shall attempt to describe the political authority possessed by the leaders of Communist China, including the origins, basis of, and changes in that authority. I shall also attempt to make a contribution to the analysis of authority itself, particularly as it makes its presence or absence felt in post-seizure-of-power revolutionary regimes. Whereas the generalizing social scientist draws upon the work of area specialists with the intention of producing generalizations—for example, "Successful defense against foreign intervention often helps to legitimatize revolutionary regimes"—and the area specialist draws upon the full range of social theory in order to try to explain the political life of a particular society at a particular time—for example, "the Chinese Communists' mandate of authority differs from that of either the Russian or Yugoslav Communists"—it seems to me that the political scientist specializing in Chinese politics should be committed to both orientations. The Chinese case, though supremely important in its own right, is of such scope and complexity that its analysis can contribute to an understanding of other revolutionary governments, both present and future.

Despite Benjamin Schwartz's dire warnings against "a large assortment of C.I.A. operatives, Pentagon strategists, professional Communist experts, games-theoreticians, political scientists, and others" who would force "narrowly conceived, rigid 'models' and 'conceptual schemes'" onto the "rich, chaotic, and infinitely varied flow of events," I am nevertheless convinced that China specialists must be prepared to attempt to theorize about revolutionary authority in general and

Chinese Communist authority in particular.[1] Although the idea of authority does constitute a kind of "conceptual scheme," I agree with de Grazia that "the subject matter of the political scientist is earthly authority," and I believe that the most serious problem of the contemporary period of the Chinese revolution is a pervasive ambiguity in the authority of the Communist regime.[2]

## INTRODUCTION

During the first two decades of Communist China's existence, the authority on which the Communist Party based its guidance of the country changed fundamentally at least three times. In the initial period, approximately 1949 to 1955, the rule of the Communist Party was legitimatized through its identification with the long-standing Chinese national revolution. In the second period, approximately 1956 to 1962, the Party moved into open administration of the economy and society, and advanced its own legitimating ideology of "socialist construction," which built upon but went considerably beyond the ideology of the Chinese national revolution. Failures in the performance of the Communist Party during this period, combined with the corrosive effects on Marxist-Leninist ideology that resulted from the breakup of the international Communist movement, ushered in an interregnum of disunity in the Communist leadership and an authority crisis for the regime. After 1965, efforts were made to resolve this crisis through the creation of an ideology of personal authority, the cult of Mao Tse-tung, as the basis of Communist government in China. The reasons for these changes and an analysis of their consequences, both intended and unintended, form the starting point for any understanding of the dynamics of Chinese Communist politics.

During all three periods the Communist Party enjoyed legitimacy —on one basis or another. That is to say, the Chinese Communist revolution differs from two of the other major archetypes of Communist success, Stalin's Russia and Tito's Yugoslavia, in that shortly after they came to power China's leaders held a mandate of authority from an overwhelming majority of the people. During its first two decades (although not uniformly over the twenty-year period), Communist China offered the rare example of a *legitimate revolution*, one in which the population genuinely authorized the exercise of political

---

[1] B. I. Schwartz, *Communism and China: Ideology in Flux* (Cambridge, Mass.: Harvard University Press, 1968), pp. 2, 192.

[2] Sebastian de Grazia, "What Authority is *Not*," *American Political Science Review*, LIII (June, 1959), 321.

power to bring about social change, and in which the changes championed by the leadership truly were aimed at restructuring the social system according to a popularly supported image. Stalinist Russia, at least until the time of the German invasion during World War II, was revolutionary but not legitimate; Yugoslavia after 1948 ceased to be revolutionary to the extent that Titoism became legitimate. The leaders of the Chinese Communist revolution were both legitimate and revolutionary.

Authority, in its earthly, political sense, is legitimate power, "power that is used in accord with the subject's values and under conditions he views as proper." [3] As de Grazia observes, "Authority itself is not force or coercion. It is a power that wants using, that is granted in order to be used, that has the support of those for whom it is used." [4] The study of authority involves, at least in part, the reasons why policy is accepted. Foreign political specialists on Communist China have typically concerned themselves with the processes by which policy is made in China, and they have often seemed guilty of regarding the mass of the population as nothing more than an infinitely malleable resource. The study of the existence and the properties of authority— of the motives and pressures that have impelled the Chinese people to follow the Party's leadership more readily than in most other comparable revolutionary regimes—seems long overdue.

Revolution is somewhat harder to define succinctly. Kirchheimer has part of the definition when he calls it "concentrated reaction to yesterday's reality." [5] However, revolution is more than mere rebellion; it is, in addition to rebellion, purposive social change guided either by an ideology of a new societal configuration that a people want to construct or by a goal or goals that a people collectively wish to achieve.[6] Revolutionary authority is thus collectively sanctioned power to bring about social change in accordance with *a people's* ideology. The leaders who exercise such revolutionary authority are legitimate leaders so long as they keep their policies within the broad limits outlined by the mandate of revolutionary authority that they have received, or have elicited, from their followers.

[3] Amitai Etzioni, *The Active Society* (New York: Free Press, 1968), pp. 360–61.
[4] de Grazia, "What Authority is *Not*," p. 329.
[5] Otto Kirchheimer, "Confining Conditions and Revolutionary Breakthroughs," *American Political Science Review*, LIX (December, 1965), 974.
[6] See Chalmers Johnson, *Revolutionary Change* (Boston: Little, Brown and Co., 1966), p. 139 *et passim*.

Strange as it seems to say, there exists some controversy over whether or not the Chinese people are revolutionary; and it is necessary at the outset to question the proper use of the notions of revolution and of revolutionary authority in the modern Chinese context. One well-informed body of opinion is impressed by the apparent continuity between traditional attitudes toward authority in China and present-day relations of authority between the Party and the Chinese people. Observers who share this opinion are drawn to the conclusion that the Communist elite is essentially a functional equivalent of the imperial bureaucracy. They do not, of course, deny that a revolution of sorts has occurred in China, but they do doubt whether the Chinese masses actually possess an ideology of revolution. The views of C. P. Fitzgerald offer an example:

So the Chinese once more feel themselves at home. There is the Party, to replace the old imperial civil service, there is Marxism, the new orthodoxy in place of old Confucianism, there is authority and obedience. In addition, there is now an expanding economy, a great range of new careers for the educated, opportunities for education which did not exist before, a chance for every bright boy. This is liberty as they have understood it, the liberty for talent to make its way to the top, the great virtue of the old system in its heyday, the great promise of the new in its hour of triumph.[7]

John Fairbank (in a review of Franz Schurmann) comes a little closer to the point with his characterization of the influence of the masses on the cadres:

The continuing present-day influence of China's still rather unknown traditions seems to me ensured by a fact that Mr. Schurmann rightly stresses in several of his case studies—that Chinese Communist organization has not been achieved purely from the top down but also from the bottom up, that is, with extensive participation by the masses and especially by millions of cadres, who may be most conscious of the new ideology but whose available options of language and style still lie within the old social matrix surrounding them. In fine, revolutionary organization must be achieved among the people and therefore largely within the limits set by their inheritance.[8]

Fairbank's point seems to me valid and of crucial importance; the question is whether or not the inheritance of the Chinese masses in-

[7] C. P. Fitzgerald, "The Historical and Philosophical Background of Communist China," *The Political Quarterly*, XXXV (July–September, 1964), 259.
[8] John Fairbank, "The State That Mao Built," *World Politics*, XIX (July, 1967), 676.

cludes revolutionary antagonism toward the "old social matrix" and revolutionary aspirations that contravene China's traditions.

As a final example of this line of reasoning, James Townsend lists first, among four reasons for Chinese Communist success in eliciting political participation from the masses, "habitual obedience to political authority. . . . Since central political authority had never held much immediacy for the Chinese people, acceptance of this authority was not a matter of great controversy." [9] According to this view the Chinese Communists possess authority and obtain compliance on the basis of it, but their authority could hardly be called *revolutionary authority* in the sense in which the term is used here. Traditional authority, to which the Chinese people may have been habituated, would have functioned to maintain the social system, whereas revolutionary authority functioned to transform it.

I believe that these interpretations are too abstract, and that they fail to account for the influence of the Chinese *national* revolution on the mass of the population. They seem to misconceive the nature of the authority possessed by the Chinese Communists and, therefore, to misinterpret the basis of the authority crisis of the 1960's—as, for example, a "dynasty in decline." [10] Central to the perspective on Chinese Communist authority advanced here is my own view that the Communist regime grew out of and built upon the Chinese national revolution, an authentic (as distinct from imposed) revolutionary movement which commenced in the late nineteenth century, underwent considerable historical development, and by 1949 had won a mass following.

It is necessary to remember, after all, that the Communist victory of 1949 was not a triumph over the political representatives of the traditional Chinese social order; the Communist forces defeated the Kuomintang (KMT)—itself a failed national revolutionary party. The victorious Communists were leaders of a mass movement, and the new government that they founded received strong support from many different sectors of Chinese society. The basis of this mass backing was not the Party's espousal of "scientific socialism"; rather, people supported the Party because the Party had made diligent efforts to identify its own public ideology with that of the fifty-year-old

[9] James R. Townsend, *Political Participation in Communist China* (Berkeley and Los Angeles: University of California Press, 1967), p. 194.

[10] For example, L. La Dany, "Mao's China: The Decline of a Dynasty," *Foreign Affairs*, XLV (July, 1967), 610-23.

Chinese revolution. The Chinese Communist Party (CCP) had exploited politically and ideologically the numerous weaknesses of the KMT and had adroitly co-opted the ideological goals of the Chinese national revolution. What were these goals?

To the extent that one can generalize about the political values of the Chinese during the 1940's, most politically conscious and mobilized Chinese were committed to two goals: (1) at a minimum, economic enhancement of their own lives through technological modernization and, maximally, economic justice for all citizens; and (2) at a minimum, genuine independence for a Chinese nation from imperialist interference and, maximally, the achievement of a truly sovereign, Great Power status for China.[11] For these goals the mass of the population was prepared to work hard and to make great sacrifices (as they have done over the past twenty years). In addition, the disappointing history of the Chinese national revolution was tending to recommend the Chinese Communist Party to them as a proper and trustworthy leader of their revolutionary cause.

Of course, these generalizations require qualification. Although China enjoys a comparative freedom from religious and ethnic cleavages, regional differences and the consequent presence of regional stereotypes in the minds of Chinese are considerable and have major political significance. Moreover, the Japanese invasion and the Communist revolution impinged upon the different parts of China in radically different ways. Any treatment of Chinese attitudes on the eve of the Communist victory must be sensitive to the problem of regional diversity. We do not deal with regional variation in detail here, first, because a major and continuing political commitment of both Chinese nationalists and Communists has been to Chinese unity; and, second, because of the danger of overemphasizing regionalism in an analysis of short compass. It might be recalled that one of the greatest foreign intelligence efforts ever directed toward China—that of the Japanese in the decades of the thirties and forties—took as its first axiom Chinese internal diversity and the falsity of generalizing about China as a whole; as a result, Japan helped forge, and totally misunderstood, the nationalistic mass movement upon which the Japanese army foundered. The study of Chinese Communist authority needs to be supplemented by the study of regional variations in it, but only folly results from

[11] Cf. Shanti Swarup, *A Study of the Chinese Communist Movement* (Oxford: Clarendon Press, 1966), pp. 3–10.

pressing the claims of regionalism while denying the existence of a Chinese political entity.

The peasants of the Japanese-occupied areas of North and East China, who had in many cases been organized into anti-Japanese guerrilla bases since approximately 1938, followed Communist leadership because the Party resisted the invaders and promised to protect their difficult livelihood by equitable taxes and rents. The student and youthful generations had been won to the Party's cause because it unequivocally championed Chinese nationalism, and many college-age men and women joined the Communist army in response to the call of *chiu-kuo* (save the nation). A significant proportion of the urban and commercial groups came to support the Party during the civil war because of their belief (or fervent hope) that the Communists might have solutions to China's numerous social and economic problems and because, in any case, the Communists were preferable to the Kuomintang, which had largely discredited itself through corruption, inefficiency, and brutality. The educated and intellectual elites backed the Party for all of these reasons and also because ever since the May Fourth period they had accepted, and had thought in terms of, particular fragments of Marxist-Leninist ideology. Whether or not Chinese intellectuals were attracted to the visionary goal of Communist society, they were impressed by Marxist explanations of what was wrong with traditional Chinese society (it was "feudal") and by Leninist explanations of the unequal treaties (they were imposed by capitalist nations at the stage of "imperialism"). This partially Marxist cast of non-Communist Chinese nationalist ideology generated a natural receptivity among nationalist intellectuals to the ideology that the Communist Party propagated during the 1940's.

It is also likely that many Chinese were drawn to the mystique of power and inevitability that communism seemed to possess during the height of Stalin's reign. Today the myth of "monolithic communism" and the Western leaders who justified anti-Communist policies in terms of countering its menace are favorite and easy targets of revisionist political critics, but it would be myopic in the extreme to suppose that the only believers in monolithic communism resided in John Foster Dulles' Washington. Twenty years ago one did not have to be a Marxist-Leninist or to know the first thing about dialectical materialism in order to imagine that communism might represent the wave of the future. Czeslaw Milosz, speaking from personal experience, describes what could be called the "romantic magnetism" of the Communist movement of the 1940's:

Mystery shrouds the political moves determined on high in the distant Center, Moscow. People speak about prominent figures in hushed voices. In the vast expanses of Euro-Asia, whole nations can vanish without leaving a trace. Armies number into the millions. Terror becomes socially useful and effective. Philosophers rule the state—obviously not philosophers in the traditional sense of the word, but dialecticians. The conviction grows that the whole world will be conquered. Great hordes of followers appear on all the continents. Lies are concocted from seeds of truth. The philosophically uneducated bourgeois enemy is despised for his inherited inability to think. (Classes condemned by the laws of history perish because their minds are paralyzed.) The boundaries of the Empire move steadily and systematically westward. Unparalleled sums of money are spent on scientific research. One prepares to rule all the people of the earth. Is all this too little? Surely this is enough to fascinate the intellectual. As he beholds these things, historical fatalism takes root in him. In a rare moment of sincerity he may confess cynically, "I bet on this horse. He's good. He'll carry me far." [12]

Rather a large number of Chinese elites, by no means all of them unsophisticated in the ways of the world, made precisely this calculation. The choice was made all the easier by the fact that the Communists openly espoused the same objectives that Sun Yat-sen had twenty-five years earlier.

The Chinese Communist Party, for its part, responded to the goals, needs, and aspirations of non-Communist Chinese with subtlety and political acumen. Throughout the decade of the 1940's, Mao Tse-tung eschewed the orthodox notion of the dictatorship of the proletariat in favor of what he called "new democracy," which directed the goals of the Communist revolution precisely toward the targets of the Chinese national revolution: "foreign imperialism," domestic agents of foreign imperialism ("compradores"), and feudal reactionaries. In the land reform movement carried out in the old liberated areas during the civil war, Party directives hammered away at cadres to avoid "leftist errors." [13] On the Double Tenth, 1947, the People's Liberation Army (PLA) adopted slogans which included: "Independence, Peace, Democracy, and Bread!"; "National Independence, Yes! Traitors,

[12] Czeslaw Milosz, *The Captive Mind* (New York: Alfred A. Knopf, 1953), p. 16.

[13] Chinese Communist Party Central Committee, "Directive Concerning Land Problems" (May 4, 1946), in Nihon Kokusai Mondai Kenkyū-sho, Chūgoku-bu (Japan International Problems Research Institute, China Section) (ed. and trans.), *Shin Chūgoku shiryō shūsei* (Collected Materials on New China) (Tokyo: Nihon Kokusai Mondai Kenyū-sho, 1963), I, Document No. 51, p. 244, s.v. par. 15.

No!"; and "The Communist Party Saves Nation and People! The Kuomintang Destroys Nation and People!" [14] A year later Liu Shao-ch'i would be explaining in "Internationalism and Nationalism" that "clearly, there is no contradiction between the true patriotism of the people of each nation and proletarian internationalism." [15] Finally, on the eve of victory Mao Tse-tung indicated that a Communist government would be a four-class "democratic dictatorship," including the working class, the peasantry, the urban petty bourgeoisie, and the "national bourgeoisie" (that is, patriotic capitalists not allied with foreign interests).[16]

A major theme in the Party's propaganda of the civil war period was the struggle of the PLA against betrayers of the nation, not necessarily against the class enemies of the proletariat. Communist publications developed and exploited the line that American imperialism had replaced Japanese fascism, that the Americans were responsible for the use of former Japanese army officers in China against "progressive" groups and the forces of liberation, and that the Americans, the Japanese, and the Kuomintang formed an unholy alliance intent upon the imperialist exploitation of China. One should not ignore the actual occurrences which lent credibility to this propaganda, but the important point is that these themes identified the Party with opposition to the same types of enemies that Chinese nationalists had been fighting since at least May 4, 1919.

As has become obvious today, the Chinese Communists' own ideology went considerably beyond that of the majority of their non-Communist followers and beyond what they propagated in the 1940's. During the Yenan period and the first few years after coming to power, Mao Tse-tung's long-range commitments were tactically but genuinely subordinated to a minimum political program. Mao had stated as much in his "Chinese Revolution and the Chinese Communist Party" (December, 1939) and in "On New Democracy" (January, 1940); and Liu Shao-ch'i reiterated, in his speech to the first plenary session of the Chinese People's Political Consultative Conference, that the so-called "Common Program" of the new government included all of the minimum objectives of the Communist Party but none of its longer-

---

[14] *Ch'ün-chung* (The Masses) (Hong Kong), No. 37 (October 9, 1947), p. 2.

[15] Liu Shao-ch'i, "Internationalism and Nationalism," *Ch'ün-chung* (Hong Kong), No. 45 (November 18, 1948), p. 12.

[16] For an article inviting the "national bourgeoisie" to support the Communists, see "The New China and the National Bourgeoisie," *Hua Shang Pao*, ed., June 27, 1949, in *Shin Chūgoku shiryō shūsei* (see n. 13), II, Document No. 116, pp. 518–20.

range goals.[17] In a more recent context, we read in the London outlet for Maoist theory:

New Democracy, *the minimum programme of the Chinese Communist Party,* was designed to eliminate feudalism and to destroy the basis of imperialist power in China by redistributing land, though without abolishing private property, and nationalizing enterprises directly or indirectly under foreign control. The latter comprised big banks and big mercantile and industrial concerns run by the so-called compradore class of Chinese.[18]

The results of these policies were phenomenal. Through its adaptation to the only genuine Chinese revolutionary movement of this century, the Party obtained a mass following, won a total revolutionary victory on the mainland, and obtained a political asset denied the Bolsheviks for at least twenty-five years after they came to power—namely, political authority. The significance of these outcomes for China and for the international Marxist-Leninist movement cannot be overstated. The Chinese case illustrates once again the fact that, historically, the circumstances that have proved propitious for the success of Communist revolutions were not the circumstances that ought to have been propitious according to Marxist ideology. Communist parties have yet to come to power when the circumstances that Marx identified as fostering revolutions were in fact propitious, as, for example, in Japan during the 1920's, a maturing industrial society with a large, exploited proletariat.[19] In concrete historical terms, Communist ideology has adapted itself to revolutions that were immensely more complicated and often of an entirely different nature than the revolutions for which it claims to be an analysis and a guide. However, in making this adaptation, Communist ideology has affected the revolutionary movement it captured as much as the ideology itself was distorted or tended to deteriorate in the adaptive process.

## AUTHORITY AND ITS FOUNDATIONS

What does it mean to say that the Communists obtained political authority as a result of their revolutionary victory? First of all, the

[17] See Miyashita Tadao, "Chūkyō ni okeru shakai-shugi kensetsu no riron" (The Theory of Socialist Construction in Communist China), in Nihon Gaisei Gakkai (Japan Foreign Policy Association), *Chūkyō seiken no genjō bunseki* (Analysis of the Chinese Communist Regime Today) (Tokyo: Nihon Gaisei Gakkai, 1961), pp. 6–7.

[18] China Policy Study Group, *The Broadsheet* (London), III, No. 4 (April, 1966), 3. Italics added.

[19] See Robert A. Scalapino, *The Japanese Communist Movement 1920–1966* (Berkeley and Los Angeles: University of California Press, 1967), pp. 328–34.

*phenomenon* of authority, which is readily observable, must be distinguished from the *bases* of authority, which are problematical and require analysis. Then phenomenon itself is a relationship of "imperative control," to use Max Weber's term, between leaders and those who are led. It is described in the Bible in this example: "I am a man under authority, having soldiers under me: and I say to this man, Go, and he goeth; and to another, Come, and he cometh; and to my servant, Do this, and he doeth it" (Matt. 8:9). As to why these relationships of imperative control exist, the quality that distinguishes the exercise of authority from other forms of power, such as coercion, remuneration, persuasion, influence, and so forth, is the existence of an *ideology,* or, more generally, of a *belief system,* which encompasses both the leaders and the led, which defines the exercise of political leadership as legitimate, and which thereby makes obedience morally incumbent upon all who share the system of beliefs. Coercion, remuneration, persuasion, and influence do not depend for their effectiveness upon the parties to a power relationship sharing the same values.

It is, of course, true that the exercise of authority does not exclude the use of other forms of power in political leadership. The alternative employment of authority, coercion, and remuneration forms the basis of Skinner's and Winckler's cyclical theory of mass movements in Communist China.[20] What Skinner calls "normative power" is similar to what is identified here as authority; and the availability of so-called "N-power" to the Communist leadership combined with the fact that it is characteristically used before the other means of eliciting compliance, support the conclusion that the Communists have enjoyed revolutionary authority.

There is a nuance of difference between authority and N-power. N-power sometimes seems to partake, at least in part, of persuasion. Yet, as Blau observes, "Authority is distinguished from persuasion by the fact that people *a priori* suspend their own judgment and accept that of an acknowledged superior without having to be convinced that his is correct." [21] As I shall try to clarify subsequently, the use of persuasion in conjunction with authority by the Communists, particu-

[20] See G. William Skinner and Edwin A. Winckler, "Compliance Succession in Rural Communist China: A Cyclical Theory," in Amitai Etzioni (ed.), *Complex Organizations, A Sociological Reader* (2nd. ed.; New York: Holt, Rinehart, and Winston, 1969), pp. 410–38.
[21] Peter M. Blau, "Critical Remarks on Weber's Theory of Authority," *American Political Science Review,* LVII (June, 1963), 307.

larly during the early 1950's, was part of a developmental process of authority building. The characteristics of N-power in the period of the cult of Mao are more authoritarian than they were, for example, in the early stages of agricultural collectivization. A model for obedience in the period of the cult is found in Wang Chieh's motto, "Whatever Chairman Mao said, I thereupon did," a motto which on November 11, 1965, became the title of an important *Chieh-fang-chün pao* (Liberation Army News) editorial.[22]

Authority rests on a belief system shared by leaders and led alike. This does not mean that followers necessarily like what they are ordered to do or that they regard every task they are directed to perform as being in their own personal interest. It does mean that they feel themselves duty-bound to obey authority. Soldiers responding to the orders of a superior officer do not necessarily like the orders they have received, but they do regard the orders as legitimate. They believe that the superior officer speaks for the common good (that is, for the purposes which the value sharers hold in common), and they are motivated to obey the superior's directives because of the directives' legitimate source. Subordinates will inevitably be influenced by the outcomes of a superior's directives. Failure by the leader to achieve common objectives always has consequences for authority. If the source and the agent of authority are identical and a failure of leadership occurs, the entire relationship of authority may be ruptured. More commonly, source and agent are separated, and it is the office or the position which a leader holds that has been legitimatized rather than the occupant himself (for example, the position of cadre rather than an individual cadre). Thus, in case of a policy failure, corruption, venality, or some other betrayal of trust by a person exercising authority, the incumbent of a position may be held responsible without damaging the authority of his office. The problem of maintaining this distinction between role and occupant is particularly acute in the Chinese Communist political system.

In a society-wide context, not everyone accepts authority equally; some political groups positively support the leadership while others only acquiesce in the leaders' commanding positions, recognizing that the leaders have significant political backing. Moreover, the leadership —no matter how attractive its ideology—must pass certain tests of its effectiveness, including possession of a capable organization, predom-

[22] See *Ts'ung Lei Feng tao Wang Chieh* (From Lei Feng to Wang Chieh) (Hong Kong: San-lien Shu-tien, 1965), pp. 17–21.

inance of political power, and some outstanding success in reaching its stated goals. Leaders always go beyond ideological appeals and consolidate their authority by giving a wide range of people posts of authority (for example, a local cadre) and thus a stake in the system. Even when the ideological or consensual bases of authority are weakened, challenges to authority will be mitigated by the longevity of the regime and by the absence of alternatives.

While all these aspects of authoritarian relationships must be considered in any realistic analysis of the phenomenon, the existence of a belief system through which the leaders and the led identify, communicate with, and motivate each other remains the *sine qua non* of genuine authority. The presence of a justifying and obligating ideology, one that legitimatizes the hierarchy which leaders and subordinates respect in common, is a necessary, if not sufficient, condition for the existence and persistence of command and obedience based on authority. This being the case, the nature of a particular grant of authority is most perceptively studied in terms of the identity, convergence, overlap, or disparity between the belief system held by part or all of the leadership and the belief system held by part or all of the people.

During the 1940's and particularly during 1949, the belief systems of the Chinese Communist leadership and of a majority of the Chinese people converged. They were never identical, since, as we have seen, the Chinese Communists purposely, for various reasons consistent with their political ambitions and ideology, held in abeyance their longer-range goals and championed the goals on which most politically mobilized Chinese had come to agree. This convergence produced sufficient power to enable the Communists, with the aid of the people, to defeat the Kuomintang; and it resulted in a grant of authority to the Communists to lead revolutionary change. The fact that the Communist victory was obtained through military means—that is, through the use of force—does not alter this conclusion. The Communists' possession of mass support is a more important political datum than their use of force against their enemies. Whether or not the use of force contravenes authority (and is therefore coercion) depends upon the content of the belief system that the parties to the relationship of authority hold. In the Chinese case, the people themselves accepted the necessity and inevitability of revolutionary violence in overthrowing the Kuomintang. As de Grazia argues, "In the obtaining of authority, the use of force will make authority impossible to achieve, if force is detested by the public. If force is esteemed [as in truly revolutionary situations], then it can lead to authority." [23] This latter form of authority we have chosen to call "revolutionary authority."

The Chinese Communists' mandate of authority of 1949 had two characteristics particularly relevant to the analysis of revolutionary authority in general and to an appreciation of the political history of Communist China over the subsequent two decades. First, the mandate of authority was *unstable* because, although the belief systems of the Chinese Communist and Chinese nationalist revolutions converged in 1949, the Chinese Communists' commitment to Marxist-Leninist goals was absolute and their accommodation to nationalist ideology was only temporary. This characteristic has caused the mandate of authority to change over time in both intended and unintended directions. Second, the mandate served to *constrain* the Chinese Communist leadership for certain particularistic and environmental reasons. Of the many particularistic factors which could be mentioned, the most important seems to me to be the fact that Mao Tse-tung is a populist (or, at any rate, that he became one in the course of his revolutionary struggle). Mao likes to have the support of the people; his whole contribution to the theory of revolutionary strategy is based upon obtaining and using the backing of the masses. And at least until the final stages of the Cultural Revolution (after the mangoes affair), when the political situation became clouded, he regarded China's huge population and its support of the Communist government as guarantees of the eventual success of his own ideological goals.

The chief environmental reason why the Chinese Communists should have felt constrained by their popular mandate of authority is the sheer size of the country and its population. Although they appear to have more effective control over the territory and the people than any previous Chinese government, the Communists are still trying to run the world's largest social system from a central government. The Chinese Communist Party is itself the world's largest Communist Party, but its effective Party-to-population ratio is smaller than that of all but one other established Communist system (Cuba). Given this problem, together with the hostile international climate in which China lives (and chooses to live) as well as its relative isolation from sources of international aid, credit, trade, and defense, the Chinese Communists have tended to be cautious (with certain exceptions) about squandering their stock of political authority, and they have generally not tried to rely on coercion (or remuneration) in achieving their ends.

[23] de Grazia, "What Authority is *Not*," p. 329.

In short, the Chinese Communists have neither wanted nor been entirely free to adopt a strategy of revolutionary development like that pursued in Russia during the height of Stalinism or in East Europe after 1948, when considerations about the attitudes of the people were certainly not a constraint on the leadership. Over the past twenty years, the Chinese Communists have appealed to values that were internalized in their followers in 1949, and they have devoted enormous amounts of time and energy toward inculcating new values. The Party's attempts to teach new values to the people, which we shall turn to subsequently, raise fundamental questions about the nature and the flexibility of belief systems which form the basis of political authority.

As stated earlier, it is relatively easy to observe relationships of authority and it is possible to study the belief systems that support such relationships, but the origins of such political belief systems—that is, their basis and psychology—have always been a subject requiring philosophical and theoretical interpretation. Weber's famous threefold typology of the bases of obedience to authority is only one of the many solutions offered to this problem. Weber argued that one form of authority, the traditional, rests on "the general and continuous belief in the sacredness of settled traditions and the legitimacy of the person or persons called to authority by such traditions." Another form of authority, the legal, rests on "the belief in the legality of a consciously created order and of the right to give commands vested in the person or persons designated by that order." A third form of authority, the charismatic, rests on "the uncommon and extraordinary devotion to the sacredness or the heroic force or the exemplariness of an individual and the order revealed or created by him." [24]

Other theories of the basis of authority include de Maistre's sombre conclusion that behind all authority stands the hangman and Arendt's apparent belief that all authority is in a certain sense traditional.[25] Her view is particularly relevant to the study of revolutionary regimes:

Those who are not only in power but in authority are aware that their (authoritarian) power depends upon its legitimacy, which is assumed and "proven" by invocation of a source beyond or above the ruler. Historically, we know of a

[24] As translated by W. G. Runciman, *Social Science and Political Theory* (Cambridge: Cambridge University Press, 1963), pp. 56–57.

[25] On de Maistre's view, see Sheldon S. Wolin, *Politics and Vision* (Boston: Little, Brown and Co., 1960), p. 398.

variety of sources to which authoritarian rulers could appeal in order to justify their powers: it could be the law of nature, or the commands of God, or the Platonic ideas, or ancient customs sanctified by tradition, or one great event in the past, such as the foundation of the body politic. . . . There exists in our political history one type of event for which the notion of founding is decisive. . . . The events are the revolutions of the modern age. . . .[26]

During their second decade in power, the Chinese Communists probably invoked the spirit and revolutionary accomplishments of Yenan in support of their authority more than any other possible source, including Marxist-Leninist ideology. When the authority of the Party was severely questioned following the failure of the Great Leap Forward, the regime launched the "Recall Bitterness" campaign, which led into the so-called "Four Histories Movement," the whole effort being designed to recall the achievements of the revolution and to insure that no one thought things were worse in 1959–61 than they were before the revolution.

Although there is an abundance of different theories about the sources of authority, the majority of them can be reduced to two fundamental schools of thought in the study of authority. One, often associated with political philosophy, stresses that authority is rationally based and that men rationally calculate the consequences of their refusal to cooperate, as well as the advantages to be gained from organized social life. The other, often associated with organization theory, stresses that authority is conditioned or learned, and that men may be "educated, indoctrinated, trained, socialized, acculturated, programmed, or brainwashed" to obey authority, depending upon one's preferences in vocabulary.[27] The rational theory of authority would include Weber's legal type and de Maistre's hangman; the learning theory of authority would include Weber's traditional type and Arendt's ancient events of foundation. The charismatic theory appears to partake of both, but as we shall see, it may, because of its inherent instability, be incommensurable with any other form. Although the rational and learning theories of authority have often been seen as antithetical, nothing emerges more clearly from the Chinese Communist experience than the fact that both views need to be combined and that a rational acceptance of authority facilitates a conditioning to authority.

[26] Hannah Arendt, "What Was Authority?" in C. J. Friedrich (ed.), *Authority* (Cambridge, Mass.: Harvard University Press, 1958), pp. 83, 106.

[27] Cf. Herbert Kaufman, "Organization Theory and Political Theory," *American Political Science Review*, LVIII (March, 1964), 5–14.

The post-"liberation" period of the New Democracy was dominated by the rational acceptance of the new authority, while the period of socialist transformation, approximately 1953–56, saw the population being conditioned to the full potentialities of the new authority. During the first period, the Party fulfilled its New Democratic commitments by using revolutionary violence to eliminate alleged agents of "feudalism" (the landlords) and "imperialism" (the compradores). At the same time it won supporters through programs which directly served the interests of particular groups. Land reform is the most obvious of these, but the Marriage Law, which was promulgated on May 1, 1950, should also be mentioned. It has proven strong enough to obtain continued support for the new order from emancipated women, and its Article 10 had the desirable consequence of virtually destroying any legal basis for lineage organizations.

The process of conditioning to authority depends upon the capacity of the leadership to enmesh the population in a web of obligation to the new regime through policies that appeal to their interests and then, gradually, to lead the people into habits of obedience that do not result in an immediate, personal payoff to them. Blau conceives the process in these terms:

In general, a situation of collective dependence is fertile soil for the development of authority, but its development is contingent on judicious restraint by the superior in the use of his power. If he alienates subordinates by imposing his will upon them against their resistance, they will obey only under duress and not freely follow his lead. If, on the other hand, he uses some of his power to further their collective interests, the common experience of dependence on and obligation to the superior is apt to give rise to shared beliefs that it is right and in the common interest to submit to his command, and these social norms of compliance legitimate and enforce his authority over them.[28]

People who have been obligated to a new regime can be led to undertake new programs in which the payoffs are delayed or nonexistent, but the question still remains as to when and how this initial suspension of judgment by the people becomes transformed into a recognition that they are accepting the judgment of their legitimate authorities. Richard Merelman has given the greatest thought to this problem, and it seems useful to me to introduce and outline here his conceptual framework for dealing with it.[29] Merelman sees legitimacy

[28] Blau, "Critical Remarks," p. 313.
[29] Richard Merelman, "Learning and Legitimacy," *American Political Science Review*, LX (September, 1966), 548–61.

as "the result of a learning sequence in which secondary reinforcement substitutes for primary reinforcement for populations and in which the entire learning effort is rationalized into a sense of legitimacy." Synthesizing learning theory and the theory of cognitive dissonance, Merelman develops a six-stage learning paradigm for political regimes. His six stages are:

1. *The stage of unconditioned reinforcement.* In this stage the regime provides a stimulus for its population, normally a material inducement, to learn new political behavior; in Communist China the clearest example is land reform.

2. *The stage of classical conditioning.* "The regime associates itself with the stimuli that provide the behaviors [elicited] in the stage of unconditioned reinforcement, [and it] elaborates a series of institutions whose processes precede or are paired with the appearance of the unconditioned stimulus." To continue the land reform example, one of the main distinctions between the land reform in China after 1950 and in Russia after 1917 is that the Chinese Communists sponsored, controlled, and directed the Chinese land reform, whereas in Russia it was an uncontrolled, elemental process.

3. *The stage of intermittent reinforcement.* During this stage material payoffs are provided less frequently than in the first stage—for example, the various Communist-directed peasant institutions persist and are now associated with the campaign to create mutual aid teams, which benefitted the peasants but less directly than did land redistribution.

4. *The stage of secondary reinforcement.* The institutional processes (Stage 2) which were associated with the stage of unconditioned reinforcement and which symbolize its achievements and rewards are now used as the stimulus to produce a new set of learned behaviors. For example, the praise, encouragement, or wisdom of the Communist Party and of Chairman Mao, or the collective, but engineered, decisions of the peasant associations, are used to elicit the initial movement toward collectivization. As Merelman puts it, "Now the symbol of unconditioned reinforcement, government behavior, has become a positive end for the population, not simply a signal for material rewards."

5. *The stage of cognitive dissonance.* During the later part of the New Democracy period and particularly during the socialist transformation period, the Party involved the population in numerous mass movements of one kind or another—movements which could be in-

terpreted by the population as further extensions of the already highly beneficial reforms that had been implemented. These movements are well-known and need not be detailed. What is important to note is that the movements were relatively moderate and that they involved the population in an extraordinary outpouring of political participation. One result of this participation was that people began to rationalize their compliance more in terms of the regime's moral authority than in terms of an immediate material payoff. Arthur Cohen offers one widely accepted interpretation of the relevant process:

It has often been demonstrated that forcing a person to express an opinion discrepant from what he privately believes results in a change of private opinion. According to [Leon] Festinger's analysis, expressing an opinion discrepant from one's privately held position creates "dissonance," or psychological tension having drive character. The tension may be reduced by changing one's private position to coincide more nearly with the position expressed.[30]

When such a forcing process is carried out on a society-wide, totalistic scale with the full pressures of government and of an engineered public environment behind it, both the dissonance and the willingness to change in order to relieve the resultant tensions are at their maximum. Unquestionably the greatest achievement of this process in China was the full collectivization into Soviet-style collective farms of the world's largest peasant population—a process which in the USSR required the use of force and produced unimaginable suffering, but which in China was accomplished with relatively little opposition.

6. *The stage of condensation symbols.* Merelman writes:

Once the cognitive dissonance stage has been passed through and the government is considered to be legitimate, the regime can signify the governmental processes which provide secondary reinforcement by elaboration of a series of condensation symbols which stand for those processes. Hence, such terms as "our way of life" or "the Constitution" reinstate quickly in the minds of the public the symbolic reinforcement now considered legitimate. . . . Once such a process of legitimizing has occurred within a population, it need not be repeated for each successive generation. Legitimacy is passed on from generation to generation. . . .

This stage does not appear to have been reached in China, largely because of the failure of the Great Leap Forward. Nevertheless, the Great Leap Forward remains the greatest testimonial to the trust that

[30] Arthur Cohen, "Attitudinal Consequences of Induced Discrepancies Between Cognitions and Behavior," in Martin Fishbein (ed.), *Readings in Attitude Theory and Measurement* (New York: Wiley, 1967), p. 332.

the people had placed in the Communist Party. On the orders of the Party, some 120 million peasant households of 752,113 high level agricultural producers cooperatives reorganized themselves into 26,000 communes with their 500,000 production brigades and three million production teams, all within a period of perhaps two months.[31] The Party can never claim that the Chinese people did not follow it down the road to socialist construction; the people followed readily enough, but many soon came to have grave doubts about whether the Party knew where it was going.

Merelman's theory has been presented here to illustrate one conception of the learning theory of authority, not necessarily to serve as an accurate and comprehensive portrayal of the process of Chinese Communist authority building. Certainly Merelman's paradigm would have to be supplemented with an analysis of the means by which a contemporary revolutionary regime is *able* to direct the political learning of the population under its control. Generally speaking, revolutionary regimes of the nineteenth century and earlier did not have the social tools to do so. Kirchheimer, for example, isolates the following modern elements, which, if the revolutionary leadership knows how to use them, can facilitate revolutionary reconstruction after the seizure of power:

(a) the technical and intellectual equipment is now at hand to direct [the masses] toward major societal programs rather than simply liberating their energies from the bonds of tradition;

(b) [modern revolutionaries] have the means at hand to control people's livelihood by means of job assignments and graduated reward unavailable under the largely agricultural and artisanal structure of the 1790's and still unavailable to the small enterprise and commission-merchant-type economy of the 1850's and 1860's;

(c) [modern revolutionaries] have fallen heir to endlessly and technically refined propaganda devices substituting for the uncertain leader-mass relations of the previous periods; and

(d) [modern revolutionaries] faced state organizations shaken up by war dislocation and economic crisis.[32]

We would want to add to item (c) what Robert Lifton has called "milieu control"—the physical isolation of populations from today's incredibly expanded international media of communications. For ex-

---

[31] As of 1963, there were a total of seventy-four thousand communes, divided into seven hundred thousand brigades and five million teams. *Shin Chūgoku nenkan, 1964* (New China Yearbook, 1964) (Tokyo: Kyokutō Shoten, 1965), p. 319.

[32] Kirchheimer, "Confining Conditions," p. 973.

ample, most of us have yet to grasp fully the consequences of the fact that the population of Communist China reads more about Albania in its public press than about any other foreign nation.

Merelman's paradigm is suggestive; and the Chinese Communist case, at least with regard to the peasantry, appears roughly to illustrate it. His work could form the theoretical basis for further research into Chinese Communist authority, an investigation that not only might illuminate the process of legitimization in China, but also might serve to refine further the theory of learning and legitimacy. However, it should be stressed again that authority and the belief systems which support it have both rational and conditioned foundations. Furthermore, the policies carried out by the Communists between 1949 and 1955 may have had the effect of conditioning a part or all of the people to the Party's authority, but it is not at all clear that this was the Party's intention or that the Communist leaders were properly sensitive to the capabilities and limitations of the authority that was granted to them.

## PERIOD OF THE NATIONALISTIC BELIEF SYSTEM

The initial period of the People's Republic of China—from 1949 until approximately the end of the Korean War—was one of New Democracy, in name and in fact. The CCP delivered on its promises to eliminate imperialism and feudalism, and it championed the goal of unity above all others. Non-Communist personages were welcomed into the government. The Party newspaper published articles on the need to "unite and advance under the great banner of patriotism," and it reported fully on the so-called "democratic parties" and their efforts to rally old KMT functionaries, intellectuals, scientific workers, and tradesmen to support the "Central People's Government [as it was then called] in the joint struggle to resist the United States, aid Korea, and to build up a New China." [33] It is sometimes forgotten that even the first round of ssu-hsiang kai-tsao (thought reform) directed against the professors was justified in terms of the traditional enemies of the Chinese national revolution. Practically all of the early confessions followed the same pattern: the intellectuals stated that the "distortion" of their minds was due either to a "feudalistic" family background or to studies in imperialist countries.[34] The demand that

[33] JMJP, ed., January 24, 1951.
[34] Cf. "The Communists and the Intellectuals: Stage One (September 1951–January 1952)," American Consulate General, Hong Kong, CB, No. 169 (April 2, 1952).

they undergo thought reform was new, but the contents of the process were not. A Chinese nationalist would not have had the slightest difficulty in rationally giving his allegiance to this new regime.

In addition to the New Democratic policies of the regime, a fortuitous occurrence (but one encountered in the histories of many great revolutions) lent credibility to some possibly dubious elements in the ideology of New Democracy. The Communists had been verbally attacking the United States throughout the civil war, and Mao Tse-tung had allied the new Chinese government with the Soviet Union. If any Chinese nationalist had doubts about Mao's motives on either of these scores, however, the Korean War helped to eliminate them. I do not wish to imply that the United Nations' aid to the government in Seoul, which the U.N. itself had created in 1948, was unwarranted or constituted foreign intervention against the Chinese Communist revolution, but it is necessary to acknowledge that the regime treated it as such and that the Resist America, Aid Korea campaign was of major importance in consolidating the regime's authority on *traditional nationalistic grounds*. The fact that the People's Liberation Army was more effective against the "imperialists" in Korea than Chinese armies had usually been in the past only heightened the effect. "It is difficult," concludes Whiting, "to think of any single course of action that could have so enhanced the stature of the new regime as did [its] intervention in Korea." [35]

The Chinese Communists made good use of the Korean War in projecting to the population the regime's peaceful but patriotic intentions in foreign policy, the threatening nature of the international environment, and the genocidal tendencies of China's enemies. An example was the two-part motion picture *K'ang-Mei Yüan-Ch'ao* (Resist America, Aid Korea), which was made in 1952 and 1953 and shown all over China during its first year of release. The climax of Part II had the Chinese People's Volunteers (a name the Chinese do not bother to use any more today) annihilating fifty-two thousand American troops in one great battle, followed by scenes of peace talks at Panmunjom and interviews with Kim Il-sung and P'eng Teh-huai.[36]

Immediately following the Korean truce, the regime published its "general line of the state during the period of transition to socialism."

[35] Allen S. Whiting, *China Crosses the Yalu* (Stanford, Calif.: Stanford University Press, 1968), p. 166.

[36] See Ōshiba Takashi, *Shin Chūgoku eiga* (Cinema of New China) (Kyoto: Hōritsu Bunka Sha, 1956), pp. 60–61 *et passim*. Cf. Alan P. L. Liu, *The Film Industry in Communist China* (Cambridge, Mass.: M.I.T. Center of International Studies, 1965).

On October 27, 1953, Li Wei-han asserted that, according to Mao Tse-tung, the entire period from the founding of the People's Republic until the establishment of socialist relations of production in China was one of "transition." Although this new definition of the essential character of the government marked the formal end of New Democracy in terms of the goals of the state (but not in terms of its political relations with the people), there were two reasons why the majority of the people easily accepted the "general line" as a logical and rational next step. First, until 1953, New Democracy had included only the negative or minimum objectives of the Chinese national revolutionary belief system—that is, elimination of feudalism and imperialism. Socialist transformation, as defined at the time by the leadership, was clearly consonant with the maximum goals of the Chinese revolution: it included as first priority the heavy industrialization of the country in accordance with an announced (but not yet published) "first five-year plan." Other elements of socialist society, such as a state-operated economy, collectivization of agriculture, and the transformation of private bourgeois enterprises into state capitalist enterprises, were all portrayed as both subordinate and prerequisite to "transforming China from an agrarian nation into an industrial nation." [37]

Second, on the political rather than the economic front, the regime not only did not unveil the quintessential institution of socialist transformation as it existed in the then-current Marxist-Leninist doctrine —namely, the dictatorship of the proletariat—it in fact began a movement to create a rational, legal, constitutional government which in principle would keep the Communist Party under considerable democratic restraints. The regime actually launched its movement toward constitutional government simultaneously with publicizing its new economic objectives. The effect was to disarm any nationalist who might be suspicious of the motives of the "Communist" leadership and to inaugurate in earnest the learning phase of authority-building in China.

As every commentator on the period 1949 to 1956 has observed, there is difficulty in assigning dates to the end of the New Democracy period, to the beginning and the end of the socialist transformation period, to the beginning of the dictatorship of the proletariat, and to

[37] Miyashita, "Chūkyō ni okeru," pp. 5–6. Cf. Yamamoto Hideo, "Chūgoku ni okeru seiji-ishiki no henkaku" (Change of Political Consciousness in China), in Kuraishi Takeshirō (ed.), *Henkaku-ki Chūgoku no kenkyū* (Research on China in Transition) (Tokyo: Iwanami Shoten, 1958), pp. 132–54.

the beginning of the period of socialist construction.[38] What has not been fully appreciated is that the Communists are quite aware and proud of the fact that these boundaries are blurred. On the fifteenth anniversary of the regime, *Jen-min Jih-pao* argued editorially:

Why is it that we were able to surmount the numerous difficulties left over by imperialism and the reactionary Kuomintang rule and rapidly make great achievements after the founding of the People's Republic of China? It is primarily because our Party resolutely opposed the erroneous view that a distinct break should be made between the democratic revolution and the socialist revolution.

. . . After the regime of the dictatorship of the proletariat was established [exactly when this was is never made clear], we not only carried through to the end the democratic revolution, but also moved ahead without interruption to the socialist transformation in various fields, liberating the social productive forces to a great extent.[39]

Although the process was not as indistinct as this statement suggests, it seems to me that the Communists' gradualness and the blurring of Marxist-Leninist stages contributed greatly to the growth of the regime's authority and at the same time reflected the constraints imposed on the regime by its initial, primarily nationalistic mandate of leadership.

A year after the onset of socialist transformation the Constitution of the People's Republic of China was adopted. Although publicized as the basic law of the land, the Constitution has received its least support from those who wrote it. Party leaders have almost never invoked it as the source of their authority, and at least two of its institutions—the National People's Congress and the office of Chairman of the Chinese People's Republic—appeared during 1970 to be moribund. (The National People's Congress has not met since December, 1964; and the Twelfth Plenum of the Party's Eighth Central Committee, although it had no constitutional power to do so, "adopted a resolution to expel Liu Shao-ch'i from the Party once and for all [and] to dismiss him from all posts *both inside and outside the party.*" [40] Therefore, since October 31, 1968, constitutionally speaking, China has not had a head of state.) In Maoist terms, the Constitution was a united front or-

---

[38] Cf. Miyashita, "Chūkyō ni okeru," p. 13; Schwartz, *Communism and China;* Tokuda Noriyuki, "Mō Taku-tō no 'shin minshu-shugi' gainen ni tsuite" (Concerning Mao Tse-tung's Concept of "New Democracy"), *Ajia Keizai* (Asian Economy), VII (September, 1966), 100–111.

[39] *JMJP*, ed., October 1, 1964.

[40] *Peking Review,* Supplement to No. 44 (November 1, 1968), p. vi.

ganizational device: it provided a smoke screen behind which the policies of socialist transformation could be carried out, and it helped educate the masses through controlled political participation to support Party-initiated policies. The vast series of elections and congresses authorized by the Constitution were pure mass line inspirations; they were not to be taken literally as expressions of the popular will since, as we know today, "blind faith in elections is conservative thinking" (*Hung-ch'i* [Red Flag], editorial, October 16, 1968). Similarly, the increased use of judicial tribunals authorized by the Constitution bolstered the trust that people placed in the regime—unless, of course, a citizen happened to run afoul of a Party member, in which case he might be denounced as a counterrevolutionary, something that happened with great frequency during 1955.

The Constitution itself does not differ in political philosophy from the "Common Program" of 1949, except that the latter does not refer to the "building of a socialist society," whereas the Constitution of 1954 does (Art. 4). Modeled after the Stalinist constitution of 1936, the Chinese Constitution represented the last manifestation of New Democratic ideology (Chinese nationalists had put pressure on Chiang Kai-shek for twenty years to end "tutelage" and to promulgate a democratic constitution), and its location of sovereignty with the National People's Congress was ideologically nullified two years later when the "dictatorship of the proletariat" came into being.

Nevertheless, the Constitution was not insignificant. It was the Communists' final payoff to the nationalists for their continuing support, and it probably contributed as much as the Party's gradualism in economic affairs to the legitimization of the new regime. If the Party had only listened, the comments of a Chinese citizen known to us as "student number 5302095 at Peking University" were not counterrevolutionary; they reflected a truly liberal commitment to the new government of China:

There are two kinds of leadership: one is "administrative;" it not only actually leads but has the authority to lead. For instance, the Ministry of Higher Education leads the university. The other kind of leadership is "educational;" for instance, propagandizing to boost morale, calling for action, drawing up draft plans, etc. The latter kind of leadership carries no compulsion; the success of this kind of leadership depends on its "correctness."

The National People's Congress has not delegated the first kind of leadership to the Communist Party. In fact, no matter how advanced the Communist Party may be, it is not entitled to this kind of leadership. Communist Party members engaged in administrative duties should base their decisions on the laws of the State and the wishes of the people; it's not necessary to compel every citizen to accept such decisions. The Communist Party can only strive to win the masses of people to accept its leadership; it cannot demand that they must necessarily obey its leadership. If the Party leads successfully, the masses of people will accept voluntarily.[41]

Within less than five years time, the Party would have good reason to ponder these remarks. By treating the "double track" (that is, the parallel Party and state hierarchies) as a mere convenience during the second five-year plan period, the Party inevitably broke down the distinction that existed in the minds of the people between the agent and the source of authority. When the Great Leap Forward failed, the people naturally held Party leaders responsible—and to have allowed that to happen in revolutionary China was, as we shall see, a serious political mistake. The state machinery created by the Constitution offered the means which could have prevented this blunder, but these means were allowed to atrophy, for reasons that relate to the dramatic transformation in both the Chinese and international Communist movements that took place during the pregnant year, 1956.

### PERIOD OF THE SOCIALIST CONSTRUCTION BELIEF SYSTEM

While studying in Peking during 1961–62, Sven Lindqvist made the following discovery:

In a copy of *All Men are Brothers,* Mao's favorite novel, which I borrowed at Peking University, I found that a student had underlined the following passage: "In those years the country was at peace and the harvests of the five grains were plentiful and the people went merrily to their work. If anything was dropped upon the road, none picked it up, nor were doors of houses locked at night. *So it was during the first nine years.*" [42]

If, as Lindqvist concluded, the student had read a modern meaning into this old passage, his periodization was approximately correct, although the problems that made the tenth year go sour began in 1956. During that year three things happened, all of them interrelated, which set in motion policies and processes that are still reverberating throughout China and the international Communist movement. First, following the relative success of full collectivization, the regime

---

[41] Trans. by Dennis J. Doolin, *Communist China, The Politics of Student Opposition* (Stanford, Calif.: Hoover Institution, 1964), p. 51.

[42] Sven Lindqvist, *China in Crisis* (London: Faber, 1965), pp. 39–40. Italics in original.

achieved its highest levels of legitimization among the people that it was to attain between 1949 and 1969. Second, the Party launched socialist construction. And, third, Khrushchev planted some seeds that would ripen into both the Sino-Soviet dispute and the cult of Mao Tse-tung.

The interrelation between all three of these elements is crucial, although we shall delay discussion of the third element until the period of the cult of Mao, when its full implications became manifest. It is well-known that Mao himself decided to push collectivization in 1955 and 1956, and thereby created the basis for disagreement and ultimately for factions within the Political Bureau concerning the means and speed with which to proceed with socialist construction. Franz Schurmann characterizes the basis of these incipient factions in terms of Mao's "fast but risky" strategy versus Ch'en Yün's "slow but safe" strategy.[43] Mao's strategy appeared, at least in his own mind, to have succeeded with full collectivization, and the fact that collectivization was achieved with such *comparatively* little opposition from the masses tended to support his conclusion. The extraordinary legitimization of the regime in 1956, as evidenced by the confidence which the success of the first five-year plan had generated and by the willingness of the people to undertake new initiatives on the Party's orders alone, laid the groundwork for the Great Leap Forward—the most Maoist and the most disastrous socioeconomic experiment undertaken in China.

If Mao's hand was evident in all the important economic decisions of the period, it was nevertheless the Party that ratified and implemented them. Responding to the confusing and disturbing statements coming from the Soviet Party's Twentieth Congress, the Chinese Party, on April 5, 1956, identified its own regime of "people's democratic dictatorship" as being, in fact, a "dictatorship of the proletariat." Although the primary intent of the Chinese Political Bureau's statement ("On the Historical Experience of the Dictatorship of the Proletariat") was to express its misgivings about Khrushchev's speech on Stalin, the effect of the statement was to move the Communist Party further toward open administration of China's society and economy, with attendant risks to its then considerable assets of authority.

This process of increased political exposure for the Communist

---

[43] Franz Schurmann, "Politics and Economics in Russia and China," in Donald W. Treadgold (ed.), *Soviet and Chinese Communism: Similarities and Differences* (Seattle: University of Washington Press, 1967), pp. 306–7.

Party accelerated with the split-session Eighth Congress of the CCP (September, 1956, and May, 1958). Regardless of the Party leaders' varying assessments of what the targets and the pace of the second five-year plan should be—a disagreement that necessitated two meetings of the Congress and that finally resulted in Mao's view prevailing—the significance of the Congress from the point of view of the regime's authority was that the divergence between the Chinese national revolutionary belief system and the Chinese Communist revolutionary belief system became open and irrevocable. At the second session of the Eighth Congress, Liu Shao-ch'i presented the "general line of socialist construction" as the new, legitimating ideology of the People's Republic of China.

The ideology of the general line was different from that of Chinese nationalism, but it built on it and was accepted by the people as growing out of the successes of the 1949–56 period. Although the general line called for the final elimination of all vestiges of capitalism and began to point to some visionary goals of Communist society, it still envisioned China's "overtaking Great Britain in steel production within fifteen years" (not strictly a Marxist objective), the elimination of illiteracy, improvements in public health, and the simultaneous development of industry and agriculture with priority given to industry. As Liu Shao-ch'i stated:

Some say that speeding up construction makes people feel "tense," and so it's better to slow down the tempo. But are things not going to get tense if the speed of construction is slowed down? Surely one should be able to see that a really terribly tense situation would exist if more than 600 million people had to live in poverty and cultural backwardness for a prolonged period, had to exert their utmost efforts just to eke out a bare living, and were unable to resist natural calamities effectively, unable to put a quick stop to possible foreign aggression and utterly unable to master their own fate. It was to pull themselves out of such a situation, that the hundreds of millions of our people summoned up their energies to throw themselves, full of confidence, into the heat of work and struggle.[44]

So long as socialist construction was conceived in these terms rather than in terms of the explicit molding of "new socialist man," it was not difficult for the Chinese people to give their allegiance to it. There

[44] Liu Shao-ch'i, "Report on the Work of the Central Committee of the Communist Party of China to the Second Session of the Eighth National Congress, May 5, 1958." Text in Harvard University, East Asian Research Center, *Communist China 1955–1959* (Cambridge, Mass.: Harvard University Press, 1962), p. 429.

is every indication that they did so during the Great Leap—until the schemes of the leadership produced disaster.

When the post-Great Leap food crisis was upon them, the people—including both peasants and hungry city dwellers—held the Party, and particularly its local representatives, the cadres, responsible. (It should be recalled that the Pei-tai-ho resolution—or the "Resolution of the Central Committee of the Chinese Communist Party on the Establishment of People's Communes in the Rural Areas, August 29, 1958"—was not a government but a Party order.) Party intellectuals such as Teng T'o and Wu Han tried to place the blame on the Party leadership, including Party Chairman Mao. The Party itself placed public blame on the Russians and the weather, but it tried to shift responsibility internally onto the cadres, saying that many of them harbored "bourgeois tendencies" and were divorced from the masses. The cadres themselves went to earth, spending more time cultivating their constituents and less time trying to please their superiors; a few of them even took advantage of the relaxation of controls to make a little money on the side. Several thousand common people—peasants and city dwellers from the southeastern provinces—flooded across the borders of Hong Kong into exile. It was certainly not the end of Party authority, but there was a crisis of authority. As T. D. Weldon once remarked, "However 'authority' is being used, it is true that when a number of people begin to ask in a mutinous and not a theoretical tone of voice 'Why should I obey X?' X has already lost, or is in the process of losing, his authority, for his orders are not being treated as the orders of those who are correctly said to have authority are treated." [45] The problem was made all the more acute in China because, as hard as the regime's propagandists might try to protect Political Bureau leaders and to shift blame onto local cadres, the distinction between agent and source of Party authority in China had never been seriously institutionalized.

A good deal of evidence exists on the extent of dissatisfaction in the wake of the Great Leap. The PLA General Political Department's *Kung-tso t'ung-hsün* (Bulletin of Activities) recorded in unimpeachable detail peasant hostility to the communes. [46] As for local conditions

[45] T. D. Weldon, *The Vocabulary of Politics* (Harmondsworth, Eng.: Penguin, 1953), p. 56.

[46] See Chalmers Johnson, "Building a Communist Nation in China," in Robert A. Scalapino (ed.), *The Communist Revolution in Asia* (Englewood Cliffs, N.J.: Prentice-Hall, 1965), pp. 58–59.

of Party authority and the attitudes of cadres, a Party directive of 1962 from Lienchiang *hsien* (county), Fukien Province, revealed:

If the upper-level Party directives suit the lower levels, then they obey them. If they do not suit them, they do not obey. It has reached the point where disorganization and disorder have already occurred among a minority of cadres. When the commune Party Committee called a meeting of branch secretaries, they could refuse to attend without sufficient cause. There was one brigade chief who refused to participate in a commune distribution meeting because he was building his house. Some commune Party Committee members have reported that most recently a very perverse spirit has developed, and that the more they oppose it, the further it develops. There are also some persons who have found a pretext for extreme democracy in what they call "demands of the masses" and "general opinion," and on these pretexts they have openly opposed the upper levels. This situation also exists among the masses. They do not obey the directions of the cadre, even going to the point where they beat the cadre without being punished.[47]

Possibly the most sensational locus of questioning authority was in the official newspaper of the Peking Municipal Committee of the Chinese Communist Party. It is important to remember that the first shot in the Cultural Revolution—Yao Wen-yüan's article of November 19, 1965, in the Shanghai *Wen-hui Pao* (*JMJP*, November 30, 1965) —was directed against Wu Han and brought charges that he had lampooned Chairman Mao and the Party for their leadership of the Great Leap Forward. Teng T'o's work, even more than Wu Han's, however, offers evidence of alienation and the questioning of authority "in a mutinous and not a theoretical way." Here are excerpts from some of Teng T'o's articles in the *Peking Jih-pao, Peking Wan-pao,* and *Ch'ien-hsien* (Frontline), which were later gathered to form his notorious book, *Evening Chats at Yen-shan:*

Some people have the gift of gab. They can talk endlessly on any occasion, like water flowing from an undamned river. After listening to them, however, when you try to recall what they have said, you can remember nothing.

The wisdom of a man is never unlimited. Only an idiot fondly imagines that he knows everything. . . .

Suppose we look into *Aesop's Fables.* For example, there is the following fable: "A pentathlon athlete was often criticized by the people in a city state for his lack of courage. So he went abroad for a time and on his return boasted of the

[47] C. S. Chen (ed.) and Charles P. Ridley (trans.), *Rural People's Communes in Lien-chiang, Documents Concerning Communes in Lien-chiang County, Fukien Province, 1962–1963* (Stanford, Calif.: Hoover Institution, 1969), p. 107.

many feats he had performed in various city states, and especially of a long jump he had made at Rhodes, a jump unequalled by any Olympic victor. He said, 'If any of you here goes to Rhodes next time, the eye-witnesses there will testify to my feat.' At this one of the bystanders said, 'Hey! If what you say is true, my man, you don't need witnesses. The place you stand on will do as well as Rhodes. Let us see the jump!' "

I would advise those friends given to great empty talk to read more, think more, say less and take a rest when the time comes for talking, so as to save their own as well as other people's time and energy!

As Chia Tao wrote in his short poem "The Swordsman:"

> For ten years I have been whetting my sword,
> Its cold blade never once put to test;
> In showing it to you, I ask today:
> Tell me who has been wronged.

"*Evening Chats* has been serialized in this newspaper and said practically nothing about newspapers. Why? Is it because you take no interest in them?" When [thus] reproachfully questioned by some intimate friends, I could not help breaking into laughter.[48]

## PERIOD OF THE CULT OF PERSONALITY

The Party leaders' answer to the authority crisis was a strong injection—in Skinner's vocabulary—of "R-power" (remuneration), with "C-power" (coercion) standing not too far in the background (for example, the increased use of "*lao-kai*," or "reform through labor," and of *hsia-fang,* or "downward transfer," to outlying areas). Teng Hsiao-p'ing's comment of 1962 typified the basic approach: "So long as it raises output, private farming is permissible. White or black, so long as the cats can catch mice, they are good cats." [49] The Party leaders recognized the disincentive features of Mao's Great Leap methods, and they, in effect, shelved his quasi-Communist communes in favor of a balanced strategy of economic development—one that relied significantly on various kinds of material incentives and that stressed *investment* in agriculture in order to bring its output up to the point where it would sustain industrialization. Although the

---

[48] As cited in "Teng T'o's *Evening Chats at Yenshan* is Anti-Party and Anti-Socialist Double-Talk," *Chieh-fang-chün pao* and *Kuang-ming jih-pao,* May 8, 1966, and translated in *The Great Socialist Cultural Revolution in China* (Peking: Foreign Languages Press, 1966), II, 12–49.

[49] Cited in "Struggle in China's Countryside Between the Two Roads," *JMJP,* November 23, 1967. Cf. Parris H. Chang, "Struggle Between the Two Roads in China's Countryside," *Current Scene,* VI (February 15, 1968).

Maoists would later borrow Lenin's old term "economism" (from *What Is To Be Done?*) in order to discredit the Party's approach, the excellent performance of the Chinese economy in the period 1962–65 suggests that some Party leaders had indeed learned from the Great Leap experience and that their new policies were proper antidotes for the regime's ailments, both economic and political.

To be sure, the Party leaders never had a completely free hand during 1962–65. Throughout this period, Mao kept taking time off from his primary preoccupations with the Sino-Soviet dispute and reform of the People's Liberation Army to promote one or another scheme of "socialist education," the training of "revolutionary successors," the popularizing of a model Communist (usually a soldier and usually dead by the time of his apotheosis), or an investigation of the cadres' political morality. There is no evidence that the Party opposed these measures in theory, but in practice socialist education usually took second place to economic recovery and growth. The result was that by 1964 and 1965, a sizable gap had appeared between the public rhetoric of the nation's press and the actual practice of production teams, factories, and commercial enterprises. The propaganda mills churned out one story after another about the triumphs of Communist willpower at Tachai and Tach'ing, but the factories of Shanghai continued to chalk up production records on the basis of regular wages and workers' bonuses.[50] Party leaders did not seem to be willfully crossing Mao (they even began to eliminate bonuses in some areas during 1965); it was rather that having once before been burned when they relied too much on "normative incentives," they must have had doubts about whether either they or China could survive another such adventure. Besides, economic performance was good; the Chinese leaders appeared finally to have perfected a realistic strategy (that is, agriculture as the foundation and industrialization as the objective) for the economic development of China in terms of its own economic geography.

At the higher reaches of the leadership, however, people were being more outspoken, though always in private. We have to rely on Maoist sources (that is, *ta-tze-pao* or "wall posters" and Red Guard tabloids) for information on this subject, but there is no reason to believe that

---

[50] Note Barry M. Richman's observation: "[A]ll of the 9 factories [I] visited in Shanghai [in the period April to June, 1966] still had worker monetary schemes in effect." Barry M. Richman, *A Firsthand Study of Industrial Management in Communist China* (Los Angeles: Graduate School of Business Administration, University of California, 1967), p. 39 *et passim*.

many of the Maoist charges against the Party establishment are not substantially accurate. Here are some representative samples:

On February 21–23, 1962, at an enlarged conference of the Standing Committee of the Political Bureau, Liu Shao-ch'i, Teng Hsiao-p'ing, and Ch'en Yün staged a joint performance. They totally denied the achievements of the Great Leap Forward and put on a show to besmirch the three red banners [that is, the General Line of Socialist Construction, the Great Leap Forward, and the People's Communes] and decry Chairman Mao. . . . Ch'en Yün said that "the present salient problems are lack of food, . . . very little oil and not enough clothing, . . . inflation, . . . speculation, . . . and a fall in living standards. . . ."[51]

In 1962 China's Khrushchev [Liu Shao-ch'i] warned the Party to learn the lesson of Stalin, not to extol the individual, not to shout Hail.[52]

T'ao Chu had a well-known saying: "Follow the Party, don't follow that man." . . . We can see he was vainly attempting to incite the masses not to follow our great leader, Chairman Mao.[53]

When we had a meeting, Teng Hsiao-p'ing always sat in the place farthest away from me. Since 1959, he has not briefed me once on the work of the Central Committee Secretariat.[54]

Other instances of alleged opposition to Mao included the so-called "Peking Zoo Incident" of 1961, in which P'eng Chen and Liu Shao-ch'i reportedly compiled a twenty-thousand-word indictment of Mao's errors during the Great Leap Forward.[55] Significantly, however, the opposition never became public until the Maoists themselves revealed it. The Party leaders, it seems, were genuinely concerned to prevent Mao from having any further influence on economic policy, and they no doubt thought they had "kicked him upstairs" at the Sixth Plenum (December, 1958). They also undertook to launch a miniature cult of Liu Shao-ch'i with the republication in *Hung-ch'i*[56] of his *How to Be a Good Communist,* apparently an attempt to offset the cult of Mao then being propagated strongly within the People's Liberation Army. However, there is no concrete evidence that they joined with anti-Maoist Russian intriguers or attempted to move directly against the Chairman. It seems certain that had Mao been content in 1958 to accept his retirement, the Party leaders would have protected his

51 *Pei-ching Kung-she,* January 28, 1967.
52 *JMJP,* May 8, 1967.
53 Radio Canton, October 26, 1967.
54 Mao Tse-tung at a central committee meeting, January, 1967, *ta-tze-pao,* January 9, 1967.
55 *Kuang-ming jih-pao,* August 9, 1967.
56 *Hung-ch'i* (nos. 15 and 16, 1962).

name and prestige as precious assets of the Chinese Communist revolution.

Mao Tse-tung, however, appears to have had his own ideas on how both to overcome the authority crisis and to modify the over-all approach to socialist construction in light of the Great Leap Forward. His policy, in essence, was to promote a cult of his own personal genius and of his indispensability as a substitute for the authority of either the Chinese national revolution or the Chinese Communist Party, to implement a new interpretation of the stage of proletarian dictatorship in terms of a defense against "peaceful evolution back into capitalism," and to begin cultivating on a long-term basis "new socialist men" who would be fit to live in and prerequisite to a genuinely socialist society.

From the point of view of the authority of the regime, the development of the cult of personal authority is more significant than Mao's latest distillation of Marxist-Leninist ideology. This fact is often obscured by descriptions of the cult of Mao in the passive voice, as if Mao himself were merely the recipient of its adulation and had nothing personally to do with promoting it.[57] By contrast, Meyer, on the basis of his study of authority in Communist systems, argues that charismatic relations of authority are "engendered by a deep authority crisis from which individuals or entire masses of citizens seek escape by endowing a leader (or an elite) with superhuman qualities or by allowing themselves to be convinced that he is so endowed." [58] This seems to me a proper approach from which to begin studying charismatic authority in Communist China, even though the Chinese case does not necessarily support Meyer's further beliefs that such a crisis is inevitable or that it is caused by the difficulties in trying to transform Marxist-Leninist ideology from a revolutionary belief system into the belief system of a maturing governmental system.

Weber's theory of charismatic authority is less useful because Weber was more concerned with how loyalty to a charismatic leader became "routinized" into loyalty to a government, institution, or priesthood, whereas the student of Communist systems is more concerned with how people loyal to a highly rational ideology transfer their loyalty to

[57] Cf. Stuart R. Schram's comment: "It may or may not be possible to manufacture charisma for any national leader, even though he be entirely lacking in remarkable personal qualities. Surely no one imagines that this happened in Mao's case." Stuart R. Schram, "Mao Tse-tung as a Charismatic Leader," *Asian Survey,* VII (June, 1967), 383.

[58] Alfred G. Meyer, "Authority in Communist Political Systems," in Lewis J. Edinger (ed.), *Political Leadership in Industrialized Societies* (New York: Wiley, 1967), p. 99. See also Claude Ake, *A Theory of Political Integration* (Homewood, Ill.: The Dorsey Press, 1967), pp. 51, 55, 66–67.

a single man. In view of the inherent and well-known instabilities of charismatic rule—the source and agent of authority are identical here (agents who are appointed by and who are in effect "disciples" of the leader cannot be easily distinguished from him) and succession struggles are virtually inevitable—it would seem that a crisis is required to discredit rational bases of authority and to cause people to turn to a single leader in their stead.

It is also not necessary to accept Weber's idea that the man who resolves (or exploits) such an authority crisis by promoting his own personal, uncommon claims necessarily possesses some quality that we can identify as charisma or grace. The case of Mussolini, Stalin, Kim Il-sung, Nkrumah, and Sukarno can be understood without positing the existence of personal charismatic qualities. As Ernst Nolte has noted, with regard to Mussolini, for example:

[He] had long ago stressed the importance of the "choreographic and picturesque side." That which in April, 1921, in Bologna had still to a great extent been a spontaneous upward surge *following upon extraordinary events,* was a year and a half later in Cremona a well-staged theatrical performance, capable of being repeated at any time, with uniforms (even for women), solemn consecration of flags, parading of columns with raised arms before the saluting Duce, roll call of the fallen (*Appello dei martiri*), and finally the glorification of Mussolini (*nostro amato capo e maestro*). The degree of calculating knowledge and cool manipulation of emotional material already in existence in the top leadership is evident fro a remark made by Mussolini at about that time: "Democracy has deprived the life of the people of 'style': that is, a line of conduct, the color, the strength, the picturesque, the unexpected, the mystical; in sum, all that counts in the soul of the masses. We play the lyre on all its strings: from violence to religion, from art to politics." [59]

## Mao displayed much the same awareness in his 1965 interview with Edgar Snow:

[59] Ernst Nolte, *Three Faces of Fascism,* trans. Leila Vennewitz (New York: Holt, Rinehart, and Winston, 1966), p. 258. Italics added. The songs of Communist China have always reflected both the current policy line and the current locus of authority. During the second five-year plan, the leading song was "Socialism is Good!" introduced in 1957, with words by Hsi Yang and music by Huan Chih. Its second stanza runs:

> The Communist Party is good, the Communist Party is good!
> Communists are good as the people's leaders.
> They are as good as their words.
> They put their all into doing good for the people.
> We must resolutely follow the Communist Party in order
>     to be good at building up the great motherland;
> And to be good at capital construction.

Chairman Mao is not mentioned once in any of the three stanzas. Seven years later, during 1965, "Tung Fang Hung" (The East is Red) was introduced and rapidly became virtually the national anthem of the nation. Its opening lines run:

"In the Soviet Union," I [Snow] said, "China has been criticized for fostering a 'cult of personality.'" Mao thought that perhaps there was some. It was said that Stalin had been the center of a cult of personality, and that Khrushchev had none at all. The Chinese people, critics say, have some (feelings or practices of this kind). There might be some reasons for saying that. Was it possible, he asked, that Mr. K. fell because he had no cult of personality at all? [60]

It is probably true that Mao Tse-tung is an exceptional leader of men, but we do not need this hypothesis in order to understand the growth of the contemporary cult of Mao, and it is quite misleading to base our appreciation of the origins of the cult on Mao's personal qualities. Signs have existed since the Yenan days that he enjoys being flattered, but the cult of Mao—as an alternative basis of authority— began, it seems to me, in approximately 1960, within the People's Liberation Army, and it was consciously spread by Mao and Lin Piao from and through the army to the rest of society. Its origins with Lin and the army are certainly no mystery: Lin Piao is the one leader in China whose present political position is both wholly owed to Mao's patronage and obtained as a result of the falling out among leaders precipitated by the failure of the Great Leap Forward (that is, as a result of the P'eng Teh-huai incident).

Regardless of whether Mao personally possesses "charisma," the belief that he does so constitutes the basis of all political authority in China today. All political figures, including Lin Piao and Chou En-lai, not only display the new symbols of authority on every public occasion (amuletic book and Mao badge), but also invoke Mao's name and his writings in order to elicit compliance to any and all orders. In a highly authoritative context, the communique of the Eleventh Plenum (August 12, 1966) informed the Chinese people that:

Comrade Mao Tse-tung is the greatest Marxist-Leninist of our era. Comrade Mao Tse-tung has inherited, defended and developed Marxism-Leninism with genius,

> The east is red
> Rises the sun;
> China has brought forth
> A Mao Tse-tung!

Interestingly enough, a group of students wrote a letter to *Chung-kuo ch'ing-nien pao* (*China Youth News*) in February, 1965, suggesting that the old song "Socialism is Good" was out of date and should be withdrawn. The editors did not agree (so much the worse for them during 1966, when *China Youth News* was suppressed) and argued that the song, although it was "not flawless and one hundred percent perfect," should continue to be sung. See *CKCNP*, February 25, 1965.

[60] Edgar Snow, "Interview with Mao," *New Republic*, January 20, 1965; reprinted in Franz Schurmann and O. Schell (eds.), *Communist China* (New York: Vintage Books, 1967), p. 370. Mao did not permit direct quotation during the interview; this accounts for the odd form in which Snow reports Mao's answer to his question.

creatively and in an all-round way, and has raised Marxism-Leninism to a new stage. Mao Tse-tung's thought is Marxism-Leninism of the era in which imperialism is heading for total collapse and socialism is advancing to worldwide victory. It is the guiding principle for all the work of our Party and country.[61]

This was not, of course, an exceptional statement. A year later *Jen-min jih-pao* announced: "Every sentence uttered by Chairman Mao is truth. Mao Tse-tung's thought is universal truth tested in revolutionary practice and is living Marxism-Leninism at its highest stage in the present era." [62] "The hallmark," writes the *Wen Hui Pao*, "of a person supporting Chairman Mao is that he honestly implements these words: 'Chairman Mao gives instructions and I carry them out accordingly; Chairman Mao gives the signal and I advance.' " [63] Mao Tse-tung is said personally to have "founded and nurtured" the Chinese Communist Party and to have saved China during the Sino-Japanese War: "The historical fact is that without Chairman Mao there would have been no victory in the War of Resistance." [64] Most important, these encomiums are not mere flattery of a national hero. During October, 1967, the authority of Mao took on a quasi-institutional form with the issuance of the first of "Chairman Mao's Latest Instructions," a series of at least thirty statements (as of the end of 1968) that outline basic policy for the regime.

### THE THOUGHT OF MAO TSE-TUNG

Unquestionably, Mao Tse-tung had more than one motive in the conscious propagation of a cult of his own personal authority. These may have included: (1) filling the void left by the weakening of Party authority; (2) establishing the political basis upon which he could attack and remove deeply entrenched Party leaders who had become his political enemies; (3) emulating Stalin, to whom he has always shown loyalty, even when Stalin was not acting in his interests and despite his mild criticism of Stalin in the polemics with the USSR; and (4) rewarding his own vanity. It should also be noted that the cult of Mao is not without precedent in the Chinese national revolutionary tradition: the posthumous cult of Sun Yat-sen also made

---

[61] Text in Union Research Institute, *CCP Documents of the Great Proletarian Cultural Revolution, 1966–1967* (Kowloon: Union Research Institute, 1968), p. 69.

[62] *JMJP*, June 19, 1967.

[63] *Wen-hui Pao*, December 9, 1967.

[64] Founding of Party: *JMJP*, July 1, 1966; Resistance War: *Hung-ch'i*, December 14, 1966.

elaborate use of books written by the prophet, songs about him and his thought (for example, the Nationalist anthem "San-min Chu-i"), and pictures of him. This element of political culture is, of course, perfectly familiar to Mao. However, until his policy in the Cultural Revolution becomes clearer, it seems that the main reason for promotion of the cult was to obtain for Mao the personal political power with which to implement his post-Great Leap analysis of the dictatorship of the proletariat.

During the Cultural Revolution, the thought of Mao Tse-tung began to display both defensive and offensive facets, in the military sense of those terms. The defensive aspect was oriented to an analysis of the danger of the "peaceful evolution" of socialist states back into capitalist states, a phenomenon that, Mao concluded on the basis of his deep immersion in the Sino-Soviet dispute, had already occurred in Russia and Yugoslavia and that he feared was happening in China because of the Party leaders' outright rejection of his Great Leap strategy and because of the material incentives they had reintroduced into China's economy. The offensive aspect was oriented to the direct remolding of the people's consciousness in order to instill in them the beliefs of "new socialist man"; this aspect entailed a complete reconceptualization of priorities in the stage of proletarian dictatorship. It is possible, as we shall see, that part of Mao's offensive strategy was temporarily aborted during the later phases of the Cultural Revolution—because of disappointing performances by the Red Guards and revolutionary committees—but as of 1970 this outcome was still neither clear nor inevitable.

Both defensive and offensive orientations derived from an ideological innovation Mao made back in 1957 or even earlier. In Lin Piao's report to the Ninth Congress of the Party (adopted April 14, 1969), Mao's designated successor stated:

In 1957, shortly after the conclusion of the Party's Eighth National Congress, Chairman Mao published his great work *On The Correct Handling of Contradictions Among the People,* in which, following his *Report to the Second Plenary Sessions of the Seventh Central Committee of the Communist Party of China,* he comprehensively set forth the existence of contradictions, classes and class struggle under the conditions of the dictatorship of the proletariat, set forth the thesis of the existence of two different types of contradictions in socialist society, those between ourselves and the enemy and those among the people, and set forth the great theory of continuing the revolution under the dictatorship of the proletariat. Like a radiant beacon, this great work illuminates the course of China's socialist revolution and socialist construction and has laid the theoretical foundation for the current Great Proletarian Cultural Revolution.[65]

This is a sensational revelation. It is clear, on the one hand, that Lin Piao is reinterpreting the past with benefit of hindsight and, on the other, that the events which came after 1957—above all the split in the Party leadership and the Sino-Soviet dispute—have lent greater significance in Mao's mind to the events of 1957 than they had at the time or during the immediately succeeding years. Nevertheless, the speech may mark one of the important ideological departures of mid-century communism.

At the time, Mao's declarations in the Correct Handling speech were an ideological cover for the 1957 Party rectification campaign, for the call to "let a hundred flowers bloom," and for the anti-rightist mopping up operation against the intellectuals who had "bloomed" and who appeared to be standing in the way of socialist construction. Mao had written the speech in response to Khrushchev's anti-Stalin revelations at the Twentieth Congress and in response to the Hungarian Revolution. His purpose at the time appeared to be to provide a more sophisticated Marxist explanation than Khrushchev's for the existence of Stalinism and for revolts in socialist countries. The fact that Mao then acted on his speech in the Hundred Flowers campaign seemed to be an attempt to head off the potential (but probably non-existent) danger of Hungarian-type disturbances in China. The campaign proved to be a political blunder, but one that was quickly recouped in the anti-rightist campaign and that did no lasting damage to the authority of the regime—except among intellectuals, for whom Mao has never had much regard anyway.

Meanwhile, the main emphasis of Mao's policies during the late 1950's continued to be on rapid industrialization and not on what Lin Piao called "the great theory of continuing the revolution under the dictatorship of the proletariat." In 1958, Mao was still committed to the classical Soviet definition of socialist construction: laying the material foundations of socialist society. His divergence from Soviet precedents was not in terms of goals but in terms of methods; whereas the first five-year plan had pursued Soviet-style capital-intensive industrialization, the second five-year plan pursued Mao's Yenan-style labor-intensive industrialization.

It was the split in the leadership following the Great Leap, combined

65 *Peking Review,* Special Issue (April 28, 1969), pp. 11–12.

with the ever more insistent demands of the Sino-Soviet dispute, that made the latent principles of the Correct Handling of Contradictions speech manifest. As the authority crisis settled on the regime and deepened, Mao began asking what had gone wrong. He never blamed himself or his ideas, at least not publicly. Rather, as the labeling of Liu Shao-ch'i as "China's Khrushchev" suggests, Mao began to suspect that some of the problems he saw in Russia and Yugoslavia existed in his own party; he found that his analyses of the errors of foreign Communist parties, including his Correct Handling speech, were simultaneously analyses of his own party. In the entirely different political atmosphere of post-Great Leap China, Mao appears to have concluded that in 1957 he had made a Marxist discovery—one that looks very much like Milovan Djilas' "new class." It was this new class, or in Maoist jargon, "a small handful of Party people in authority taking the capitalist road," who were causing all the trouble and who had to be stopped.

One of the great coincidences of modern Marxism is that both Mao's "On the Correct Handling of Contradictions Among the People" and Milovan Djilas' *The New Class: An Analysis of the Communist System* were published in 1957. It suggests something analogous to the frequent occurrence in the physical sciences of almost simultaneous discoveries by independent researchers working thousands of miles apart. Mao and Djilas have one other biographical similarity: both have been high-ranking leaders of Communist revolutionary movements who clashed with Communist Party organizations because they claimed to put Marxist ideals ahead of the demands of the Party's bureaucratic life.

In his most recent work, Djilas summarizes his theory of the new class as follows:

[T]he society that has arisen as the result of Communist revolutions, or as a result of the military actions of the Soviet Union, is torn by the same sort of contradictions as are other societies [that is, classes and contradictions persist after socialist revolutions]. The result is that Communist society has not only failed to develop toward human brotherhood and equality, but also out of its Party bureaucracy there arises a privileged social stratum, which, in accord with Marxist thinking, I named "the new class." [66]

There are two main differences between Mao and Djilas: (1) Mao has a different explanation for the origin and persistence of the new class,

[66] Milovan Djilas, *The Unperfect Society,* trans. Dorian Cooke (New York: Harcourt, Brace, and World, 1969), p. 8.

and (2) whereas they agree on their diagnoses of the problem, they differ radically in their remedies.

Djilas explains his new class in traditional Marxist terms: the Communist Party literally *possesses* the means of production in the societies where it has come to power, and it is therefore set off from the rest of society as a ruling class—one that like all other possessing and ruling classes governs in terms of its own interests, primarily its material comfort and self-perpetuation. Mao has a different theory. He believes that abolishing private property in the means of production does not create a classless society (as Stalin contended) but that, instead, the superstructure of bourgeois society—its attitudes, institutions, and state of mind—persists with tremendous inertia for long periods of time after its material roots have been cut. In contemporary Maoist thought, as Joan Robinson tells us, "Class is defined by a state of mind, and the state of mind is revealed in conduct." [67] According to Mao, the bourgeois state of mind not only infects socialist society, it is also capable of contaminating members of the Communist Party, with the unfortunate results that could be witnessed—from Peking—in Russia and Yugoslavia.

Clearly Mao's interpretation departs further from the spirit of Marxism than does Djilas'. Mao appears to have set Hegel back on his feet and to have reconciled himself with idealist philosophy. Although this contemporary Maoist idealism infuriates the Soviet Union, it does not appear to bother Mao or his supporters in the slightest. Mao could not accept Djilas' theory, since it is an attack on the Communist Party, and Mao has never repudiated the Party as the most advanced element of the proletariat. Instead, Mao's supporters claim that Mao's theory is actually a new development of Marxism-Leninism, one that places Mao on a par with Marx and Lenin as a theoretician—although, as an idealist attack on Marxism, Mao's theory would appear to be an even more radical heresy than Djilas'.

One possible explanation as to why Mao developed this particular line of analysis is its clear congeniality with his military philosophy. Mao has consistently argued that, although weapons are necessary tools of the soldier, it is the soldier himself—his morale, state of mind, aggressiveness, and military outlook—that determines the qualities of an army. This is only one of several possible strands, including concrete historical problems, that have helped shape Mao's contemporary

[67] Joan Robinson, *The Cultural Revolution in China* (Harmondsworth, Eng.: Penguin, 1969), p. 15.

views, but it seems significant that he first implemented and tested these views, with Lin Piao's able supervision, within the People's Liberation Army.

Mao and Djilas, of course, differ diametrically in terms of their remedies for the "new class" phenomenon. Whereas Djilas today has abandoned Marxist categories entirely and stresses only his commitment to the struggle to expand human freedom, Mao is prepared to operate surgically on the "new class" whenever it crops up and, more importantly, to try to change men's minds so that there will be no more new classes. Mao's London followers explain his position this way:

What has been demonstrated by these recent experiences of social development in the USSR is that altering the economic base of society by expropriating the private owners of the means of production only establishes the basic *possibility* of Socialism. Bourgeois habits of thought, bourgeois motivation, the whole bourgeois world outlook still have to be fought and conquered ideologically to bring into existence socialist man. Without socialist man, motivated by socialist impulses of putting others first, not oneself, of working for the good of society, and not one's own material benefits, a socialist system cannot be consolidated. That is what the Cultural Revolution in China is all about. . . . The Cultural Revolution is the socialist answer to the reactionary bourgeois dictum: "You can't change human nature." [68]

Given this view of Mao's and three years of Cultural Revolution in China, the real question during 1970 is, "What has been accomplished?" The answer can only be ambiguous. On the one hand, the creation of revolutionary committees throughout the country suggests that Mao has succeeded to a remarkable degree in erecting a new structure that will help both to inhibit the growth of "modern revisionism" and to inculcate some "Paris Commune" type principles of radical socialist egalitarianism. On the other hand, Mao appears to have been disappointed in the revolutionary committees and in the mass organizations that contributed to them. He has allowed the revolutionary committees to be heavily staffed with conservative army officers, and during 1968 he began to send millions of his Red Guards to the rural areas, there to live and be supervised by the peasantry.[69] It is possible that Mao, in his old age, has become disillusioned, like many Communist idealists of the past, and that he is trying to rebuild

[68] China Policy Study Group, *The Broadsheet*, V (March, 1968), 4. Italics in original.
[69] See Klaus Mehnert, *Peking and the New Left: At Home and Abroad* (Berkeley: Center for Chinese Studies, University of California, China Research Monographs, No. 4, 1969).

the Party which he himself shattered. These questions cannot be answered until more time passes and considerably more information on the Cultural Revolution becomes available.

Whatever the ultimate outcome of the Cultural Revolution, Mao's China continued to function during 1969 primarily because the Party, the army, the bureaucracy, and the revolutionary committees were all portrayed to the people as agents of and subordinate to a living, personal source of authority—namely, "the greatest Marxist-Leninist of our era," Mao Tse-tung. However, as I have tried to argue, Mao's personal authority rests on an earlier authority crisis and on his having skillfully filled the vacuum created by that crisis. The only long-standing and indigenous basis of political authority in China remains the nationalistic awakening of the Chinese people and the history of their prodigious labors to bring about revolutionary change in their lives and nation. It is unlikely that Mao's successors will be able to rule long in China without appealing to that authentic popular will, and it is even possible that Mao himself, before he leaves the stage, will once again have to acknowledge its existence. As the Sino-Soviet dispute evolves further toward warfare between peoples rather than ideologies and as the call for war preparedness to defend the motherland is once again heard in China, there can be no doubt that Mao knows—like Stalin during World War II—that the ultimate appeal he can make in asserting his claims to authority is to Chinese nationalism.

# PART II

*Politics Within Political Hierarchies*

❦❦❦❦❦❦❦❦❦❦❦❦❦❦❦❦❦❦❦❦❦❦❦❦❦❦❦❦❦❦❦❦❦❦

MICHEL C. OKSENBERG

# Policy Making Under Mao, 1949-68: An Overview[1]

With the information about the policy making process revealed during the Cultural Revolution and the growing number of case studies of policy formulation in the Chinese People's Republic prior to the Ninth Party Congress,[2] perhaps it is appropriate to codify the findings: to present a generalized description of the policy making process,

[1] I have tapped liberally the wisdom of Philip Bridgham, Parris Chang, Roderick MacFarquhar, and Richard Sorich in the preparation of this paper. The participants of the Cuernavaca Conference, Harry Harding, and Nathan Leites trenchantly criticized a first draft. Errors of fact and interpretation remain my responsibility.

[2] A partial listing of these studies includes Philip Bridgham, "Mao's 'Cultural Revolution': Origin and Development," *CQ*, No. 29 (January–March, 1967), pp. 1–35; Philip Bridgham, "Mao's Cultural Revolution in 1967: The Struggle to Seize Power," *CQ*, No. 34 (April–June, 1968), pp. 6–37; Parris Chang, "Patterns and Processes of Policy Making in Communist China, 1955–1962: Three Case Studies" (Ph.D. dissertation, Columbia University, 1969); David A. Charles, "The Dismissal of Marshal P'eng Teh-huai," *CQ*, No. 8 (October–December, 1961), pp. 63–76; Merle Goldman, *Literary Dissent in Communist China* (Cambridge, Mass.: Harvard University Press, 1967); Harold Hinton, "Intra-Party Politics and Economic Policy in Communist China," *World Politics*, XII (July, 1960), 509–24; Alice Langley Hsieh, *Communist China's Strategy in the Nuclear Age* (Englewood Cliffs, N.J.: Prentice-Hall for the RAND Corporation, 1962); Roderick MacFarquhar, "Communist China's Intra-Party Dispute," *Pacific Affairs*, XXXI (December, 1958), 323–35; Michel C. Oksenberg, "Policy Formulation in Communist China: The Case of the 1957–8 Mass Irrigation Campaign" (Ph.D. dissertation, Columbia University, 1969); Franz Schurmann, *Ideology and Organization in Communist China* (rev. ed.; Berkeley and Los Angeles: University of California Press, 1969), esp. chap. i; J. D. Simmonds, "P'eng Te-huai: A Chronological Re-examination," *CQ*, No. 37 (January–March, 1969), pp. 120–38; Kenneth R. Walker, "Collectivization in Restrospect: The 'Socialist High Tide' of Autumn 1955–Spring 1956," *CQ*, No. 26 (April–June, 1966), pp. 1–43; Allen Whiting, *China Crosses the Yalu: The Decision to Enter the Korean War* (New York: Macmillan, 1960); Donald S. Zagoria, "Peking's Hawks, Doves, and Dawks," in his *Vietnam Triangle: Moscow/Peking/Hanoi* (New York: Pegasus, 1967), pp. 63–98. *China News Analysis* also contains many informative articles on policy making.

79

to explore how the policy making process tended to vary with the type of issue being considered, to chart the major changes in the way policy was formulated, and to mention some of the factors producing these changes. At the same time, an attempt to systematize existing knowledge must identify the many areas of disagreement and ignorance.

## INFLUENCES UPON MAO

Mao Tse-tung has dominated the policy making process over the past twenty years. The extent of his dominance, however, has fluctuated as a result of a combination of his own choice, the extent of opposition he faced, and the socioeconomic constraints upon him. A study of the policy making process must, therefore, start with Mao *and* the influences upon him.

Although Mao dominated the policy making process, he had to respond to specific problems pressing upon him and make use of the limited opportunities available to him; at the same time, of course, his perception and evaluation of these problems and opportunities were determined by his beliefs, his health, and the demands of his role as the acknowledged leader of China. In sum, role demands, his beliefs, the social and economic problems of the country, and the resources at hand shaped the choices available to Mao.

### ROLE DEMANDS

Of these forces working on Mao, least is known about the expectations which may have gradually developed among his policy making associates, the bureaucrats, and the populace concerning how the chairman of the Chinese Communist Party (CCP) and the national leader should behave. As the first incumbent of his office, Mao probably was less encumbered by such expectations than leaders of older organizations. Nonetheless, widely shared norms circumscribed his alternatives and defined some of his tasks.

For example, Mao had to act at least partially in accordance with what he thought the people of China wanted of him. Without the ability to poll the Chinese people, it is risky to estimate the beliefs of Chinese citizens. But as a working hypothesis, we can assume that most of the population in rural areas, at least, where tradition still seemed strong even in the late 1960's, expected their leader to play a role similar to the emperor in traditional China—a wise and benevolent ruler who, while far removed from them, was responsible for ordering their universe. Many youths in China saw Mao as embodying their aspirations, sought communion with him, and longed for him to respond to their desires. His conduct in office—his regal aloofness, his blend of reigning and ruling—suggests a studied response to and manipulation of a widely held desire for him to personify the unity and hopes of the nation.

Through their long service in the governmental apparatus and their study of Mao's leadership doctrines, Chinese bureaucrats probably wanted something else from the Chairman and his top associates: firm policy to guide their daily administrative acts. In fact, tension existed between Mao and the bureaucrats, especially those on the middle and lower levels. Bureaucrats tended to be reluctant to develop policies which later could be condemned by their superiors; they wanted precise but manageable directives. Adhering to norms evolved in the course of waging guerrilla war, the top policy makers and particularly Mao wanted to foster bureaucratic initiative and flexibility. Top policy makers, therefore, were reluctant to offer detailed directives, thereby also enabling them to blame subordinates for poorly conceived policies. Nonetheless, Mao grudgingly responded to the role demanded of him by bureaucrats, most distinctively by formulating pithy slogans relevant to the current situation which were supposed to orient bureaucrats to their jobs—"More, Better, Faster, More Economically," "Catch up with Great Britain," "Remember Class Struggle," "Grasp Production, Promote Revolution," and so on. At any given time, the prevailing slogans defined the spirit of public administration.

Bureaucrats also expected Mao to abide by the unwritten rules governing administrative practice.[3] For instance, if he called for a campaign to raise the ideological level of the Chinese people, bureaucrats believed that he wanted the campaign organized as previous campaigns. Or, basing their conduct on previously rewarded virtues, bureaucrats counted on Mao's continued recognition of these virtues. In short, bureaucrats wanted Mao to be predictable.

But most important is the role which his closest colleagues expected of him. The evidence from CCP writings on the theory of leadership and from reports of Party meetings allows several inferences to be made.[4] Evidently, Mao's associates—including Liu Shao-ch'i, Teng

---

[3] For a lengthier discussion, see my "The Institutionalization of the Chinese Communist Revolution," *CQ,* No. 36 (October–December, 1968), pp. 61–92.

[4] The subject is more fully explored in John W. Lewis, *Leadership in Communist China* (Ithaca, N.Y.: Cornell University Press, 1963), and Harry Harding, *Maoist Theories of Policy-Making and Organization: Lessons from the Cultural Revolution* (Santa Monica: RAND Corporation, R-487-PR, September, 1969).

Hsiao-p'ing, and others purged during the Cultural Revolution—believed that he had the ultimate responsibility for establishing a hierarchy of short-run preferences among the many conflicting long-run goals, and for initiating new policies. They were also willing, at least overtly and in the short run, to abide by his judgments about personnel. Mao's often testy remarks about the errors of his comrade-subordinates suggest that these people may have felt that their conduct legitimately could be subjected at any moment to the scrutiny of their chairman. But the expected relationship between Mao and others at the Politburo level did involve important mutual obligations. Mao's associates expected him to exercise his important prerogatives in consultation with them. They expected him basically to work within the established institutional framework and to tolerate and even foster policy debate. And they expected that Mao would rely upon them to provide much of his information, to brief him on his policy options through written reports and speeches at meetings, and to supervise the implementation of his policies.

To what extent did Mao feel encumbered by the expectations of his three broadly defined constituencies—the public, the bureaucracy, and his associates? Apparently, he enjoyed latitude precisely because of the conflicting demands made upon him. Many Chinese seemed to want a ruler writ larger than life, whose glory they could share through mystical bonds with him. Bureaucrats seemed to want to limit Mao to issuing precise but totally predictable orders. Policy making associates wanted him to bear responsibility for necessary policy innovations, after consultations with them; they wanted him to be first among partners. Mao selected a changing combination of these roles, sometimes playing off one constituency against another. In the classic instance, during the Cultural Revolution, he fulfilled the role demanded by many Chinese, particularly the young, and ignored the role demanded by the bureaucrats, thereby enabling him to mobilize many citizens and to pit them against the bureaucrats. But since his rule ultimately depended upon some undeterminable level of support from all three constituencies, he could not long ignore the demands of any of them.

MAO'S BELIEFS

A second set of influences affecting the way Mao behaved, obviously, were his own attitudes and beliefs. The salient issues in the political arena were defined by Mao's chief intellectual concerns, which included the type of social structure and economy the Communist revolution was producing, the potentiality of human beings who had experienced a spiritual transformation, and the organizational techniques for retaining a society's commitment to the achievement of social change. Mao's intellectual concerns, in fact, were the quests of a restless, vigorous mind trying to reconcile some of the apparently irreconcilable conflicts of the modern age—between egalitarianism and industrialization, freedom and bureaucracy, participation and order. He had faith that ultimately these and other qualities which seemed to be incompatible could be reconciled. During his rule, he groped for the synthesis.

Mao's biases—that bureaucracy, intellectuals, and cities were evil, that man with proper motivation could transform his environment, that struggle was inherently valuable, that a modern society need not have status systems or a high division of labor—led him continually to seize upon data which seemed to confirm them. Those of his counselors who argued their case in response to Mao's concerns were more likely to prevail.

Although he was not always successful, Mao also attempted to make policy making procedures conform to his doctrine.[5] A stress upon investigation of actual conditions; the necessity of remaining attuned to public opinion; the value of clarity, conciseness, and precision of expression; a distrust of highly institutionalized decision making mechanisms; the need for open debate within Party committees followed by discipline after decisions were made; a belief that policy formulation and implementation are intertwined and, hence, the wisdom of fusing these two phases of the policy process—these were the hallmarks of Mao's approach to policy making.

PERSONAL FACTORS

Hidden from public view, such personal factors as whom Mao trusted and his health shaped Mao's approach to policy making. Although reliable information is unavailable, tantalizing evidence sug-

[5] Mao's ideal decisional model can be constructed from these major statements: "Rectify the Party's Style in Work," in Mao Tse-tung, *Selected Works* (hereafter *SW*) (Peking: Foreign Language Press, 1965), III, 35–52; "Oppose the Stereotyped Party Writing," in *SW*, III, 53–68; "Some Questions Concerning Methods of Leadership," in *SW*, III, 117–22; "On Strengthening the Party Committee System," in *SW*, IV, 267–68; "Methods of Work of Party Committees," in *SW*, IV, 377–82; and "Kung-tso fang-fa liu-shih-t'iao" (Sixty Points on Work Methods), in an untitled "Collection of Statements by Mao Tse-tung, 1956–1967" (in Chinese) (n.p., n.d.), pp. 29–38, held by the East Asian Institute, Columbia University. This collection has been translated in *CB*, No. 892 (October 21, 1969). Page citations to this work are to the Chinese text.

gests, for example, that memories of earlier disputes continued to affect interpersonal relations. For instance, Mao apparently criticized P'eng Teh-huai on several occasions during the Yenan period, and he may have felt that P'eng was involved in Kao Kang's illicit maneuvers of the early 1950's.[6] These prior experiences with P'eng may have made Mao more willing to question P'eng's motives for condemning his policies at Lushan in 1959, whereas P'eng clearly voiced long suppressed hostility toward Mao when he said to the Chairman, "You [dumped on me] for forty days in Yenan; why can't I dump on you now for twenty days?"

In a similar manner, Mao's marriage to Chiang Ch'ing in Yenan is rumored to have caused severe displeasure among his colleagues.[7] Mao allegedly promised that he would not involve Chiang in politics. Perhaps this hostility to Chiang and her possible jealousy of Liu Shaoch'i's wife, Wang Kuang-mei, were basic factors in Cultural Revolution politics.

Mao seemed to have had definite opinions about his colleagues. He also remembered how they came to his attention. For instance, addressing a January, 1967, gathering of top officials, Mao is alleged to have recalled, "T'ao Chu was introduced into the Central Committee by Teng Hsiao-p'ing. At first, I said that T'ao lacked candor, but Teng said that he was all right." [8] At another Party meeting, Mao is supposed to have asked what regional Party leader Liu Lan-t'ao intended to do when he returned to the Northwest. When Liu replied, "I'll see when I get back," Mao retorted, "You always equivocate, don't you?" [9] Such concise evaluations of his associates—more could be cited—clearly affected Mao's conduct.

Last, Mao's health crucially affected the policy process. Did he have the physical strength to dominate policy making? Did his colleagues perceive him to be gravely ill and begin to struggle over succession?

6 The discussion here is based upon *The Case of P'eng Teh-huai, 1959–1968* (Hong-Kong: Union Research Institute, 1968), esp. pp. 183–208; and "Mao chu-hsi tui P'eng, Huang, Chang, Chou fan-tang chi-t'uan ti p'i-pan" (Chairman Mao's Criticism of the P'eng-Huang-Chang-Chou Anti-Party Clique) (n.p., n.d.), translated in *Chinese Law and Government* (hereafter *CLG*), I, No. 4 (Winter, 1968–69), esp. 85–94. Page citations to this work are to the translation.

7 This rumor circulated even prior to the Cultural Revolution. See Anna Wang (the former Mrs. Wang Ping-nan), *Ich Kämpfe für Mao* (Hamburg: Christian Wegner Verlag, 1964), pp. 121–22.

8 "Kung-tso fang-fa liu-shih-t'iao," p. 11. T'ao Chu, former first secretary of the CCP's Central-South Bureau, had fallen from power days before Mao delivered these remarks.

9 In Jerome Ch'en, *Mao* (Englewood Cliffs, N.J.: Prentice-Hall Spectrum Paperbacks, 1969), p. 92.

In old age, did he lose keenness and sagacity? These are all vital questions. Again, firm evidence is lacking, but several prolonged absences from the limelight, discussions by historians in the mainland press in the 1960's concerning the fate of aged rulers suffering from amnesia, pointed mention of his radiant health (as if to refute rumors of his illness), and public appearances with a nurse at his side all suggest that particularly in the 1960's, Mao was not always vigorous. Clearly, when the data become available, scholars will have to reconstruct the policy process with due weight given to factors of health and interpersonal relations.

STATE OF THE ECONOMY

The range of alternatives available to Mao could be no greater than the resources available to him. He had little control over the immediate problems pressing upon him, although many were the unanticipated consequences of his previous policies. The impoverished Chinese nation yielded only a small amount of government revenue, in contrast to enormous demands upon that revenue. Moreover, a significant portion of government revenue probably was committed years in advance (for example, to the nuclear program).

Perhaps the major influence upon the policy making process, then, stemmed from economic conditions, particularly the performance of agriculture, with a bountiful harvest increasing the range of policy options available to Mao. Lagging agricultural production, on the other hand, demanded immediate attention.[10] A documentable instance of the impact of visions of a bountiful harvest upon policy formulation came with the launching of the Great Leap Forward. At the March, 1958, Chengtu conference, decisions were made to increase the size of collectives, further decentralize industrial development, and so on. At this Chengtu meeting, as agricultural spokesman T'an Chen-lin later disclosed, the Party Center had calculated that 1958 agricultural production would increase by approximately 17 to 20 per cent over 1957.[11]

[10] Alexander Eckstein has attempted to trace the impact of agricultural production upon other domestic policies in his "Economic Fluctuations in Communist China's Domestic Development," in Ping-ti Ho and Tang Tsou (eds.), *China in Crisis* (Chicago: University of Chicago Press, 1968), I, Book One, 691–729.

[11] T'an Chen-lin, "Cheng-ch'ü tsai liang-san-nien nei tso-tao feng-nung tsu-liang" (Struggle for Two to Three Years to Obtain a Bountiful Agriculture and a Surplus of Grain), *Hung-ch'i* (Red Flag), No. 6 (August 16, 1958), p. 8.

Fostering and manipulating social tensions was Mao's method of producing social change. The major options that he perceived were thus determined by the cleavages in society. Mao came to power through his use of the tensions between rich and poor and between natives and foreigners. But by 1956, with nationalization of private wealth and the absence of foreigners (with the exception of Russians and East Europeans), these tensions had been reduced. In 1956 and the first half of 1957, Mao attempted to move society by unifying it, but he abandoned the attempt after the May, 1957, criticisms of his rule. Afterward, he tried first to foster class struggle in the late 1950's, then to create tensions in society in the early 1960's,[12] and finally to exploit the generation gap, the conflicts among bureaucracies, and the tensions between state and society during the Cultural Revolution.[13] His technique of rule, then, made him dependent upon the cleavages in society and the forces which they unleashed if he chose to tap them.

BUREAUCRATIC INFLUENCES

One other factor had an impact upon Mao—the conduct of the bureaucracies over which he presided. The alternatives available to him were shaped by his staff and bureaucratic subordinates. They provided the information which governed Mao's perceptions. In fact, Mao had to devote considerable energy to retain control over the bureaucracy and to secure adequate flows of information. For example, evaluating the conduct of his erstwhile closest associates who previously were responsible for day-to-day decisions, Mao in October, 1966, complained, "On many things, I wasn't even consulted . . . [examples cited]. . . . All these things could have properly been done through a discussion at the Party Center. But Teng Hsiao-p'ing never paid me a visit." [14] Earlier, during the Lushan Conference, Mao had noted, "During the past decade, not a single comrade suggested and dared to expose analytically and systematically to the Center the defects in our plan in order to seek adjustments. I have never seen

[12] The point is well argued in John W. Lewis, "Revolutionary Struggle and the Second Generation in Communist China," *CQ*, No. 21 (January–March, 1965), pp. 126–47.

[13] For an explanation of the Cultural Revolution in terms of Mao's attempt to exploit the tensions between state and society, between those with and without authority, see Tang Tsou, "The Cultural Revolution and the Chinese Political System," *CQ*, No. 38 (April–June, 1969), pp. 63–91.

[14] Ch'en, *Mao*, p. 94.

such a man. I know there are such people, but they dared not appeal to the top echelon by bypassing proper echelons." [15] Thus, one purpose of the purges, rectification campaigns, and administrative reorganizations which Mao sponsored was to ensure that the bureaucracy would remain responsive to him.

Unfortunately, little is known about the bureaucratic environment in which Mao worked—how information flowed to him, what he read, how his subordinates competed to gain access to him, how he organized his personal staff. Edgar Snow, the American journalist who interviewed Mao on many occasions, reported in 1960 that Mao had a staff of secretaries,[16] but Mao's often-expressed distrust of staff assistants ("To entrust everything to secretaries is a sign of decline in revolutionary spirit" [17]) suggests that he tried to minimize his dependence upon his staff. Clearly, a large number of reports flowed across his desk, many from basic level units, such as reports from a production brigade to a commune or from a factory to a municipal organ.[18] How Mao obtained such reports is unknown, but he frequently ordered them widely distributed, to serve as positive or negative examples of his desired policy. The available evidence of Mao's reading habits tends to confirm Snow's statement: "He may spend as much as a whole week reading." [19]

Of course, Mao did not read everything sent to him. For example, in an address to discussion leaders of the enlarged Military Affairs Committee session on June 28, 1958, he disclosed:

This meeting has been conducted not badly. The speeches of some comrades are very good. XX [name not disclosed in the text of Mao's speech] requested the Chairman to read the speeches of nine comrades. The Chairman read the speeches by Chang Tsung-hsun and Liu Ya-lou.[20]

Drafts of *People's Daily* editorials were submitted (how often is not known) for approval to the Chairman, but at least one was returned

[15] *CLG*, I, No. 4 (Winter, 1968–69), 48.

[16] Edgar Snow, *The Other Side of the River: Red China Today* (New York: Random House, 1961), p. 154.

[17] "Kung-tso fang-fa liu-shih-t'iao," p. 36.

[18] The conclusion is based upon four recently obtained collections of Mao's works: *CLG*, I, No. 4 (Winter, 1968–69); "Collection of Statements by Mao Tse-tung"; *Mao Tse-tung szu-hsiang wan-sui* (Long Live Mao Tse-tung's Thought) (n.p., April, 1967), translated in *CB*, No. 891 (October 8, 1969) (page citations to this work are to the Chinese text); and *Mao chu-hsi wen-hsüan* (Selections from Chairman Mao) (n.p., n.d.), translated in *JPRS*, No. 49826 (February 12, 1970), and No. 50792 (June 23, 1970).

[19] Snow, *The Other Side of the River*, p. 156.

[20] *CLG*, I, No. 4 (Winter, 1968–69), 15.

with the marginal notation, *"pu kan-le"* (did not read it).[21] The *Work Bulletin (Kung-tso T'ung-hsün)*, a secret military journal, also contained reports with the comments Mao had written in the margins. Predictably, those seeking to influence him attempted to monitor what he read.[22]

## MAO'S ROLE

To list the influences upon Mao tells us little, however, about the roles he played. Though there were noticeable exceptions such as 1958 and 1966, Mao appears not to have been immersed in day-to-day decision making and in the supervision of administration. Rather, he attempted to keep his eyes on the broader picture. His was an interventionist role, stepping into the ongoing policy making process in order to bring initiatives and to bend the course of events to accord with his vision.

It may be that every important policy initiative over the past twenty years has been prompted by Mao. Some major instances include his July 31, 1955, speech to a specially convened group of regional Party secretaries, which initiated the collectivization drive; his July, 1957, address to the Tsingtao conference, where he resurrected his shelved National Agricultural Development Program, thereby initiating the sequence of events leading to the Great Leap; [23] his remarks to the August, 1962, Pei-tai-ho central work conference on the necessity of fighting bureaucracy and fostering class antagonisms in society, which led to the socialist education campaign; [24] and his launching of the Cultural Revolution at the September, 1965, meeting of the Standing Committee of the Politburo.[25] All these are examples of initiatives that radicalized Chinese politics. But equally important, the major initiatives for moderating Chinese politics—for consolidating

21 *Kung-jen P'ing-lun* (Workers Review), No. 5 (June 1–10, 1968), in *SCMM*, No. 662 (July 28, 1969), p. 5.

22 Radio Chengtu, September 5, 1957.

23 For the Tsingtao Conference, see especially Teng Tzu-hui, "Tsai ch'üan-kuo ti-erh-tzu shui-t'u pao-chih hui-i shang ti pao-kao" (Report at the Second National Water and Soil Conservation Conference), in *Chung-kuo shui-li* (Chinese Water Conservancy), No. 1 (January 14, 1958), p. 7. There are many other references to this conference, as well as to quotations from the speech Mao delivered to it. See also *SCMP*, No. 4000 (August 14, 1967), p. 18; *Hsin-hua pan-yüeh-k'an* (New China Fortnightly) (hereafter *HHPYK*), No. 120 (November 25, 1957), p. 49; and *HHPYK*, No. 137 (August 10, 1957), p. 66.

24 See *CLG*, I, No. 4 (Winter, 1968–69), 85–93; also Lin Piao, "Report to the Ninth National Congress of the Chinese Communist Party," *Peking Review*, No. 18 (April 30, 1969), p. 19.

25 "Circular of the Central Committee of the Chinese Communist Party," *Peking Review*, No. 21 (May 19, 1967), p. 6.

gains rather than advancing further—were also attributable to Mao. His important speech on Ten Great Relationships to the late April, 1956, Politburo meeting,[26] his Sixty Point Program outlined to the March, 1961, Canton work conference,[27] and his September, 1967, tour of the provinces were of this kind. In the latter instances, to be sure, Mao was yielding to difficulties, but he demonstrated his prudence in adversity.

Mao's role was not limited to providing new initiatives, however. He also had to intervene to give renewed vitality to favorite programs encountering difficulty. His convening of a Supreme State Conference from February 27 to March 1, 1957, should be seen in this light, for it came at a time when Mao's efforts to launch a rectification campaign within the Party and to invite intellectuals to participate more fully in national political life were languishing and when the agricultural collectives—an institution with which he was closely identified—were under attack. His speech "On the Correct Handling of Contradictions among the People" dealt with all these problems. Similarly, Mao's twenty-three point instruction of January, 1965, was an attempt to spur the socialist education campaign, the implementation of which displeased him.[28]

Mao exercised his initiatives through several devices. When chairman of the republic, until 1959, he was able to convene a Supreme State Conference, which he did on fifteen occasions. He also wrote programmatic statements, which could be published either under his name or anonymously. Further, Mao dealt directly with a large number of political figures, either sending them short notes or seeing them in person. In 1960, Edgar Snow learned that Mao visited the big cities regularly and kept in close touch with provincial Party leaders and the lower ranks.[29] Mao's comments while visiting new projects also became the basis for policy. For instance, recounting the origins of the communes, Mao recalled, "I did not claim the right of inventing

[26] In Ch'en, *Mao*, pp. 66–85.

[27] Mao's role at the March, 1961, Central Work Conference was mentioned in *Tung-fang hung* (The East Is Red), No. 20 (February 18, 1967). The summer, 1960, Pei-tai-ho Conference was a crucial conference initiating the 1960–64 period of "readjustment, consolidation, filling out, and raising standards." Presently unavailable information on Mao's activities at this meeting would be a litmus test of Mao's role in decisions to retrench or consolidate.

[28] On the December, 1964–January, 1965, Party Work Conference and the 23-Point Document, see Lin Piao, "Report to the Ninth Party Congress," p. 20, and Richard Baum and Frederick C. Teiwes, *Ssu-ch'ing: The Socialist Education Movement of 1962–1966* (Berkeley: Center for Chinese Studies, University of California, 1968), pp. 118–26.

[29] Snow, *The Other Side of the River*, p. 156.

communes, but I had the right to suggest. In Shantung [while inspecting the new organization in the summer of 1958], a reporter asked me: 'Is the commune good?' I said, 'Good,' and he immediately published it in the newspaper." [30] Mao also sometimes ordered ancient Chinese poetry or the writings by Marx and Lenin which he was reading to be circulated among his comrades, appending notes explaining their relevance to the current situation.

Mao, in addition, often penned marginal comments on reports submitted to him—correcting them here, criticizing them there, occasionally praising. Here is an example of Mao at work:

> Comrade Lin Piao: I have received the report by the General Logistics Department which you forwarded on May 6th. I think this scheme is very good. I should like you to call together all cadres at Army and Division level in the Military Districts to debate the matter. . . . After their opinions have been reported to the Military Affairs Commission and to the Central Committee for approval, arrange for the issue of a suitable directive to the entire armed forces.[31]

In another instance, Mao commented upon a summary by Ch'en Po-ta of the Cultural Revolution from August to October, 1966:

> Comrade Ch'en Po-ta: I have read the revised draft and it is splendid. Please consider where it would be best to add these two sentences, "Grasp revolution and boost production." A great number of these booklets must be printed and they must be distributed to all branches and at least a proportion of Red Guard platoons.[32]

Many other examples exist of Mao's decisive intervention in the policy process through comments on reports submitted to him.[33]

But perhaps Mao's most significant forum was the informal Party meeting which he was able to summon.[34] The history of China since 1954 (references exist to only a few Party meetings before this date) can be written in terms of Mao's remarks to these meetings which

---

[30] CLG, I, No. 4 (Winter, 1968–69), 41. Undoubtedly the decision to launch the commune movement was more complicated than this quotation suggests.

[31] Mao Tse-tung szu-hsiang wan-sui, p. 34.

[32] Ibid., p. 42.

[33] See, for example, ibid., pp. 25, 31, 42; also CLG, I, No. 4 (Winter, 1968–69), 52.

[34] Other leaders could convene Party meetings. For example, Liu Shao-ch'i, who convened Supreme State Conferences as chairman of the CPR from 1959 to 1966, also gathered Politburo meetings. (See Ching-kang-shan [Ching-kang Mountain], No. 46 [May 13, 1967], translated in JPRS, No. 41,858 [July 17, 1967], p. 190.) The Party Secretariat was also able to convene Party meetings; these may have been gathered on the initiative of Teng Hsiao-p'ing or Yang Shang-k'un. (See SCMM, No. 639 [January 6, 1969], p. 3.) But the available evidence suggests that at most of these Party conclaves, Mao played the pivotal role. See below for further discussion.

drew upon the freewheeling discussions to set forth new policy. No instance has been identified when his concluding statement at the meeting was rejected overtly. On the contrary, Mao's prescriptions were soon transformed into specific directives, and his words reverberated throughout China.

His role in policy formulation was, in essence, dual. Bringing initiatives, establishing priorities, and giving coherence to ongoing policies, Mao played a definitive role. On the other hand, his search for a synthesis of goals that seemed to be irreconcilable raised as many questions as he answered; he was disquieting and provocative.

### Informal Party Meetings

References have been found to over eighty gatherings of top level Party officials from 1953 to late 1967.[35] Informal groups assembled, frequently at one of Mao's favorite resort retreats, to discuss the latest turn of events and issue new policy guidelines. These meetings often were referred to by the name of the place in which they were held. For the leaders of China, such names as "the Chengtu meeting," "First Chengchow," "Second Chengchow," "Nanning," and "Shanghai 1965" must evoke in vivid fashion policies, slogans, and debates, as Cairo, Yalta, and Potsdam do for Western diplomats. Perhaps this was especially true of Mao. He could recall that "superstitions were destroyed at the Nanning and Chengtu meetings."[36]

On some occasions, such meetings had an institutional label, such as a Politburo meeting, an enlarged Politburo meeting (meaning the Politburo plus others), Politburo Standing Committee meeting, or enlarged Politburo Standing Committee meeting. On other occasions, such as the July 31, 1955, gathering or the July, 1957, Tsingtao Conference, the participants were primarily regional Party officials along with selected officials of the national political apparatus. On yet other occasions, meetings were labeled a "Party work conference under the jurisdiction of the Central Committee." Exactly who extended the invitations to these meetings and who prepared the agenda are not known. But Mao's speech to the September, 1962, Tenth Plenum, in which he described his activities at the August, 1962, Pei-tai-ho Party work conference, suggests that he may have set the agenda: "At Pei-tai-ho, I raised three problems: the class situation, current conditions,

---

[35] For a list of these meetings, compiled with the assistance of Richard Sorich and this author, see Parris Chang, "Research Notes on the Changing Loci of Decision in the CCP," *CQ*, No. 44 (October–December, 1970), pp. 181–94.

[36] *CLG*, I, No. 4 (Winter, 1968–69), 17.

and existing contradictions. I raised these problems because the problem of classes has not been solved." [37]

The format of the meetings appears to have encouraged blunt talk and ample policy debate. Position papers could even be circulated for discussion. Opposition to Mao's view was expressed, although of course not in terms personally insulting to Mao. Nor could the opposition establish even an informal coalition against the Chairman, if the opposition were to retain its legitimacy.[38] The clearest example of spirited debate occurred at the Lushan meeting in July–August, 1959, when Politburo member and Minister of Defense P'eng Teh-huai sharply attacked Mao's Great Leap policy. In addition to labeling this attack as "unprincipled," Mao complained that P'eng had not voiced his opposition early enough:

> Comrades guilty of rightist opportunism did not put forth their opinions in the Chengchow meeting of November last year, much less did they express their displeasure with the supreme directives and instructions at the Pei-tai-ho Conference [of August, 1958, where Mao formally proclaimed his desire to see communes established throughout China]. Nor did they raise objections at the December [1958] Wuchang meeting, nor at the February [1959] Chengchow meeting, nor at the March-April Shanghai meeting, but it was only at this Lushan meeting that they voiced their opinions.
>
> Why did these comrades not offer their opinions then, but only at this time? Because their views had not yet been formulated. If they had correct insights, and been more intelligent than us, then they would have said something at Pei-tai-ho. . . .[39]

The length of these meetings varied, but some lasted as long as a month. The pivotal 1958 Chengtu conference may have lasted a good portion of the month of March, punctuated by inspection visits by the participants to factories, farms, and regional Party headquarters so that they could acquire a personal feel for the situation in the country.[40] According to Mao, the meetings prior to the Tenth Plenum took more than two months.[41] Other meetings were briefer. The July, 1957, Tsingtao conference and the January, 1958, Nanning conference could not have lasted more than ten days, whereas during the Cultural Revolution—though Politburo-type meetings were frequently

[37] *Ibid.*, p. 86.

[38] The point is well made in Schurmann, *Ideology and Organization*, pp. 54–57.

[39] *CLG*, I, No. 4 (Winter, 1968–69), 45.

[40] Based upon daily appearances of Chinese Politburo members during 1958, as recorded by the United States Consulate General in Hong Kong. See also *SCMP*, No. 4000 (August 14, 1967), p. 20; *CB*, No. 838 (October 13, 1967), pp. 17, 18.

[41] *CLG*, I, No. 4 (Winter, 1968–69), 86.

convened—they usually lasted only two to three days. (An exception was the seventeen-day October, 1966, meeting, which discussed the Cultural Revolution and heard a draft of a self-confession by Liu Shao-ch'i.) [42] Informal regional meetings sometimes preceded the central ones. The 1959 Lushan Plenum was preceded by such gatherings, and conferences of provincial Party officials from a particular region were also a frequent phenomenon in late 1957. Practice seemed to follow Mao's earlier dictum: "On important problems which are complicated and on which opinions differ, there must, in addition, be personal consultations before the meeting to enable the members to think things over, lest decisions by the meeting become a mere formality or no decision can be reached." [43]

Since these meetings were so crucial and debate was permitted, it becomes important to know something about the participants and their efforts to persuade Mao to incorporate their views in his summary of the meeting. The participants tended to be the top regional and central Party officials, with the bulk of the central officials having special responsibilities in a particular field (agriculture, finance, public security, and so on). With a few exceptions, these men had occupied their specialized positions for a long period of time, and had probably developed considerable expertise.[44] In addition, many at the center had career and personal ties to particular regions (for instance, Teng Hsiao-p'ing to the Southwest and Ch'en Yi to the East).[45] But Mao expected his associates to rise above their specialities and to judge issues in terms of China at large. Anything less was a manifestation of "localism" or "sectarianism." Yet, at these meetings, he also tapped his associates for their expert advice. In short, he expected them to perform two somewhat conflicting roles simultaneously—to evaluate policy as experts and to evaluate it in terms of the national interest.

Participants of the informal meetings probably experienced stress between these two roles. Moreover, as the leaders became ever more immersed in their particular jobs from 1953–54 through 1965 (after which most were purged), this role stress may have increased. The Cultural Revolution brought a new group of participants in small Party meetings to power. For a short time, these people may have

[42] On the October, 1966, plenum, see *Hung-hsien pan* (Red Line Edition), December 19, 1966, in *CLG,* I, No. 1 (Spring, 1968), 7–12.

[43] *SW,* IV, 268.

[44] A. Doak Barnett emphasized this point in his *China after Mao* (Princeton, N.J.: Princeton University Press, 1967).

[45] The significance of this is demonstrated in William Whitson, "The Field Army in Chinese Communist Military Politics," *CQ,* No. 37 (January–March, 1969), pp. 1–30.

experienced less role stress and may have been more able to conduct themselves as the Chairman wished. But already by late 1968, they began to assume specialized functions, and the process which unfolded from 1953–54 through 1966 seems to have begun again.

How did the participants attempt to influence the Chairman? Perhaps the standard technique was to develop experimental units that implemented the advocate's programs. The "advanced experience" of these "model units" was then introduced at the conference as a living example of the feasibility and desirability of the program. In the 1957–58 water conservancy campaign, for example, T'an Chen-lin and Honan official Wu Chih-p'u used the irrigation program in the Mang River Valley in this way. And Liu Shao-ch'i was later said to have paid excessive attention to a specific school system in Kirin Province to demonstrate the attractiveness of his educational policy. This leadership style introduced an innovative and experimental note to the policy process, but it also was misleading. Often, the level of support given these model projects could not be sustained on a nationwide basis.

Mao's associates also apparently hoped to influence him through flattery. Available excerpts from transcripts of Party meetings frequently contain passages such as these three examples:

Mao: ". . . Struggle means smashing and reform means starting. The school curricula were compiled by mid-year, but . . . the erroneous parts should be eliminated, while newspaper editorials and Central directives should be inserted.
Interjection from the floor (speaker not identified):
    The Chairman's works should be included.[46]

Mao: Teaching materials should be slashed to eliminate the useless. Chop one-third to one-half that is mistaken or redundant.
Wang Jen-chung: Two-thirds should be eliminated and Chairman Mao's sayings studied.[47]

Mao: All of us here are students of a sort.
Ch'en Po-ta: Except the Chairman.[48]

To a certain extent, then, policy formulation involved the politics of sycophancy.

In addition, while trying to avoid the charge of forming a clique, top Party officials may have attempted to cultivate supporters prior to

---

[46] "Collection of Statements by Mao Tse-tung," p. 8.
[47] *Mao Tse-tung szu-hsiang wan-sui,* p. 43.
[48] "Collection of Statements by Mao Tse-tung," p. 3.

Party meetings. Although P'eng Teh-huai disavowed evil intent, he admitted consulting others on the eve of the Lushan meetings.[49] The charges against Kao Kang included his alleged cultivation of supporters.[50] The allegations made about the Southwest Bureau First Secretary Li Ching-ch'üan are convincing in their description of his contacts with Ho Lung, P'eng Chen, and Teng Hsiao-p'ing, frequently sharing his opinions prior to or during a Party center conference (without conspiring against Mao).[51] In addition, Li was charged with censoring unfavorable reports by his subordinates, which they were trying to submit to the Central Committee and to Party gatherings.

Finally, participants circulated position papers both before and during the Party meeting. Their number could be numerous; thirty-four reports were delivered to an extended, two-month Politburo meeting in March and April, 1956.[52] (P'eng Teh-huai even submitted such a paper—an eighty thousand-character document—to a 1962 Party meeting three years *after* he had been purged of his government positions.) In his talk at these meetings, Mao occasionally praised position papers that influenced his thinking.

Documents obtained during the Cultural Revolution reveal two other important aspects of Mao's closest policy making associates. As the active heads of large bureaucracies, they had their own personal staffs of advisors, secretaries, and so on. How Politburo officials organized and used their staffs, how the staffs attempted to influence the men they served, and what the personal relations were among and within the staffs of the top leaders, are major questions for an understanding of Chinese politics, but the available information does not allow them to be answered. In addition, the top leaders were in constant contact with each other. Thus, when gathering for a Party meeting the participants were well briefed and were aware of the attitudes of many of their colleagues.

What attributes and strategies did Mao possess to lead his associates? His major weapon was his ability to declare that an associate had deviated from his doctrine. Since his beliefs formed the value system upon which the regime based its legitimacy, such a declaration stripped an associate of his right to rule. But Mao's eminence was

---

[49] *The Case of P'eng Teh-huai,* pp. 1, 36–38.

[50] In fact, this probably was Kao's major "crime." See Frederick C. Teiwes, "Purges and Rectification Campaigns in Communist China, 1942–1962" (Ph.D. dissertation, Columbia University, forthcoming), chap. vi.

[51] Based upon many reports broadcast over Radio Chengtu and Radio Kweiyang in 1967 and 1968.

[52] Ch'en, *Mao,* p. 66.

due to more positive qualities than fear. In fact, recently acquired documentation supports Snow's conclusion: "It was Mao's ability to analyze the experience common to his generation—rather than the uniqueness of his own experience—plus his messianic belief in the correctness of his own generalizations of that experience, which distinguished him from compatriots who became his followers." [53] His rambling talks to the small Party gatherings reveal an impressive grasp of Chinese history, a wide-ranging interest in world history, and a capacity for humor and invective. According to P'eng Teh-huai, "Mao Tse-tung is more familiar with Chinese history than any other comrade in the Party, and . . . the first emperor of any dynasty is always strong handed and brilliant." [54]

His talks frequently betray a condescending air—teacher Mao lecturing his student-colleagues. Perhaps deliberately, he projected an image of a passionate, slightly humble, earthy, irascible, and shrewd man. He peppered his speeches to Party colleagues with such sentences as, "First I want to speak; second, I want to listen"; "Being an unpolished man, I am not too cultured"; "If you have caught me in the wrong, you can punish me"; "I am like Chang Fei [a general of the Three Kingdoms period in Chinese history] who, although crude, was careful at times"; "I am a native [Chinese] philosopher"; and so on.[55] He maintained, in short, the vigorous posture of a formidable adversary.

At least seven tactics added to the sheer forcefulness of his personality. First, similar in result to Stalin's tactic of disorganizing his Politburo into several decision making bodies [56] and Khrushchev's tactic of convening "expanded" meetings of Party bodies, Mao may have retained the initiative by gathering constantly changing groups of policy advisors. By convening *ad hoc* Supreme State Conferences or conferences of regional Party officials and by inviting non-Politburo members to Politburo meetings (that is to say, an "expanded" Politburo meeting), Mao may have prevented the formation of a cohesive, difficult-to-control small group. The apparent fluidity of the informal Party meetings made them, in an important sense, *Mao's* decision making group. Second, Mao personally attended, read the transcripts,

[53] Snow, *The Other Side of the River*, p. 145.
[54] *The Case of P'eng Teh-huai*, p. 37.
[55] These passages come, in order, from *CLG*, I, No. 4 (Winter, 1968–69), 36; *ibid.*; *ibid.*, p. 40; *ibid.*, p. 41; and "Collection of Statements by Mao Tse-tung," p. 2.
[56] For this aspect of Stalin's rule, see "Secret Speech of Khrushchev Concerning the 'Cult of the Individual,'" in *The Anti-Stalin Campaign and International Communism* (New York: Columbia University Press for the Russian Institute, 1956), p. 83.

or otherwise kept in close touch with the proceedings of the Party meetings. His presence probably was always felt. His approach here might be contrasted to President John Kennedy's absence from some deliberations of the group he had assembled during the Cuban missile crisis so that the discussions would not be muted. Third, Mao kept close track of the normal activities of his associates. For example, he was able to describe the content of a letter from Liu Shao-ch'i to Chekiang Party secretary Chiang Wei-ch'ing,[57] while in another instance, he mentioned how many ounces of meat one Politburo member ate daily.[58] During the Cultural Revolution, he referred to the political positions taken by the Red Guard children of several Politburo members.[59] Mao devastatingly employed such knowledge in exchanges with his colleagues. Fourth, realizing his basic strength, he sometimes threatened to withdraw from the political system in order to build a new revolutionary movement. (Threats and actual withdrawals from the political system have long been major gambits in Chinese politics.) [60] Fifth, Mao cunningly applied his general strategy of "unity-struggle-unity." Whenever he perceived himself in a weak position, it seems, he proclaimed that comrades should unite for the common cause. He attacked his enemies when he was politically secure, announcing that an era of struggle had begun. Sixth, when he was attacked, Mao often bided his time, waiting for his opposition fully to expose itself. Mao termed this strategy, "stiffening the scalp to stand it." At Lushan, he urged his supporters to "listen to them [his opponents] for a couple weeks and then counterattack." [61] In this tactic, Mao simply was applying guerrilla strategy to Politburo level debates. His counterattack could be swift and harsh. Mao wrote Chang Wen-t'ien after Chang's attack at Lushan:

What can you do now? Let me think for you. There are two words for you: "Rectify painfully." Since you [profess to] respect me, have phoned me several times, and have wanted to come to my place for a talk, I am willing to talk to you. But I am busy these days. Please wait for some time. I am writing you this letter to express my sentiments.[62]

[57] *Mao Tse-tung szu-hsiang wan-sui*, p. 44.
[58] *CLG*, I, No. 4 (Winter, 1968–69), 30.
[59] *Mao Tse-tung szu-hsiang wan-sui*, p. 44.
[60] The stratagem reoccurs in monographs covering such different eras as the Sung (see James Liu, *Reform in Sung China* [Cambridge: Cambridge University Press, 1959]); Ch'ing (Frederic Wakeman, Jr., *Strangers at the Gate* [Berkeley and Los Angeles: University of California Press, 1966]); and Republican (James Sheridan, *Chinese Warlord: The Career of Feng Yü-hsiang* [Stanford, Calif.: Stanford University Press, 1966]).
[61] *CLG*, I, No. 4 (Winter, 1968–69), 29, 33.
[62] *Ibid.*, p. 55.

Effectiveness in counterattack no doubt was an essential ingredient of Mao's success in the Party meetings. Seventh, in time of need Mao apparently turned to his most trusted supporters, especially Ch'en Po-ta. Indeed, every time Mao initiated policies of social change, Ch'en received special assignments. In 1955, Ch'en made a major speech on agricultural collectivization to the Central Committee and temporarily became deputy director of the Party's Rural Work Department. In 1958 he became editor of the new Party theoretical journal *Red Flag*. In 1962, when rural developments disturbed Mao, Ch'en delivered the agricultural report to the Tenth Plenum.[63] And in 1966, he headed the Cultural Revolution Group. These seven tactics ensured Mao's dominance of the Party meetings, particularly since he blended them effectively as well.

To conclude, the small Party gatherings were a pivotal part of the policy making machinery. Here, Mao confronted social forces and bureaucratic interests in the speeches and reports of the participants. The policies scrutinized at these meetings through the years covered the entire range: educational policy, agricultural policy, Party life, foreign policy, and so on. Out of these meetings came Mao's guidelines, which were sometimes vague and at other times precise. But they usually established a spirit which had nationwide impact. In addition, specific directives sometimes were drafted at these meetings. Central Committee plenums usually were preceded by such Party meetings, indicating perhaps that the roles of the plenums were to legitimatize, to explain, to justify, and slightly to modify (if plenum participants seemed dissatisfied) policy and particularly innovations in policy.

## SPECIFYING POLICY

Policy guidelines formulated at the small Party meetings and sometimes then legitimated by a Central Committee Plenum were hammered into more specific directives by three key bodies: the Military Affairs Committee (MAC), the Standing Committee of the State Council, and the Party headquarters Secretariat. These three small groups (none having more than twenty members) presided over the activities of the major hierarchies in China—the military, the government, and the Party. (In addition, during such movements as the 1955 *su-fan* rectification campaign and the Cultural Revolution, *ad hoc* groups with plenipotentiary powers directed and coordinated the nationwide drives.) Before the Cultural Revolution, different individuals

---

[63] This aspect of Ch'en's career was only recently revealed. See *ibid.*, pp. 85–86.

(all Politburo members) headed each: Lin Piao the MAC, Chou En-lai, Standing Committee of the State Council; Liu Shao-ch'i, Teng Hsiao-p'ing, and P'eng Chen at CCP headquarters.[64] Quite probably, the particular styles and concerns of these leaders affected the policy making processes of their units, though to be sure these men labored under Mao's shadow.

Unfortunately, little information is available on how decisions were made within these bodies, how they were linked to their subordinate agencies, what directives they drafted (as opposed to ratified), and so on.[65] The available evidence suggests that policy at this level followed established procedures. Each body apparently used its large staffs to prepare position papers, to draft regulations, and to help administer its

[64] "CCP headquarters," rather than a more precise term, is employed because the exact group leading Party activities is unknown. The Secretariat probably was involved in this task, but intriguing passages by Liu Shao-ch'i (who was not on the Secretariat), which detail how the crucial work team issue was handled during the early stages of the Cultural Revolution, suggest a more complicated process:

> During a certain period prior to July 18 [1966] when Chairman Mao was absent from Peking, the Central Committee's daily work pivoted around me. I made decisions affecting the conduct of the cultural revolution in all quarters of Peking and made reports to *the Central Committee meetings.* . . . At that time, requests came from many quarters for work teams. . . . The masses would not have been satisfied merely with the dispatch of liaison men. However, at that time, we should not have done anything more than to handle the situation by sending some liaison men. At the time, some comrades discovered that the work teams were in conflict with the masses, and taking up this issue, proposed that the dispatch of work teams was unnecessary. For instance, Comrade Ch'en Po-ta made such a proposal. He understood Mao's thinking. Had we also understood Chairman Mao's thought, we would have suspended these activities, and would not have pursued a mistaken line and direction. . . . Precisely at this critical moment when I was directing *the Central Work Meetings,* I committed the above mentioned mistakes. [*Collected Works of Liu Shao-ch'i, 1958–1967* (Hong Kong: Union Research Institute, 1968), pp. 357–59; emphasis added.]

What men were included in the "Central Work Meetings" is unknown, but clearly Liu referred to routine procedures which he assumed his readers knew, for he also noted, "For some time prior to July 18 [1966], the daily work of the Party Central Committee was in my charge. Those erroneous decisions mentioned above were made at meetings of the Central Committee held to hear reports—meetings at which I presided. Chairman Mao and the Party Central Committee asked me to take charge of the daily routine of the Party Central Committee" (*ibid.,* pp. 371–73). Clearly, the procedures of Party headquarters remain a mystery.

[65] For preliminary descriptions of each, see especially for the MAC: John Gittings, *The Role of the Chinese Army* (London: Oxford University Press, 1967), especially pp. 282–88, and Ralph L. Powell, *Politico-Military Relationships in Communist China* (Washington, D.C.: External Research Staff, Bureau of Intelligence and Research, United States Department of State, 1963); for the State Council: Chang Wang-shan, "The State Council in Communist China: A Structural and Functional Analysis, 1954–65" (Master's essay, Columbia University, 1968), esp. pp. 65–75, and Donald Klein, "The State Council and the Cultural Revolution," *CQ*, No. 35 (July–September, 1968), esp. pp. 93–95; for Party headquarters: Schurmann, *Ideology and Organization,* pp. 140–49.

directives.[66] The programs adopted by each group also acquired greater legitimacy and force through the convening of larger, more representative bodies, which endorsed these programs.[67]

Each body was concerned with particular spheres: the MAC with national security and the role of the military in society; the State Council with economic policy, educational affairs, and diplomatic matters; Party headquarters with ideology, social policy (particularly in rural areas), and international Communist affairs. The responsibilities of these bodies, however, overlapped. The State Council's direction of the formal education system and the Party's concern for ideology (raising the social consciousness of the Chinese people) were intertwined. All three bodies were involved with foreign affairs. The MAC's role in maintaining domestic tranquillity gave it an interest in rural social policy, since ill-advised policies produced peasant unrest.

Assuming the universality of bureaucratic phonomena, a logical inference is that each of these bodies was willing to expand its sphere of operations. Overlapping jurisdictions and a certain amount of rivalry may have characterized the relationship among these bodies. (On the other hand, the overlapping membership of these groups probably dampened rivalries.) Hence, a vigorous Mao enjoyed flexibility. He could choose among these three bodies to transform his general policies into administrative procedures. To some extent, he could use one group to check another. Or, as he did on several occasions, he could establish special advisory groups to make policy recommendations.[68] But, an infirm Mao could become the victim of competition

---

[66] The bodies performing staff functions for the MAC were in the Ministry of Defense (the Logistics Department, the General Staff Department, and the Political Department). See J. Chester Cheng (ed.), *The Politics of the Chinese Red Army: A Translation of the Bulletin of Activities of the People's Liberation Army* (Stanford, Calif.: Hoover Institution, 1966). For the State Council, the Secretariat (*mi-shu t'ing*), the Office of the Premier (*tsung-li pan-kung-shih*), and the specialized staff offices under the State Council, see "Organic Law of the State Council of the People's Republic of China" in Albert P. Blaustein (ed.), *Fundamental Legal Documents of Communist China* (South Hackensack, N.J.: Fred B. Rothman & Co., 1962), pp. 127–31, and Chang, "The State Council." For the Party headquarters, the general office under Yang Shang-k'un, and the specialized departments under the Central Committee (Finance and Trade, Rural Work, and so on).

[67] Meetings of military officials convened by the MAC performed this role for the MAC; the National People's Congress (NPC), the Standing Committee of the NPC, and plenary sessions of the State Council performed this role for the Standing Committee of the State Council; and a National Party Congress and Central Committee plenum, for Party headquarters.

[68] Ch'en Yün headed such a group in the early 1960's, P'eng Chen in the mid-1960's.

among these groups; without his vigilance, these groups inevitably would encroach upon his power. On the basis of available evidence, however, it is impossible to determine the extent to which the distribution of power and authority among these three groups at any given moment resulted from Mao's deliberate choice and the extent to which it was the product of inter-group struggle.

## THE POLICY CYCLE

The broad picture that emerges centers on Mao, constrained by his economic resources and the range of tensions he could tap. Acting in accord with his consciously held beliefs as well as his more primordial sentiments, and manipulated to an undeterminable degree by the bureaucracies over which he presided, Mao constantly intervened in the decision making processes to bring fresh policy initiatives to areas of concern to him and to give renewed vigor to languishing pet programs. The major way in which he brought his will to bear was to convene informally a small group of Party officials. There, he heard the range of opinions of his associates in remarkably lively policy debates, and then he issued a summary of his views, which he expected to be translated into action. Through time, Mao's associates had become immersed in particular sectors of society. When he heard their views, then, he was in contact with imperfect embodiments of many of the social forces in society.

Policy guidelines adopted at these meetings were transferred into specific policies by the State Council, Party headquarters, and the MAC, and were communicated across the nation through diverse means: Central Committee plenums, editorials and articles in the Party controlled press, various types of national congresses, legal edicts of ministries, and dispatch of squads of officials to local units. To be sure, Mao's associates occasionally harbored doubts about the wisdom of his latest directive and sometimes delayed enforcing it, or when they were translating vague guidelines into specific policy prescriptions, interpreted the guidelines to suit their purposes. This was particularly the case from 1962 through 1965, when the intent of Mao's directives was not always obvious. As Lin Piao himself allegedly stated:

> Chairman Mao gives full consideration to handling problems and he is farsighted and has his ideas. There are many ideas we do not understand. We must firmly execute the Chairman's directives. . . . Sometimes I cannot avoid making mis-

takes and cannot follow the Chairman's thoughts. . . . The Chairman is the genius of the world revolution. There are wide gaps between him and us.[69]

Nonetheless, in general, Mao and his associates did establish the parameters within which bureaucratic politics were played and did attempt to exercise vigorous leadership to secure compliance.

Compliance was not automatic, however. Directives from above were not always easy to integrate with the routine, day-to-day decisions that an agency was issuing. The communication networks often distorted or blocked the flow of information. Lower level officials pursued sophisticated strategies to bend the directives to suit their own short-run needs and long-run career plans. The compliance patterns of lower officials and of the populace became part of the policy making process.[70]

These patterns were soon monitored by officials on tour and in reports filtering up the bureaucratic hierarchy. Although the Party Secretariat and later the Cultural Revolution Group were pivotal monitoring agencies, Mao's avid reading of reports meant that he was involved personally in the monitoring process as well. With the information gathered from these monitoring devices, Mao and his comrade-subordinates constantly re-evaluated their broad policy guidelines. Probably at Mao's initiative, if it were felt necessary, the top Party officials would gather again informally to reformulate these guidelines, usually making only marginal adjustments to policy but occasionally introducing substantial change. With this process, the policy making cycle was complete.

### VARIATIONS IN MAO'S INVOLVEMENT

Mao's involvement in policy making varied considerably. Sometimes he was intimately involved, while at other times power seems to have gravitated to Party headquarters, the State Council, or the MAC on the national level. What explains the variations? One previously mentioned factor was Mao's health. Another factor, to be explored in the concluding section of this essay, was the degree of confidence that his associates had in him. But Mao's strategic orientation also affected which policies he perceived to be pivotal and, hence, which ones he

[69] From a poster at Tsinghua University, prepared by the Fan-fen Eighth Branch corps of Huai-chou, the Wei-tung Combat Group of Ta-hsing *hsien*, and the Part-work, Part-study Supply and Marketing Cooperative school, Peking.

[70] My Ph.D. dissertation attempts to document this theme. See Oksenberg, "Policy Formulation in Communist China," chaps. xii and xiii.

wished to control. Three considerations appear to have governed his behavior: (1) the problem involved (was the policy closely linked to the pivotal problem of defining the current situation?), (2) the issue-area (finance, foreign affairs, rural affairs, and so on), and (3) the phase in the policy cycle (was China in a period of advance or consolidation?). How did each of these considerations affect him specifically?

## THE PROBLEM INVOLVED

To Mao, tensions and conflicts of interest are inherent in all situations. In his Manichaean view, "positive" forces (those assisting socialist advance) perpetually are either oppressed or threatened by "negative" forces. Positive groups and individuals always must struggle to eliminate the negative forces among them and to remain militant against pernicious external forces. This world view generates the hierarchy of problems demanding a leadership's attention. First, it must confront several interrelated questions concerning the current situation: Exactly which groups and individuals in society comprise the positive forces, and which the negative? Does the situation call for a period of advance and struggle, or for consolidation and unity? What tensions can best be manipulated to advance the cause, and does the resolution of these tensions call for the use of violence? Then, in the light of answers to these questions, a leadership must establish priorities among conflicting goals and must determine the relative importance of different sectors of society. Next, it must develop organizational strategies—how to arouse and mobilize the positive forces in society and how to isolate, reform, or vanquish the negative forces. Finally come tactical matters: how to apply general strategy toward each sector of society.

Mao considered decisions about defining the current situation to be his, although he was willing to discuss them with his Politburo level associates. But he clearly believed that he had special insight into such questions as: What role could intellectuals play; had the time come to collectivize agriculture; was violence necessary to rid China of its remnant capitalist class; should the tension between state and society be tapped? Mao considered such problems to be of the utmost importance. He did not hesitate to stipulate policy on such matters, even in the face of considerable opposition.

Mao also deemed it his prerogative to settle matters of priorities, although he seemed less strong-willed and more prepared to widen the circle of his advisors on these problems. For example, the relative weight assigned to agricultural and industrial development, the balance to be struck between conflicting ideological and economic considerations in foreign affairs, and the short-run choice between increasing peasant income or increasing tax revenue in the countryside, seem to have been issues Mao preferred to resolve, though only after prolonged discussions and even compromises with his colleagues.

Mao was less involved with organizational matters—as long as bureaucratic practice did not violate his well-established norms. Hence, the decentralization edicts of 1957 were the product of long debate within the State Council, and Liu Shao-ch'i drafted the important section on administrative procedures in the 1958 document on work methods.[71] Although Mao was concerned with tactical matters, his guerrilla experience taught him that lower level bureaucrats required flexibility. Thus, while he was ready to praise model units (for example, the Ta-chai Brigade) whose *spirit* deserved emulation, he left the details of national regulations to the State Council and its ministries, the MAC and the military apparatus, and so on.

ISSUE-AREAS

Mao believed that issue-areas varied in importance, but through time his evaluations changed. Until the mid-1950's Mao placed a high value upon technology and believed that he could achieve his goals through rapid industrialization; hence, he paid special attention to issues dealing with industry, labor, and intellectuals. From the mid-1950's to the early 1960's, he placed a high value upon sheer manpower and the capabilities of proper organization, devoting more attention to the agricultural and organizational issues. Increasingly through the 1960's, Mao worried about the survival of the revolution, and pinned his hopes upon securing attitudinal change. Moreover, he became concerned about his foreign and domestic enemies. His attention became riveted upon issues involving culture and education, youth, the military, and foreign affairs.

Mao concentrated upon policy issues that he considered vital. Even tactical matters in these areas were placed on the agenda of the informal Party gatherings. Politburo level debates on these issues were open, however, for they were not perceived to involve matters of ideological orientation. Mao approached these problems with a greater degree of flexibility. Decision making in issue-areas which he deemed

71 "Collection of Statements by Mao Tse-tung," p. 29.

less vital, however, became largely a matter of routine bureaucratic processes.

Mao also felt more confident handling some issues than others. In his speech On the Correct Handling of Contradictions, for example, Mao said: "I do not propose to talk at length on economic questions today. With barely seven years of economic construction behind us, we still lack experience and need to get more." [72] And at Lushan in 1959, he observed: "Before August of last year [1958], I devoted my main energy to revolution. Being basically not versed in [economic] construction, I knew nothing about industrial planning." [73] Mao appears to have been more tolerant of disagreement and of experimentation in such areas, and less tolerant of disagreement in areas in which he felt competent—culture and education, agriculture, and organization.

The concept of "issue-areas" requires that the general picture of policy making be refined because "issue-areas" were interrelated. Decisions made on public security or on financial issues had implications for decisions made on the agriculture front, for example. Decisions in low priority areas ultimately may have had a significant impact upon high priority areas. Thus, although Mao attempted to concentrate upon strategically important issues, his solutions were always in danger of being swamped by the unanticipated consequences of decisions taken in areas that he had neglected.

POLICY PHASE

The Chinese political system tended to fluctuate between a phase of advance, struggle, and mobilization and a phase of consolidation, proclaimed unity, and "normalcy." Mao's own involvement followed this swing in policy. During an advance, he increased his personal involvement in policy formulation, particularly by convening lengthy informal Party meetings. His lengthy speeches at the moments of advance in 1955, 1958, and 1966 convey his sense of enthusiasm and energy. But he became less active during a consolidation phase. The whole purpose of the consolidation phase was to institutionalize gains of previous advances, which was in part to be accomplished through more routine, bureaucratic decision making. One firm indication of this fluctuation was that the number of known *ad hoc* Party gather-

[72] In Robert Bowie and John K. Fairbank (eds.), *Communist China, 1955–1959: Policy Documents with Analysis* (Cambridge, Mass.: Harvard University Center for International Studies and East Asian Research Center, 1961), p. 294.
[73] *CLG,* I, No. 4 (Winter, 1968–69), 38.

ings dropped during the consolidation phases, while the relative importance of routine ministerial activities appeared to increase.

The significance of the variance in Mao's involvement in the making of policy hardly needs to be stated. The interests of mortal men seemed to govern decisions in China when he was missing. But Mao left his indelible mark upon those policies involving problems of concern to him, particularly during the mobilization phases. The quest for an egalitarian society was unmistakable when he was active.

### TRENDS: SOME HYPOTHESES

Policy making under Mao changed from the early 1950's through 1968. These trends should be specified, though of necessity the analysis must be impressionistic. Insufficient data require this section to be offered in the form of hypotheses.

#### CHANGES IN INFLUENCES UPON MAO

The relative importance of the various influences upon Mao—the role demands upon him, his beliefs, personal factors, economic considerations, the tensions in society, and bureaucratic practices—appears to have changed. To be sure, such judgments are difficult, but reference to the roles expected of him, to his beliefs, and to the existing tensions in society appear to provide the basic explanation for his policies in the 1950's. The unifying role that Mao played in Chinese society and politics; the "mass line" and the theory of contradictions; and the tensions between urban and rural areas, between "red" and "expert," and between the central government and the localities—these, after all, are the key factors which Franz Schurmann persuasively used in *Ideology and Organization in Communist China* to illuminate Chinese politics of the 1950's. But these factors seem less crucial in explaining Mao's behavior in the 1960's. Rather, personal factors, economic conditions, and bureaucratic influences become more salient. The ambitions of his wife, the economic constraints placed upon him by the sluggish growth in national productivity and the military build-up of hostile powers on China's periphery, and Mao's perception that the pre-Communist social structure and values persisted and were represented in the Party, are crucial in explaining his actions during the 1960's, as Schurmann recognized in the supplement to the revised edition of his book.[74]

The changes can be described in another way. The dominant influ-

[74] Schurmann, *Ideology and Organization*, pp. 501–92.

ences upon Mao in the 1950's could in turn be shaped by him. He could modify his beliefs. He could select which roles to fulfill. He could choose the tensions to be manipulated. But Mao could only respond to the dominant influences of the 1960's; they were beyond his control. The differences between the 1950's and the 1960's should not be drawn too starkly; after all, Mao faced economic and bureaucratic constraints in the 1950's. But the trend unmistakably was there—a Mao being overwhelmed by his environment, finding himself less powerful, fearing that the initiative was no longer his. From this vantage, the Cultural Revolution was Mao's desperate attempt to acquire power—less from Liu Shao-ch'i than from society at large.

CHANGES IN MAO'S ROLE

Earlier, it was noted that Mao had a dual impact upon the policy making process. On the one hand, as the authority responsible for establishing priorities for a goal-oriented movement, Mao played a definitive role. But his restless quest to reconcile the probably irreconcilable introduced a disquieting note. Moreover, Mao was expected to satisfy several roles, particularly as chairman of the Party and as the acknowledged ruler of his people. The role of chairman was organizational and involved Mao's role in the policy making process. The role of leader was societal and involved his role in social processes.

Through time, it seems, Mao moved from playing a definitive to playing a provocative role in the policy process. In the early years of his rule, he was interested in perfecting techniques of rule, and as his Ten Great Relationships and On the Correct Handling of Contradictions speeches indicate, his mind was occupied with the problems of identifying real tensions in society and defining short-term objectives. But by the mid-1960's, he had imported into and impressed upon the Politburo his search for the classless and industrialized, participatory and controlled, ordered and revolutionary society. This problem dominated his thinking in the 1960's, as his *On Khrushchev's Phony Communism* tends to demonstrate.

Concomitantly, Mao shifted his emphasis from the policy making role expected by his colleagues to the role of father of the country. In the first role, he worked within the confines of the organization; in the second, he transcended them.

Accompanying the change in Mao's role orientation was his willingness to treat his own personal entourage—people with whom he felt more at ease—as Politburo level associates. The elevation of Madame

Mao, Ch'en Po-ta, and Yao Wen-yüan (perhaps Lin Piao's wife, Yeh Chün, should be included) to the Politburo in 1969 capped a long-term trend of Mao's increasing reliance and dependence upon friends rather than upon comrades.

These changes in Mao had wide ramifications upon the policy making process. By the mid-1960's the policy making machinery was headed by someone who no longer felt responsible to the institutional processes that had gradually emerged, and Mao was willing to wreak havoc upon that machinery in the Cultural Revolution. Moreover, if his associates perceived the changes in him—and some of the admittedly less reliable Red Guard documents suggest that they did—then they had an interest in trying to isolate him in order to minimize the provocative consequences of his intervention in the policy making process. Thus, through time, the proper role for Mao in the policy making process became, not openly discussed perhaps, but felt by all. A major trend in the policy making process, therefore, was the increasing problem of Mao's proper role in it.

CHANGES IN INFORMAL PARTY MEETINGS

Available evidence does not allow any charting of trends with respect to procedures, frequency, or the participants and their strategies in the Party meetings. But inferences can be made about changes in the basis of Mao's authority. The attributes that seem to be responsible for Mao's success have already been mentioned: his control of the legitimizing symbols in society, his vision, his knowledge, his dominating personality, his stratagems in Party meetings to retain initiative, and his reliance upon trusted supporters. As to trends, consider the implications of these disparate clues: The incisiveness and brilliance so obvious in Mao's speeches in the 1950's (The Question of Agricultural Cooperation; Ten Great Relationships; On the Correct Handling of Contradictions) seem less evident in his speeches of the 1960's (for example, to the Tenth Plenum and the October, 1966, work conference). Also, P'eng Teh-huai's 1959 and 1962 position papers and the statements by others supporting P'eng severely challenged Mao's judgment. Further, Mao apparently engaged in a series of ruses from September, 1965, and possibly earlier to launch the Cultural Revolution (for instance, the attack upon Wu Han to weaken P'eng Chen, the use of the Shanghai base, and so on). In addition, in the 1960's many of Mao's associates seemed to feel a need to flatter him. Also, Mao's associates appear to have gradually identified their interests with those of their bureaucracies and constituencies. Moreover, especially after the Great Leap, Chinese policy makers retreated into secrecy. Confident of their performance in the fifties, they gathered and released firm statistics, held many publicized meetings, and issued explicit directives and policy statements. Fearful of the performance in the sixties, their statistical network fell into disrepair, their economic performance went unreported, meetings were fewer and less publicized, and policies were not well articulated. Finally, in the second decade of his rule, Mao increasingly disciplined his policy making associates by proclaiming them to be ideological deviants. This form of discipline, rarely used from 1949 through 1958, made Mao's associates more reluctant to express heterodox views. Taken together, these clues imply that Mao's power among his colleagues increasingly was based on fear rather than respect, and that he prevailed through stratagems rather than reasoned arguments. More and more, tension may have pervaded the informal Party gatherings. To the extent that a small group requires considerable mutual trust in order to make sound decisions, the sketchy evidence raises the hypothesis that a major mechanism in the policy making process was losing its effectiveness.

CHANGES IN POLICY SPECIFYING BODIES

The State Council met frequently in the 1950's, but less often in the 1960's. Nine of the fifteen Central Committee plenums convened since 1949 met in the five years from 1956 to 1961. The MAC, with few publicly announced meetings in the 1950's, came into the spotlight with its meetings during the 1960's. The variations in the frequency of meetings appear to reflect the shifting political powers and responsibilities of these bodies. The State Council particularly was active when the governmental apparatus it headed played the dominant administrative role. The peak of Central Committee activity corresponded roughly with the height of the CCP's involvement in day-to-day administration. The increased prominence of the MAC accompanied the rise of the PLA in Chinese politics. The shift was from economic, to ideological, to coercive organizations.

The implications of these changes upon the policy formulation process were at once subtle and profound. Each organization had its own approach to policy making. The agendas, directives, and procedures of the State Council suggest a well-organized, pragmatic institution at work: sifting reports, searching for realistic options, calm and unhurrying, competently responding to problems by adjusting on-going policies at the margins. Reports from Party plenums and the informal Party meetings suggest another policy making style: tumul-tuous, hurried, concerned with relating means to ideological ends. Finally, although the image of the PLA is extremely ill-defined, the PLA *Kung-tso T'ung-hsün* (Work Bulletin) as well as PLA actions in 1967–68 reflect an organization that was proud of its tradition and impatient with civilian society, which had relatively good communica-tion channels and a capacity to handle problems pragmatically, but which may have been plagued by inter- and intra-service rivalries.

## CONCLUSION

In the 1950's, the policy making process in China resembled the situation in American government when the President has a compliant bureaucracy and Congress—although to be sure the importance of ideology and the dominance of Mao were significant differences. In the 1960's, the comparison is with a President who faces an obstructive bureaucracy and Congress.

But a series of limited comparisons can be made between Mao and particular aspects of American presidents. As Roosevelt, Mao fostered conflict among several policy-specifying bodies in order to increase his options. As Truman in 1948, Mao attempted to manipulate the ten-sions in society. As Eisenhower, Mao believed in the value of gathering his specialized subordinates together to elicit advice on general topics, although unlike Eisenhower, who relied upon the Cabinet and the National Security Council, Mao wished to avoid routine procedures. As Kennedy, Mao commanded the respect of his associates through his intelligence and vision. As Johnson, he engendered a fear among his associates through his wile and personality. As Nixon, he spent much time reading official reports and drawing the attention of his subordinates to those that impressed him. As all presidents since FDR with his Harry Hopkins, Mao apparently relied upon a chief assistant —Ch'en Po-ta.

Yet the Chinese process of the 1960's also seems more alien. The possibly reduced effectiveness of the small Party gatherings meant that Mao may have increasingly lacked a major mechanism for mak-ing direct contact with social and bureaucratic forces in society. As Mao himself complained, he became somewhat isolated from the reali-ties of Chinese politics. Thus, the chance that he might act capriciously increased. At the same time, in part through Mao's deliberate transfer of responsibility to his subordinates, the policy specifying bodies became more powerful. Their increasing power, when it was combined with the economic constraints upon the system, meant that Mao's capricious acts could be circumvented, blunted, or challenged covertly. In the 1950's, Mao's interventions, such as his launching of agricultural collectivization and initiating the Great Leap, elicited immediate and obedient responses from the bureaucracy. His interventions in the 1960's, while earning overt responses, became the focal points of bureaucratic conflict.

In a curious way, the policy making process appears to have changed from one familiar to students of American government to one reminiscent of the imperial institution in traditional China. Intrigue by the emperor's wife, tension between the inner and outer courts, competition between the Grand Secretariat and the Grand Council, the contrast between the remoteness of the emperor and the omnipresence of his influence, the difficulty of distinguishing between loyal and disloyal opposition, the embodiment by bureaucrats of the interests of their constituencies, the inability of the emperor to obtain reliable information, the alleged machinations of cliques, and the inability to devise widely accepted methods for handling succession— these were the hallmarks of politics in Peking in the eighteenth and nineteenth centuries. They find ready analogs in Peking in the 1960's.

Why the seeming reversion to tradition? Three explanations can be suggested: the politics of a gerontocracy, the demands of Chinese society, and the politics of poverty.

Certainly, policy making in China has been controlled by an aged group: Mao, born in 1893, Liu Shao-ch'i in 1898, Chou En-lai in 1899, and so on. Born in 1907, Lin Piao was among the youngest of the Politburo officials until the 1966–69 changes in Politburo membership. The question then becomes: what are the characteristics of small groups of aged Chinese when they are engaged in solving problems? Does the group become more inflexible as each member becomes more committed to his previous record? Do old battles tend to be re-enacted? Drawing upon Robert Lifton's work,[75] we can ask whether it is possible that as Mao aged, he became more concerned with preserving his claim to immortality as a revolutionary. Did the old comrades find it more difficult to accept criticism as they aged? These questions seem realistic enough to suggest that the consequences

[75] Robert Lifton, *Revolutionary Immortality: Mao Tse-tung and the Chinese Cultural Revolution* (New York: Vintage Books, 1968).

of the aging process in Chinese culture may help to explain the political trends. Unfortunately, there is no firm analysis on the psychology of aging in China to sustain the inquiry here.

There is another way to explain the trends. If the parallels between the traditional and post-1960 policy making process are drawn correctly, then perhaps the similarities reflected continuities in the values and structural needs of the society: China cannot be unified unless it has a strong leader; the traditional emphasis upon hierarchy and harmony make such institutions as informal Party meetings not viable over the long run; and so on. According to such an argument, what has occurred is the remolding of a revolutionary organization by the society it seeks to change. The same argument was offered to explain Stalin: a reassertion of the czarist style. But this attractive argument is easier to state than to document. After all, the way policy was made in traditional China varied considerably; for instance, compare the K'ang-hsi era and the T'ung-chih Restoration. Moreover, similar phenomena need not have similar causes. Further, even if the values and structural needs of society have permeated the national policy machinery of the CCP, those values and requisites must be specified and the linkages must be established. That task is beyond the scope of this essay.

Turning to another factor, the politics of poverty may well have the greatest explanatory power for the trends.[76] That the aspirations of the Chinese leaders far exceed their resources is obvious. Less obvious, there is reason to believe that the total amount of resources which Mao actually could allocate annually to new programs decreased from 1956–58 to 1966–68. Foreign aid to Peking from the Soviet Union terminated in that time span. The sources of wealth confiscated during the three-anti and five-anti campaigns of 1951–52 and the socialist transformation of industry and commerce of 1955–56 could not be tapped again. The commitment of the government to rather extensive welfare and education programs, with a growing population, may have required annual increases in appropriations. The military build-up of the United States, India, and the Soviet Union around China's

[76] The discussion in this section draws from, but alters, Theodore Lowi, "American Business, Public Policy, Case Studies, and Political Theory," *World Politics,* XVI (July, 1964), 677–715; Lewis A. Froman, Jr., "The Categorization of Policy Contents," in Austin Ranney (ed.), *Political Science and Public Policy* (Chicago: Markham Press, 1968); Raymond Bauer (ed.), *The Study of Policy Formulation* (New York: The Free Press of Glencoe, 1968), introduction and *passim;* and Gabriel A. Almond and G. Bingham Powell, Jr., *Comparative Politics: A Developmental Approach* (Boston: Little, Brown and Co., 1966).

periphery could not be ignored. And during this time, although firm statistics are lacking, the nation did not enjoy sustained, rapid economic growth.

In the 1950's, Mao and his associates enjoyed abundant resources—when compared to the sums available to them in Yenan. The newness of their bureaucratic positions and their suddenly increased wealth perhaps enabled the policy makers to allocate resources without fully caring that one bureaucracy or sector of society could be given resources only at the cost of another bureaucracy. Perceived abundance produces the process of logrolling so familiar on the American congressional scene. But the consequences of the Great Leap and the long tenures in specific bureaucracies shattered illusions of abundance. The politics of poverty held sway.

An economically impoverished system cannot offer vast material rewards; it must rely more heavily upon symbols to secure compliance, and the symbols become ever more grandiose. This has been the trend since 1958, and the policy making processes reflect this trend: increased political intrigue, a seemingly greater concern with rank in the political hierarchy, and a tendency to deal with words rather than meaning. This is the trend which made the Chinese political system appear to be essentially weak and susceptible to breakdown in the late 1960's.

Under the politics of poverty, policy makers perceive that the allocation of rewards to some entails depriving others. Funds for one bureaucracy mean less for another. Allocations are perceived to involve redistribution. Though discussing American politics, Theodore Lowi's description of redistributive politics echoes Mao's analysis:

> Issues that involve redistribution cut closer than any others along class lines and activate interests in what are roughly class terms. . . . In redistribution, there will never be more than two sides and the sides are clear, stable, consistent. Negotiation is possible, but only for the purpose of strengthening or softening the impact of redistribution.[77]

Lowi implies that the resolution of redistributive issues in favor of the weaker members of society can only occur when strong leadership unilaterally enforces its will upon the privileged strata of society. This kind of politics is highly centralized, involves coercion, and is motivated by ideological conviction.

Under conditions of poverty, then, the Chinese leaders had to de-

[77] Lowi, "American Business," pp. 710–11.

cide whether to redistribute resources or simply to regulate the behavior of individuals, groups, and bureaucracies in order to prevent their encroaching upon the rights of others. Obviously, the responsibility for regulating behavior fell upon the bureaucracy. Hence, the choice was whether to emphasize the redistribution of resources through strong leadership or to regulate competing interests through bureaucracy.

Mao saw himself as the representative of the "have nots": the rural areas, the poorer peasants, the uneducated, and the temporary laborers. For these people to get their just rewards, he insisted, redistribution had to be at the core of the political process. And this involved the need for strong, willful leadership and class conflict. But he met the opposition of bureaucracy.

Nowhere was the conflict more clearly revealed than in the handling of the issue of public health.[78] Mao saw it as a redistributive issue; he wanted to reduce the level of care available in China's cities and to allocate more doctors to the countryside. He saw the issue in class terms. People in the public health field saw the issue in regulative terms: how to protect the health field from encroachments so that, *as a field*, it might prosper—more doctors, better wages, higher skills, more research.

The scarcity of resources, in sum, seems to explain a great deal about the policy making process in China. In spite of their scarcity, according to Mao, resources had to be redistributed. Mao forged an alliance with the dispossessed; he emphasized his relationship with society, not with his policy making associates. His associates, responsible for the large bureaucracies under their command, were reluctant to allocate funds to the poor or to other bureaucracies, for such allocations came at the cost of developing their own bureaucracies. Further, some of Mao's associates believed that egalitarian redistribution was shortsighted and that increasing the total wealth of society was more important. And this could only be done, they argued, by investing in the advanced sectors of society and properly regulating industry, agriculture, and commerce.

The divergence between Mao's emphasis upon redistribution and his colleagues' emphasis upon regulating society produced the policy making process described earlier: A vigorous Mao pressed his egalitarian vision upon his colleagues. They responded because they feared and respected him. They realized that he had special links with the

[78] See "Mao's Revolution in Public Health," *Current Scene,* VI (May 1, 1968) pp. 1–10.

dispossessed, whom they also claimed to champion. But these policy making associates also acquired vested interests in the system; in the 1960's they began to be interested in regulating the system as well as changing it. Tension developed between Mao and his policy making associates. During the Cultural Revolution, Mao purged those associates whom he perceived to be reluctant to support his redistributive policies.

But the purge did not eliminate the underlying causes of the problem. As long as the dreams far exceed government revenue in China and the leader feels impelled to build alliances with the poorer sectors of society, the gap between the Chinese leader and his top level policy associates in the bureaucracy will persist. The leader will try to shift funds to the dispossessed; the top level bureaucrats will try to retain their resources and hope for an era of greater calm.

🏵🏵🏵🏵🏵🏵🏵🏵🏵🏵🏵🏵🏵🏵🏵🏵🏵🏵🏵🏵🏵🏵🏵🏵🏵🏵🏵

### FREDERICK C. TEIWES

# Provincial Politics in China:
# Themes and Variations[1]

In recent years, scholars have given increasing attention to the pre-viously neglected subnational levels of the Chinese political system. Coincident with questioning of the more monolithic aspects of the totalitarian model, studies appeared on provincial and sub-provincial politics.[2] Moreover, research on national policies and campaigns has manifested concern with problems of local implementation and regional variation.[3] The apparent growth of military-based regional power dur-ing the Cultural Revolution has intensified the already significant in-terest in local government and politics.

Despite the growing interest in local government, many basic ques-

[1] Many people have aided in the preparation of this study. I am particularly indebted to David L. Denny, Roderick MacFarquhar, and Michel Oksenberg for their generosity in allowing me the use of their personal files, and to Jane Barneke, Patrick G. Maddox, and Alberta Wang for their research assistance.

[2] For provincial politics, see, for example, Frederick C. Teiwes, *Provincial Party Per-sonnel in Mainland China 1956–1966* (New York: East Asian Institute, Columbia Uni-versity, 1967); Frederick C. Teiwes, "The Purge of Provincial Leaders 1957–1958," *CQ*, No. 27 (July–September, 1966), pp. 14–32; and Ezra Vogel, "Land Reform in Kwang-tung 1951–1953: Central Control and Localism," *CQ*, No. 38 (April–June, 1969), pp. 27–62. For sub-provincial politics, see, for example, A. Doak Barnett, with a contribution by Ezra Vogel, *Cadres, Bureaucracy, and Political Power in Communist China* (New York: Columbia University Press, 1967), Parts II and III; Ying-mao Kau, "The Urban Bureaucratic Elite in Communist China: A Case Study of Wuhan, 1949–65," in A. Doak Barnett (ed.), *Chinese Communist Politics in Action* (Seattle: University of Washington Press, 1969), pp. 216–67; and Michel C. Oksenberg, "Local Government and Politics in China, 1955–58," in Andrew W. Cordier (ed.), *Columbia Essays in International Affairs* (New York: Columbia University Press, 1967), II, 223–45.

[3] An excellent example is Michel C. Oksenberg, "Policy Formulation in China: The Case of the 1957–8 Water Conservancy Campaign" (Ph.D. dissertation, Columbia Uni-versity, 1969).

tions remain unanswered. This study deals with a number of fundamental questions concerning the largest administrative level continuously in existence under the Communist regime—the province.[4] For example, what are the main tasks and functions of provincial administration? To what degree and under what circumstances are provincial interests articulated? How responsive have the provinces been to central policies during different periods? How do the provinces differ in terms of such variables as political stability, socioeconomic indexes, degree of dependence on the center for finances and resources, Party membership, and so forth, and how are these variables interrelated?

A study of provincial politics is feasible because of the existence of a significant amount of virtually unused source material.[5] This material is discussed in the first section. The second section treats in broad perspective some major aspects and tensions of provincial politics. The third section summarizes a detailed analysis of official statements by provincial authorities with particular attention to the questions raised above. The final section examines relationships among various sets of quantifiable political, socioeconomic, and organizational data on China's provinces.

## SOURCES ON PROVINCIAL POLITICS: THE WORK REPORT AND RELATED MATERIAL

Prior to the ban by the People's Republic of China (CPR) on the export of local newspapers at the start of the 1960's, the major daily papers of each province were the key source of information for provincial developments.[6] Although holdings of provincial newspapers available in the West are incomplete, and although there are important differences in the number of issues available for different provinces, a rich vein of material exists for most provinces.[7] The provincial press

[4] The provincial level, as defined for the purposes of this paper, includes the twenty-one provinces (*sheng*) and five autonomous regions (*tzu-chih ch'ü*) of China, but not the centrally administered municipalities (*chih-hsia shih*) of Peking, Shanghai, and Tientsin.

[5] An extensive bibliography of major provincial and municipal documents, including work reports, budget reports, economic development plans, and speeches and articles by leading officials, is being compiled by Robert M. Field, Larry Lau, Michel C. Oksenberg, and Frederick C. Teiwes.

[6] Since that time, monitored provincial radio broadcasts have been the most important source of provincial data. While extremely valuable, these broadcasts suffer from the same decline in quality of information that has marked all CPR communications media during the 1960's.

[7] The two most important holdings are those of the Library of Congress and the Union Research Institute (URI), Hong Kong. The URI holdings are listed in *Catalogue of Mainland Chinese Magazines and Newspapers Held by the Union Research Institute* (Hong Kong: Union Research Institute, 1962). Draft listings of the Library of Congress

contains many authoritative reports, editorials, and directives. Of these, the most comprehensive statements of governmental activities and political conditions are work reports (*kung-tso pao-kao*) delivered at Provincial People's (government) and Party Congresses. In addition, work reports provide a manageable amount of material for cross-provincial comparisons. For these reasons, government and Party work reports have served as the basic sources of this study. Tables 1 and 2 indicate the known dates of Provincial People's and Party Congresses and the work reports which are available.[8]

Provincial People's Congresses (*sheng jen-min tai-piao ta-hui*), theoretically the highest organs of state power at the provincial level, are occasions for reviewing work and tasks, and thus provide opportunities to express provincial perspectives on a wide variety of issues. The Congresses also have the function of transmitting national policies to key personnel of the provincial and lower levels. The work report of the provincial government, that is, of the People's Council (*sheng jen-min wei-yüan-hui*), is the major report of the congressional sessions. Delivered by the governor or a vice-governor, the work report examines the achievements and shortcomings of the previous year's work and lays down the policies, tasks, and goals to be pursued in the coming year. Provincial government work reports are heavily weighted toward economic concerns. These reports, which range from roughly nine thousand to thirty-five thousand characters, generally devote at least two-thirds of their contents to agriculture, industry, transportation and communications, commerce, and public finance. Measures for raising production are described in great detail, and plans for longer-range economic development are often elaborated at length. Moreover, detailed statistics are generally provided on a wide range of economic matters. Besides economic affairs, probably the greatest attention is given to the social organization of the countryside, that is, the Agricultural Producers' Cooperatives (APCs) and the People's Communes, which are intimately related to agricultural production. Education and

holdings were prepared in 1965 by Edwin G. Beal, Jr., and are available at the Library of Congress.

[8] To determine the dates of the various Congress sessions, the following sources were consulted: the publications of the American Consulate General, Hong Kong (*CB, ECMM, SCMP*); *JPRS;* the URI Classified Files on Communist China, No. 11243143; and *Ch'üan-kuo chu-yao pao-k'an tzu-liao so-yin* (Index to Major Newspapers and Periodicals of China) (Shanghai: Shang-hai shih pao-k'an t'u-shu kuan, Nos. 1–57, March, 1955–July, 1960). The availability of work reports was determined by examining the holdings of the consulate publications, *JPRS*, URI, and the Library of Congress.

public health also receive considerable comment, and their relevance to economic development generally is stressed. Perhaps the most surprising aspect is the relative lack of attention to political and legal work. Although calls for vigilance against counterrevolutionaries and for strengthening the people's democratic dictatorship are common, they are usually very general.

In addition to government work reports, People's Congresses also regularly hear budget reports which give detailed breakdowns of actual revenues and expenditures during the previous year and projections for the coming year, and equally detailed reports on provincial economic development plans. Other reports transmit the resolutions and the spirit of sessions of the National People's Congress and review the work of the People's Courts. Although these reports are frequently unavailable in the West (see Table 1), New China News Agency dispatches on the congressional sessions provide an indication of their content as well as some provincial statistics, even though they are decidedly on the skimpy side. Thus some rudimentary indications of provincial developments can be obtained even in the absence of the major reports.

Government work reports are available only for the 1954–60 period, a fact undoubtedly related to the formalization of the government's reporting system in conjunction with the establishment of People's Congresses from national to township (*hsiang*) levels in the summer and fall of 1954.[9] Table 1 demonstrates that during the 1950's the terms of Provincial People's Congresses adhered to the four-year period stipulated by the CPR Constitution [10] and the Second Congresses were convened precisely on schedule in 1958. However, the Third Congresses were convened a year or two behind schedule in 1963–64.[11] The frequency of Provincial People's Congress sessions was not set by the Constitution, but most provinces held at least one session annually throughout the 1950's, and several provinces appear to have kept that standard in the 1960's. Although provincial differences in the timing

[9] Article 66 of the Constitution of the CPR (1954) stipulates that local People's Councils report to the People's Congresses of the same level. See *Chung-hua jen-min kung-ho-kuo fa-kuei hui-pien* (Compendium of Laws and Regulations of the People's Republic of China) (Peking: Fa-lü ch'u-pan she, No. 1, September, 1954–June, 1955), p. 24. Prior to the establishment of People's Congresses, meetings of Provincial Political Consultative Conferences (*sheng hsieh-shang wei-yüan-hui*) served similar purposes; scattered press reports on these conferences are available. See URI Classified Files on Communist China, No. 1124114.

[10] Article 57, Constitution of the CPR (1954).

[11] At the national level, the Third National People's Congress was nearly two years behind schedule when it met in December, 1964.

TABLE 1
PROVINCIAL PEOPLE'S CONGRESSES

| Province | 1954 | 1955 | 1956 | 1957 | 1958 | 1959 | 1960 | 1961 | 1962 | 1963 | 1964 | 1965 |
|---|---|---|---|---|---|---|---|---|---|---|---|---|
| Anhwei | | 2-2s/1C† | 5-3s/1C | 9-4s/1C* | 11-1s/2C | | | | | | 9-1s/3C | |
| Chekiang | | 1-2s/1C<br>12-3s/1C | 6-4s/1C<br>12-5s/1C | 12-6s/1C* | 10-1s/2C* | | 2-2s/2C* | | | | 9-1s/3C | |
| Fukien | | 2-2s/1C | 3-3s/1C | 5-4s/1C | | | | | 12-2s/2C | | | |
| Heilungkiang | | 1-2s/1C<br>12-3s/1C | 12-5s/1C | 8-6s/1C* | 8-1s/2C* | 8-2s/2C | | | | | 9-1s/3C | |
| Honan | | 1-2s/1C<br>8-3s/1C | 3-4s/1C<br>11-5s/1C | 8-6s/1C | 12-1s/2C* | | 2-2s/2C* | | | | 9-1s/3C | |
| Hopeh | | 2-2s/1C*<br>9-3s/1C | 3-4s/1C<br>10-5s/1C | 8-6s/1C* | 4-7s/1C<br>10-1s/2C* | | 2-2s/2C | | | | 10-1s/3C | |
| Hunan | | 2-2s/1C<br>12-3s/1C | 12-4s/1C | 12-5s/1C | 7-1s/2C* | | | | 2-4s/2C | | 9-1s/3C | |
| Hupeh | | 1-2s/1C | 1-3s/1C | 1-4s/1C | 12-1s/2C | | | | | | | |
| Inner Mongolia | | 4-2s/1C | | 4-4s/1C | 6-1s/2C | 8-2s/2C* | 8-3s/2C | | 6-4s/2C | | 9-1s/3C | |
| Kansu | 8-1s/1C<br>12-2s/1C | | 3-3s/1C* | 4-5s/1C | 4-5s/1C<br>10-1s/2C* | 12-2s/2C | | 12-3s/2C | | | 9-1s/3C | |
| Kiangsi | | 2-2s/1C<br>8-3s/1C | 5-4s/1C<br>10-5s/1C | 3-6s/1C* | 6-1s/2C* | 6-2s/2C* | | | | | 10-2s/3C | |
| Kiangsu | | 2-2s/1C<br>11-3s/1C | 8-4s/1C | 1-5s/1C* | 10-1s/2C* | 12-2s/2C* | | | | | 9-1s/3C | |
| Kirin | | 2-2s/1C<br>12-3s/1C | 4-4s/1C<br>12-5s/1C | | 7-1s/2C* | 6-2s/2C* | 5-3s/2C* | | | | 9-2s/3C | |

| | 1C·1 | 1C·2 | 1C·3 | 1C·4 | 1C·5 | 1C·6 | 2C·1 | 2C·2 | 2C·3 | 2C·4 | 3C·1 | 3C·2 |
|---|---|---|---|---|---|---|---|---|---|---|---|---|
| Kwangsi ‡ | | | | | | | | | | | | |
| Kwangtung | 8-1s/1C | 2-2s/1C* | 7-3s/1C | 7-4s/1C | | 7-6s/1C | 9-1s/2C* | 10-2s/2C* | 11-3s/2C* | 11-4s/2C | 12-4s/1C | 9-2s/2C |
| Kweichow | | 2-2s/1C | 11-3s/1C | 9-5s/1C | 12-5s/1C | | 9-1s/2C* | 9-2s/2C | | 11-4s/2C* | 12-1s/3C | 9-2s/3C |
| Liaoning | | 2-2s/1C* | 10-3s/1C | 3-4s/1C | | 8-6s/1C | 12-1s/2C* | 12-2s/2C* | | | 12-1s/3C | 10-2s/3C |
| Ninghsia § | 10-1s/1C | | | | | | 9-1s/2C | | | | | |
| Shansi | 8-1s/1C | 2-2s/1C | 9-3s/1C | 4-4s/1C | | 8-6s/1C | 11-1s/2C* | 7-2s/2C* | 5-3s/2C | | 10-1s/3C | |
| Shantung | | 2-2s/1C* | 9-3s/1C | 8-4s/1C | | 8-6s/1C* | 10-1s/2C* | 5-2s/2C | 5-3s/2C | | | 9-2s/3C |
| Shensi | 9-1s/1C | 12-2s/1C | 10-3s/1C | 11-4s/1C | 7-5s/1C | | 7-1s/2C | 7-2s/2C* | | 5-4s/2C | | 9-2s/3C |
| Sinkiang ‖ | | 9-2s/1C | 1-3s/1C | 5-4s/1C | | | 1-1s/2C* | | | | | |
| Szechwan | | 1-2s/1C | 12-3s/1C | 11-4s/1C* | 8-5s/1C | | 6-1s/2C | 6-2s/2C* | 5-3s/2C | | | 10-2s/3C |
| Tibet # | 9-1s/1C | | | | | | | | | | | |
| Tsinghai | | 12-2s/1C* | 8-3s/1C | 8-4s/1C | 8-5s/1C* | | 6-1s/2C* | 6-2s/2C* | | 12-2s/2C* | | 9-2s/3C |
| Yunnan | 8-1s/1C | 2-2s/1C* | 4-3s/1C | 8-4s/1C | 3-5s/1C | | 11-1s/2C | 7-2s/2C* | | | | 9-2s/3C |

* Work report available in full or excerpts.

† 2-2s/1C = February (month of congress opening), first session of First People's Congress.

‡ Kwangsi Province became the Kwangsi Chuang Autonomous Region in March, 1958, and the congresses were renumbered accordingly.

§ The Ninghsia Hui Autonomous Region was established in October, 1958.

‖ Sinkiang Province became the Sinkiang Uigur Autonomous Region in October, 1955, and the congresses were renumbered accordingly.

# The Tibetan Autonomous Region was established in September, 1965.

## TABLE 2
### PROVINCIAL PARTY CONGRESSES *

| Province | 1954 | 1956 | 1957 | 1958 | 1959 | 1960 | 1961 | 1963 | 1964 |
|---|---|---|---|---|---|---|---|---|---|
| Anhwei | | 7-1s/1C† | 12-2s/1C | | 1-3s/1C‡ | | | | |
| Chekiang | | 7-1s/2C | 12-2s/2C‡ | | | 1-1s/3C | | | |
| Fukien | | 6-1s/1C | | 1-2s/1C | | | | | |
| Heilungkiang | | 7-1s/1C | 9-2s/1C | 12-3s/1C‡ | | | | 4-2s/2C | |
| Honan | | 7-1s/1C | 11-2s/1C | 12-3s/1C | | | | | |
| Hopeh | | 7-1s/1C | | | | | | | |
| Hunan | | 6-1s/1C | 11-2s/1C | | | | | | |
| Hupeh | | 6-1s/1C | 12-2s/1C | | | | | | |
| Inner Mongolia | | 7-1s/1C | | 2-2s/1C | | | | | |
| Kansu | 8-1s/1C | 6-1s/2C | 12-2s/2C‡ | | | | | | |
| Kiangsi | | 7-1s/5C | | | 1-3s/5C‡ | | | | |
| Kiangsu | | 7-1s/3C | 12-2s/3C | | 1-3s/3C‡ | | | | |
| Kirin | | 6-1s/1C | | | | 3-1s/2C | | | |

| | | | | | | | |
|---|---|---|---|---|---|---|---|
| Kwangsi | 6-1s/1C | | 6-3s/1C | | | | |
| Kwangtung | 7-1s/1C | 11-2s/1C ‡ | | 2-3s/1C | | 12-1s/2C | 7-2s/2C |
| Kweichow | 6-1s/1C | | | | | | |
| Liaoning | 7-1s/1C | 11-2s/1C ‡ | | | | | |
| Ninghsia | | | | | | | |
| Shansi | 7-1s/1C | 11-2s/1C | | | | | |
| Shantung | 7-1s/1C | 12-2s/1C | | 2-3s/1C ‡ | | | |
| Shensi | 6-1s/1C  6-1s/2C | 11-2s/2C | | | | | |
| Sinkiang | 7-1s/1C | | | | 2-2s/1C | | |
| Szechwan | 7-1s/1C | | 4-2s/1C | | | | |
| Tibet | | | | | | | |
| Tsinghai | 6-1s/2C | | | | | | |
| Yunnan | 6-1s/1C | 11-2s/1C | 9-3s/1C | | | | |

* No data available on Party congresses in 1955 or 1962.
† 7-1s/1C = July (month of Congress opening), first session of First Party Congress.
‡ Work report or summing-up report available in full or excerpts.

of congressional sessions may have political relevance,[12] the over-all frequency of meetings in the 1950's was basically a reflection of routinized governmental patterns. In the first year and a half after the establishment of provincial congresses in the summer of 1954, nearly all provinces met three times. For the remainder of the First Congress, however, there was greater variation among the provinces in the frequency and the timing of sessions, with some meeting at annual or slightly longer intervals and with others meeting more frequently. This variation seemed to continue during the term of the Second Congress. In any case, because of the regime's restrictions on local news, no work reports are available after 1960, and press dispatches on Provincial People's Congresses in that period contain little useful information.

Provincial Party Congresses (*tang tai-piao ta-hui*) were first held throughout China in June–July, 1956, in anticipation of the National Party Congress in September of that year.[13] The Party Constitution provides that Provincial Party Congresses, which are elected for three-year terms, meet annually, and this was apparently the case from 1956 through 1959.[14] Although the evidence is fragmentary for the 1960's, it seems that Provincial Party Congresses were not held as regularly in that period. The Party work report, or alternatively the summing-up report (*tsung-chieh pao-kao*), is the main document issued by the congressional sessions. Normally delivered by the provincial first secretary, it takes a comprehensive view of both past achievements and future tasks, and has a broader range of concerns than its government counterpart. In addition to economic affairs, the Party report gives particular attention to such matters as rectification campaigns, erroneous ideas within the Party, and questions of work style. These

[12] It may be that provinces where People's Congresses met more frequently in the 1956–57 period had special political problems at that time. Chekiang, Honan, Hopeh, Kwangtung, Liaoning, and Shantung held the sixth sessions of their First Congresses in the latter part of 1957 and underwent high-level purges in 1957–58. However, two other provinces which experienced purges in that period—Anhwei and Yunnan—held only the fourth sessions of their First Congresses in August and September, 1957, while Heilungkiang, Kiangsi, and Shansi, which held their sixth sessions in mid-1957, were unaffected by the purges. Thus, any link between the frequency of People's Congress sessions and political instability must be suggested with caution.

[13] It is not clear why Party Congresses were held in only a few provinces in earlier years. Prior to 1956, the major provincial Party meetings were Party Conferences (*tang tai-piao hui-i*). According to the 1945 Party Constitution, Party Conferences were to be held in the intervals between Party Congresses. In fact, they apparently replaced the Congresses. In any case, the 1956 Party Constitution eliminated any reference to Party Conferences and they were not held subsequently. See *CB*, No. 417 (October 10, 1956), pp. 60–62.

[14] Article 38, *The Constitution of the Communist Party of China* (1956) (Peking: Foreign Languages Press, 1965), p. 29.

matters are also dealt with in government work reports, however, and the basic similarity of the two documents should not be overlooked. As in the case of Provincial People's Congresses, press dispatches on the work of Provincial Party Congresses are often available in the absence of work reports.

Several gaps in the data for the 1954–60 period should be mentioned. First, no work reports (and extremely little other information) are available for the Ninghsia Hui and Tibetan Autonomous Regions. In both cases this results partially from administrative facts—the Ninghsia Hui Autonomous Region was not set up until the latter part of 1958, and the Tibetan Autonomous Region was not formally established until 1965.[15] More serious is the uneven distribution of available work reports over the 1954–60 period, particularly the small number of such reports from the spring of 1955 to the spring of 1957. Therefore, to supplement the work reports I have drawn on speeches and articles by leading provincial figures, economic development plans, budget reports, communiqués of provincial Party conferences and Party Committee plenums, major editorials of provincial papers, and New China News Agency dispatches on Provincial People's and Provincial Party Congresses. In this manner, I have compiled a data base broad enough for a meaningful examination of provincial politics.

## AN OVERVIEW OF PROVINCIAL POLITICS

Given the size and diversity of China's provinces, significant political and administrative problems are inevitable. Here I shall examine briefly some of the key sources of tension between the provinces and central authority, the various roles of provincial leaders, and the major provincial purges in the decade preceding the Cultural Revolution.

### CENTRAL-PROVINCIAL TENSIONS

One of the oldest Chinese Communist Party (CCP) principles is that of flexibly applying policy to suit local conditions (*yin-ti chih-i ling-huo yün-yung*). Although this principle legitimizes the idea that policies must be adjusted to local needs, it does not, however, clearly indicate the adjustments that are permissible and those that are not. On the one hand, it is clear that rigid implementation of central policies results in losses and setbacks to the state. Production losses resulting from the

---

[15] Ninghsia, which existed as a separate province in the early 1950's, was carved out of Kansu in 1958. Tibet, although it has been an administrative entity since 1951, had only preparatory status prior to 1965.

mechanical implementation of specific farming measures, regardless of regional differences, and popular resistance resulting from the enforcement of social measures that were particularly offensive to local customs, are common examples. Thus, it is not surprising that the failure of higher-level authorities to heed the advice of basic-level cadres who are most sensitive to local conditions has been severely criticized:

> When we meet resistance in carrying out directives from above, we do not seek the reason in the directives themselves, but criticize cadres at the basic levels. We are proud of our "resoluteness" in implementing tasks assigned from above. We listen to opinions only when they conform to our "framework," and we express indignation when they do not. . . . We were greatly shocked when we read Chairman Mao's teaching that "to carry out directives from upper levels blindly and without reservation is the most subtle way of opposing or sabotaging such directives." [16]

Conversely, it is equally clear that policies can be and are "adjusted" to local conditions in a manner which subverts their intent. Local officials have been repeatedly denounced for failing to carry out Party directives under the pretext that concrete conditions required alterations in those directives. This has been the case particularly where local leaders have argued that "conditions are not ripe" in their areas for the rapid realization of national policy. Thus, provincial leaders have been caught between conflicting pressures. On the one hand they are expected to implement central measures strictly, without distorting the intent of those measures; on the other hand they are urged to administer policies flexibly, taking due account of local conditions. The principle of *yin-ti chih-i ling-huo yün-yung* only delineates the problem without solving it.

Another source of tension in central-provincial relations is the allocation of resources. This multifaceted problem, which also places the provinces in the position of competing among themselves, comprises such diverse elements as the location of centrally controlled investments, the assignment of economic tasks to provincial authorities, revenue transfers to and from the center, interprovincial grain flows, and the setting of regional price differentials. Accusations made during the Cultural Revolution are particularly revealing in this regard. Concerning the allocation of funds for modern industry, T'ao Chu, the long-

[16] *JMJP,* October 18, 1965. This statement, which was a self-criticism by a county (*hsien*) Party secretary from Fukien, could apply equally well to provincial level officials.

time leader of Kwangtung Province, was charged with being over-zealous in promoting the development of his area:

> The foundation of industry in Kwangtung, especially light industry, is com-paratively good. If we resolutely implement Chairman Mao's instructions to make use of the original industry, then we can do a better job in supporting industry in the interior of China. However, the counter-revolutionary T'ao Chu stubbornly resisted and opposed Chairman Mao's instructions . . . . T'ao said: "We should build a complete industrial system in Canton." . . . [T'ao] blindly chased after the "big," "foreign," and "new," trying his best to demand capital and equipment from the center.[17]

Another Cultural Revolution accusation sheds light on the tensions involved in determining a province's economic activities. Liu Chien-hsun, the first secretary of Honan since 1961 who weathered Red Guard attacks to become head of the Honan Revolutionary Committee, was denounced for encouraging the planting of peanuts, an economic crop. This peanut production increased provincial revenues at the expense of grain output and led to demands on the center for grain shipments to offset the deficits reportedly resulting from Liu's policies.[18] Different tensions exist for grain surplus provinces, as demonstrated by Cultural Revolution attacks on Li Ching-ch'üan, the former leader of Szechwan Province. Li was accused of taking a niggardly attitude toward sending Szechwan's large grain surplus to grain deficit provinces, and of in-stituting measures to restrict the amount actually exported. Li's atti-tude was illustrated by the following accusation:

> In the autumn of 1962, Li Ching-ch'üan, at a Szechwan Provincial conference of secretaries of special district CCP committees, said, on behalf of the Food Bureau: "Some people eat Szechwan grain and insult us too." At that time, some said to him: "The center has directed that some grain be shipped out of Szechwan to support disaster areas elsewhere." Li Ching-ch'üan replied angrily: "Am I to be regarded as a little State Council?" This black talk completely exposed the counter-revolutionary features of this local emperor.[19]

Thus the cases of T'ao, Liu, and Li clearly indicate that the allocation of scarce resources can be a major cause of conflict in provincial politics.

[17] Radio Canton (Kwangtung), December 1, 1967 (cited in Michel C. Oksenberg et al., *The Cultural Revolution: 1967 in Review* [Ann Arbor: Center for Chinese Studies, University of Michigan, 1968], p. 28).

[18] *JPRS*, No. 43,357 (November 16, 1967), pp. 29–30 (cited in Oksenberg, *The Cultural Revolution*, p. 28).

[19] Radio Kweiyang (Kweichow), June 4, 1967.

Another source of tension is the deviation of "localism" (*ti-fang chu-i*). Leading Party officials are not immune to traditional provincial loyalties and to the distrust which natives of one province have for those of another. For example, former governor Chao Chien-min of Shantung allegedly proclaimed, "I am a native of Shantung, I am for the people of Shantung and the cadres of Shantung." [20] One consequence of localist sentiment is organizational disunity as native cadres form cliques to pursue particularist goals. Chiang Hua, the former first secretary of Chekiang, addressed himself to this problem in a December, 1957, Party work report:

Persons imbued with serious bourgeois individualism are often characterized by serious sectarianism and localism. This is because they need such tendencies to fulfill their personal ambitions and carry on their anti-Party activities. . . . In order to build their personal prestige, they manipulate old comrades and subordinates and make use of contacts with local cadres to draw them together. When they attack the Party, they carry on small clique activities, find their support inside and outside the Party, and make trouble for the Party. Localism, one of the expressions of sectarianism, is just as dangerous to the Party. . . . In the past, the Party raised the "localization [of cadres]" slogan, the main spirit of which is aimed at building close ties between cadres and the local people. . . . The "localization" slogan must not be used as an excuse for developing localism. *On no account are those with ulterior motives allowed to exploit this slogan to sow dissention between outside cadres and local cadres or carry on sectarian activities.* Some people err in acting as "representatives of local cadres" or in stressing the employment of local people as secretaries of the Party committees. As pointed out by Comrade Teng Hsiao-p'ing, "the 'localization' of cadres is not the highest principle of the Party's policy relating to cadres. The highest principle of the Party's cadres policy is 'communization,' and provincialism is incompatible with Communism." [21]

Localist deviations also cause severe problems of policy implementation. Because of their ties to the local population, including the "exploiting classes," native leaders have frequently been lukewarm to basic social reforms.[22] Moreover, native cadres are especially prone to argue that local conditions are unsuited to rapid economic development. A case in point occurred in Kansu where a localist clique allegedly ad-

[20] *Ch'ing-tao Jih-pao*, November 4, 1958, in *SCMP*, No. 1924 (December 31, 1958).
[21] *JMJP*, December 28, 1957, in *CB*, No. 487 (January 10, 1958); also cited in Franz Schurmann, *Ideology and Organization in Communist China* (Berkeley and Los Angeles: University of California Press, 1966), pp. 214–15 (emphasis added). It should be noted, however, that outside cadres also formed cliques and frequently were guilty of ignoring local conditions.
[22] See Vogel, "Land Reform in Kwangtung."

vanced the "theory of Kansu's backwardness" in order to justify a slower pace of development. These localists reportedly emphasized the complex social problems and diverse nationalities of the province, as well as poor natural conditions, and deplored central policies as being too "left" and "impetuous." They feared to change the *status quo* and argued that violent deviations had occurred during land reform because none of the leading regional officials were natives of Kansu. They also objected to large-scale construction on the grounds that it entailed the immigration of workers from other provinces, with the result that "Lanchow is no longer the Lanchow of the natives of Kansu." [23]

To prevent localist deviations while guaranteeing sufficient familiarity with local conditions, the CCP assigns a mixture of natives and outsiders to key provincial posts, with outside cadres generally predominating.[24] This measure has, on the whole, kept localism in check, but significant tensions still exist between natives and outsiders.

THE ROLE OF PROVINCIAL LEADERS

The role of a provincial leader in the above conflicts and in the general affairs of government is ambiguous. He is the spokesman and the representative of provincial interests before the central authorities, and at the same time he is the arm of those authorities in dealing with the people and the functionaries of his province. The careers of the men who led China's provinces before the Cultural Revolution provide graphic illustrations. Not only were most provincial first secretaries also Central Committee members,[25] but three of the most powerful regional figures—Li Ching-ch'üan, Ulanfu, and T'ao Chu—held key national positions as Politburo members (Li, Ulanfu) and Vice-Premiers (T'ao, Ulanfu).[26] While their day-to-day responsibilities identified them with provincial interests, the national positions of provincial leaders provided additional perspectives to influence their actions. Moreover, to the degree that provincial leaders represent provincial interests, it is by no means clear what those "interests" are. Thus, while T'ao Chu pushed Kwangtung's local interests by building up modern industry, localist leaders in Kansu resisted large-scale industrial development. Indeed, provincial officials are frequently under con-

---

[23] *Kan-su Jih-pao*, August 16, 1958, in *CB*, No. 528 (October 28, 1958).
[24] See Teiwes, *Provincial Party Personnel*, chap. ii.
[25] See *ibid.*, p. 67.
[26] Another figure who fits this category is K'o Ch'ing-shih, the former mayor of Shanghai who was a Vice-Premier and Politburo member at the time of his death in 1965.

flicting pressures from both conservative and radical forces within their own bailiwicks.[27]

The role of provincial leaders in major national decisions deserves mention. Such a role is suggested both by their Central Committee membership and by the substantial provincial interests affected by national policies. It is conceivable that one side or another in Peking has enlisted provincial leaders to tip the balance in a policy debate. Thus, Parris H. Chang argues that when Mao, in July, 1955, called for an upsurge in agricultural cooperativization by convening a special meeting of provincial secretaries rather than summoning a more formal body, he mobilized the support of the provincial officials to overcome resistance to the new policy at the center.[28] (This case is examined in greater detail in the third section of this study.) Moreover, provincial authorities may have been an important force behind Mao at the September, 1957, Central Committee Plenum which adopted some of the main features of the Great Leap Forward. The decentralization measures decided at that meeting considerably increased provincial control over industry, finances, and planning. While such measures were logical in terms of the Great Leap strategy, they no doubt had a political appeal to some provincial leaders as well.[29]

Finally, the implications for provincial officials of the CCP's emphasis on experimentation and investigation should be noted. For example, in the spring and summer of 1958 several provinces, most notably Honan, set up experimental communes, to the accompaniment of widespread publicity in the national press. Although the precise effect of these experiments on the policy process cannot be determined, they apparently were influential in the August, 1958, decision to proceed with the universal establishment of communes.[30] In general, both by ostensibly demonstrating the feasibility of new policies and by identifying problems requiring adjustments, provincial leaders have considerable potential for affecting the ultimate shape of policy.

[27] For example, in Chekiang the leadership of the Provincial Party Committee reportedly was attacked for both rightist and leftist errors by cadres within the province. See *JMJP*, December 28, 1957, in *CB*, No. 487 (January 10, 1958).

[28] See Parris H. Chang, "Patterns and Processes of Policy Making in Communist China, 1955–1962: Three Case Studies" (Ph.D. dissertation, Columbia University, 1969), chap. ii.

[29] See *ibid.*, chap. iii; and Schurmann, *Ideology and Organization*, pp. 195–210.

[30] See Chang, "Patterns and Processes" chap. iv.

PROVINCIAL PURGES [31]

Although provincial leadership was generally stable in the decade before the Cultural Revolution, a number of purges did take place. The most significant provincial purges occurred in late 1957 and 1958, and affected leading personnel in twelve provinces: Anhwei, Chekiang, Honan, Hopeh, Kansu, Kwangsi, Kwangtung, Liaoning, Shantung, Sinkiang, Tsinghai, and Yunnan.[32] Among those purged were: P'an Fu-sheng, first secretary of Honan; Chao Chien-min, governor of Shantung; Sha Wen-han, governor of Chekiang; Sun Tso-pin, governor of Tsinghai; and Tu Che-heng, governor of Liaoning. In two-thirds of these cases, charges of localism (or local nationalism) were raised against provincial leaders.[33] In addition, accusations of rightist policy deviations were leveled in most cases. Most significant were allegations that leading officials had advocated conservative economic policies in 1956, arguing against "reckless advance," large APCs, and so forth. These purges, most of which took place in the months following the September, 1957, Central Committee Plenum, were apparently designed to ensure a provincial leadership that would be fully responsive to central control and to the new Great Leap policies by dismissing those who had previously been most skeptical of radical policies.

At least two leading provincial figures were purged as a result of the August, 1959, Lushan Central Committee Plenum and the anti-right opportunist campaign which followed. Chou Hsiao-chou, the first secretary of Hunan, was one of the leading voices joining P'eng Teh-huai at Lushan to criticize the communes and Great Leap Forward and to argue the case for more moderate economic policies.[34] Cultural Revolution sources indicate that Chang K'ai-fan, a secretary in Anhwei, held similar views, and he apparently was removed from office as a consequence.[35] Thus, the policy orientations of the provincial leaders

[31] In addition to the purges discussed below, two cases involving provincial first secretaries are worthy of note. In 1957, Kwangsi's Ch'en Man-yuan was dismissed for mishandling a famine situation. See *JMJP*, June 18, 1957, in *SCMP*, No. 1562 (July 3, 1957). In 1965, Chou Lin of Kweichow was removed for errors in implementing the socialist education movement. See Radio Kweiyang (Kweichow), June 3, 1967.

[32] These purges are discussed in detail in Teiwes, "The Purge of Provincial Leaders."

[33] The provinces in question were Chekiang, Kansu, Kwangsi, Kwangtung, Liaoning, Shantung, Sinkiang, and Yunnan.

[34] See "Resolution of the CCP Central Committee Concerning the Anti-Party Clique Headed by P'eng Te-huai," NCNA, Peking, August 15, 1967, in *SCMP*, No. 4004 (August 18, 1967).

[35] See *The Case of Peng Teh-huai 1959–1968* (Hong Kong: Union Research Institute, 1968), pp. 321–22; and Chang's file in the biographical files of the American Consulate General, Hong Kong.

purged in 1959 and of those ousted in 1957–58 were similar; both advocated a slower pace of economic development and modification of rural social organization.

A number of key provincial leaders were quietly removed from their posts as national policy retreated from the radicalism of the Great Leap in the 1960–61 period. First secretaries Chang Chung-liang of Kansu, Kao Feng of Tsinghai, Shu T'ung of Shantung, and Tseng Hsi-sheng of Anhwei, and Governor Liu Ko-p'ing of Ninghsia were dismissed from office while Wu Chih-p'u, the first secretary of Honan, was demoted to second secretary.[36] While no public charges were made against these men, it seems likely that they were prominent examples of the "good hearted and well intentioned" cadres without "adequate ideological consciousness" who were criticized at the January, 1961, Central Committee Plenum.[37] The implication of excesses in implementing the commune and the Great Leap policies seems particularly pertinent in the case of Wu Chih-p'u, who had been in the forefront of commune experimentation in Honan.[38]

Thus, provincial leaders fell for both rightist and leftist deviations. The men in charge of China's provinces had to cope with shifting national policies, and some were unable to navigate successfully in the rapidly changing situation. The uncertainties resulting from reversals in central policy, together with recurrent tensions caused by the need for flexibility in policy implementation, competition for scarce resources, and localist tendencies, shaped the context of provincial politics in the pre–Cultural Revolution period.

### PROVINCIAL POLITICS IN ACTION: AN ANALYSIS OF WORK REPORTS

How have leading officials responded to the variegated pressures of provincial politics? How has provincial government performed in the context described above? An analysis of Party and government work reports, together with related material, is one approach to these questions.

---

[36] See Teiwes, *Provincial Party Personnel,* pp. 29–30, 42, 86.

[37] See "Communique of the Ninth Plenum of the Eighth Central Committee," NCNA, Peking, January 20, 1961, in *CB,* No. 644 (January 27, 1961).

[38] *JMJP,* September 2, 1961, and July 3, 1962, carried articles critical of commandism in Honan at about the time of Wu's demotion.

PICK UP STO

LIBRARY (R)KTSA
L.R. CLAIM

SERIES S202 21105

VOLUME/ED.
AUTHOR/TITLE

1971/ 0012 50
01/20/72

DATE 06/26/72

Conference on Government in
China; 1969.
China; management of a
revolutionary society, ed. by
J.M.H.Lindbeck. (Studies in
Chinese Government & politics,
2)

A1784525

PUBLISHER
31105

U of Washington Pr

COPIES

PRICE 1

PRE-BILLED

RICHARD ABEL & CO., INC.

PRE-BUFFED

A METHODOLOGICAL NOTE

A number of comments on the analysis of work reports and supplementary material which follows are in order. First, the availability of material limits the conclusions to the 1954–60 period; they are not necessarily valid for the 1960's. Nevertheless, the fact that the 1954–60 period spans a variety of political circumstances—including both phases of cautious consolidation and mass mobilization drives—enhances the salience of the analysis. Similarly, although cross-provincial comparisons are limited by the incompleteness of data, significant comparative statements are possible because of the availability of material on a variety of provinces in any given period.

The nature of work reports, development plans, key speeches, and the like also causes problems. Focusing on singular documents that appear at substantial intervals of time does not provide a detailed analysis of the way that a province treats a particular issue. Only a careful examination of the provincial press would reveal the full, day-by-day response of different provinces to specific central directives. Moreover, with the exception of several attacks on the 1957–58 purge victims, the sources used are marked by the impersonality which afflicts most official statements prior to the Cultural Revolution. Thus, the entire dimension of personal relationships and conflicts, always a crucial aspect of politics in any culture, is missing from my analysis.

Finally, it is necessary to recognize the methodological dilemma posed by the functional bias of work reports. As I noted in the first section, a basic function of the work report is to transmit national directives to provincial and lower level cadres. The resulting expositions of central policy tend both to create a picture of provincial responsiveness and to blur provincial differences. The facts that provincial work reports are highly visible and undoubtedly are monitored by the central authorities reinforce these tendencies. In this regard, it is significant that manipulation of information to deceive the center was a key aspect of the 1957–58 provincial purges.[39] For the purposes of my analysis, these considerations pose the question of whether work reports and related documents reflect actual developments or mere words. Do strong advocacy of a policy and claims of achievements indicate genuine implementation or are they simply an effort to appear loyal to Peking?

The use of public statements to project loyalty and to build political credit with higher officials is undeniable. But the very function of

[39] See Teiwes, "The Purge of Provincial Leaders," pp. 25–26.

transmitting policy to those responsible for its implementation does suggest a link between word and deed, however imperfect that link may be. That is, the subjective impressions of the audience which hears a work report affect subsequent policy implementation. Moreover, the detail and the apparent candor of examinations of work performance demonstrate close attention to real problems. Finally, critical references to earlier periods in all cases indicate a political orientation consistent with that suggested by reports from the periods in question. In sum, although the line between fact and appearance is ambiguous, work reports are at least an approximate measure of actual provincial developments.

THE CHANGING PRIORITIES OF PROVINCIAL GOVERNMENT

The tasks of provincial level administration cover the entire range of governmental activity in China. In the 1954–60 period, however, a basic shift in duties and priorities occurred following the September, 1957, Central Committee Plenum which sanctioned the Great Leap Forward and adopted far-reaching decentralization measures. Prior to the September, 1957, Plenum, provincial authorities repeatedly cited agricultural production and rural organization as their main tasks. This reflects the division of labor of the economic strategies and administrative arrangements then in effect. The key features of the industrialization program—heavy industry and Soviet-aided projects—were placed under the authority of central ministries. Despite the emphasis on heavy industry, it was recognized that industrial growth could not be sustained without accompanying agricultural growth, and the task of agriculture fell largely to the provinces. In addition, the main function of local industry under provincial control was to support agriculture and the rural economy.[40]

The Great Leap Forward created new tasks. The Great Leap policy of simultaneous development of industry and agriculture, with priority to heavy industry, combined with industrial and financial decentralization to create unprecedented provincial concern with industrial development. The new order of priorities was reflected in a September, 1958, work report by Governor Ch'en Yü of Kwangtung:

From now on, our province like other areas of the nation can, according to the directive of the Central Committee and Chairman Mao, shift the center of leader-

---

[40] See, for example, *Yun-nan Jih-pao,* February 11, 1955, in *SCMP,* Supplement 1015 (March 25, 1955).

ship work from agriculture and rural work to industrial construction. Our policy is to grasp industry with one hand and agriculture with the other, with the key point in industry and first of all iron and steel and the machine-building industry.[41]

Thus, provincial responsibilities were no longer restricted to light industries supporting agriculture but focused instead on the sinews of modern industry. Although provincial authorities began to give more attention to agriculture in 1960, this was part of a national reordering of priorities brought about by the dislocations of the Great Leap. At the time work reports ceased to be available, however, it was unclear whether the earlier division of labor was being re-established.[42]

THE ARTICULATION OF PROVINCIAL INTERESTS

On the whole, statements of provincial leaders contained strikingly little overt articulation of provincial interests, and that which did occur was largely veiled and indirect. For example, Szechwan pointed out that it had exported enough grain to feed thirty million people for half a year; while Kiangsu noted that its cotton yarn, silk, oils, and fats were national assets important both for daily necessities throughout the country and for foreign exchange.[43] Such observations may be implicit claims on central resources as rewards for services rendered, but they fall far short of open statements of provincial needs.

There was one major exception in the material examined. This was a remarkable set of speeches delivered by provincial leaders at the Eighth National Party Congress in September, 1956, where provincial interests were expressed with remarkable frankness.[44] One major demand was for more leeway from central authorities in carrying out directives. The leaders of Honan and Shantung appealed directly to the responsible ministries for an end to excessive rigidity in setting sowing plans and in fixing other matters related to agricultural production.[45]

[41] Ch'en Yü, *Kuang-tung sheng jen-min wei-yüan-hui kung-tso pao-kao* (Work Report of the Kwangtung Provincial People's Council), September, 1958, p. 1.

[42] There is evidence that considerable industrial decentralization continued in the 1960's. See Franz Schurmann, "China's 'New Economic Policy'—Transition or Beginning," *CQ*, No. 17 (January–March, 1964), pp. 74–75.

[43] NCNA, Chengtu, December 8, 1955, in *SCMP*, No. 1194 (December 22, 1955); and *Hsin-hua Jih-Pao* (Nanking), September 10, 1955, in *SCMP*, Supplement 1162 (November 2, 1955).

[44] These speeches by leaders of all provinces except Liaoning appeared in *Hsin-hua pan-yüeh-k'an* (New China Fortnightly) (hereafter *HHPYK*), Nos. 20–21, 1956. I am grateful to Roderick MacFarquhar for his notes on many of these speeches. Much of the analysis which follows is similar to MacFarquhar's in an informal paper, "Aspects of the CCP's Eighth Congress," Columbia University Seminar on Modern East Asia: China, February 19, 1969.

[45] *HHPYK*, No. 21, 1956, pp. 183, 218.

On the question of the relation of grain and economic crops, T'ao Chu strongly defended Kwangtung's plans to increase the acreage sown to economic crops by converting land formerly devoted to grain. He argued that economic crops were particularly important for increasing peasant incomes in his overpopulated province. T'ao revealed the extent to which such plans reflected provincial interests by saying that *from the point of view of Kwangtung alone* it would be best to devote every *mou* of land to economic crops and to import grain from other provinces. However, he tacitly recognized national priorities by declaring such a wish to be a fantasy and completely impractical.[46]

Many provincial spokesmen directly requested Central Government support for projects of particular importance to their areas. Lin T'ieh, then first secretary of Hopeh, pointed out that the control of the Hai River was a basic requirement for the development of his province, and expressed the hope that the center would support Hopeh's water control plans. Similarly, T'an Ch'i-lung hoped that the Ministry of Water Conservancy would provide technological and investment support as well as an over-all plan for the regulation of Shantung's chief rivers. Concerning another problem, Li Ching-ch'üan cited the problems caused by poor communications with the remote minority areas of Szechwan and suggested that the state increase its investments to correct this situation.[47]

Yeh Fei of Fukien argued his province's case on the basis of backwardness. He stated that Fukien's weak industrial base required powerful state support if industrial development were to succeed, and requested that the relevant central ministries select the "method of supporting backward areas" and aid Fukien's plans for building up large-scale light industry.[48]

Perhaps the most interesting speech was by Yang Shang-k'uei, first secretary of Kiangsi. Yang made ample use of Kiangsi's history as an old base area to present his case. Pointing out that Kiangsi's role in the revolution had cost dearly, that its population had been reduced by one-fourth, and that its fields had been laid waste by Chiang Kai-shek, he asked for special attention on these grounds. Yang also cited current

---

[46] *Ibid.*, p. 69. The problem of the proper balance between grain and economic crops was repeatedly raised by provincial leaders at the Congress. The predominant view was that emphasis on grain targets had resulted in neglect of economic crops. Although it was recognized that overemphasis on economic crops adversely affected the food supply, most provincial officials urged greater attention to economic crops to offset the prior stress on grain.

[47] *Ibid.*, pp. 170–71, 183, 198; *HHPYK*, No. 20, 1956, pp. 54, 66.

[48] *HHPYK*, No. 21, 1956, pp. 202–203.

problems—Kiangsi's labor shortage, poor communications, low standard of living, underdeveloped cultural and educational conditions, and backward health facilities—in order to appeal for central support. He further argued that the province had suffered from the regime's price policies and claimed that its tax burden was higher than the national average. Summing up this catalog of difficulties, Yang said that the burdens were a little heavy and caused dissatisfaction among the masses, and that state assistance would be required for a comparatively long period.[49]

Several factors appear to have influenced this spate of special pleading. First, the fact that the speeches were given at a national forum may be significant. In contrast to provincial meetings where local leaders are especially conscious of their roles as arms of the center, Peking seems a logical place to advance claims for central support. Even more important, however, was the over-all context of the Eighth Party Congress. At that time, the CCP leaders believed that the basic victory of the socialist revolution had been attained through the co-operativization of agriculture and the socialization of industry. The Congress was in large measure a celebration of what was termed the unprecedented unity and stability of the regime. It was also an occasion for the frank assessment of problems, and the top national leaders themselves raised such matters as excessive centralization. In sum, the setting was appropriate for pressing claims to share in the fruits of victory.[50]

Apart from the Eighth Party Congress, the general tendency was for provincial leaders to emphasize the need to accept the center's priorities and policies. This frequently required arguing against substantial opinion. Thus, when provincial five-year plans were announced in late 1955, provincial spokesmen appeared to be countering the feeling that local interests were insufficiently protected. For example, the report on Szechwan's plan defended the provincial investment figures that had been stipulated by the center on the grounds that the low utilization rate of industrial equipment meant that the province could use its existing capacity to advance production.[51] Ironically, in view of Cultural Revolution charges (see p. 127), T'ao Chu was one of the most

[49] *Ibid.*, pp. 198–99.

[50] For statements by national leaders setting the tone of the Party Congress, see *Eighth National Congress of the Communist Party of China* (Peking: Foreign Languages Press, 1956), I, especially 7, 66–67, 77–78, 82, 190–92, 310–12. The speeches of provincial leaders were well within the guidelines established by these statements.

[51] *Chung-ch'ing Jih-pao*, December 8, 1955, in *SCMP*, Supplement 1216 (January 26, 1956).

vigorous defenders of central policies. In the course of justifying the policy of agriculture as the key point of provincial development, T'ao discussed why little heavy industry was planned for Kwangtung:

At present, Kwangtung is not yet ready for the construction of heavy industry but has excellent conditions for the development of such light industries as sugar, paper, . . . foodstuffs, etc. But these conditions all rest on the development of agricultural production. . . . The State [central government] could have built larger light industries in Kwangtung but for the impossibility of guaranteeing the supply of raw materials. If we want to develop industry in Kwangtung, therefore, we must first of all make a success of agricultural production.[52]

Later, when discussing revenue sources, he bluntly stated that "As the State is concentrating its efforts on construction of key projects, we should not and cannot ask the State to increase appropriations for our province."

The assertion of the primacy of national interests was particularly forceful in periods of mass mobilization. Thus, a major target of strident attacks on "rightist conservativism" which accompanied the emergence of the Great Leap Forward was the tendency to stress local conditions. People who stressed local conditions argued that factors peculiar to their areas made high targets and rapid development unattainable. T'ao Chu, who was ever the one to emphasize the current line, had a ready answer for such comrades:

In the past year, departmentalism began to germinate in some areas under the "suit the local conditions" slogan. Too much complaint was voiced about difficulties and inadequate attention was paid to subordination to over-all interests. This must also be examined and rectified. . . . Our Communist Party stands for democratic centralism and our partial interests should be subordinate to the over-all interests, otherwise our work cannot be done well. . . .[53]

This theme, as well as the concomitant campaign against localism (see p. 131), was undoubtedly linked to the decentralization measures of the September, 1957, Plenum. With the economy and government administration increasingly under local control, intensified political efforts were required to check the centrifugal pressures inherent in such an arrangement.

In sum, the public posture of provincial leaders placed more em-

[52] *NFJP*, September 24, 1955, in *SCMP*, Supplement 1237 (February 29, 1956).
[53] *Wen-hui Pao* (Hong Kong), December 18, 1957, in *SCMP*, No. 1682 (January 2, 1958).

phasis on their role as an arm of the central authorities than on their
position as the representative of provincial interests. There apparently
was a shift in emphasis according to political phases, however. The
only overt articulation of provincial interests in the material analyzed
came at a time of consolidating past gains. In contrast, provincial
leaders especially emphasized the primacy of central interests during
periods of rapid advance. Thus, provincial leaders balanced their conflicting roles according to the dictates of the changing political situation.

COOPERATION AND COMPETITIVENESS

A corollary of the primacy of national interests and a frequent theme
of provincial pronouncements was the need for cooperation between
provinces. Work reports cited the support of "brethren provinces and
municipalities" as important to provincial achievements. For example,
Tsinghai authorities reported how manpower and material resources
from the northeastern provinces and Inner Mongolia had helped in the
fight against livestock disease.[54] The emphasis on interprovincial cooperation was strongest during the Great Leap Forward when the
threat of autarchy was most severe. Under the slogans of "Communist
cooperation" and "the entire nation as a chessboard," provincial reports proclaimed the need for planned coordination not only among
counties and communes but among provinces and regions as well. The
implications of "Communist cooperation" for the allocation of resources during the Great Leap were clear—wealth would be redistributed and equalized. Thus, a Heilungkiang work report, after at-
tributing unbalanced economic development to the lack of essential
industrial bases in some regions, pointed out that Heilungkiang and the
other northeastern provinces had received large amounts of state aid
for industrial construction during the first five-year plan, and declared
the time had come to render strong support to the rest of the nation.[55]

Interprovincial competitiveness also marked the Great Leap period.
For example, Hopeh exhorted its cadres to "Follow Honan, overtake
Honan"; Party members in Honan were urged to emulate the drought
fighting activities of cadres in Kansu; Lunghsi special district, Fukien,
advanced the slogan, "Catch up with Swatow [Kwangtung] special
district" in grain output; and leading personnel in Kansu were told to

[54] *Ch'ing-hai Jih-pao*, January 6, 1955, in *SCMP*, Supplement 1011 (March 19–21,
1955).
[55] *Hei-lung-chiang Jih-pao*, September 17, 1958, in *JPRS*, No. 1518-N (April 28,
1959); see also *ibid.*, January 25, 1959, in *JPRS*, No. 1878-N (September 4, 1959).

learn from the working methods of the Hupeh Provincial Committee.[56] Moreover, Kiangsu organized visits of cadres to Shanghai, Shantung, Anhwei, Chekiang, Fukien, Kansu, Honan, Shansi, Hunan, Hupeh, and Liaoning to learn from advanced experiences in those areas.[57] It is impossible to judge how successful these methods were in stimulating a "leap forward" in production, but there is evidence that the comparative performance of provinces was taken seriously. Thus, Liaoning vice-governor Ch'iu Yu-wen was forced to admit that "compared with the fraternal provinces, the work . . . was not outstanding in industry [despite a 50 per cent increase in industrial output value] and even less outstanding in agriculture." [58] While work reports contained no detailed descriptions of the tensions caused by interprovincial competition, the Cultural Revolution report that Honan's energetic Wu Chih-p'u (see p. 132) made other leaders nervous, suggests that the strain was considerable.[59]

THE PROVINCIAL ROLE IN POLICY MAKING: THE CASE OF
AGRICULTURAL COOPERATIVIZATION

The question raised earlier (p. 130) regarding the role played by provincial leaders in key national decisions can now be examined on the basis of provincial documents. The most complete data concern the decision to speed up agricultural cooperativization in July, 1955. As previously noted, the use of a forum of provincial leaders to announce the decision might indicate provincial support for the move. Yet Mao also used the occasion to criticize Chekiang Province for a policy of "drastic compression" and for disbanding fifteen thousand APCs in the spring of 1955.[60] This suggests alternative possibilities. Were some provinces striving for more rapid cooperativization in the first half of 1955, and thus making themselves natural allies for Mao? Or was Chekiang, although perhaps an extreme case, representative of a "go-slow" attitude in the provinces? Were provincial leaders an active force for a basic policy change, or did they simply ratify decisions made by Mao? The view of the provinces as adopting a "go-slow" posture in

56 Ho-pei Jih-pao, October 29, 1958, in JPRS, No. 1877-N (September 9, 1959); NCNA, Chengchow, December 4, 1957, in SCMP, No. 1671 (December 13, 1957); NCNA, Fukien, February 3, 1958, in SCMP, No. 1712 (February 13, 1958); and Kan-su Jih-pao, August 16, 1958, in CB, No. 528 (October 28, 1958).

57 HHPYK, No. 7, 1959, in ECMM, No. 170 (June 1, 1959).

58 NCNA, Shenyang, December 19, 1958, in SCMP, No. 1925 (January 2, 1959).

59 See The Case of Peng Teh-huai, p. 23.

60 Mao Tse-tung, "On the Cooperativization of Agriculture," JMJP, October 17, 1955, in CB, No. 364 (October 19, 1955).

1955 and only ratifying Mao's call for faster cooperativization appears closest to the truth.

The policy of "active leadership and steady progress" adequately reflected the moderate provincial posture toward the cooperativization movement in early 1955. The provincial attitude was indicated by frequent criticisms voiced at Provincial People's Congress sessions. While some criticism was directed at conservative and "laissez-faire" attitudes toward APC work, the thrust of the attacks was directed against haste and rough practices. According to a work report by Lin T'ieh of Hopeh:

> The main problem in the development of the mutual aid and cooperative movement was that in the course of establishing APCs some cadres had been too impatient, having a desire for quantity, size and higher forms of APCs. They overlooked the actual degree of the masses' consciousness and their own capabilities and violated the voluntary principle. In some places, commandism was practiced. Although local authorities paid attention to correcting this practice, it is still a problem which should be attended to hereafter.[61]

In view of such shortcomings, careful, systematic development was called for. According to the communiqué of the February, 1955, Sinkiang Party Conference: "There must be adopted the method of making plans for the whole year, seeking development in stages, building up one batch of APCs, consolidating the batch, and proceeding to build up a second batch, so as to fulfill the year's plans. . . ."[62]

Reports on provincial developments demonstrate that Chekiang was not alone in curbing the development of APCs in the spring of 1955. Hopeh officials called a halt to development of new APCs in April, 1955, and directed all efforts to the task of readjusting existing APCs. Hopeh further stipulated that APCs without a solid organizational base should be either reduced or suspended, and that cooperative members who retained misgivings despite education should be allowed to withdraw.[63] In another case, the February Provincial People's Congress in Shansi called for a substantial increase from 42 per cent to 60–65 per cent of peasant households in APCs. At a Party conference in May and June, however, this goal was not mentioned, whereas blind progress was criticized, and the need to focus on consolidating existing APCs was stressed.[64] These were not backward provinces; both Hopeh and

[61] *Ho-pei Jih-pao*, February 2, 1955, in *SCMP*, Supplement 1056 (May 26, 1955).
[62] *Hsin-chiang Jih-pao*, March 2, 1955, in *SCMP*, Supplement 1028 (April 15, 1955).
[63] NCNA, Paoting, May 14, 1955, in *SCMP*, No. 1051 (May 19, 1955).
[64] NCNA, Taiyuan, February 10 and June 11, 1955, in *SCMP*, No. 988 (February 15, 1955) and in *SCMP*, No. 1069 (June 15, 1955).

Shansi were leaders in the cooperativization of agriculture (see p. 168). Moreover, the slowdown in APC development apparently was in response to central directives. Specifically, the State Council's "Decision on Spring Farming and Production" of March 3, 1955, stipulated that "in order to insure the healthy and normal development of the cooperativization movement, the pace . . . should be slowed down a bit. Before spring farming, development of new APCs should be stopped and efforts concentrated on reorganizing existing APCs. . . ." [65] Thus, while Chekiang may have gone too far,[66] its direction seems "correct" in terms of the policies then in force.

Provincial documents issued during the high tide of cooperativization provided another kind of evidence on provincial attitudes prior to the July decision. Criticisms of spring work performance echoed Mao's July 31 speech by focusing on rightist conservatism as the main deviation of the earlier period. In addition to fairly standard criticisms of cadres for failing to perceive rural class struggle or to understand the "active demands" of the peasant masses for more rapid development of APCs, self-criticisms by several provincial Party committees were particularly revealing. Most striking were the self-criticisms of the Kwangtung Provincial Committee contained in a report by T'ao Chu. T'ao admitted that when the upsurge of the rural socialist revolution was imminent, the provincial leadership "had not the slightest idea of it." His account indicated that Mao's initiative was the key to the committee's enlightenment:

We have been guilty of oscillation in leading the agricultural cooperativization movement. Only after receiving a directive and assistance from the Party Central Committee and Chairman Mao did we decide to set up 70,000 APCs in 1955. Before May 1955, the Provincial Party Committee planned to develop only a small number of new APCs and to devote its major efforts to consolidating a not very large number of old APCs for 1955, a year of such decisive significance to the accomplishment of the Five-Year Plan. This was evidently wrong. . . .[67]

While the above analysis suggests that provincial leaders did not play a major role in the decision to speed up agricultural cooperativization, subsequent developments indicate that the provinces played a substantial role in the ultimate pace of the movement. From the time

65 *CB*, No. 373 (January 20, 1956), p. 9.

66 Mao claimed that the Central Committee issued an April, 1955, warning against mass dissolutions of APCs, but Chekiang authorities preferred not to listen. See *JMJP*, October 17, 1955, in *CB*, No. 364 (October 19, 1955).

67 *NFJP*, September 24, 1955, in *SCMP*, Supplement 1237 (February 29, 1956).

of Mao's speech until the end of the year, China went through a cycle of the center establishing goals, the provinces outstripping those goals, the center revising its targets upward, and the provinces once again overfulfilling central targets.[68]

On July 31, Mao called for the establishment of 1.3 million APCs by the fall of 1956, and set a target of 50 per cent of agricultural households in APCs by the spring of 1958. In August and September, after a period of study of the July speech and of organizational activity, the provinces issued new targets which surpassed Mao's guidelines. The combined total of APCs that the provinces planned for the spring of 1956 exceeded Mao's fall, 1956, target. Moreover, the proportion of agricultural households scheduled for inclusion in APCs in 1957 was substantially above Mao's goal for the spring of 1958. More than half of the sixteen provinces that publicized 1957 targets had set targets of 60 per cent or greater, and only in Hupeh, which had been hard hit by floods in 1954, was the target under 50 per cent.[69]

In this context, a Central Committee Plenum met in October and set new, more ambitious targets. The Plenum stipulated that "relatively well advanced" areas, where 30 to 40 per cent of peasant households were in APCs by the summer of 1955, should achieve "basic completion" of cooperativization, that is, of 70 to 80 per cent of peasant households, by the spring of 1957. Moreover, the majority of the country, where 10 to 20 per cent of peasant households were cooperativized by the summer of 1955, was to attain "basic completion" by the spring of 1958.[70] Following the Plenum, the provinces issued new targets consistent with its policy.[71] In late November, however, most of the provinces began to issue new plans that would make the end of 1955 the target date for "basic completion" by relatively advanced provinces and the end of 1956 the goal for other provinces, thereby advancing the Central Committee's October targets by one year.[72] This completed the cycle of central initiative and provincial response.

[68] The following analysis basically follows *CB,* No. 373 (January 20, 1956), with some exceptions. I have also found useful an informal memorandum prepared by Roderick MacFarquhar.

[69] For the targets province by province, see *CB,* No. 373 (January 20, 1956), pp. 14–15.

[70] *Decisions on Agricultural Cooperation* (Peking: Foreign Languages Press, 1956), pp. 29–30.

[71] For provincial targets publicized in October and early November, see *CB,* No. 373 (January 20, 1956), pp. 19–20.

[72] See *ibid.,* pp. 21–24; also NCNA, Tsinan, January 11, 1956, in *SCMP,* No. 1214 (January 24, 1956).

To summarize, the case of the agricultural cooperativization movement in 1955 suggests that the role of provincial leaders in major national decisions is peripheral. The initiatives to halt development in March and to launch a high tide in July both came from the center. Once the direction is set, however, the provinces can significantly alter policies in the course of implementing them. In the spring, at least in some areas, dissolutions of APCs apparently exceeded expectations, which resulted in what was later termed a "rightist conservative" deviation. When the radical phase began in the summer, the provinces raised targets to display the zeal that was considered to be the mark of political loyalty. While the spring deviation had no lasting impact, provincial overperformance in the second half of 1955 caused a major acceleration of national policy.

PROVINCIAL RESPONSIVENESS TO PEKING

The preceding analysis suggests a high degree of provincial responsiveness to the center. This impression is strengthened by the almost total accord of provincial statements with prevailing national policy. Although methodological problems exist (see p. 133), this matter is worth pursuing.

The pattern of central initiative and provincial response illustrated by the cooperativization movement appears generally valid. This is the case even where the first manifestations of a new policy appear at the provincial level. Thus, although output targets were revised downward in a number of provinces in the summer of 1959 before national targets were lowered, the provincial revisions were explicitly in response to a central directive.[73]

As demonstrated earlier, self-criticisms by provincial leaders provide particularly revealing insights into provincial politics. These self-criticisms, when given after a shift in policy, deal with shortcomings and deviations prior to the change in line. In all cases, provincial officials criticized themselves for going too far in the direction set by the former policy, never for having opposed it. The late 1955 admissions of "rightist conservatism" during the previous spring were followed a year later by self-criticisms of performance during the high tide of cooperativization. Reflecting the moderate perspective of the Eighth Party Congress, Lin T'ieh acknowledged the error of the Hopeh Provincial Committee in setting up overly large

[73] See *Hsin-hua Jih-pao* (Nanking), December 30, 1959, in *SCMP*, No. 2190 (February 5, 1960).

APCs, while T'ao Chu and other provincial leaders accepted responsibility for setting excessively high production targets.[74] By the winter of 1957–58, however, self-criticisms of a different color referred to events from mid-1956 to mid-1957. The Kansu Provincial Committee admitted lowering irrigation targets four times; the Honan Committee apologized for denying rural class struggle and for stimulating spontaneous capitalism; and Hunan authorities criticized themselves for going too far in adjusting oversized APCs.[75] In this regard, it is important to recall that the 1957–58 purge victims were accused of pushing conservative views *in 1956,* a period when national policies were moderate and cautious. Finally, in early 1959 as the regime began to moderate some aspects of the Great Leap, the Kiangsu Provincial Committee acknowledged "some extent" of bureaucratism and subjectivism, which was a tacit admission of excessive enthusiasm during the earlier stages of the "leap forward." [76]

A corollary to the high level of responsiveness to the center is the low level of divergence among the provinces. Provincial work reports indicate differing provincial tasks according to local conditions (for example, handling minority problems in Szechwan and livestock production in Tsinghai), but not conflicting political orientations. In only one case—educational policy following the August, 1959, Lushan Plenum—did clear differences appear. One tendency was to consolidate past gains and to overhaul existing institutions. Excessively fast educational development, which used resources and manpower needed for agriculture, was criticized. Moreover, the educational policies of the Great Leap reportedly resulted in lowering the quality of education. Thus, Shansi undertook a number of measures to improve teaching and learning. New arrangements increased time for teaching as opposed to time for labor; the "forceful combination" of politics and education was prohibited; classroom teaching was made primary and field teaching secondary; and emphasis was placed on establishing "normal order" in schools, laying down a code of academic principles, and developing the habit of hard study and discipline among students.[77]

[74] *HHPYK,* No. 20, 1956, pp. 65–66; and *ibid,* No. 21, 1956, pp. 69, 175, 183.

[75] *Kan-su Jih-pao,* August 16, 1958, in *CB,* No. 528 (October 28, 1958); NCNA, Chengchow, December 4, 1957, in *SCMP,* No. 1671 (December 13, 1957); and *Hsin Hu-nan Pao,* December 15, 1957, in *SCMP,* No. 1712 (February 13, 1958).

[76] *HHPYK,* No. 7, 1959, in *ECMM,* No. 170 (June 1, 1959).

[77] *Shan-hsi Jih-pao,* August 30, 1959, in *SCMP,* No. 2141 (November 23, 1959); see also *Hsin-hua Jih-pao* (Nanking), December 30, 1959, in *SCMP,* No. 2190 (February 5, 1960); and *NFJP,* December 4, 1960, in *SCMP,* No. 2419 (January 18, 1961).

A contrary tendency emphasized bringing productive labor into teaching plans, the massive expansion of spare-time education, and strengthening Party leadership over education. According to a Liaoning work report:

> Our main defect in the Great Leap in cultural and educational work was that politics did not assume adequate command and some cadres did not carry out firmly the Party's policies concerning cultural and educational work. . . . In carrying out the policy of walking on two legs in cultural, educational and health work, fear of difficulties was shown and efforts were slackened. These rightist ideas must be overcome.[78]

This divergence, however, may have reflected ambiguities in national policy. The period following the Lushan Plenum was marked by a growing contradiction between continued fidelity to the aims and slogans of the Great Leap Forward and cautious measures to modify Great Leap policies. In general, provinces could not be classified according to contrasting conservative and radical tendencies on the basis of public statements.

In sum, the provincial politician is a man eminently sensitive to shifting winds from Peking. Although jealous of provincial interests, he is careful to tailor his articulation of those interests to the prevailing policy line. He emphasizes the primacy of national interests and shapes provincial policy according to central directives. When the provincial politician errs, it is more likely by going too far in implementing "infallible" central policies than by opposing them.[79] Still, the "correct" policy stance is a reasonable guarantee of survival, and the provincial politician understands this dictum well.

### VARIATIONS AND CORRELATIONS: SOME QUANTIFIABLE INDEXES OF PROVINCIAL POLITICS

Despite the high degree of responsiveness to the center, a number of factors guarantee diversity in provincial politics. The variation in socioeconomic conditions poses different tasks for provincial governments. Whatever the similarities of policy orientation, officials in urban, industrial Liaoning cannot function in the same manner as

---

[78] *Liao-ning Jih-pao,* December 21, 1959, in *SCMP,* No. 2193 (February 10, 1960); see also *Ho-nan Jih-pao,* March 1, 1960, in *JPRS,* No. 3823.

[79] Clearly, there have been problems of securing compliance to particular central directives. At times, this has even gone against the grain of over-all national policy. See Teiwes, "The Purge of Provincial Leaders," pp. 25–30. However, the general pattern is for "rightist conservative" deviations in moderate phases and for "leftist adventurism" during radical periods.

officials in backward, agrarian Kweichow. Nor are the problems that face the leaders of an ethnically homogeneous Han Chinese province comparable to those of an area heavily populated by minorities. Some implications of diverse conditions were indicated in the previous section as different provinces presented their cases in different ways. Thus, Kiangsu pointed to the importance of its wealth in an apparent effort to build political credit with Peking, while the leader of Fukien used backwardness to argue for more central support. Moreover, inevitable differences exist in the politics of rich and poor provinces, and policies such as "Communist cooperation" have markedly different implications for each. Last, the course of the Chinese revolution, the international situation, and the Party's organizational development are but three of the nonsocioeconomic factors that variously affect different areas.

The existence of quantifiable data on a range of variables allows this study to proceed beyond impressionistic statements to more precise measures of provincial differences. Moreover, simple statistical methods can be used to reveal relationships which may help to explain the dynamics of provincial politics. In this section, following a brief methodological note, I will examine a number of political, socioeconomic, and organizational variables, differences in campaign implementation, and the degree of dependence on or independence of the central government, and will attempt to explain correlations among these factors.

A METHODOLOGICAL NOTE

Besides the data extracted from various work reports and the like, I have used several Western compilations of economic statistics that draw on the same or similar sources. These include figures which have been calculated by simple arithmetic on the basis of available data, and I also have made such calculations. In addition, official sources have published extensive province-by-province data on the implementation of several major campaigns. Last, a number of scholars have gathered scattered provincial data on political, organizational, and other variables, and I have also used this material.

A general comment on the reliability of official CPR statistics is in order. Since China's statistical system is still in the early stage of development, any official statistics must be used with great caution. There is considerable variation in quality according to the economic sector, with the Chinese themselves considering the range to be from "fair" in industry, to "worse" in trade, to "worst" in agriculture.[80] Nevertheless, for the first five-year plan period, official statistics can be regarded as dependable in the sense that there is no evidence of systematic politically inspired bias. They are adequate for this study since I am interested in rough orders of magnitude rather than precision. In 1958 and 1959, however, statistics on economic performance were grossly inflated by the enthusiasm of the Great Leap Forward. Although some figures from this period are included in the appendixes for reference purposes, they have not been used for purposes of analysis. Therefore, I am limited to socioeconomic data for the years 1952–57, and even for that period there is considerable variation in the data available for each province. But despite significant gaps, comparable data have been gathered on a majority of provinces for all the socioeconomic indexes analyzed.

The criteria for the selection of data should be made explicit. All data which seemed reasonable in terms of what is known about a province and which seemed consistent with other data were used. Where secondary sources were used and the primary reference was readily available, a check for accuracy was made. In the fair number of cases where conflicting figures exist, I chose on the basis of the following criteria: (1) consistency with other data, (2) primary sources were preferred to unverifiable references in secondary sources, (3) the most recent reference was used, and (4) data from a series in one primary source were favored over scattered figures for individual years. In each case, the data used represent my best estimate after examining all alternatives.

While correlations between all sets of data are examined, the central thrust of the following analysis is to determine relationships between political variables and other factors. This raises a major methodological problem since the political variables analyzed in part or in whole refer to the 1960's. How meaningful is any correlation of socioeconomic data from the 1950's with political data from the 1960's? [81]

---

[80] See Choh-ming Li, *The Statistical System of Communist China* (Berkeley and Los Angeles: University of California Press, 1962), pp. 63–64.

[81] This problem is further complicated by changes in provincial boundaries between 1954 and 1958. In most cases, Chinese sources have adjusted the data to administrative divisions as of the end of 1957, which generally existed unchanged in the 1960's. There are two major exceptions, however. First, Kansu and Ninghsia were amalgamated into the single province of Kansu in 1954, but they again became separate entities with the establishment of the Ninghsia Hui Autonomous Region in October, 1958. With the few exceptions indicated, the Kansu data presented below refer to the combined areas

This question is particularly acute because of the major economic and political changes following the failure of the Great Leap Forward. While this problem makes my conclusions more tentative, the reasons for attempting the analysis are persuasive. First, studies of contemporary China must use the data available and must not be paralyzed by the difficulties involved. Second, the basic socioeconomic variations of the 1950's may be presumed to be generally valid for the 1960's. For example, the most urban and industrial provinces of the 1950's will still rank high in urbanization and industrialization in the next decade. Last, the key political variable of the following analysis—stability of Party personnel—covers the entire period from 1956 to 1966, and thus includes a substantial period for which data on other variables are available. This fact is particularly relevant since the purges of the 1957–61 period are major factors in determining provincial variations in stability.

To measure correlations between different variables, I have adopted the Spearman rank correlation coefficient.[82] This method consists of using a mathematical formula to determine a coefficient of correlation for the rank orders of two variables ranging from $+1.0$, a perfect positive relationship, to zero, no relationship, to $-1.0$, a perfect negative relationship. The significance attached to a correlation coefficient is a matter of personal judgment. In order to adopt a standardized practice, however, I will regard as significant those coefficients which could not have occurred by chance more than five times out of one hundred if China's twenty-six provinces were a sample from an infinite universe of political systems. For all twenty-six provinces ($N=26$), the critical value of significance is .33; for the fewest number of

of Kansu and Ninghsia. Because of Ninghsia's relative backwardness, this results in a slight downward bias in ranking Kansu by various indexes, but the bias is not enough to affect the validity of my findings in most cases. Concerning the relationship of grain output per capita and personnel stability (see p. 164), however, this downward bias may cause the correlation coefficient to exceed the critical value of significance. Second, Tientsin was a centrally administered municipality until February, 1958, when it was placed under the jurisdiction of Hopeh. The city regained its separate status in 1967. The Hopeh data presented below exclude Tientsin through 1957 and include the city for the 1958–66 period. Clearly, the inclusion of Tientsin causes considerable variation in various indexes derived for Hopeh. In the correlations undertaken, however, the ranking of Hopeh is altered only in the case of urbanization, where 1958 data are used. The use of these data provides the most accurate measure for examining the relationship of urbanization and personnel stability in the 1960's. In any case, the use of Hopeh data excluding Tientsin would not affect the validity of the correlation discussed (p. 163).

[82] For a technical discussion of this tool, see Sidney Siegel, *Nonparametric Statistics: For the Behavioral Sciences* (New York: McGraw-Hill, 1956), pp. 202–13.

provinces used in any correlation, eight (N=8), the critical value is .64. Although I apply this guideline flexibly, it is the rule of thumb generally followed in the subsequent analysis.[83]

In sum, despite the vagaries of Chinese statistics, the data are sufficient for rank order analysis. While this form of analysis cannot prove causation, it can support explanations and can demonstrate the lack of a relationship. In addition, the analysis also indicates prominent exceptions to correlations. The fact that a province diverges sharply from a pattern may be as significant as the relationship indicated by the pattern itself.

POLITICAL VARIABLES

Quantifiable "political variables" are not easy to come by in the study of contemporary China. The two analyzed here—the degree of personnel stability of provincial Party secretariats from 1956 to 1966 and the order of establishment of provincial revolutionary committees in 1967–68—refer not only to different periods of time but to radically different political phenomena as well. A third factor, the influence of international tension, is also examined below, although no attempt is made to "quantify" or to assign ranks to provinces according to this variable.

*Stability of Provincial Party Secretariats, 1956–66.* Despite sudden changes in policy, the period from 1956 to the full-scale initiation of the Cultural Revolution was marked by a considerable degree of personnel stability at both the national and the provincial levels. As it was suggested earlier, the rules of the game were more or less clear to the political leaders of China's provinces, and, on the whole, they had a remarkable capacity for survival. There was, however, significant variation in personnel stability among provinces, which ranged from virtually no change in the top provincial leadership over the entire period to a total turnover of that leadership.

In an earlier work, I used an extensive study of the careers of nearly 350 Party secretaries and more than 600 officials serving in departments of provincial Party secretariats to classify and to rank the twenty-six provinces of China in terms of personnel stability. The four categories adopted were: I—highly stable; II—basically stable; III—limited continuity; and IV—unstable. A number of criteria were

[83] This discussion draws heavily on Thomas R. Dye, *Politics, Economics, and the Public: Policy Outcomes in the American States* (Chicago: Rand McNally, 1966), pp. 22–26, 34–38. I also acknowledge the assistance of Steven Hendricks and Richard I. Hofferbert.

used to classify and to rank provinces. First, to measure the continuity of provincial leadership, I determined the size of two different "core groups" of secretaries who worked together for extended periods. One consisted of secretaries who served together during at least the 1958–64 period. The second comprised secretaries active at the start of the Cultural Revolution in late 1965 and early 1966 who had served continuously since 1956–57. The existence of these "core groups" allowed stable political relationships and administrative patterns to develop. An important consideration in ranking was whether the provincial first secretary was included in a "core group." Another criteria was whether a provincial secretariat had been purged and the extent of organizational disruption caused by a purge. Again, an important consideration was whether the first secretary was dismissed. Also bearing on the classification and the rank of a province was the average tenure and turnover of its secretaries, especially the degree to which they were transferred into or out of the province. Table 3 summarizes the results of this examination.[84]

*Provincial Revolutionary Committees.* After a decade of what was on the whole remarkable personnel stability, the provinces were subjected to massive purges during the Cultural Revolution. Every provincial Party and government apparatus was affected. In only Honan and Kwangsi did the pre-Cultural Revolution first secretaries survive and take over as chairmen of provincial revolutionary committees, and even in those two provinces there was extensive purging of other Party secretaries.[85] There were considerable provincial differences in the replacement of the shattered Party and government apparatuses by revolutionary committees, however. More than nineteen months elapsed between the establishment of the first and the last provincial revolutionary committees. Moreover, the revolutionary committees were formed under a variety of political circumstances as the Cultural Revolution oscillated through a number of "radical" and "conservative" phases. Reconstructing the Cultural Revolution in the provinces from the time of its first major impact in the fall of 1966, seven major

[84] One significant change appears in Table 3 compared to the version published in 1967: Anhwei was lowered from twenty-first to twenty-third in rank order of stability and Kweichow and Honan were raised correspondingly to take into account the purge of Secretary Chang K'ai-fan (see p. 131) which had not been revealed when the original table was compiled.

[85] Liu Chien-hsün in Honan and Wei Kuo-ch'ing in Kwangsi. Heilungkiang, where P'an Fu-sheng assumed the first secretaryship sometime in early 1966, might technically be considered another case of a pre-Cultural Revolution leader surviving. However, since P'an did not have a long record of service in Heilungkiang prior to the Cultural Revolution his case is clearly different. See the discussion of the Heilungkiang case below.

## TABLE 3
### Stability of Provincial Party Secretariats, 1956–66 *

| Rank Order of Stability | Province | Stability Category | Number of First Secretaries | Size of Core Group With Continuous Service Since 1956–57 | Size of Core Group 1958–64 | Total Number of Additions and Removals of Secretaries | Number of Purges | Number of Secretaries Purged | Number of Department Leaders Purged | Region | National Defense Area |
|---|---|---|---|---|---|---|---|---|---|---|---|
| 1 | Kiangsu | I | 1 | 5 ‖ | 6 ‖ | 5 | 0 | 0 | 0 | EC | No |
| 2 | Kiangsi † | I | 1 | 4 ‖ | 5 ‖ | 9 | 0 | 0 | 0 | CS/EC | No |
| 3 | Szechwan | I | 2 | 4 # | 5 ‖# | 8 | 0 | 0 | 0 | SW | No |
| 4 | Kirin | I | 1 | 4 ** | 5 ‖# | 10 | 0 | 0 | 0 | NE | No |
| 5 | Shansi | I | 2 | 4 # | 6 ‖# | 10 | 0 | 0 | 0 | NC | Yes |
| 6 | Tibet | I | 2 | 4 # | 5 ‖# | 11 | 0 | 0 | 0 | SW | Yes |
| 7 | Inner Mongolia | I | 1 | 3 = | 3 ‖ | 9 | 0 | 0 | 0 | NC | Yes |
| 8 | Fukien | I | 1 | 5 = | 5 ‖ | 19 | 0 | 0 | 0 | EC | Yes |
| 9 | Hupeh | I | 1 | 3 = | 4 ‖ | 13 | 0 | 0 | 0 | CS | No |
| 10 | Heilungkiang | I | 2 | 4 | 6 ‖ | 9 | 0 | 0 | 0 | NE | Yes |
| 11 | Hopeh | II | 1 | 3 =# | 5 ‖# | 12 | 1 | 0 | 1 ## | NC | No |
| 12 | Kwangtung | II | 2 | 5 = | 6 ‖# | 16 | 1 | 2 | 0 ## | CS | No |
| 13 | Sinkiang | II | 1 | 3 ‖ | 4 ‖ | 10 | 1 | 1 §§ | 3 ## | NW | Yes |
| 14 | Chekiang | II | 1 | 2 ‖ | 4 ‖ | 8 | 1 | 1 §§ | 3 ## | EC | No |
| 15 | Shensi | II | 3 ‡ | 0 | 4 ‖ | 22 | 0 | 0 | 0 | NW | No |
| 16 | Liaoning | III | 2 § | 2 | 4 †† | 14 | 1 | 3 §§ | 1 ## | NE | No |
| 17 | Ninghsia | III | 2 | 2 | 3 | 11 | 1 | 3 §§ | 0 | NW | No |
| 18 | Yunnan | III | 2 | 0 ** | 4 | 26 | 1 | 0 | 2 ## | SW | Yes |
| 19 | Hunan | III | 2 | 2 ** | 3 # | 15 | 1 | 1 | 0 | CS | No |
| 20 | Kwangsi | III | 3 ‡ | 4 # | 4 # | 11 | 2 | 3 | 3 ## | CS | Yes |
| 21 | Kweichow | III | 3 ‡§ | 1 | 3 ‖ | 20 | 1 | 1 | 0 ## | SW | No |
| 22 | Honan | III | 3 § | 2 | 4 | 20 | 1 | 2 | 0 ## | CS | No |
| 23 | Anhwei | III | 2 | 2 | 4 | 22 | 3 | 3 ‖ | 1 ## | EC | No |
| 24 | Tsinghai | IV | 3 ‡ | 0 . | 2 # | 16 | 2 | 2 §§‖ | 0 ## | NW | No |
| 25 | Shantung | IV | 3 ‡ | 1 # | 2 # | 22 | 2 | 2 §§‖ | 0 ## | EC | No |
| 26 | Kansu | IV | 2 | 0 | 1 | 26 | 2 ‡‡ | 2 ‖ | 0 ## | NW | No |

\* Source: Frederick C. Teiwes, *Provincial Party Personnel in Mainland China 1956–1966* (New York: East Asian Institute, Columbia University, 1967), pp. 38–39.

† Kiangsi was in the Central-South region in the 1950's but was placed under the East China Party Bureau in 1961.

‡ Including one acting first secretary.

§ Including one first secretary demoted to second secretary.

‖ Including the first secretary serving in 1956.

\# Including a first secretary appointed after 1956 who was a secretary in same province since 1956.

\*\* In Kirin, including First Secretary Wu Te who was transferred to Peking in June, 1966; in Hunan, including First Secretary Chang P'ing-hua who was transferred to the CC Propaganda Dept. in July, 1966.

†† Including Huang Huo-ch'ing, first secretary since 1958.

‡‡ Including a major 1958 purge not affecting any secretaries or department leaders.

§§ Including the purge of a governor.

‖‖ Including the purge of a first secretary.

\#\# Officials in lower posts also purged.

stages can be identified.[86] These are: (1) the fall of 1966 to early January, 1967—provincial authorities under heavy attack, chaotic attempts to "seize power" by revolutionary groups; no revolutionary committees formed; (2) mid-January to mid-March, 1967—initial "seizures of power" backed by military support, efforts to curb anarchistic tendencies; five revolutionary committees formed; (3) late March to early July, 1967—attacks on conservative tendencies, restrictions on military authority by Peking, and growing violence among revolutionary groups; one (municipal) revolutionary committee formed; (4) mid-July and August, 1967—centrally encouraged attacks on military authority, extreme violence; one revolutionary committee formed; (5) September, 1967, to early March, 1968—curbing of the "extreme left," military suppression of disorders, and reinstatement of cadres; nine revolutionary committees formed; (6) late March to mid-July, 1968—attacks on the "right" as the main danger, increasingly widespread violence; eight revolutionary committees formed; (7) late July to October, 1968—disgrace of the Red Guards, reaffirmation of military control; five revolutionary committees formed. Table 4 indicates the order in which the revolutionary committees were established and the periods of their formation.

The timing of the formation of revolutionary committees is an important index of provincial politics. As an explicit act by the center legitimizing a new provincial leadership, the creation of a revolutionary committee reflects both central priorities and provincial conditions. Committees established in each period were formed in response to different pressures and resulted in different power constellations. While a full examination of the complex relationships involved is not possible here, a few hypotheses can be offered. First, the provinces which were the earliest to establish revolutionary committees appeared to be particularly responsive to the "Maoist" faction at the center. Although efforts to bring excesses under control marked the mid-January to mid-March, 1967, period, it was definitely a time when the "Maoist" forces in Peking were riding high. The committees established at that time were meant to be models of the correct way to seize power, to break down the old order, and to establish the new. Moreover, committees established later probably reflect the "conservative" or "radical" orientation of their respective periods, since it seems logical that

[86] This reconstruction of the various phases of the Cultural Revolution is primarily based on Philip Bridgham, "Mao's Cultural Revolution in 1967: The Struggle to Seize Power," *CQ*, No. 34 (April–June, 1968), pp. 6–37; and Richard Baum, "China: Year of the Mangoes," *Asian Survey*, IX (January, 1969), pp. 1–17.

the forces carrying the day in Peking would sanction similarly oriented leaderships in the provinces. Last, it is reasonable to assume that the greater the delay in setting up a revolutionary committee the more likely that other priorities were considered to be more important.

*National Defense Areas.* While international tension and domestic politics are related in frequently obscure ways, it is clear that some provinces are affected more than others by their proximity to hostile powers and to areas of conflict. I have classified seven provinces as national defense areas: Fukien, where troops are heavily concentrated facing Taiwan; Heilungkiang, where major border clashes with the Soviet Union have occurred; Inner Mongolia, which has a long border with the Soviet-dominated Mongolian People's Republic; Kwangsi, located in close proximity to the Vietnam War; Sinkiang, scene of

TABLE 4

ESTABLISHMENT OF PROVINCIAL REVOLUTIONARY COMMITTEES *

| Order of Establishment | Province | Date of Establishment | Cultural Revolution Period | National Defense Area | Stability Category and Rank |
|---|---|---|---|---|---|
| 1 | Heilungkiang | 1/31/67 | 2 | Yes | I-10 |
| 2 | Shantung | 2/3/67 | 2 | No | IV-25 |
| 3 | Kweichow | 2/13/67 | 2 | No | III-21 |
| 4 | Shansi | 3/18/67 | 2 | No | I- 5 |
| 5 | Tsinghai | 8/12/67 | 4 | No | IV-24 |
| 6 | Inner Mongolia | 11/1/67 | 5 | Yes | I- 7 |
| 7 | Kiangsi | 1/5/68 | 5 | No | I- 2 |
| 8 | Kansu | 1/24/68 | 5 | No | IV-26 |
| 9 | Honan | 1/27/68 | 5 | No | III-22 |
| 10 | Hopeh | 2/3/68 | 5 | No | II-11 |
| 11 | Hupeh | 2/5/68 | 5 | No | I- 9 |
| 12 | Kwangtung | 2/21/68 | 5 | No | II-12 |
| 13 | Kirin | 3/6/68 | 5 | No | I- 4 |
| 14 | Kiangsu | 3/23/68 | 6 | No | I- 1 |
| 15 | Chekiang | 3/24/68 | 6 | No | II-14 |
| 16 | Hunan | 4/8/68 | 6 | No | III-19 |
| 17 | Ninghsia | 4/10/68 | 6 | No | III-17 |
| 18 | Anhwei | 4/18/68 | 6 | No | III-23 |
| 19 | Shensi | 5/1/68 | 6 | No | II-15 |
| 20 | Liaoning | 5/10/68 | 6 | No | III-16 |
| 21 | Szechwan | 5/31/68 | 6 | No | I- 3 |
| 22 | Yunnan | 8/13/68 | 7 | Yes | III-18 |
| 23 | Fukien | 8/19/68 | 7 | Yes | I- 8 |
| 24 | Kwangsi | 8/26/68 | 7 | Yes | III-20 |
| 25 | Sinkiang | 9/5/68 | 7 | Yes | II-13 |
| 26 | Tibet | 9/5/68 | 7 | Yes | I- 6 |

* Source: *Directory of Chinese Communist Officials: Provincial, Municipal and Military* (Washington: April, 1969), pp. 1–55. Municipal revolutionary committees were established in Shanghai on February 5, 1967, in Peking on April 20, 1967, and in Tientsin on December 6, 1967.

important clashes with both India and the Soviet Union; Tibet, scene of long-standing friction with India; and Yunnan, the base of small-scale military operations in Burma and Laos as well as neighboring North Vietnam.[87] The role of the military was particularly strong in most of these provinces before the Cultural Revolution. In all national defense areas except Heilungkiang and Kwangsi, the posts of regional military commander and Party leader were held by the same person at some point, and in Sinkiang and Tibet three additional secretaries also were military figures.[88] This presumably had profound implications for provincial administration and politics.

*Correlations.* Although rank correlation analysis is not appropriate in the case of national defense areas, Tables 3 and 4 point to interesting relationships in terms of both stability and revolutionary committees. All of the provinces in the last group to establish revolutionary committees are national defense areas, which suggests that considerations of military security postponed the formation of committees in those provinces.[89] The high priority given to military tasks may have diverted energies from the conciliation of different revolutionary groups which preceded the establishment of committees. Heilungkiang, the first province to set up a revolutionary committee, and Inner Mongolia are exceptions to this pattern. In terms of stability, four national defense areas—Tibet, Inner Mongolia, Fukien, and Heilungkiang—are in the "highly stable" category for the pre-Cultural Revolution decade, while Sinkiang is rated "basically stable." It could be hypothesized that military priorities contributed to stability by reducing the importance attached to other tasks. Yunnan and Kwangsi, however, are exceptions. In any case, it is intriguing that both before and during the Cultural Revolution national defense areas appear to have been insulated to some extent from the pressures of provincial politics.

The correlation coefficient for stability in the 1956–66 period and the establishment of revolutionary committees ($-.11$, $N=26$) does not indicate a significant relationship. A closer look at Table 4, however, reveals some interesting patterns. Many of the less stable provinces formed revolutionary committees in periods of "Maoist"

---

[87] Since the Korean War ended in 1953, Kirin and Liaoning which both border on North Korea are not listed. Moreover, Chinese troops stationed in Korea, rather than forces in these provinces, served as the front line of national defense until 1957. The withdrawal of those troops apparently reflected the view that international tension had eased considerably in the area.

[88] Teiwes, *Provincial Party Personnel*, p. 46.

[89] Cf. Baum, "Year of the Mangoes," p. 9.

ascendancy: Shantung and Kweichow during the initial formation of committees; Tsinghai during the "ultra-left" period of the summer of 1967; and Hunan, Ninghsia, Anhwei, and Liaoning during the "leftist" revival in the spring and early summer of 1968. Conversely, six of the ten "highly stable" provinces established revolutionary committees during "conservative" phases of the Cultural Revolution. This pattern leads me to suggest that in provinces where the leadership had been most deeply entrenched it was particularly difficult to create a new, purified elite. The cohesion of the ruling group complicated the task of finding leading "revolutionary cadres" who had the necessary skills and yet were free of close ties to the old provincial leaders, to provide administrative personnel for the new revolutionary structures. On the other hand, provinces with a history of heavy turnover of personnel lacked such cohesion, and ambitious cadres not tainted by prolonged association with the leading provincial "powerholders" were available for leadership roles.

This hypothesis, moreover, is supported by what on the surface appear to be exceptions to the pattern. Heilungkiang, the first province to set up a revolutionary committee, and Shansi, the fourth, were "highly stable" in terms of personnel. However, both P'an Fu-sheng, who became first secretary of Heilungkiang in early 1966 and survived to become chairman of the Provincial Revolutionary Committee, and Liu Ko-p'ing, who came to Shansi in 1965 as a vice-governor and then rose to head its Revolutionary Committee, were newcomers to their provinces without long-standing ties to the old power elite. As a result, they did not have to bear the onus for past "crimes" committed by "capitalist roaders" in their respective provinces, but instead could make cause with rebellious Red Guards.[90] Although other exceptions (Kiangsu, Szechwan) cannot be explained in these terms, there does appear to be a significant relationship between the availability of experienced leaders who were relatively free of involvement in local politics and the establishment of "Maoist" oriented revolutionary committees.

SOCIOECONOMIC VARIABLES

*National Minority Areas.* The problem of localism is intensified in areas inhabited by national minority peoples. Both "local nationalism" —separatist tendencies on the part of minority cadres—and "Great

[90] The cases of P'an and Liu are also notable in that both are former purge victims. The lessons which they learned from past experience may have stood them well in the turbulent times of the Cultural Revolution.

Hanism"—discrimination toward minorities by Han Chinese cadres—have been involved in provincial purges, which indicates that the presence of minorities can contribute to instability. Sixteen provinces have significant minority populations, that is, either more than 1 per cent of the total provincial population or sufficient concentrations to cause the formation of special "autonomous" administrative subdivisions. Of course, there are great differences among these sixteen provinces. Here it is only possible to classify them into two categories, major and minor minority areas. I have defined major minority areas as provinces with a minority population of more than 10 per cent of the total population. All major minority area provinces have at least one autonomous subdivision of the *chou* level (comparable to the special district or *chuan ch'ü*), and half of these provinces are autonomous regions themselves. Minor minority areas are provinces with a minority population of 1 to 10 per cent of the total population or at

TABLE 5
NATIONAL MINORITY AREAS *

| | Province | Stability Category | Revolutionary Committee Period | National Defense Area |
|---|---|---|---|---|
| Major Minority Areas | Inner Mongolia | I | V | Yes |
| | Kansu | IV | V | No |
| | Kirin | I | V | No |
| | Kwangsi | III | VII | Yes |
| | Kweichow | III | II | No |
| | Ninghsia | III | VI | No |
| | Sinkiang | II | VII | Yes |
| | Tibet | I | VII | Yes |
| | Tsinghai | IV | IV | No |
| | Yunnan | III | VII | Yes |
| Minor Minority Areas | Heilungkiang | I | II | Yes |
| | Hopeh | II | V | No |
| | Hunan | III | VI | No |
| | Kwangtung | II | V | No |
| | Liaoning | III | VI | No |
| | Szechwan | I | VI | No |

* Sources: Nai-Ruenn Chen (ed.), *Chinese Economic Statistics: A Handbook for Mainland China* (Chicago: Aldine Publishing Co., 1967), p. 126; *Economic Geography of Central China,* in *JPRS,* No. 2227-N (February 10, 1960); *Economic Geography of the East China Region,* in *JPRS,* No. 11438 (December 7, 1961); *Economic Geography of South China,* in *JPRS,* No. 14954 (August 24, 1962); *Economic Geography of Southwest China,* in *JPRS,* No. 15069 (August 31, 1962); *Economic Geography of Northeast China,* in *JPRS,* No. 15388 (September 21, 1962); and *1965 Jen-min Shou-ts'e* (People's Handbook) (Peking: Ta-kung Pao, 1965), pp. 108–14.

least one autonomous subdivision of the county level, or both. The provinces are classified in Table 5.

*Urbanization.* The process of modernization has differentially affected China's provinces, with the greatest impact on Northeast and North China and on the coastal areas generally. Urbanization and industrialization have been two related aspects of this process. Data on urbanization are of particular value for my purposes since, in contrast to industrial data, they are available for all provinces in a single series. The measure of urbanization used here is the mid-1958 urban population in municipalities of one hundred thousand or more people as a percentage of total provincial population.[91] This information, together with data on the increase in the urban share of the total population from 1953 to 1958 and on the annual over-all rate of population growth (urban and rural), is given in Table 6.

*Industrialization.* The high priority which the CCP attaches to industrial development has many ramifications for provincial politics. Although their efforts centered on agriculture in the pre-Great Leap period, provincial authorities were deeply involved in tasks that supported industry. Moreover, industrial development creates its own social and administrative problems. The third section of this paper further indicates that the more industrialized areas were favored in terms of resource allocation before the Great Leap Forward, but were required to aid less developed areas during that period.

The best index of industrialization available is industrial output value per capita. Although data are incomplete for this variable, scattered information is available for most provinces. (See Appendixes B and C for all available data.) The data for 1957, the last year of reliable figures, are used in Table 7 to rank fourteen provinces.

*Agriculture.* Agriculture plays a key role in Chinese politics for a number of reasons. The overwhelmingly rural nature of the country makes the role of agriculture crucial for economic development. (The CCP leadership learned in the 1950's that Soviet-style neglect of the

---

[91] The procedure adopted was to add the mid-1958 populations of all municipalities over one hundred thousand people, to take 83.13 per cent of the total as the *urban* population of those municipalities (that is, using the ratio derived from 1953 data to exclude nonurban residents of municipalities—see Morris B. Ullman, *Cities of Mainland China: 1953 and 1958* [Washington: Bureau of the Census, August, 1961], p. 9) and calculating this figure as a percentage of total provincial population in mid-1958. There are major problems with this. The use of the 83.13 ratio is arbitrary. Moreover, municipal populations were affected by the redrawing of administrative boundaries as well as by actual growth. See *ibid.*, pp. 42–44. Nevertheless, the data are presented in the belief that they serve to convey a rough order of magnitude.

agricultural sector was not suitable for China.) Moreover, the peasant-based nature of the Chinese revolution creates particular sensitivities to agricultural matters among CCP leaders and cadres. The aspect of provincial agriculture that provides the most data is the output of grain, the food staple of the nation. (See Appendix D for a complete summary.) Two grain indexes are summarized in Table 8; these are the per capita output and the percentage of increase in total output for 1952–57.

The average per capita grain output for 1952–57 (yearly figures in Appendix E) is an important measure of rural living standards. More-

TABLE 6
PROVINCIAL URBANIZATION: MID-1958

| Rank by Percentage of Urban Population, 1958 | Province | Percentage of Urban Population, Mid-1958 * | Increase in Percentage of Urban Population, Mid-1953– Mid-1958 † | Annual Rate of Total Population Growth, 1953–58 ‡ | Stability Category and Rank |
|---|---|---|---|---|---|
| 1 | Liaoning | 26.1 | 1.7 | 3.58 | III-16 |
| 2 | Heilungkiang | 19.3 | 6.7 | 5.07 | I-10 |
| 3 | Kirin | 13.3 | 1.0 | 2.38 | I- 4 |
| 4 | Hopeh § | 11.3 | 2.1 | 2.18 | II-11 |
| 5 | Shansi | 9.1 | 2.6 | 2.45 | I- 5 |
| 6 | Kiangsu | 8.8 | .8 | 2.24 | I- 1 |
| 7 | Inner Mongolia | 8.0 | 4.6 | 5.15 | I- 7 |
| 8 | Shensi | 7.0 | 2.2 | 2.99 | II-15 |
| 9 | Kwangtung | 6.6 | 1.2 | 0.73 | II-12 |
| 10 | Hupeh. | 6.3 | 1.7 | 2.30 | I- 9 |
| 11 | Sinkiang | 6.1 | 1.9 | 3.30 | II-13 |
| 12 | Kansu | 6.0 | 3.1 | 2.94 | IV-26 |
| 13 | Tsinghai | 5.9 | 1.2 | 4.58 | IV-24 |
| 14 | Fukien | 5.8 | .2 | 2.44 | I- 8 |
| 15 | Chekiang | 5.5 | .9 | 2.26 | II-14 |
| 16 | Szechwan | 5.0 | .0 | 2.11 | I- 3 |
| 17 | Shantung | 4.9 | 1.4 | 2.25 | IV-25 |
| 18 | Yunnan | 4.7 | .6 | 2.00 | III-18 |
| 19 | Honan | 4.0 | 1.2 | 2.16 | III-22 |
| 20 | Kweichow | 3.5 | 2.0 | 2.62 | III-21 |
| 21 | Hunan | 3.5 | .2 | 1.94 | III-19 |
| 22 | Kiangsi | 3.5 | 1.5 | 2.34 | I- 2 |
| 23 | Anhwei | 3.3 | .4 | 2.03 | III-23 |
| 24 | Kwangsi | 3.1 | .2 | 2.19 | III-20 |
| 25 | Ninghsia | 0 | 0 | 1.55 | III-17 |
| 26 | Tibet | 0 | 0 | —0.07 | I- 6 |

* Derived from Ullman, *Cities*, pp. 11, 35–36.
† Derived from *ibid.;* adjusted to 1958 administrative divisions.
‡ Derived from Appendix A.
§ Including Tientsin.

over, it is also an important factor in determining provincial imports and exports of grain, which are discussed below (pp. 174–76). The percentage of increase in total grain output from 1952 to 1957 provides a useful index of provincial agricultural performance. (See Appendix F for yearly growth rates.) Provincial government is vitally concerned with both the agricultural performance and the peasant living conditions reflected by these indexes.

*Correlations.* Minority nationalities inhabit China's borderlands, and only Fukien of the seven national defense areas does not have a significant minority population. Although four of the five provinces in the last group to establish revolutionary committees are major minority

TABLE 7
PROVINCIAL INDUSTRIAL OUTPUT VALUE PER CAPITA, 1957 *

| Rank by Value Per Capita | Province | Industrial Output Value Per Capita | Stability Category and Rank † |
|---|---|---|---|
| 1 | Liaoning | 737 | III- 9 |
| 2 | Heilungkiang | 271 | I- 5 |
| 3 | Kwangtung | 94 | II- 6 |
| 4 | Kiangsu | 92 | I- 1 |
| 5 | Chekiang | 91 | II- 8 |
| 6 | Sinkiang | 80 | II- 7 |
| 7 | Inner Mongolia | 70 | I- 4 |
| 8 | Kiangsi | 64 | I- 2 |
| 9 | Szechwan | 60 | I- 3 |
| 10 | Tsinghai | 52 | IV-14 |
| 11 | Anhwei | 45 | III-13 |
| 12 | Hunan | 35 | III-10 |
| 13 | Kweichow | 34 | III-11 |
| 14 | Honan | 32 | III-12 |

* Source: Appendix C. Unit: *Yuan.*
† Rank adjusted to N=14.

areas, the fact that they are also defense areas appears to be more significant. Revolutionary committees were formed in minority areas during all other periods, "radical" and "conservative" alike. There may be, however, a significant negative relationship between major minority areas and stability. Although four of the ten major minority areas are "highly stable" or "basically stable," three are also defense areas. Conversely, four of the five major minority areas without national defense priorities are in the "limited continuity" or "unstable" categories. Thus, it does appear that the problems caused by ethnic tensions significantly disrupt personnel patterns, although provinces

TABLE 8

PROVINCIAL GRAIN OUTPUT PER CAPITA AND GROWTH OF TOTAL PRODUCTION, 1952–57 *

| Rank of Average Per Capita Output | Province | Average Per Capita Output | Percentage of Increase in Total Output | Rank | Stability Category and Rank † |
|---|---|---|---|---|---|
| 1 | Heilungkiang | 959 | — 4.7 | 22 | I- 9 |
| 2 | Inner Mongolia | 873 | —14.7 | 24 | I- 6 |
| 3 | Sinkiang | 716 | 26.7 | 10 | II-12 |
| 4 | Kiangsi | 704 | 18.8 | 13 | I- 2 |
| 5 | Kirin | 683 | 3.3 ‡ | 21 | I- 4 |
| 6 | Hupeh | 635 | 33.7 | 7 | I- 8 |
| 7 | Chekiang | 621 | 10.8 | 17 | II-13 |
| 8 | Hunan | 609 | 9.8 | 18 | III-17 |
| 9 | Kwangsi | 604 | 6.4 | 20 | III-18 |
| 10 | Anhwei | 601 | 37.4 | 5 | III-21 |
| 11 | Szechwan | 589 | 36.2 | 6 | I- 3 |
| 12 | Fukien | 587 | 19.5 | 12 | I- 7 |
| 13 | Kwangtung | 585 | 29.1 | 9 | II-11 |
| 14 | Yunnan | 574 | 50.6 | 4 | III-16 |
| 15 | Kansu § | 567 | 58.6 | 2 | IV-24 |
| 16 | Shensi | 566 | 13.2 | 16 | II-14 |
| 17 | Tsinghai | 562 | 72.3 | 1 | IV-22 |
| 18 | Kiangsu | 551 | 16.4 | 15 | I- 1 |
| 19 | Kweichow | 539 | 54.6 | 3 | III-19 |
| 20 | Shansi | 532 | — 6.2 | 23 | I- 5 |
| 21 | Liaoning | 512 | 21.0 | 11 | III-15 |
| 22 | Honan | 480 | 32.9 | 8 | III-20 |
| 23 | Shantung | 460 | 18.3 | 14 | IV-23 |
| 24 | Hopeh ‖ | 430 | 7.3 | 19 | II-10 |
|  | China |  | 19.8 |  |  |

* Source: Derived from Appendixes D and E.
† Rank adjusted to N=24.
‡ Percentage of increase for 1953–57; 1952 data unavailable.
§ Including Ninghsia.
‖ Excluding Tientsin.

with less than a 10 per cent minority population seem little affected.

As anticipated, there is a high positive correlation (+.81, N=14) between industrialization as measured by 1957 per capita industrial output value and urbanization as of mid-1958. In addition, the high correlation between urbanization in mid-1958 and urban growth in 1953–58 (+.65, N=26) [92] suggests that despite the importance attached by the first five-year plan to the development of backward inland areas (as reflected in the case of Kweichow, which ranks twentieth in the level of urbanization but which has the seventh highest

[92] Urban growth, in turn, is highly correlated to the annual growth rate of the total provincial population (+. 75, N=26).

rate of urban growth), the net result of the plan was to strengthen the advanced areas.

The most striking relationship to emerge from the socioeconomic data is a positive correlation between modernization and personnel stability. Both the coefficient of urbanization and stability (+.35, N=26) and that of industrialization and stability (+.53, N=14) demonstrate this relationship. There are important exceptions to the trend, however. Liaoning, China's most industrialized and urbanized province, had only "limited continuity" of personnel during the 1956–66 period. Conversely, "highly stable" Kiangsi and Szechwan rank middle to low on both industrialization and urbanization indexes.

The following tentative hypothesis is offered to explain the prevailing pattern. Central support for advanced areas may significantly ease the burdens on provincial leaders and thus may contribute to personnel stability. It is plausible that central support involves, in addition to material resources, the assignment of especially competent cadres to staff the administrative machinery of these areas. Moreover, the Party leaders themselves may have been selected with particular care, in view of the importance of industrial development. Conversely, backward areas may be neglected in terms both of resource allocation and of the assignment of less talented personnel. Despite the Great Leap Forward, the Cultural Revolution emphasis on the need for giving more attention to backward areas suggests that favoritism for advanced regions had soon reasserted itself. With such favoritism a basic feature of provincial politics, leaders of advanced provinces enjoy considerably enhanced opportunities for success and survival.[93]

One significant correlation to emerge from the agricultural data is a negative relationship (−.48, N=24) between the increase in grain output from 1952 to 1957 and personnel stability. While I am unable to offer an explanation for the negative nature of this correlation, it does demonstrate that agricultural performance was not a key to political stability. This point is reinforced by yearly grain output growth data in Appendix F. For example, Kweichow, classified in the "limited continuity" category, not only had a steady annual growth rate of 7 to 10 per cent from 1952 to 1957, but in each year ranked in the top half of all provinces in terms of growth of grain output. In

---

[93] Positive correlations exist between the order of establishing revolutionary committees and both urban growth 1953–58 (+.63, N=26) and annual growth rates of the total population (+.39, N=26). No significant correlation exists between the urbanization level in mid-1958 and revolutionary committees, however. I am unable to offer a satisfactory hypothesis to explain the relationships.

contrast, the top-ranking province in terms of stability, Kiangsu, actually declined in grain output in three out of five years. But if success in increasing grain output did not help the careers of provincial officials, there is evidence that a high per capita grain output did. There is a positive correlation ($+.37$, $N=24$) between per capita grain output and personnel stability.[94] This is especially worth noting because of its implication for grain exports (see pp. 174–76). For the present, I offer the tentative hypothesis that personnel stability becomes more difficult to maintain as peasant living standards become increasingly stringent. Where the peasantry is relatively better off, the burdens on provincial leaders lessen and they are better able to perform in a manner judged adequate by Peking.

ORGANIZATIONAL VARIABLES

*Party Membership.* An important factor in the performance of provincial leaders should be the organizational resources available to them. Presumably, the capacity to carry out mass movements and to obtain compliance from the population is related to the numbers of reliable cadres at hand. One index of organizational resources is the ratio of Party members to total provincial population. Substantial Party membership data are available at the provincial level only for 1956.[95] This information is summarized in Table 9.

Party membership ratios are clearly related to the course of the Chinese revolution; they are highest in those areas of North China where key victories were won over the Japanese and the Kuomintang (KMT). Moreover, the old guerrilla base area of Kiangsi ranks relatively high despite Chiang Kai-shek's many suppression campaigns (see p. 136). Conversely, Party membership ratios are lowest in the Central-South and Southwest regions, which were last to come under CCP control.

*Demobilized Servicemen.* One of the most dependable groups in the population, and a major target for Party recruitment, are demobilized People's Liberation Army (PLA) men. Having served in an organization marked by a highly nationalistic orientation, tight discipline, and systematic ideological training, the ex-serviceman is a valuable resource for shock tasks. Michel Oksenberg and Carol Tryon have com-

[94] See note 81.

[95] Many of these figures were released in conjunction with the Provincial Party Congresses of mid-1956. In this regard, I am indebted to Michel C. Oksenberg for the use of his Party membership file.

TABLE 9

PARTY MEMBERSHIP BY PROVINCE *

| Rank by Percentage of Population in CCP, Mid-1956 | Province | Region | CCP Membership, Mid-1956 † | Percentage of Population in CCP, Mid-1956 |
|---|---|---|---|---|
| 1 | Hopeh ‡ | NC | 1,280,000 § | 3.18 |
| 2 | Shansi | NC | 450,000 ‖ | 2.92 |
| 3 | Shantung | EC | 1,120,000 | 2.14 |
| 4 | Inner Mongolia | NC | 151,700 | 1.78 |
| 5 | Liaoning | NE | 400,000 | 1.75 |
| 6 | Kirin | NE | 195,700 | 1.62 |
| 7 | Kansu # | NW | 216,400 | 1.54 |
| 8 | Kiangsi | CS/EC | 250,000+ | 1.39 |
| 9 | Heilungkiang | NE | (190,000) | 1.38 |
| 10 | Kiangsu | EC | 600,000+ | 1.37 |
| 11 | Sinkiang | NW | 68,000+ | 1.27 |
| 12 | Shensi | NW | 200,000+ | 1.15 |
| 13 | Honan | CS | 509,500 | 1.08 |
| 14 | Fukien | EC | (150,000) | 1.06 |
| 15 | Tsinghai | NW | 20,000 | 1.04 |
| 16 | Yunnan | SW | 182,000 | .98 |
| 17 | Kwangtung | CS | 350,000 ** | .93 |
| 18 | Kweichow | SW | 139,000 | .86 |
| 19 | Kwangsi | CS | (160,000) | .85 |
| 20 | Anhwei | EC | (270,000) | .83 |
| 21 | Hunan | CS | 282,000 | .80 |
| 22 | Chekiang | EC | 190,000+ | .78 |
| 23 | Hupeh | CS | (230,000) | .77 |
| 24 | Szechwan | SW | (500,000) | .71 |

* Sources: Michel C. Oksenberg, "Local Government and Politics in China," Columbia University Seminar on Modern East Asia: China, May 4, 1966, p. 31, unpublished; *CB,* No. 411 (September 27, 1956).

† Figures in parentheses are estimates in *CB,* No. 411 (September 27, 1956).

‡ Excluding Tientsin.

§ Derived from *HHPYK,* No. 21, 1956, p. 70.

‖ My estimate based on *Shan-hsi Jih-pao,* September 25, 1959.

# Including Ninghsia.

** Ezra F. Vogel, *Canton Under Communism: Programs and Politics in a Provincial Capital, 1949–1968* (Cambridge, Mass.: Harvard University Press, 1969), p. 371.

piled data on demobilized servicemen in ten provinces for the 1957–59 period. The results are summarized in Table 10.

Although the data are less complete than those for Party membership, some similarities are apparent.[96] The ratio of demobilized servicemen is highest where soldiers were recruited during the anti-Japanese

[96] The correlation between Party membership ratios and ratios of demobilized servicemen is +.55 (N=10). This, however, is slightly below the critical value of .56 for N=10.

and revolutionary wars. History combines with the policy of returning demobilized soldiers to their native areas in favoring North and Northeast China and conversely in holding the ratios of ex-servicemen low in South China. As Tryon suggests, other factors may be at work, such as sending former soldiers to strategic areas (Heilungkiang) and giving preference to veterans in newly built or expanded industrial enterprises (Liaoning). Whether the above pattern for the 1950's has been altered by nationwide conscription, which presumably equalizes the provincial military burden, cannot be determined.[97]

TABLE 10
DISTRIBUTION OF DEMOBILIZED SERVICEMEN BY PROVINCE *

| Rank Order of Demobilized Servicemen as Per Cent of Population | Province | Region | Year | Total Demobilized Servicemen (thousands) | Demobilized Servicemen as Per Cent of Population ‡ |
|---|---|---|---|---|---|
| 1 | Heilungkiang | NE | 1959 | 307 † | 1.92 |
| 2 | Shansi | NC | 1959 | 200+ | 1.21 |
| 3 | Shantung | EC | 1957 | 610 | 1.14 |
| 4 | Liaoning | NE | 1957 | 265 | 1.12 |
| 5 | Chekiang | EC | 1957 | 190 | .76 |
| 6 | Honan | CS | 1958 | 310 | .63 |
| 7 | Kiangsu | EC | 1957 | 283 | .63 |
| 8 | Hunan | CS | 1959 | 210 | .56 |
| 9 | Kiangsi | CS/EC | 1958 | 78 | .41 |
| 10 | Kwangtung | CS | 1957 | 30 | .08 |

* Sources: Michel C. Oksenberg, "Local Leaders in Rural China, 1962–65: Individual Attributes, Bureaucratic Positions, and Political Recruitment," in Barnett (ed.), *Chinese Communist Politics in Action,* p. 197; and Carol Gillespie Tryon, "The Role of Demobilized Soldiers in the People's Republic of China" (East Asian Institute Certificate essay, Columbia University, 1969), p. 33.
† Does not include one hundred thousand in state farms.
‡ Adjusted to year of data.

*Correlations.* Urbanization as measured in mid-1958 correlates positively to both Party membership ratios (+.55, N=24) and ratios of demobilized servicemen (+.62, N=10).[98] In the case of Party membership, this reflects the overrepresentation of urban groups in the

[97] See Tryon, "The Role of Demobilized Soldiers," pp. 34–35.
[98] There is also a positive correlation between 1957 per capita industrial output value and both Party membership and demobilized servicemen data, but in both cases it falls short of the critical value of N. The figures are: for Party membership data, +.44 (N=14), where the critical value is .46; for demobilized servicemen data, +.46 (N=8), where the critical value is .64.

Party.[99] The data on demobilized servicemen suggest a similar phenomenon within the PLA.

Of interest is the lack of a significant correlation between Party membership and personnel stability (+.15, N=24). Although one could expect the availability of a large corps of Party members to aid provincial leaders in the performance of their duties and thus to contribute to stability, this does not prove to be the case. There is, however, a positive relationship between Party membership ratios and the establishment of revolutionary committees (+.42, N=24). Moreover, the three top provinces in ratios of former servicemen to total population were also among the first to set up revolutionary committees.[100] It may be that large numbers of Party members and ex-servicemen guaranteed the availability of an ample supply of "revolutionary cadres" even after widespread purges. This, in turn, could have facilitated the establishment of revolutionary committees.

CAMPAIGN IMPLEMENTATION

Mass movements are characteristic of the CCP's approach to both social reform and economic development. Socioeconomic variables and differences in organizational resources provide the basis for considerable variation in campaign implementation. Moreover, large-scale movements give provincial leaders the opportunity to display activism, and to demonstrate loyalty and responsiveness to the center.

Below, I examine campaign implementation in two very different periods. The agricultural cooperativization drive of 1955–56 was essentially an acceleration of a movement which had been under way for several years. In contrast, the Great Leap Forward and the People's Communes marked a fundamental break with the past and a leap into the unknown.

*Agricultural Cooperativization.* The third section of this paper discussed the over-all provincial response during the 1955 upsurge in cooperativization. Here variation in that response is measured by the percentage of peasant households organized into higher stage APCs by the summer of 1956. These data are supplemented in Table 11 by the percentage of households in APCs in the summer of 1955 and by the change in each province's rank from 1955 to 1956.

[99] In 1956, national figures showed that 69.1 per cent of Party members were peasants (compared to 80–85 per cent of the population), while industrial workers with 14 per cent and intellectuals with 11.7 per cent were overrepresented. See NCNA, Peking, September 13, 1956, in *CB,* No. 411 (September 27, 1956).

[100] The correlation of +.45 (N=10), however, falls short of the critical value of .56.

A basic factor determining achievements by the summer of 1956 was the work done in building APCs prior to the high tide, as indicated by the high positive correlation (+.70, N=24) between the percentages of peasant households in APCs in 1955 and 1956. Not all provinces adhered to the pattern, however. Kwangsi, Tsinghai, Hupeh, and Honan all substantially improved their performances by 1956, while Chekiang and Shantung lagged noticeably. The political implications of these exceptions are discussed below.

TABLE 11
IMPLEMENTATION OF AGRICULTURAL COOPERATIVIZATION BY PROVINCE *

| Rank by Percentage of Households in Higher APCs, Summer 1956 | Province | Percentage of Peasant Households in Higher APCs, Summer 1956 | Percentage of Peasant Households in APCs, Summer 1955 † | Rank | Change in Rank, 1955–56 |
|---|---|---|---|---|---|
| 1 | Hopeh ‡ | 99.4 | 34.8 | 3 | + 2 |
| 2 | Heilungkiang | 98.7 | 36.6 | 2 | 0 |
| 3 | Kwangsi | 98.2 | 9.5 | 15 | +12 |
| 4 | Shansi | 97.9 | 40.8 | 1 | − 3 |
| 5 | Honan | 97.2 | 12.8 | 12 | + 7 |
| 6 | Kirin | 95.7 | 34.1 | 4 | − 2 |
| 7 | Tsinghai | 92.0 | 8.7 | 17 | +10 |
| 8 | Liaoning | 91.8 | 28.9 | 5 | − 3 |
| 9 | Anhwei | 80.7 | 13.6 | 11 | + 2 |
| 10 | Kiangsu | 78.9 | 11.2 | 13 | + 3 |
| 11 | Inner Mongolia | 77.5 | 18.1 | 7 | − 4 |
| 12 | Hupeh | 69.0 | 5.0 | 21 | + 9 |
| 13 | Shantung | 67.2 | 18.4 | 6 | − 7 |
| 14 | Shensi | 65.2 | 15.5 | 9 | − 5 |
| 15 | Fukien | 62.2 | 15.1 | 10 | − 5 |
| 16 | Kiangsi | 62.2 | 9.9 | 14 | − 1 |
| 17 | Chekiang | 60.0 | 17.0 | 8 | − 9 |
| 18 | Kweichow | 51.6 | 5.5 | 20 | + 2 |
| 19 | Kwangtung | 44.1 | 6.7 | 19 | 0 |
| 20 | Sinkiang | 42.1 | 4.5 | 23 | + 3 |
| 21 | Kansu § | 34.5 | 9.2 | 16 | − 5 |
| 22 | Yunnan | 27.9 | 4.8 | 22 | 0 |
| 23 | Hunan | 13.8 | 3.3 | 24 | + 1 |
| 24 | Szechwan | 7.4 | 7.4 | 18 | − 6 |
|  | China ‖ | 62.6 | 14.2 |  |  |

\* Source: Shih Ching-t'ang, et al. (eds.), *Chung-kuo nung-yeh ho-tso hua yün-tung shih-liao* (Historical Materials on China's Agricultural Cooperativization Movement) (Peking: Sheng-huo tu-shu hsin-chih san-lien shu-tien, 1959), pp. 1011, 1019.

† In all provinces except Heilungkiang and Chekiang, the percentage of households in higher APCs was less than 1/10 of 1 per cent. The figures were .189 per cent for Heilungkiang and .145 per cent for Chekiang.

‡ Excluding Tientsin.

§ Including Ninghsia.

‖ Including Peking, Shanghai, and Tientsin.

*The Great Leap Forward and the Communes.* The Great Leap Forward and creation of People's Communes was the most significant
mass mobilization effort in the history of the CPR. Despite the high
degree of unreliability, data from the Great Leap period on the
achievements that were claimed and on the targets that were set are
important as an index of provincial response under unprecedented conditions.

The water conservancy campaign of 1957–58 played a key role in
the Great Leap strategy by creating conditions for a "leap forward"
in agriculture. Michel Oksenberg's study of this campaign reveals a
process whereby the provinces set modest irrigation targets in August,
1957, then raised the targets drastically in October and November, and
subsequently, with one exception, claimed even greater accomplishments in January, 1958. The relationship between the targets set in
August and the claims made in January suggests different degrees of
provincial activism in response to the center's demand for a "leap
forward." Oksenberg's data for the expansion of irrigated area are
summarized in Table 12.[101]

TABLE 12
PROVINCIAL CLAIMS OF EXPANSION IN IRRIGATED AREA DURING 1957–58
WATER CONSERVANCY CAMPAIGN *

| Rank of Percentage of Increase Late January over August Target | Province | August 1957 Target | Revised Target, October–November, 1957 | Completed and Nearing Completion, January, 1958 | Percentage of Increase Late January over August Target |
|---|---|---|---|---|---|
| 1 | Hupeh | .80 | | 10.00 | 1150 |
| 2 | Anhwei | 1.01 | 3.00 | 7.80 | 672 |
| 3 | Kansu † | 1.00 | | 5.30 | 430 |
| 4 | Hunan | .40 | .60 | 1.90 | 375 |
| 5 | Hopeh ‡ | 5.47 | | 25.42 | 365 |
| 6 | Honan | 5.54 | 20.00 | 22.52 | 306 |
| 7 | Kiangsi | 1.60 | 8.20 | 5.43 | 239 |
| 8 | Shantung | 4.00 | 10.00 | 13.33 | 233 |
| 9 | Kwangtung § | 5.00 | | 14.10 | 182 |
| 10 | Kwangsi § | 5.00 | 8.00 | 12.09 | 142 |
| 11 | Szechwan | 5.30 | | 8.90 | 68 |
| 12 | Kirin | 1.35 | | 1.71 | 27 |

* Source: Oksenberg, "Policy Formulation in China," chap. xiii. Unit: Million *mou*.
† Including Ninghsia.
‡ Excluding Tientsin.
§ Data include area of improved irrigation.

[101] Data are also available on increases targeted and claimed for the area of improved
irrigation in four provinces. In three cases the magnitude of increase closely parallels the

Targets for the planned purchase of grain are another indicator of provincial activism during the Great Leap. The 1958 purchase targets for all provinces except Tibet were published in November, 1958. I have determined an index of activism by calculating the ratio of those targets to the actual grain procurement in 1956. (Although procurement data are available for seventeen provinces in 1956, they are extremely sparse for 1957.) These are not entirely comparable figures; total grain procurement (*cheng kou*) includes agricultural taxes collected in grain as well as planned purchases (*shou kou*). My assump-

TABLE 13

RATIO OF 1958 GRAIN PURCHASE TARGETS TO ACTUAL
1956 PROCUREMENT *

| Rank | Province | Ratio | Stability Category and Rank † |
|------|----------|-------|-------------------------------|
| 1 | Tsinghai | 3.13 | IV-16 |
| 2 | Hopeh ‡ | 2.34 | II- 7 |
| 3 | Kweichow | 1.91 | III-13 |
| 4 | Shensi | 1.74 | II- 9 |
| 5 | Honan | 1.67 | III-14 |
| 6 | Shantung | 1.62 | IV-17 |
| 7 | Kwangsi | 1.57 | III-12 |
| 8 | Szechwan | 1.56 | I- 2 |
| 9 | Shansi | 1.46 | I- 4 |
| 10 | Heilungkiang | 1.38 | I- 6 |
| 11 | Anhwei | 1.35 | III-15 |
| 12 | Kirin | 1.30 | I- 3 |
| 13 | Hupeh | 1.25 | I- 5 |
| 14 | Kiangsi | 1.23 | I- 1 |
| 15 | Liaoning | 1.13 | III-10 |
| 16 | Yunnan | 1.08 | III-11 |
| 17 | Chekiang | .79 | II- 8 |

* Source: See note 102.
† Rank adjusted to N=17.
‡ Ratio derived from 1956 data excluding Tientsin and 1958 data including Tientsin.

tion is that the greatest increases in total procurements resulted from planned purchases. In any case, the ratios computed in Table 13 give an indication of provincial efforts to extract grain from the countryside.[102]

expansion data. In Hunan, however, the increase in January claims over August targets in improved irrigation was only 75 per cent. On this index Hunan would rank low in contrast to its position in Table 12.

[102] I am indebted to David L. Denny both for suggesting this measure of activism and for allowing me the use of his grain file to derive the ratios. Each ratio is based on references in the local press for 1956 *cheng kou* figures and in *JMJP*, November 19, 1958, for 1958 *shou kou* figures. I alone am responsible for the accuracy of the ratios given.

Another indication of provincial activism in this period was the response to the late August, 1958, decision to build communes on a universal basis. By the end of September, all but three provinces had organized over 90 per cent of peasant households into communes, and fifteen provinces claimed 100 per cent. A better measure of provincial variation is the size of the average commune as measured by the number of peasant households. The initial Party resolution on communes left each province responsible for setting its own standard of size.[103] In view of Mao's dictum that the commune is "distinguished by two main characteristics: its *bigger size* and more socialist nature," the provincial response is especially significant.[104] Provincial achievements by the end of September, 1958, together with related data, are summarized in Table 14.

As one would expect, the variations in commune size are highly correlated ($+.76$, $N=25$) to population density.[105] It is also noteworthy that the three provinces which lagged in the percentage of peasant households in communes were all major minority areas. While a number of these areas claimed a 100 per cent record, it appears that the presence of large numbers of minority people complicated the task of organizing communes. Last, the data show considerable variation in the readjustment of communes from September, 1958, to December, 1959. The possible significance of this is examined below.

*Correlations.* The data on the agricultural cooperativization movement supports the assumption that the availability of organizational resources substantially aids campaign implementation. On the eve of the high tide in mid-1955, a high correlation ($+.67$, $N=24$) existed between Party membership ratios and the percentage of peasant households in APCs. By mid-1956, the correlation was lower, but it still was significant ($+46$, $N=24$). The decrease illuminates an aspect of activism during the APC drive. The provinces that made the greatest relative advances from 1955 to 1956 ranked middle to low in Party membership ratios;[106] their performances outstripped the organiza-

---

[103] NCNA, September 9, 1958, in *SCMP*, No. 1853 (September 15, 1958).

[104] For an excellent discussion of the pressures to build large communes, see G. William Skinner, "Marketing and Social Structure in Rural China," Part III, *Journal of Asian Studies*, XXIV (May, 1965), 388–94.

[105] Skinner's hypothesis of a relationship between modernization and commune size is not borne out by my data. There is no significant correlation between either urbanization in 1958 or industrial output per capita in 1957, and the size of communes. See *ibid.*, p. 393.

[106] The converse is not true. The provinces with the sharpest drop in relative position from 1955 to 1956 did not necessarily rank high in Party membership ratios.

## TABLE 14

### IMPLEMENTATION OF COMMUNALIZATION BY PROVINCE*

| Rank by Number of Households Per Commune, September, 1958 | Province | Number of Peasant Households Per Commune, September, 1958 | Percentage of Peasant Households in Communes, September, 1958 | Number of Communes, September, 1958 | Number of Communes, December, 1959 | Percentage of Change in Number of Communes, 1958–59 | Population Density, 1958† |
|---|---|---|---|---|---|---|---|
| 1 | Kwangtung | 9,845 | 100.0 | 803 | 1,134 | 41.2 | 165 |
| 2 | Hopeh ‡ | 8,836 | 100.0 | 951 | 927 | — 2.5 | 223 |
| 3 | Hupeh | 8,286 | 96.1 | 729 | 687 | — 5.8 | 166 |
| 4 | Honan | 7,994 | 100.0 | 1,285 | 1,210 | — 5.8 | 295 |
| 5 | Liaoning | 7,627 | 100.0 | 428 | 472 | 10.3 | 162 |
| 6 | Chekiang | 7,487 | 100.0 | 761 | 638 | — 16.2 | 251 |
| 7 | Shantung | 7,182 | 100.0 | 1,580 | 1,382 | — 12.5 | 356 |
| 8 | Anhwei | 6,849 | 100.0 | 1,054 | 1,048 | .6 | 242 |
| 9 | Hunan | 6,365 | 100.0 | 1,284 | 1,134 | — 11.7 | 174 |
| 10 | Kiangsu | 6,126 | 99.4 | 1,490 | 1,558 | 4.6 | 447 |
| 11 | Kwangsi | 5,155 | 100.0 | 784 | 1,054 | 34.4 | 89 |
| 12 | Fukien | 4,297 | 95.1 | 622 | 579 | — 6.9 | 120 |
| 13 | Yunnan | 4,135 | 31.0 | 275 | 1,284 | 366.9 | 44 |
| 14 | Kirin | 3,980 | 100.0 | 481 | 494 | 2.7 | 68 |
| 15 | Ninghsia | 3,808 | 67.3 | 53 | 120 | 126.4 | 27 |
| 16 | Shansi | 3,573 | 100.0 | 975 | 942 | — 3.4 | 103 |
| 17 | Kiangsi | 3,000 | 92.0 | 1,240 | 1,276 | 2.9 | 114 |
| 18 | Szechwan | 2,833 | 99.1 | 4,827 | 5,427 | 12.4 | 128 |
| 19 | Heilungkiang | 2,710 | 100.0 | 718 | 661 | — 7.9 | 33 |
| 20 | Kansu | 2,527 | 100.0 | 794 | 565 | — 28.8 | 35 |
| 21 | Tsinghai | 2,456 | 100.6 | 144 | 207 | 43.8 | 3 |
| 22 | Shensi | 1,932 | 100.0 | 1,673 | 681 | — 59.3 | 94 |
| 23 | Inner Mongolia | 1,922 | 98.6 | 812 | 733 | — 9.7 | 8 |
| 24 | Sinkiang | 1,607 | 59.3 | 389 | 452 | 16.2 | 3 |
| 25 | Kweichow | 1,413 | 94.5 | 2,194 | 537 | — 75.5 | 98 |
| | China § | 4,614 | 98.2 | 26,425 | 25,450 | — 3.3 | 98 |

* Sources: State Statistical Bureau, *T'ung-chi Kung-tso* (Statistical Work) (Peking: Chi-hua t'ung-chi tsa-chih she), No. 20, 1958, p. 23; *Handbook of Administrative Divisions of the People's Republic of China*, in *JPRS*, No. 10342 (October 11, 1961), pp. d–f; Chen (ed.), *Chinese Economic Statistics*, p. 123; Appendix A.

† Population per square kilometer.

tional resources available to them. However, the general pattern in 1956 was a positive relationship between accomplishments and organizational resources. In contrast, during the Great Leap period neither achievements claimed during the water conservancy campaign, nor grain purchase targets, nor the size of communes had a significant correlation to Party membership ratios. Thus, one feature of the unprecedented mass mobilization of 1957–58 was disregard for the tested practice of relating work tasks to the availability of reliable personnel.

Searching the data on campaign implementation for political implications reveals no positive relationships. There is, however, evidence that outstanding displays of political activism do not in the long run benefit the careers of provincial leaders and, in fact, may be detrimental. It is suggestive that of the four provinces that substantially improved their relative positions during the high tide of agricultural cooperativization, three (Kwangsi, Tsinghai, and Honan) were classified "limited continuity" or "unstable" in terms of personnel. Moreover, there is a significant negative correlation ($-.53$, $N=12$) between claims for expanded irrigation area and personnel stability.[107] Similarly, the correlation between the ratio of 1958 grain purchase targets to 1956 procurements and stability is also negative ($-.40$, $N=17$), although it is slightly below the critical value of significance.[108] While no relationship exists between the size of communes and stability, a suggestive correlation ($-.49$, $N=22$) was discovered between stability and the absolute change in number of communes from September, 1958, to December, 1959.[109] That is, provinces that made the fewest administrative changes were more stable in terms of personnel than provinces that made the most changes by either enlarging or reducing commune size.

All of the above data point in the same direction. Whatever the benefits of displaying "skyrocketing zeal" during mass movements, they are temporary. A Wu Chih-p'u may have his moment of glory, but he will most likely pay the price later. A more appropriate strategy for political survival is a steady and lasting performance, for example, communes which, once established, are sufficiently related to actual

---

[107] The problem of Hunan (see note 101) complicates this correlation. If Hunan is excluded from the correlation, the coefficient is still negative ($-.22$, $N=11$), but it is below the critical value of .53.

[108] For $N=17$, .41.

[109] For this correlation Ninghsia, Sinkiang, and Yunnan were excluded because of the small percentage of peasant households organized in September, 1958.

conditions so that they require a minimum of readjustment. While success in provincial politics demands responsiveness to the visions and goals of the center, it also requires respect for the concrete realities of the local scene.

## CENTRAL-PROVINCIAL RELATIONS

Throughout this study a recurring focus has been central-provincial relations. This relationship is greatly affected by the degree of a province's dependence on the center, that is, whether it is over-all a donor or a recipient of revenue, raw materials, and food. Several questions arise. Does dependence result in high responsiveness to Peking's policies? Are surplus areas more able to maintain a measure of autonomy, or does recurrent tension over the extraction of surpluses (see p. 127) prove detrimental to provincial leaders?

*Grain Imports and Exports.* A key index of central-provincial relations is whether a province is an importer or an exporter of grain. Does a province depend on central allocations for critical amounts of this staple, or does it regularly send grain to other areas at the behest of Peking? Nearly every province must both import and export grain each year to take account of crop and seasonal variations and of marketing patterns. The net balance is decisive. Although data are scattered, enough exist to classify twenty-four provinces into four grain categories: I—consistent substantial exporter; II—normal exporter except in particularly bad years; III—exporter or importer depending on harvest conditions; and IV—consistent substantial importer.

To elaborate, Group I exports on the average 7 to more than 20 per cent of its grain output, and maintains a comfortable surplus in every year for which data exist. Group IV averages grain imports in excess of 20 per cent of total provincial output. It is more difficult to distinguish Categories II and III, however. If a province generally exports grain but in a single year shows a minimal surplus or a deficit, it is placed in Category II. But if a province seems to be a deficit area in more than one year, it is placed in Category III. The data for provinces in these two categories vary considerably, and some classifications are markedly firmer than others.[110] Admittedly, most of the data are from the first five-year plan period. This poses severe prob-

---

110 In the absence of data on imports and exports, a number of other criteria were used: descriptive statements of grain conditions, per capita grain output figures (see Appendix E), and the net balance of grain in a province as determined by the difference between total procurements (*cheng kou*) and total retail sales (*t'ung hsiao*).

lems, since China changed from a net exporter in the 1950's to a net importer in the 1960's. But whatever changes this caused in inter-provincial grain flows, it is unlikely that major export areas ran grain deficits, and it is certainly unlikely that perennial importers changed their position. The province classifications are given in Table 15.[111]

A striking relationship between grain exports and personnel stability emerges from Table 15.[112] All substantial exporters are "highly stable"

TABLE 15

PROVINCES AS IMPORTERS AND EXPORTERS OF GRAIN *

| Grain Category | Province | Stability Category | Cultural Revolution Period |
|---|---|---|---|
| I | Heilungkiang | I | II |
| I | Inner Mongolia | I | V |
| I | Kiangsi | I | V |
| I | Kirin | I | V |
| I | Szechwan | I | VI |
| II | Chekiang | II | VI |
| II | Fukien | I | VII |
| II | Hunan | III | VI |
| II | Hupeh | I | V |
| II | Kansu | IV | V |
| II | Kiangsu | I | VI |
| II | Kwangtung | II | V |
| II | Kweichow | III | II |
| II | Shensi | II | VI |
| II | Sinkiang | II | VII |
| III | Anhwei | III | VI |
| III | Honan | III | V |
| III | Kwangsi | III | VII |
| III | Shansi | I | II |
| III | Shantung | IV | II |
| III | Tsinghai | IV | IV |
| III | Yunnan | III | VII |
| IV | Hopeh | II | V |
| IV | Liaoning | III | VI |

* Source: See note 111; and Tables 3 and 4.

provincials. Moreover, by applying the Kendall correlation coefficient to a case of "tied ranks," I have found a significant positive correla-tion ($+.43$, N$=24$) between grain export areas and personnel stabil-

[111] I have made these classifications on the basis of extensive references from the local press in the grain file of David L. Denny. I alone am responsible for the categories adopted.

[112] No significant relationship exists between grain exports and the establishment of revolutionary committees, however. The data do not confirm Oksenberg's suggestion (*The Cultural Revolution*, p. 7) of a link between the early establishment of revolutionary committees and grain deficits, since Heilungkiang and Kweichow are grain surplus areas.

ity.[113] This correlation may also help explain exceptions to the positive relationship of stability and modernization. "Highly stable" Kiangsi and Szechwan, although they rank middle to low in urbanization and industrialization, are both substantial exporters of grain; while highly industrial Liaoning, which has "limited continuity" of personnel, is a consistent importer of grain. Conversely, exceptions to the relationship between grain category and stability might be explained by modernization. The only "highly stable" province not falling under grain categories I or II is Shansi, the fifth ranking urban province in 1958. Moreover, "basically stable" Hopeh, although it is a consistent grain importer, ranked fourth in urbanization. Thus, both modernization and grain exports are potent factors which explain exceptions as well as patterns of personnel stability.

What are the ramifications of the relationship between grain exports and stability? Although it could be argued that the personnel stability of grain exporting provinces reflects relative political independence born of an abundance of natural resources, I do not believe that Peking in the pre-Cultural Revolution period would have tolerated a significant degree of provincial autonomy. The evidence analyzed in the third section of this paper strongly suggests a preoccupation with central primacy. My interpretation stresses the advantages grain surpluses give provincial leaders in intra-provincial politics and in meeting central tasks. Officials in surplus areas have a margin of safety in dealing with the requirements of peasant livelihood. For example, although grain output actually declined in Heilungkiang from 1952 to 1957, the high per capita output guaranteed both relatively high peasant consumption and substantial exports. Even a poor agricultural performance was sufficient to meet both central demands and provincial needs. In contrast, leaders in grain deficit provinces faced greater peasant demands and made more frequent calls for central assistance. Unable to meet local needs, these leaders, who were a repeated source of irritation to Peking, were less able to survive the pressures of provincial politics.

---

[113] The Kendall coefficient is used because it is more accurate in cases of tied ranks than the Spearman coefficient. The Kendall coefficient is always lower than Spearman's when it is applied to the same data. The Spearman coefficient for grain exports and stability is also significant ($+.58$, $N=24$). For a discussion of the Kendall coefficient, see Siegel, *Nonparametric Statistics,* pp. 213–23.

SUMMARY AND CONCLUSIONS

The behavioral relationships suggested by the quantifiable data analyzed above are summarized as follows: (1) There appears to be a negative relationship between personnel stability in the 1956–66 period and the establishment of "Maoist" oriented revolutionary committees in 1967–68; (2) national defense areas were significantly insulated from the priorities of the Cultural Revolution; (3) national defense areas tended to be stable in personnel during the pre-Cultural Revolution decade; (4) there is an apparent relationship between large minority populations and personnel instability when national defense considerations are discounted; (5) a positive correlation exists between modernization and stability; (6) there is a positive relationship between per capita grain output and stability; (7) both Party membership ratios and numbers of demobilized servicemen are greatest in areas of pre-1949 revolutionary activity; (8) density of Party membership and ex-servicemen is positively correlated to urbanization; (9) Party membership was positively related to implementation of the cooperativization movement, but no relationship was found during the Great Leap period; (10) density of Party membership and demobilized soldiers may be positively correlated to the early establishment of revolutionary committees; (11) instances of high activism during mass movements do not promote personnel stability and may have the opposite effect; and (12) a positive correlation exists between grain exports and stability.

The strongest explanatory variables in terms of personnel stability are military priorities, modernization, and grain exports. All "high stability" provinces are either national defense areas or Category I grain areas or rank in the top quarter of provinces in urbanization, with the exception of Hupeh which ranks tenth in urbanization and which is a Category II grain province. Conversely, the six least stable provinces do not meet any of these criteria. Last, of the three provinces in the "limited continuity" of personnel category which meet one of these requirements, Liaoning is a substantial grain importer, while both Kwangsi and Yunnan are Category III grain areas and rank low in urbanization.

In sum, while the rules of the game stressing provincial responsiveness to the center are clear, local conditions impinge significantly on how well provincial leaders can abide by those rules. The game is easiest to play under certain conditions—where overriding military priorities insulate provincial authorities from other demands, where central authorities concerned with industrial development display favoritism in the allocation of resources, and where key agricultural surpluses exist. Moreover, where conditions are less favorable and where officials seek prominence by conspicuous displays of activism which fail to take account of actual local conditions, short-run gains are followed by the inevitable reckoning. Underlying the continuities and diversities of provincial politics is a phenomenon not unknown in other societies: the haves prosper, the have nots struggle as best they can. For Mao Tse-tung, a man romantically identified with the have nots, the Cultural Revolution may have been the only way out of this dilemma.

# APPENDIX A

## TABLE 16
### POPULATION BY PROVINCE, 1952–59 *

| Province † | 1952 | 1953 | 1954 | 1955 | 1956 | 1957 | 1958 | 1959 |
|---|---|---|---|---|---|---|---|---|
| Anhwei | 30,053 | 30,663 | 31,285 | 31,920 | 32,568 | 33,229 | 33,904 | 34,592 |
| Chekiang | 22,361 | 22,866 | 23,383 | 23,911 | 24,451 | 25,004 | 25,569 | 26,147 |
| Fukien | 12,830 | 13,143 | 13,464 | 13,793 | 14,130 | 14,475 | 14,828 | 15,190 |
| Heilungkiang | 11,323 | 11,897 | 12,500 | 13,134 | 13,800 | 14,500 | 15,235 | 16,007 |
| Honan | 43,280 | 44,215 | 45,170 | 46,146 | 47,143 | 48,161 | 49,201 | 50,264 |
| Hopeh | 39,688 | 40,580 | 41,482 | 42,394 | 43,315 | 44,243 | 45,177 | 46,116 |
| Hunan | 32,595 | 33,227 | 33,872 | 34,529 | 35,199 | 35,882 | 36,578 | 37,288 |
| Hupeh | 27,165 | 27,790 | 28,429 | 29,083 | 29,752 | 30,436 | 31,136 | 31,852 |
| Inner Mongolia | 6,979 | 7,338 | 7,716 | 8,113 | 8,531 | 8,970 | 9,432 | 9,918 |
| Kansu | 10,918 | 11,239 | 11,569 | 11,909 | 12,259 | 12,619 | 12,990 | 13,372 |
| Kiangsi | 16,389 | 16,773 | 17,165 | 17,567 | 17,978 | 18,399 | 18,830 | 19,271 |
| Kiangsu | 40,036 | 40,933 | 41,850 | 42,787 | 43,746 | 44,726 | 45,728 | 46,752 |
| Kirin | 11,028 | 11,290 | 11,559 | 11,834 | 12,116 | 12,404 | 12,699 | 13,001 |
| Kwangsi | 17,214 | 17,591 | 17,976 | 18,370 | 18,772 | 19,183 | 19,603 | 20,032 |
| Kwangtung | 36,474 | 36,740 | 37,008 | 37,278 | 37,550 | 37,824 | 38,100 | 38,378 |
| Kweichow | 14,653 | 15,037 | 15,431 | 15,835 | 16,250 | 16,676 | 17,113 | 17,561 |
| Liaoning | 19,855 | 20,566 | 21,302 | 22,065 | 22,855 | 23,673 | 24,520 | 25,398 |
| Ninghsia | 1,663 | 1,689 | 1,715 | 1,742 | 1,769 | 1,796 | 1,824 | 1,852 |
| Shansi | 13,972 | 14,314 | 14,665 | 15,024 | 15,392 | 15,769 | 16,155 | 16,551 |
| Shantung | 47,801 | 48,877 | 49,977 | 51,101 | 52,251 | 53,427 | 54,629 | 55,858 |
| Shensi | 15,420 | 15,881 | 16,356 | 16,845 | 17,349 | 17,868 | 18,402 | 18,952 |
| Sinkiang | 4,718 | 4,874 | 5,035 | 5,201 | 5,373 | 5,550 | 5,733 | 5,922 |
| Szechwan | 64,328 | 65,685 | 67,071 | 68,486 | 69,931 | 71,407 | 72,914 | 74,452 |
| Tibet | 1,275 | 1,274 | 1,273 | 1,272 | 1,271 | 1,270 | 1,269 | 1,268 |
| Tsinghai | 1,603 | 1,676 | 1,753 | 1,833 | 1,917 | 2,005 | 2,097 | 2,193 |
| Yunnan | 17,130 | 17,473 | 17,822 | 18,178 | 18,542 | 18,913 | 19,291 | 19,677 |

* Sources: *Ti-li Chih-shih* (Geographical Knowledge), No. 9, 1957, pp. 390–91; State Statistical Bureau, *Ten Great Years* (Peking: Foreign Languages Press, 1960), p. 11; Robert Michael Field, "A Note on the Population of Communist China," *CQ*, No. 38 (April–June, 1969), pp. 162–63. Unit: thousands of people.

† All figures are mid-year. Figures for Hopeh, Kansu, and Ninghsia are according to administrative divisions as of the end of 1958; all others are according to administrative divisions as of the end of 1957. With the exception of Kansu and Ninghsia, all figures are extrapolated from official mid-1953 and end-1957 data. Since the 1953 data subsume Ninghsia under Kansu and the 1957 data treat Ninghsia separately, official end-1954 data for Kansu and Ninghsia are used in combination with the 1953 and 1957 data to estimate figures for those provinces. Although there are inconsistencies in the three sets of data, the above figures are reasonable approximations.

# APPENDIX B

## TABLE 17
### Total Value of Provincial Industrial Output*

| Province | 1952 | 1953 | 1954 | Rank | 1955 | 1956 | 1957 | Rank | 1958 | Rank | 1959 |
|---|---|---|---|---|---|---|---|---|---|---|---|
| Anhwei | 631 | | (782) | 10 | (911) | 1,158 | 1,501 | 8 | 4,000 | 8 | |
| Chekiang | (1,137) | (1,501) | (1,613) | 5 | | 2,000 | 2,274 | 6 | | | |
| Fukien | | | (728) | 11 | | | | | 1,330 | 10 | |
| Heilungkiang † | (1,891) | | 2,461 | 3 | | | 3,930 | 4 | 6,840 | 4 | |
| Honan | | | 1,227 | 7 | | | (1,560) | 7 | 4,330 | 7 | |
| Hopeh ‡ | | | (1,673) | 4 | | | | | | | |
| Hunan § | (444) | | | | | | 1,258 | 9 | | | |
| Hupeh | | | | | | | | | | | |
| Inner Mongolia | 160 | 243 | 358 | 13 | 421 | 570 | 631 | 11 | 1,157 | 13 | |
| Kansu ‖ | | | (302) | 15 | | | | | | | |
| Kiangsi # | | | | | | | (1,171) | 10 | 1,880 | 9 | |
| Kiangsu ** | | | | | | | (4,124) | 3 | 7,540 | 2 | |
| Kirin | | | (1,494) | 6 | | | | | | | (4,270) |
| Kwangsi | | | | | | | | | 1,238 | 11 | |

| | | | | | | | | |
|---|---|---|---|---|---|---|---|---|
| **Kwangtung** | | (336) | | | (3,571) | 5 | (5,800) | 6 |
| **Kweichow ††** | | | 14 | | (562) | 12 | 1,180 | 12 |
| **Liaoning ‡‡** | | (7,459) | 1 | | (17,442) | 1 | (26,303) | 1 |
| **Shansi** | | (926) | 8 | | | | | |
| **Shantung** | | | | 1,341 | 1,634 | | | 7,000 | 3 |
| **Shensi** | | (785) | 9 | | | | | |
| **Sinkiang** | 169 | | | | 446 | 13 | 740 | 14 |
| **Szechwan** | | (2,659) | 2 | | (4,283) | 2 | 6,668 | 5 |
| **Tsinghai** | 32 | | | | 104 | 14 | 399 | 15 |
| **Yunnan** | | 630 | 12 | | | | | |
| **Number of Provinces Ranked** | | | 15 | | | 14 | | 15 |

\* Principal Source: Chen (ed.), *Chinese Economic Statistics*, pp. 214–16. Figures in parentheses are calculated from other data. Unit: million *yuan*.

† 1952 and 1957: *Hei-lung-chiang Jih-pao*, September 19, 1958, in *JPRS*, No. 1518-N (April 28, 1959).

‡ Excluding Tientsin.

§ 1952 and 1957: derived from *Economic Geography of Central China*, p. 230.

‖ Including Ninghsia.

# 1957 and 1958: *Chiang-hsi Jih-pao*, July 1, 1959, in SCMP, No. 2110 (October 6, 1959).

** 1957: derived from *HHPYK*, No. 7, 1959, in *ECMM*, No. 170 (June 1, 1959).

†† 1957 and 1958: *Kuei-chou Jih-pao*, September 30, 1959, in *SCMP*, No. 2143 (November 25, 1959).

‡‡ 1957 and 1958: derived from *Economic Geography of Northeast China*, p. 85, and Chen (ed.), *Chinese Economic Statistics*, p. 365.

# APPENDIX C

## TABLE 18
### Per Capita Value of Provincial Industrial Output *

| Provinces | 1952 | 1953 | 1954 | Rank | 1955 | 1956 | 1957 | Rank | 1958 | Rank | 1959 |
|---|---|---|---|---|---|---|---|---|---|---|---|
| Anhwei | 21 | | 25 | 13 | 29 | 36 | 45 | 11 | 118 | 9 | |
| Chekiang | 51 | 66 | 69 | 4 | | 82 | 91 | 5 | | | |
| Fukien | | | 54 | 6 | | | | | 90 | 12 | |
| Heilungkiang | 167 | | 197 | 2 | | | 271 | 2 | 449 | 2 | |
| Honan | | | 27 | 12 | | | 32 | 14 | 88 | 13 | |
| Hopeh † | | | 43 | 9 | | | | | | | |
| Hunan | 14 | | | | | | 35 | 12 | | | |
| Hupeh | | | | | | | | | | | |
| Inner Mongolia | 23 | 33 | 46 | 8 | 52 | 67 | 70 | 7 | 123 | 8 | |
| Kansu ‡ | | | 23 | 14 | | | | | | | |
| Kiangsi | | | | | | | 64 | 8 | 100 | 10 | |
| Kiangsu | | | | | | | 92 | 4 | 165 | 4 | |
| Kirin | | | 129 | 3 | | | | | | | 328 |
| Kwangsi | | | | | | | | | 63 | 15 | |
| Kwangtung | | | | | | | 94 | 3 | 152 | 5 | |
| Kweichow | | | 22 | 15 | | | 34 | 13 | 69 | 14 | |
| Liaoning | | | 350 | 1 | | | 737 | 1 | 1073 | 1 | |
| Shansi | | | 63 | 5 | | | | | | | |
| Shantung | | | | | 26 | 31 | | | 128 | 7 | |
| Shensi | | | 48 | 7 | | | | | | | |
| Sinkiang | 36 | | | | | | 80 | 6 | 129 | 6 | |
| Szechwan | | | 40 | 10 | | | 60 | 9 | 91 | 11 | |
| Tsinghai | 20 | | | | | | 52 | 10 | 190 | 3 | |
| Yunnan | | | 35 | 11 | | | | | | | |
| Number of Provinces Ranked | | | | 15 | | | | 14 | | 15 | |

\* Source: Derived from Appendixes A and B. Unit: *yuan*.
† Excluding Tientsin.
‡ Including Ninghsia.

# APPENDIX D

## TABLE 19
### PROVINCIAL GRAIN OUTPUT *

| Province | 1952 | Rank | 1953 | Rank | 1954 | Rank | 1955 | Rank | 1956 | Rank | 1957 | Rank | 1958 | Rank | 1959 |
|---|---|---|---|---|---|---|---|---|---|---|---|---|---|---|---|
| China † | 3,088 | | 3,138 | | 3,209 | | 3,496 | | 3,650 | | 3,700 | | 5,000 | | |
| Anhwei ‡ | 167 | 8 | 145 | 9 | 155 | 7 | 230.58 | 5 | 218 | 6 | 229.5 | 6 | 320 | 4 | |
| Chekiang | 140.8 | 10 | 143 | 10 | 137 | 9 | 151.8 | 10 | 153 | 10 | 156 | 10 | 203 | 9 | |
| Fukien | 73.26 | 18 | 76.7 | 19 | | | 76.8 | 20 | 87.4 | 20 | 87.54 | 18 | 108 | 17 | |
| Heilungkiang | 129 | 11 | 114 | 12 | 111 | 13 | 133 | 11 | 125 | 13 | 123 | 13 | 177 | 10 | |
| Honan | 184.3 | 6 | 199.1 | 4 | 217.4 | 5 | 233.8 | 4 | 238.8 | 5 | 245 | 3 | | | |
| Hopeh § | 181.7 | 7 | 153.2 | 8 | 150.2 | 8 | 172 | 9 | 155.6 | 9 | 195 | 9 | 240 | 7 | |
| Hunan ‖ | 204.96 | 3 | 206 | 3 | 185 | 6 | 224 | 6 | 206 | 8 | 225 | 7 | 450 | 3 | |
| Hupeh # | 164 | 9 | 181.3 | 7 | 136 | 10 | 188 | 8 | 210 | 7 | 219.3 | 8 | 244 | 6 | |
| Inner Mongolia | 65.9 | 20 | 67.6 | 21 | 73.9 | 20 | 61.9 | 22 | 87.5 | 19 | 56.2 | 22 | 96 | 18 | |
| Kansu ** | 53.58 | 21 | 60 | 22 | 75.8 | 19 | 78.5 | 19 | 108.6 | 15 | 85 | 20 | 120 | 15 | |
| Kiangsi †† | 115 | 12 | 115 | 11 | 115 | 12 | 123 | 12 | 130 | 12 | 136.6 | 11 | 240 | 7 | |
| Kiangsu ‡‡ | 202.4 | 4 | 235 | 2 | 230 | 3 | 257.4 | 2 | 240 | 2 | 235.6 | 5 | 460 | 2 | |
| Kirin §§ | | | 82.8 | 18 | 77.2 | 18 | 88.5 | 17 | 70 | 17 | 85.5 | 19 | | | |
| Kwangsi ‖‖ | 101 | 13 | 109 | 13 | 118 | 11 | 118 | 13 | 105 | 13 | 107.5 | 15 | 142 | 13 | |

TABLE 19 (*Continued*)
PROVINCIAL GRAIN OUTPUT

| Province | 1952 | Rank | 1953 | Rank | 1954 | Rank | 1955 | Rank | 1956 | Rank | 1957 | Rank | 1958 | Rank | 1959 |
|---|---|---|---|---|---|---|---|---|---|---|---|---|---|---|---|
| Kwangtung | 189 | 5 | 194 | 5 | 220 | 4 | 218 | 7 | 240 | 3 | 244 | 3 | 320 | 4 | 350 |
| Kweichow | 67.9 | 19 | 74 | 20 | 80.3 | 17 | 86 | 18 | 95 | 18 | 105 | 18 | 150 | 12 | |
| Liaoning ## | 98.1 | 14 | 100.1 | 14 | 106.3 | 14 | 112.2 | 14 | 133.2 | 11 | 118.7 | 11 | 150.3 | 11 | |
| Shansi *** | 76 | 17 | 86.4 | 17 | | | 74.5 | 21 | 86.7 | 21 | 71.3 | 21 | 110 | 16 | |
| Shantung | 219 | 2 | 193 | 6 | 231 | 2 | 240 | 3 | 256 | 2 | 259 | 2 | | 2 | |
| Shensi | 79.5 | 16 | 94.8 | 15 | 100.9 | 15 | 90.1 | 15 | 108.6 | 15 | 90 | 15 | 142 | 13 | |
| Sinkiang ††† | 32.1 | 22 | 34.4 | 22 | 36.39 | 23 | 38.25 | 23 | 38.68 | 23 | 40.68 | 23 | 60 | 19 | |
| Szechwan ‡‡‡ | 337.5 | 1 | 366.3 | 1 | 390.5 | 1 | 404.6 | 1 | 445.1 | 1 | 459.6 | 1 | 650 | 1 | |
| Tsinghai §§§ | 7.43 | 23 | 6.62 | 24 | 10.49 | 24 | 11.78 | 24 | 12.2 | 24 | 12.8 | 24 | 22.0 | 20 | |
| Yunnan \|\|\| | 83 | 15 | 88 | 16 | 98 | 16 | 104 | 16 | 125 | 13 | 125 | 13 | | 12 | |
| Number of Provinces Ranked | 83 | 23 | | 24 | | 22 | | 24 | | 24 | | 24 | | 20 | |

\* Principal source: *Provincial Agricultural Statistics for Communist China* (Ithaca, N.Y.: Committee on the Economy of China, 1969). Unit: one hundred million catties (one catty = 1.1 pounds).

† *Ten Great Years*, p. 119.

‡ 1955 and 1956: *An-hui Jih-pao*, September 28, 1957, in *SCMP*, No. 1677 (December 23, 1957); 1957: *Economic Geography of the East China Region*, p. 141.

§ Excluding Tientsin, 1952–57; including Tientsin, 1958.

\|\| 1953 and 1954: *Hsin Hu-nan Pao*, August 7, 1957; 1957: *Economic Geography of Central China*, p. 230.

## 1953 and 1954: *Chang-chiang Jih-pao*, July 14, 1957; 1957: derived from *ibid*, CKCNP, September 9, 1957, and *Hu-pei Jih-pao*, September 27, 1957.

** Including Ninghsia. 1952 and 1957: *Kan-su Jih-pao*, August 16, 1958, in *CB*, No. 528, October 28, 1958.

†† 1958: *Chiang-hsi Jih-pao*, July 1, 1959, in *SCMP*, No. 2110 (October 6, 1959).

‡‡ 1957: *Economic Geography of the East China Region*, p. 57.

§§ 1953–56: derived from *Provincial Agricultural Statistics*, p. 124, and *Chi-lin Jih-pao*, December 2, 1956 and August 21, 1957.

|||| 1952–55: *Kuang-hsi Jih-pao*, November 13, 1957.

## 1958: *Economic Geography of Northeast China*, p. 90.

*** 1952: *HHPYK*, No. 16, 1957, p. 74; 1953 and 1956; *Shan-hsi Jih-pao*, August 11, 1957.

††† 1957: *Hsin-chiang Jih-pao*, January 30, 1959, in *JPRS*, No. 1804-N (July 24, 1959).

‡‡‡ 1952–56: *Hsüeh-hsi* (Study), No. 17 (1957), p. 25.

§§§ 1952: *Ch'ing-hai Jih-pao*, July 4, 1957, in *SCMP*, No. 1864 (September 30, 1958).

|||||| 1952–56: *Chi-hua Ching-chi* (Planned Economy), No. 3 (1957), pp. 2–3 (cited in Chen [ed.], *Chinese Economic Statistics*, p. 363).

# APPENDIX E

## TABLE 20
### PROVINCIAL GRAIN OUTPUT PER CAPITA*

| Province | 1952 | Rank | 1953 | Rank | 1954 | Rank | 1955 | Rank | 1956 | Rank | 1957 | Rank | 1958 | Rank | 1959 |
|---|---|---|---|---|---|---|---|---|---|---|---|---|---|---|---|
| Anhwei | 556 | 10 | 473 | 19 | 495 | 18 | 722 | 5 | 669 | 8 | 691 | 5 | 944 | 8 | |
| Chekiang | 630 | 5 | 625 | 7 | 586 | 10 | 635 | 11 | 626 | 12 | 624 | 14 | 794 | 13 | |
| Fukien | 571 | 9 | 584 | 12 | | | 557 | 17 | 619 | 14 | 605 | 15 | 728 | 16 | |
| Heilungkiang | 1139 | 1 | 958 | 1 | 888 | 2 | 1013 | 1 | 906 | 2 | 848 | 1 | 1162 | 3 | |
| Honan | 426 | 22 | 450 | 21 | 481 | 19 | 507 | 21 | 507 | 22 | 509 | 19 | | | |
| Hopeh † | 490 | 17 | 404 | 22 | 388 | 22 | 436 | 24 | 386 | 24 | 475 | 23 | 531 | 20 | |
| Hunan | 629 | 6 | 620 | 8 | 546 | 15 | 649 | 7 | 585 | 15 | 627 | 12 | 1230 | 2 | |
| Hupeh | 604 | 7 | 652 | 6 | 478 | 20 | 646 | 8 | 706 | 6 | 721 | 4 | 784 | 14 | |
| Inner Mongolia | 944 | 2 | 921 | 2 | 958 | 1 | 763 | 2 | 1026 | 1 | 627 | 12 | 1018 | 6 | |
| Kansu ‡ | 426 | 22 | 464 | 20 | 571 | 12 | 575 | 15 | 774 | 3 | 590 | 16 | 810 | 12 | |
| Kiangsi | 702 | 3 | 686 | 5 | 670 | 4 | 700 | 6 | 723 | 4 | 742 | 2 | 1275 | 1 | |
| Kiangsu | 506 | 15 | 574 | 13 | 550 | 13 | 602 | 12 | 549 | 21 | 527 | 18 | 1006 | 7 | |

| Province | V1 | R1 | V2 | R2 | V3 | R3 | V4 | R4 | V5 | R5 | V6 | R6 | V7 | R7 | (8) |
|---|---|---|---|---|---|---|---|---|---|---|---|---|---|---|---|
| Kirin | 587 | 8 | 733 | 3 | 668 | 5 | 748 | 3 | 578 | 18 | 689 | 6 | 724 | 17 | 912 |
| Kwangsi | 518 | 13 | 620 | 8 | 656 | 6 | 642 | 10 | 559 | 20 | 560 | 17 | 840 | 11 | |
| Kwangtung | 463 | 20 | 528 | 15 | 594 | 9 | 585 | 14 | 639 | 9 | 645 | 8 | 877 | 10 | |
| Kweichow | 494 | 16 | 492 | 17 | 520 | 16 | 543 | 18 | 585 | 15 | 630 | 11 | 613 | 19 | |
| Liaoning | 544 | 11 | 487 | 18 | 499 | 17 | 508 | 20 | 583 | 17 | 501 | 21 | 681 | 18 | |
| Shansi | 458 | 21 | 604 | 10 | | | 496 | 22 | 563 | 19 | 452 | 24 | | | |
| Shantung | 516 | 14 | 395 | 23 | 462 | 21 | 470 | 23 | 490 | 23 | 485 | 22 | | | |
| Shensi | 680 | 4 | 597 | 11 | 617 | 7 | 535 | 19 | 626 | 12 | 504 | 20 | 772 | 15 | |
| Sinkiang | 525 | 12 | 706 | 4 | 723 | 3 | 735 | 4 | 720 | 5 | 733 | 3 | 1047 | 5 | |
| Szechwan | 464 | 19 | 558 | 14 | 582 | 11 | 591 | 13 | 636 | 10 | 644 | 9 | 891 | 9 | |
| Tsinghai | 485 | 18 | 395 | 23 | 598 | 8 | 643 | 9 | 636 | 10 | 638 | 10 | 1049 | 4 | |
| Yunnan | | | 504 | 16 | 550 | 13 | 572 | 16 | 674 | 7 | 661 | 7 | | | |
| Number of Provinces Ranked | | 23 | | 24 | | 24 | | 24 | | 24 | | 24 | | 24 | 20 |

* Source: derived from Appendixes A and D. Unit: catty.
† Excluding Tientsin, 1952–57; including Tientsin, 1958.
‡ Including Ninghsia.

## APPENDIX F

### TABLE 21
Annual Growth of Provincial Grain Output *

| Province | 1952-53 | Rank | 1953-54 | Rank | 1954-55 | Rank | 1955-56 | Rank | 1956-57 | Rank | 1957-58 | Rank |
|---|---|---|---|---|---|---|---|---|---|---|---|---|
| China | 1.6% | | 2.3% | | 8.9% | | 4.4% | | 1.4% | | 35.1% | |
| Anhwei | −13.2% | 21 | 6.9% | 10 | 48.8% | 1 | − 5.5% | 18 | 5.3% | 5 | 39.4% | 13 |
| Chekiang | 1.6% | 15 | − 4.2% | 19 | 10.8% | 9 | 0.8% | 17 | 2.0% | 13 | 30.1% | 16 |
| Fukien | 4.7% | 12 | | | | | 13.8% | 7 | 0.2% | 16 | 23.4% | 18 |
| Heilungkiang | −11.6% | 19 | − 2.6% | 18 | 19.8% | 4 | − 6.0% | 19 | − 1.6% | 18 | 43.9% | 9 |
| Honan | 8.0% | 8 | 9.2% | 7 | 7.5% | 10 | 2.1% | 15 | 2.6% | 11 | | |
| Hopeh † | −15.7% | 22 | − 2.0% | 16 | 14.5% | 6 | − 9.5% | 22 | 25.3% | 1 | 23.1% | 19 |
| Hunan | 0.5% | 16 | −10.2% | 21 | 21.1% | 3 | − 8.0% | 21 | 9.2% | 4 | 100.0% | 1 |
| Hupeh | 11.1% | 5 | −25.0% | 22 | 38.2% | 2 | 11.7% | 8 | 4.4% | 9 | 11.3% | 20 |
| Inner Mongolia | 2.6% | 14 | 9.3% | 6 | −16.2% | 22 | 41.4% | 1 | −35.8% | 24 | 70.8% | 5 |
| Kansu ‡ | 12.0% | 4 | 26.3% | 2 | 3.6% | 18 | 38.3% | 2 | −21.7% | 23 | 41.2% | 12 |
| Kiangsi | 0.0% | 17 | 0.0% | 15 | 7.0% | 12 | 5.7% | 13 | 5.1% | 7 | 75.7% | 3 |
| Kiangsu | 16.1% | 2 | − 2.1% | 17 | 11.9% | 8 | − 6.8% | 20 | − 1.8% | 19 | 95.3% | 2 |

| | % | Rank | % | Rank | % | Rank | % | Rank | % | Rank | % | Rank |
|---|---|---|---|---|---|---|---|---|---|---|---|---|
| Kirin | | | — 6.8% | 20 | 14.6% | 5 | —20.9% | 24 | 22.1% | 2 | | |
| Kwangsi | 7.9% | 9 | 8.3% | 9 | 0.0% | 19 | —11.0% | 23 | 2.4% | 12 | 32.1% | 14 |
| Kwangtung | 2.6% | 13 | 13.4% | 4 | — 0.9% | 20 | 10.1% | 10 | 1.7% | 14 | 31.2% | 15 |
| Kweichow | 9.0% | 6 | 8.5% | 8 | 7.1% | 11 | 10.5% | 9 | 10.5% | 3 | 42.9% | 10 |
| Liaoning | 2.0% | 14 | 6.2% | 13 | 5.6% | 14 | 18.7% | 5 | —10.9% | 20 | 26.6% | 17 |
| Shansi | 13.7% | 3 | | | | | 16.4% | 6 | —17.8% | 22 | 54.3% | 7 |
| Shantung | —11.9% | 20 | 19.7% | 3 | 3.9% | 16 | 6.7% | 12 | 1.2% | 15 | | |
| Shensi | 19.3% | 1 | 6.4% | 12 | —10.7% | 21 | 20.5% | 3 | —17.1% | 21 | 57.8% | 6 |
| Sinkiang | 7.2% | 10 | 5.8% | 14 | 5.1% | 15 | 1.1% | 16 | 5.2% | 6 | 47.5% | 8 |
| Szechwan | 8.5% | 7 | 6.6% | 11 | 3.6% | 17 | 10.0% | 11 | 3.3% | 10 | 41.4% | 11 |
| Tsinghai | —10.9% | 18 | 58.5% | 1 | 12.3% | 7 | 3.6% | 14 | 4.9% | 8 | 71.9% | 4 |
| Yunnan | 6.0% | 11 | 11.4% | 5 | 6.1% | 13 | 20.2% | 4 | 0.0% | 17 | | |
| Number of Provinces Ranked | | 23 | | 22 | | 22 | | 24 | | 24 | | 21 |

* Source: derived from Appendix D.
† 1957-58 growth rate involves comparison of 1957 data excluding Tientsin and 1958 data including Tientsin; all other rates derived from data excluding Tientsin.
‡ Including Ninghsia.

# PART III

*Strategies and Dilemmas of
Restructuring Chinese Society*

PETER SCHRAN

# Economic Management

> *Question:* What is the difference between the managerial triangle and
> the trigonometric triangle?
> *Answer:* The trigonometric triangle cannot have more than one obtuse
> angle.
>
> RADIO YEREVAN

## INTRODUCTION

The Constitution of the People's Republic of China states: "From the founding
of the People's Republic of China to the attainment of a socialist society is a
period of transition. During the transition the fundamental task of the state is,
step by step, to bring about the socialist industrialization of the country and, step
by step, to accomplish the socialist transformation of agriculture, handicrafts and
capitalist industry and commerce." It will take a fairly long time to complete this
fundamental task of the transition period—approximately fifteen years, or three
five-year plans, in addition to the three years of rehabilitation.[1]

The organizational problems which this task poses for the state are
extraordinary. As a policy instrument, the state is part of the economy.
As such it must draw on and must make do with the existing human
and natural resources, just as private business does or would do. This
necessity gives rise to a strategic problem or "contradiction" in all
backward economies that attempt to accelerate their development by
means of planning. But the problem is particularly grave in a backward economy that attempts to institute socialism prematurely by

---

[1] *First Five-Year Plan for Development of the National Economy of the People's
Republic of China in 1953–1957* (Peking: Foreign Languages Press, 1956), p. 21.

orthodox Marxist standards. Here backwardness means that relatively few persons are either politically red or technically expert and that almost no one possesses both attributes. The process of transition, therefore, cannot begin spontaneously but must be planned, directed, and controlled by those who are red with the help of those who are expert. Because their numbers are limited, however, the reds and the experts are not well able to perform such functions at the time when they need to be performed. The first strategic organizational task is the resolution of this contradiction. The "advanced experiences" of other economies may help to resolve it.

As a result of progress toward a solution, a new strategic problem or "contradiction" arises, which also appears to some degree in other developing economies under other forms of development planning. During the course of the transition to socialism, more and more persons are expected to become indoctrinated as well as trained. The process of transition, therefore, can proceed with increasing spontaneity, and it consequently need not be planned, directed, and controlled by a few persons. Indeed, progress toward the utopia requires that these functions be performed by many when they can be carried out quite well by a few.[2] The second organizational task is the resolution of this newly emerging contradiction. The experiences of other economies also may help—at least negatively—to resolve it.

The peculiarity of Maoism is that it deals with both contradictions almost simultaneously. Such an attempt conflicts with the Soviet approach, which assigns the first task to the beginning and leaves the second task for the end of the process of transition to socialism. As a consequence, Maoism arrives at solutions to organizational problems which differ from the Soviet prototype and which appear to be "antiscientific" and "voluntaristic" in the Soviet view.[3] Correspondingly, Maoism refers to the Soviet approach and its organizational solutions as "revisionist" or "taking the capitalist road," to name but two of the choice epithets in each instance.

The following pages deal with the organization of economic activities in China in this perspective. Because the principal facts have been

[2] This implication conflicts with the view which is common in the West that organizational reforms in Soviet-type economies are being introduced because the system of centralized administration has become unworkable. Similar attempts to "democratize" the management of the economy appear to be made increasingly in Yugoslavia.

[3] For the recent expression of such a criticism see V. Vyatsky and G. Dmitriev, "The Anti-Scientific, Voluntaristic Character of Mao Tse-tung's Economic Policy," *Voprosy Ekonomiki* (Economic Problems), No. 11 (1968), as translated in *Reprints from the Soviet Press*, VIII, No. 4 (1969), 3–25.

discussed repeatedly by Western students of Chinese affairs, I find it both convenient and justifiable to refer mainly to these secondary sources.

## INITIAL CONDITIONS

At the time of the founding of the People's Republic of China, the Chinese mainland appears to have been inhabited by close to 540 million persons [4] who probably resided in about 120 million households.[5] Of this total, approximately one hundred million units were peasant households which engaged primarily in agricultural production, largely for their own consumption.[6] Some members of peasant households and most of the economically active nonpeasant population were occupied in a large number of predominantly small enterprises in various branches of the economy. In particular, there were more than four million commercial establishments with about seven million occupied persons, most of whom were self-employed.[7] The numbers of handicraft establishments and of handicraftsmen as well as the share of self-employed craftsmen were similarly large.[8] There were more than 126,000 industrial establishments with more than three million employees, and most of these enterprises were small in size.[9] In addition, there were large numbers of small transport enterprises besides the state-operated railways, plus a few large shipping companies.[10]

The average size of enterprises was extraordinarily small, not only in transportation but in almost all branches of the economy. The most frequent number of employed persons per family farm was two. The averages for commercial as well as handicraft establishments ranged somewhat below this number. And the average number of employed persons per industrial enterprise was merely twenty-four. Such enter-

---

[4] See *T'ung-chi kung-tso* (Statistical Work), No. 11 (1957), p. 24.

[5] This estimate implies an average household size of 4.5 persons which is indicated for the peasant population. See Peter Schran, *The Development of Chinese Agriculture* (Urbana: University of Illinois Press, 1969), Table 3.1, and *Nung-ts'un kung-tso t'ung-hsün* (Rural Work Bulletin), No. 4 (1957), p. 1.

[6] See *ibid.*

[7] See Choh-ming Li, *Economic Development of Communist China* (Berkeley and Los Angeles: University of California Press, 1959), p. 241.

[8] See *ibid.*, p. 233, and Peter Schran, "Handicrafts in Communist China," *CQ*, No. 17 (January–March, 1964), pp. 166, 170.

[9] See Li, *Economic Development*, pp. 232–33, and Chao I-wen, *Hsin Chung-kuo ti kung-yeh* (New China's Industry) (Peking: T'ung-chi Press, 1957). Note that *large* is defined as fifteen or more employed persons in the presence of mechanical power and thirty or more employed persons in the absence of mechanical power.

[10] See Li, *Economic Development*, pp. 237–38, Notes.

prise sizes entailed a minimum of specialized and formalized managerial work. Farmers, craftsmen, and even merchants performed most of the functions personally, and they kept records largely in their heads. Industrialists as a rule ran their enterprises by themselves, often with the aid of family members. And they usually kept books to a rather limited extent. The management of most economic activities was thus highly decentralized as well as unstandardized.

The product of this multitude of ventures is not known. Official estimates, which place the net value of domestic material production in 1950 at about 70 per cent of that in 1952, and by implication at 42.5 billion *yuan* in 1952 prices,[11] probably understate the actual income level. Its structure can be approximated with data for 1952, at the risk of understating the initial share of agriculture and of overstating the initial shares of industry and construction.[12] According to these estimates, the materially productive sectors contributed as follows to the net domestic material product: [13]

| | |
|---|---|
| Agriculture | 59.2 per cent |
| Industry plus handicrafts | 18.0 per cent |
| Construction | 3.0 per cent |
| Transport and communications | 4.0 per cent |
| Commerce | 15.8 per cent |

Various service sectors, including the government, added perhaps 20 per cent to the net domestic material product.[14] The consequent estimate of total net domestic product, which may understate the actual total for 1950, is 51 billion *yuan* in 1952 prices. Close to two-thirds of the net product of agriculture was disposed of intrasectorally.[15] By implication, merely 60 per cent of the net domestic material product, as well as about two-thirds of the entire net domestic product, involved transactions.

The existing governmental apparatus had been used in the past to manage small fractions of this product and of all economic activities. For this reason its ability to intervene effectively on a larger scale was

[11] See State Statistical Bureau, *Ten Great Years* (Peking: Foreign Languages Press, 1960), p. 20, and *Ching-chi yen-chiu* (Economic Research), No. 10 (1959), pp. 17, 18.

[12] See State Statistical Bureau, *Ten Great Years,* pp. 16, 20, for rates of growth of national income which exceeded those of the gross value of production of agriculture, but which fell short of those of the gross value of production of industry.

[13] See Niu Chung-huang, *Wo kuo kuo-min shou-ju ti chi-lei ho hsiao-fei* (Accumulation and Consumption of Our Country's National Income) (Peking: Chung-kuo Ch'ing-nien Press, 1957), p. 21.

[14] See Li, *Economic Development,* pp. 102–107.

[15] See Schran, *Chinese Agriculture,* Table 5.4.

extremely limited. The Communist Party could not change this state of affairs at once. Indeed, it first had to worry about its ability to take over the apparatus and to begin reforming it in the desired direction.[16] In view of such circumstances, the Party adopted a strategy which Mao Tse-tung outlined in his "Report to the Second Plenary Session of the Seventh Central Committee of the Communist Party of China" on March 5, 1949.[17] It called for immediate expropriation of the "enemies" (notably the bureaucratic capitalists) as well as for "utilizing, restricting, and reconstructing" the relevant segments of the "people" (in particular the national bourgeoisie). In the beginning, it was unavoidably necessary to use rather than to restrict or to reconstruct existing forms of economic organization.

In accordance with this policy, the government collected in the main the established taxes through the established channels. But it also raised as well as restructured the rates of taxation in accordance with its objectives. In addition, it enforced the tax laws much more vigorously by instituting "democratic appraisal of taxes" in the absence of proper records, by prosecuting tax evasion, and so on.[18] A large share of the total, namely agriculture tax and salt tax, was collected in kind. In addition to taxes, the government received a substantial amount of revenue in the form of profit from state-owned enterprises plus relatively small amounts of foreign and domestic loans, contrary to previous periods.[19] In 1950, it thus collected a total of 6.52 billion *yuan* in current prices, which appear to have been equivalent to 7.70 billion *yuan* in 1952 prices.[20] The latter value constitutes 15 per cent

[16] See, for example, Mao Tse-tung, *Selected Works* (Peking: Foreign Languages Press, 1967), IV, 203–5: "On the Policy Concerning Industry and Commerce" (February 27, 1948); IV, 337–39: "Turn the Army into a Working Force" (February 8, 1949); IV, 361–75: "Report to the Second Plenary Session of the Seventh Central Committee of the Communist Party of China" (March 5, 1949).

[17] See *ibid.*, especially IV, 366–70.

[18] See George N. Ecklund, *Financing the Chinese Government Budget* (Chicago: Aldine Publishing Company, 1966), especially pp. 13–43. For a description of the democratic appraisal, cf. *ibid.*, pp. 37–39. Ecklund states on p. 37: "The process was designed to be 'democratic' in that the determination was made by a group that represented the government, the general community, and the trade or business concerned. Regulations establishing this procedure clearly show that the line of command from the higher units to the local appraisal team maintains a firm degree of government direction and control."

[19] See Ming-chung Tay, *Das Finanz- und Steuerwesen Chinas* (Jena: Verlag von Gustav Fischer, 1940), p. 21, for information on the importance of profits and loans during 1928–36.

[20] See note 11, and State Statistical Bureau, *Ten Great Years*, p. 21, and State Statistical Bureau, *Report on Fulfilment of the National Economic Plan of the People's Republic of China in 1955* (hereafter *1955 Report*) (Peking: Foreign Languages Press,

of the estimated net domestic product in 1950, and 23 per cent of its transacted portion. Since the actual product may have been somewhat larger than estimated, the actual share of public revenue was probably not quite as high.

The initial changes in other forms of government intervention in economic activities were similarly limited. Most important, the government socialized few of the existing enterprises at once. In industry, it owned in 1949 a total of 2,677 establishments, most of which had been nationalized in 1945. In addition, it owned 109 enterprises jointly with the Soviet Union and 193 enterprises jointly with private partners.[21] Most of these enterprises were comparatively large, however, and together they accounted for close to 50 per cent of the total industrial employment and product.[22] In handicrafts, agriculture, and most other production branches, the government limited itself to forming comparatively few state enterprises (for example, state farms) and relatively few cooperative ventures.[23] State ownership and cooperation were more common in domestic trade.[24] And the state sector predominated from the beginning in foreign trade, modern transport, communications, and finance.[25] The creation of the People's Bank of China in 1948 was perhaps the most drastic innovation.

## THE PATTERN OF TRANSFORMATION

In pursuit of its principal objectives, the government had to accomplish three tasks: (1) it had to build new sectors and in particular industry under fully socialistic auspices; (2) it had to reallocate resources from the old sectors and from agriculture in particular for this purpose; (3) it had to socialize the old sectors. The opportunities for reallocation were limited by constraints on production which were to be overcome in part by social change. The second and third tasks could be combined for this reason as soon as they were organizationally feasible. Until then, the government could attempt to manipulate the large number of small enterprises in most branches of the economy to a more limited extent.

1956), p. 46, for such an implication. It is assumed that the purchasing power of revenue changed in proportion to the index of wholesale prices.

[21] See Chao, *Hsin Chung-kuo*, p. 35.

[22] See *ibid.*, pp. 35, 64, 75 as well as Li, *Economic Development*, p. 233, and State Statistical Bureau, *Ten Great Years*, p. 38.

[23] See Li, *Economic Development*, pp. 233, 243–44, 249.

[24] See *ibid.*, pp. 239–41.

[25] See *ibid.*, p. 238, and Audrey Donnithorne, *China's Economic System* (New York: Frederick A. Praeger, 1967), pp. 251–52, 321, 402–403.

MONOPOLIZATION OF TRADE AND FINANCE

The entire economy derived its food and most of the raw materials entering into other consumer goods from agriculture. Agriculture consumed or accumulated close to three-fourths of its gross product intrasectorally.[26] The distribution and disposal of this portion could not be affected greatly by controlling trade.[27] But agriculture sold one-fourth of its gross product to the nonagricultural sector. Control over this transaction was possible as well as necessary. The government therefore developed state commerce, initially under the Ministry of Trade, to compete with private commerce. Early in 1950, it formed "eight state companies for internal trade whose task was 'to take a commanding position in the domestic market and to regulate national and local supply and demand' by buying up the lion's share of the supply of essential commodities. . . . To assist these companies, a network of 'supply and selling cooperatives' was set up all over the countryside." [28] The ministries, state companies, and marketing cooperatives proliferated during the following years. By 1952, state commerce had reached a dominant position in wholesale trade,[29] especially in the marketing of basic necessities such as grains. Soon the government felt able to solidify the organization of its monopoly.

By transacting an increasingly large share of products of agricultural origin, the government was in a position to have an increasing effect upon the operations of the nonagricultural sector as well. Foreign trade was socialized almost entirely at once, of course.[30] In the domestic sale of final products, the state wholesalers supplied a large number of private retailers in addition to growing numbers of state and cooperative retailers (state stores, rural marketing cooperatives, urban consumer cooperatives). These came to depend more and more on state commerce, again especially for the supply of most basic necessities.[31] For intermediate products, state commerce more and more

[26] See Schran, *Chinese Agriculture,* Table 5.4.

[27] Note, however, that the concomitant land reform affected the distribution of the farm product drastically. See *ibid.,* chap. vi.

[28] See Li, *Economic Development,* p. 18, where he quotes *T'ung-i kuo-chia ts'ai-cheng kung-tso* (Unify State Financial Work) (Hankow, 1951), p. 26.

[29] See *ibid.,* p. 16, and Donnithorne, *China's Economic System,* p. 278.

[30] See *ibid.,* p. 321.

[31] Note that such measures also related to efforts to arrest the inherited inflation which temporarily received new impetus during the Korean War. The index of wholesale prices, which had continued to rise until March, 1950, and had fallen after the implementation of the stabilization measures, rose again substantially from July, 1950, to November, 1950, as well as moderately during 1951. See *1955 Report,* p. 46.

often contracted with capitalist industrial enterprises for their process-
ing. By 1952, more than 50 per cent of the gross product of capitalist
industry was accounted for by state agents, that is, by capitalists who
worked exclusively for the state.[32] Soon the government thought about
consolidating these positions of power, too.

The growing dependence of private farms and businesses on state
trade was reinforced by the credit policy of the state banking system.
It provided credit through the various business affairs ministries,[33]
including those of state commerce, for example, to peasants and state
agents in the form of advance payments on sales contracts or in the
form of delayed payments on purchasing contracts.[34]

After the government had become predominant among the inter-
mediaries in the principal markets of the economy,[35] it began to transform the system of free contracting. In 1953, it instituted a system of
"planned purchase and planned supply" which imposed sales quotas on
the producers and rations on the consumers of the most basic consumer
goods of agricultural origin. It also added a system of "unified purchase" of many other products of both agricultural and nonagricultural origin which were not subject to rationing.[36] Both systems institutionalized the state monopoly by substituting previous fiscal practices for commercial practices. They apparently were fully operational
by 1955 and were applied to increasing numbers of commodities. Their
institution required the formation of an elaborate bureaucratic structure in state commerce which is evident notably for the grain trade.[37]

EXPANSION OF THE STATE BUDGET SECTOR

While the government consolidated its control over markets, it developed in addition a more comprehensive set of business affairs ministries for specific production branches of the economy, notably in the

---

[32] See Li, *Economic Development*, p. 13.

[33] See Choh-ming Li, *The Statistical System of Communist China* (Berkeley and
Los Angeles: University of California Press, 1962), for the use of this term.

[34] See Donnithorne, *China's Economic System*, pp. 418, 421.

[35] Note that according to official estimates, the value of direct retail sales by (agricultural and nonagricultural) producers to the resident population rose slowly from 1953
to 1956. The implied volume probably remained fairly stable. But the share in total
retail sales declined considerably, thus pointing to an increasing separation of trade from
production. See *T'ung-chi kung-tso*, No. 11 (1957), p. 28, and State Statistical Bureau,
*Ten Great Years*, p. 166.

[36] See Li, *Economic Development*, pp. 20–23, and Donnithorne, *China's Economic
System*, pp. 283–87, for a description of both systems. Note that Li uses the term
"centralized purchase."

[37] For a discussion of the grain marketing system with emphasis on productivity
problems, see *T'ung-chi kung-tso*, No. 8 (1957), pp. 9–10.

industrial sector. The number of ministries which concerned themselves with the traditional production branches remained relatively
small until late in 1954, that is, until the eve of their socialist transformation. Ministries which dealt with the newly developing branches,
and notably with producer goods production, became more numerous
and important.[38] This expansion of the state budget sector was reflected in the share of the state budget in the net domestic material
product, which increased from about 18 per cent in 1950 to almost
30 per cent in 1953. The share remained at this level throughout the
first five-year plan period.[39]

In order to develop new sectors and industries under socialist auspices, the government had to invest in them. It was characteristic for
the direction of change associated with the growth of the state budget,
therefore, that the increase in state expenditure on economic construction almost from the beginning provided for most of the capital formation.[40] Its share rose from 25 per cent of total state expenditures or
5 per cent of the net domestic material product in 1950 to 40 per cent
of total state expenditures or 12 per cent of the net domestic material
product in 1953, and it reached 50 per cent of total state expenditures
or 15 per cent of the net domestic material product during the remainder of the first five-year plan period.[41] By implication, the share
of all other state expenditures in the net domestic material product
remained fairly constant.

Since the transition to socialism was to be brought about by noninfla-
tionary means, these increases in expenditures had to be matched by
increases in revenues. Interestingly, the government did not raise the
rate of taxation significantly after the initial years. The share of total
tax receipts in the net domestic material product fluctuated mildly

---

[38] This pattern of development is made evident in Donnithorne, *China's Economic
System,* pp. 517 ff.

[39] Derived from State Statistical Bureau, *Ten Great Years,* pp. 20–24, and *Ching-chi
yen-chiu,* No. 10 (1959), pp. 17, 18.

[40] See Niu Chung-huang, *Wo kuo kuo-min shou-ju,* pp. 61–63, for the following information on the structure of capital formation by social sector in 1953 and in 1956:

| *Accumulating sector* | *1953* | *1956* |
|---|---|---|
| State organs and state enterprises | 80.0% | 75.5% |
| Joint state-private sector | 1.6% | 6.0% |
| Capitalist sector | 2.5% | 0.1% |
| Cooperative sector | 4.8% | 14.3% |
| Including agricultural cooperatives | 0.05% | 12.1% |
| Individual sector | 9.1% | 1.1% |
| Residential sector | 2.0% | 3.2% |
| All sectors | 100.0% | 100.0% |

[41] See note 39.

above the 16 per cent level during most of the 1950's. Their share in total state revenues declined from about 75 per cent in 1950 to 55 per cent in 1953 and to about 50 per cent during the remainder of the first five-year plan period. But the revenues from state-owned enterprises and undertakings increased drastically in absolute as well as in relative terms. Their share reached 35 per cent of all state revenues or 10 per cent of the net domestic product in 1953 and rose to 40–45 per cent of all state revenues or 12–14 per cent of the net domestic material product thereafter.[42]

A comparison of state expenditures on economic construction with revenues from state-owned enterprises and undertakings shows that the latter sufficed to finance most of the former at most times. Since the state-owned enterprises were subject to some taxation, too, it is evident that the development of new sectors, and socialist industrialization in particular, were budget-internal processes, within the limits set by the productivity of labor and the availability of wage goods.

SOCIALIST HIGH TIDE

The government may have intended to increase the transaction of agricultural goods and to improve the distribution of consumer goods by instituting planned and unified marketing.[43] The available data suggest, however, that the actual increases and improvements were not so great.[44] There remained the possibility of increases in consumer goods production in general and in agricultural production in particular, which also had been disappointing during the years of predominantly private production.[45] In these circumstances, Mao called for the acceleration of agricultural collectivization on July 31, 1955, that is, one day after the adoption of the first five-year plan. On the premise that "where there is a will there is a way," he expected organizational problems to be resolved by cadres who would be learning by doing.[46] His call was followed in 1956 by the propagation of the agricultural development program. The transformation of the other branches accelerated as well. But the tide of socialization swept very

---

[42] See *ibid.*

[43] See Donnithorne, *China's Economic System*, p. 346, for the claim that the food crisis of 1953 was the immediate cause of the introduction of rationing.

[44] For grain marketing in particular see *T'ung-chi kung-tso*, No. 19 (1957), pp. 31, 32. For changes in the relation between sales of agricultural products and agricultural production in general, see Schran, *Chinese Agriculture*, Table 5.4.

[45] See Kenneth R. Walker, "Collectivization in Retrospect: The 'Socialist High Tide' of Autumn 1955–Spring 1956," *CQ*, No. 26 (April–June, 1966), pp. 1–43.

[46] See *ibid.*, especially pp. 30–31, and Schran, *Chinese Agriculture*, chap. i.

TABLE 22
PLANNED AND ACTUAL SOCIALIZATION BY THE END OF 1957

| Economic Branch | First Five-Year Plan Target * | 1957 Result † |
|---|---|---|
| *Agriculture* ‡ | | |
| Cooperative | 33% § | 98% ‖ |
| Individual | 67% | 2% |
| *Industry* # | | |
| Socialist ** | 65.7% | 68.2% |
| State capitalist | 22.1% | 31.8% |
| Capitalist | 12.2% | 0.0% |
| *Handicrafts* | | |
| Cooperative | 38.7% # | 89.8% †† |
| Individual | 61.3% # | 10.2% †† |
| *Retail trade* ‡‡ | | |
| Socialist ** | 54.9% | 65.7% |
| State capitalist | 24.0% | 31.6% |
| Private §§ | 21.1% | 2.7% |

* Derived from *First Five-Year Plan.*

† Derived from State Statistical Bureau, *Kuan-yü fa-chan kuo-min ching-chi ti ti-i-ko wu nien (1953 tao 1957 nien) chi-hua chih-hsing chieh-kuo ti kung-pao* (Report on the Results of Implementing the First Five-Year [1953–1957] Plan for De-velopment of the National Economy) (Peking: T'ung-chi Press, 1959); State Statistical Bureau, *Ten Great Years;* NCNA, Peking, December 17, 1957.

‡ Unit: Percentage of peasant households.

§ Elementary cooperatives.

‖ 96 per cent advanced cooperatives.

# Unit: Percentage of gross value of production.

** State plus cooperative.

†† Unit: Percentage of craftsmen.

‡‡ Unit: Percentage of value of retail sales.

§§ Capitalist plus individual.

high in the traditional production branches, as the contrast between first five-year plan targets and 1957 results in Table 22 demonstrates.

As a consequence of this socialist transformation, the numbers of organizational units in production and distribution decreased dras-tically. By May, 1956, 110.1 million of the then 120.7 million peasant households had been organized into one million Agricultural Producers Cooperatives (APCs). One-third of them were members of elementary APCs with an average size of fifty-one households per APC. Two-thirds were members of advanced APCs with an average size of 247 households per APC.[47] By June, 1958, the number of cooperator

[47] See *1955 Report*, p. 38.

households had increased to 123 million while the number of (advanced) APCs had decreased to 740,000. The average size reached 166 households per APC.[48] Soon afterward, these APCs were reorganized into large production brigades of rural People's Communes. By December, 1958, 26,578 communes had been formed with an average size of 4,637 households per commune.[49] In subsequent years, the number of communes increased and their average size decreased.[50] Moreover, the more numerous agricultural production brigades, which were comparable in size and organization to the APCs, emerged as decision making units in agricultural production.[51]

In handicraft production, more than five million craftsmen had become members of handicraft production cooperatives by the end of 1956. More than three million establishments had been combined into nearly one hundred thousand units with an average number of fifty-one craftsmen per cooperative.[52] Most of these cooperatives were transformed during the Great Leap Forward, so that their members became wage laborers. By 1961, however, cooperative forms of organization began to reappear.[53]

In industry, employment increased from more than three million persons in 1949 to nearly eight million persons in 1956, while the number of establishments decreased from more than 126,000 to 60,000 during the same period. Average employment per establishment therefore grew from 24 persons to 132 persons. Most of this growth in average size occurred during 1955–56 when the large number of small capitalist enterprises was consolidated into a much smaller number of correspondingly larger, joint state-private enterprises.[54]

In commerce, the number of employed persons decreased somewhat during the course of socialist transformation, but the number of commercial establishments decreased much more. Whereas private commerce typically employed less than two persons per establishment, state commerce in 1955 counted eleven persons per organizational

[48] See Chao Kuo-chun, *Agrarian Policy of the Chinese Communist Party 1921–1959* (Bombay: Asia Publishing House, 1960), p. 293.

[49] See State Statistical Bureau, *Ten Great Years,* p. 43.

[50] See G. William Skinner, "Marketing and Social Structure in Rural China, Part III," *Journal of Asian Studies,* XXIV (May, 1965), 363–99.

[51] See *ibid.* and Cheng Chu-yüan, *Communist China's Economy 1949–1962* (South Orange, N.J.: Seton Hall University Press, 1963), pp. 37 ff.

[52] See Schran, "Handicrafts," p. 170, and Chao, *Hsin Chung-kuo,* p. 109.

[53] See John Philip Emerson, *Nonagricultural Employment in Mainland China: 1949–1958* (U.S. Bureau of the Census, International Population Statistics Reports, Series P-90, No. 21; Washington, D.C.: U.S. Government Printing Office, 1965), pp. 45, 50.

[54] See *ibid.,* pp. 134, 136.

unit. Marketing cooperatives at the same time reported a staff of about five persons per store,[55] and apparently there were several stores per cooperative.[56] Beyond these few observations, the reorganization of commerce cannot be quantified satisfactorily. Descriptions of other branches of the economy are similarly difficult. But there is no doubt that the process of socialist transformation led to the combination of organizational units almost everywhere.

In summary, the transformation of established enterprises constituted only one part of the strategy of socialist development. The other part consisted of the creation of new enterprises and undertakings, most of which were organized, owned, and operated by the state.[57] The number of such undertakings is obscure.[58] But the relative importance of the two courses of action can be gauged roughly by the data of Table 23. In the opinion of the State Statistical Bureau, the state sector grew primarily by investment of state revenues and only secondarily by expropriation of private enterprises.[59] The transformation of the capitalist sector into a joint state-private sector and the transformation of the individual sector into a cooperative sector did not prevent the growth of these two components of the economy. Most Western critics tend to object to this official interpretation, arguing that the official data understate the initial levels of production in the capitalist and the individual sectors.

### THE NEW STRUCTURE OF MANAGEMENT

The decision to socialize the economy more rapidly than originally planned was not attributable to a sudden improvement in the government's ability to administer the economy differently. The government, therefore, could not move simultaneously to the system of centralized administration of economic activities which the Soviet Union was practicing. Instead, it had to find alternative solutions to the problems

[55] See *ibid.*, p. 141, and Li, *Economic Development*, p. 241.

[56] See Donnithorne, *China's Economic System*, p. 279, for a reference to 29,600 marketing cooperatives in the autumn of 1954.

[57] Note that the number of private industrial establishments increased until 1953, while the number of individual craftsmen grew until 1954. See Emerson, *Nonagricultural Employment*, pp. 134, 136.

[58] See *First Five-Year Plan*, pp. 38–39, for references to 694 above-norm and 2,300 below-norm projects for the first five-year plan period. State Statistical Bureau, *Ten Great Years*, pp. 46–47, mentions a total of more than fifty thousand construction projects during 1950–58, more than one thousand of which were above-norm, large, and modern.

[59] See note 40 for information on the structure of capital formation.

of planning, directing, and controlling the activities of a predominantly socialist economy.

## LIMITATIONS TO THE STATE SECTOR

Most important, the government was conscious of the fact that the incorporation of many individual enterprises into a few cooperative enterprises did not integrate the management of the economy. The less than one million Agricultural Producers Cooperatives and the one hundred thousand handicraft production cooperatives, which had been created during the process of socialist transformation, were indepen-

TABLE 23
NET DOMESTIC MATERIAL PRODUCT BY SOCIAL SECTOR, 1952–57 *

| Year | All Sectors | State Owned | Joint State-Private | Capitalist | Joint Plus Capitalist | Cooper-ative | Individ-ual | Cooperative Plus Individual |
|------|------|------|------|------|------|------|------|------|
| All sectors equal to 100.0 | | | | | | | | |
| 1952 | 100.0 | 19.1 | 0.7 | 6.9 | 7.6 | 1.5 | 71.8 | 73.3 |
| 1953 | 100.0 | 23.9 | 0.9 | 7.9 | 8.8 | 2.5 | 64.8 | 67.3 |
| 1954 | 100.0 | 26.8 | 2.1 | 5.3 | 7.4 | 4.8 | 61.0 | 65.8 |
| 1955 | 100.0 | 28.0 | 2.8 | 3.5 | 6.3 | 14.1 | 51.6 | 65.7 |
| 1956 | 100.0 | 32.2 | 7.3 | 0.0 | 7.3 | 53.4 | 7.1 | 60.5 |
| 1957 | 100.0 | 33.2 | 7.6 | 0.0 | 7.6 | 56.4 | 2.8 | 59.2 |
| All sectors in 1952 equal to 100.0 | | | | | | | | |
| 1952 | 100.0 | 19.1 | 0.7 | 6.9 | 7.6 | 1.5 | 71.8 | 73.3 |
| 1953 | 114.0 | 27.2 | 1.0 | 9.0 | 10.0 | 2.9 | 73.9 | 76.8 |
| 1954 | 120.4 | 32.3 | 2.5 | 6.4 | 8.9 | 5.8 | 73.4 | 79.2 |
| 1955 | 128.3 | 35.9 | 3.6 | 4.5 | 8.1 | 18.1 | 66.2 | 84.3 |
| 1956 | 146.3 | 47.1 | 10.7 | 0.0 | 10.7 | 78.1 | 10.4 | 88.5 |
| 1957 | 153.0 | 50.8 | 11.6 | 0.0 | 11.6 | 86.3 | 4.3 | 90.6 |

* State Statistical Bureau, *Ten Great Years*, pp. 20, 42.

dent enterprises. They were not substantially more subordinate to business affairs ministries than their predecessor enterprises had been. This was true in particular in personnel matters because the coopera-tors rather than government officials were entitled to choose the co-operative management. To effect such a choice and to direct coopera-tive management in general, at least two measures could be and were taken.

On the one hand, it was possible to assign the task of directing in-dependent enterprises to organizations outside the state administrative apparatus. In the case of the Agricultural Producers Cooperatives, the

Communist Party tended to assume this function itself, not only because it had confidence in its ability to do rural work, but also because it saw no alternative. To facilitate the socialist transformation, the Party found it necessary to exclude most of the traditional rural elite from cooperative management positions.[60] At the same time, the Party lacked the numbers of qualified cadres which the staffing of parallel bureaucracies throughout the countryside required.[61] In the case of the much less numerous handicraft production cooperatives, however, a separate organization was created in the form of the Federation of Handicraft Cooperatives. Under the rules of democratic centralism, this federation could provide a chain of command apart from the Communist Party and the Handicraft Administrative Bureau. Unfortunately, little is known about the role of the federation in the administration of handicraft activities.[62]

On the other hand, it was possible to advance the process of socialist transformation beyond the cooperative stage. Such a change was initiated in 1958 in agriculture, handicrafts, rural commerce, and all other fields of cooperation. The rural People's Communes, in particular, which assumed the functions of local government in the countryside, subordinated the management of the production brigades as the successor organizations to the Agricultural Producers Cooperatives to the communal administrative organs, specifically to their newly formed departments of agriculture. The communes also transformed rural handicraft production cooperatives into brigades under communal departments of industry.[63] In the cities, the majority of handicraft production cooperatives were reorganized into state enterprises which were placed under local bureaus of handicrafts or of light industry. Only a minority of the handicraftsmen remained in cooperatives.[64]

The administrative organs for agriculture, handicrafts, and other traditional activities at the local level were created without commensurate changes in the numbers of administrative and technical experts.

[60] See Articles 8 and 9 of the model regulations for advanced Agricultural Production Cooperatives on the membership rights of former landlords, rich peasants, and counterrevolutionaries. National People's Congress, *Model Regulations for Advanced Agricultural Producers' Cooperatives, June 30, 1956* (Peking: Foreign Languages Press, 1956). See Chao, *Agrarian Policy*, pp. 312–13.

[61] See Donnithorne, *China's Economic System*, pp. 41–43. Note that the direct involvement of the Party in rural work manifested itself as well in the unusual fact that the highest parallel positions in Party and government in this sphere were held in personal union.

[62] See *ibid.*, pp. 222–23.

[63] See Cheng, *Communist China's Economy*, p. 41.

[64] See *ibid.*, pp. 41, 76–77.

As a consequence, the Communist Party had to involve itself in managerial work even more than before. Proponents of the "mass line" argued that the shortage of experts did not matter much or that it actually could be turned into an advantage. Contrary to such arguments, however, diseconomies of major proportions tended to appear in instances where management functions were centralized at the local government level. In most lines of production, management functions therefore soon reverted to the brigades and teams which also assumed once more the various other attributes of cooperatives, including in many instances the name. But these collectives apparently did not regain their previous degree of autonomy. The rural ones in particular continued to be parts of rural communes, which remained the units of local government in the countryside. And the commune administrations seemingly instituted relations to brigades and teams which resembled those between other state administrative units and state enterprises.[65] Communes concentrated especially on managing the development rather than the current operations of subordinate units, by means of communal investment funds and of producer goods production.

### LIMITATIONS TO ADMINISTRATION

So far as relations within the state sector were concerned, the government recognized from the beginning that its ability to administer enterprises centrally was rather limited. It therefore confined its efforts to exercise administrative authority. In general, the sphere of central administration was delineated both by the desire to allocate as much as possible of the surplus of the economy and by the necessity to arrange interregional transfers of goods and services for this purpose as well as to sustain the entire population.

Within the state and joint state-private sectors, this limitation is most clearly evident in industry. Of the nearly three thousand enterprises which the state owned fully or in part in 1949,[66] most seem to have been subordinated directly to the initial regional governments. During the following years, the number of centrally administered enterprises grew substantially but remained relatively small. Since these

---

[65] This statement reflects the findings of Shahid Javed Burki, *A Study of Chinese Communes, 1965* (Harvard East Asian Monograph No. 29; Cambridge, Mass.: Harvard University Press, 1969). Burki states on p. 13: "While the management of production resources within the commune hierarchy was considerably decentralized in the period 1959–1961, it does not seem right to read into this development a process of total disintegration of the system." Burki's impressions conflict with the prevailing view.

[66] See note 21.

enterprises were large as well as modern, they accounted for much more sizable shares of industrial employment and industrial product.

TABLE 24
NUMBER OF INDUSTRIAL ESTABLISHMENTS *

| | Centrally Administered | | Locally Administered | |
|---|---|---|---|---|
| Year | State | Joint State-Private | State | Joint State-Private |
| 1952 | 2,409 | 88 | 8,262 | 909 |
| 1953 | 2,722 | 101 | 9,573 | 935 |
| 1954 | 3,392 | 130 | 10,274 | 1,614 |
| 1955 | 4,077 | 147 | 11,113 | 3,046 |

* See Emerson, *Nonagricultural Employment,* p. 136.

In 1956, the total number of state enterprises increased moderately to 17,104, whereas the number of joint state-private enterprises rose to 32,166.[67] Their distributions on central and local administrations are not known. But it may be assumed that most of the newly formed joint state-private enterprises were placed at once under local authority, because most of them were small and were engaged in consumer goods production. Moreover, the Central Administration for Commerce and Industry, which had to direct the transformation, had only been formed in November, 1954. The number of enterprises which could be transferred from central to local jurisdiction at a later time must have been correspondingly small.

At the local level, enterprises were administered either by provincial departments or by lower local (district, city) organs. The distribution of enterprises on the various levels is not known. But it seems reasonable that the provincial administrations concentrated on the larger and more modern enterprises, thus leaving many of the smaller and more traditional enterprises to the districts and the cities. Prior to the socialist high tide, most of the local state and joint state-private enterprises were large, whereas most of the private (and cooperative) enterprises were small. After their transformation, many of the new joint state-private enterprises probably came under district and city jurisdiction, even though their average size must have increased drastically as a result of the merging of enterprises.[68]

The administrative structure was decentralized further by the No-

[67] See Emerson, *Nonagricultural Employment,* p. 136. Note that Emerson derives the number of state enterprises in 1956 as a residual.
[68] *Ibid.,* pp. 134, 136.

vember, 1957, decree on the reform of the industrial management system. It limited the jurisdiction of the central government in the main to enterprises in producer goods production, which accounted for the majority of centrally administered enterprises at all times. Enterprises in consumer goods production were to be transferred to local control. But the lion's share (80 per cent) of their profits and basic depreciation funds remained allotted to the central government, which thus preserved its ability to direct the course of development through investment more or less as before. In addition, many enterprises which remained under central authority were integrated into local economies. Local organs acquired partial authority over them and a minor share of their profits (20 per cent).[69] As a result of this reform, the pattern of central administrative work changed. Planning, facilitating, and supervising the *development* rather than the day-to-day business of their industrial branches became the primary tasks of the central organs from then on, especially in consumer goods production. There is little evidence which points to recentralization in recent years.[70]

A similar development in the limitation of central functions is indicated in the case of state commerce. Here the central ministries had control over local ministerial organs and central trade companies, both of which shared control over local trade companies.[71] The absorption of the companies by the ministerial organs at both levels destroyed the system of dual control by the center. The decentralization measures of 1957 may have diminished central influence on local affairs unduly for this reason.[72] But it is not obvious that the center exerted much influence through the system in the beginning. And the renewed division of trade among companies in the 1960's could be attributable to problems caused by the combination of specialized trade functions in the ministerial organs at both levels. Difficulties of the latter type became evident, especially in rural trade during 1958–59, as part of the problems which the rural People's Communes encountered in their efforts to centralize the administration of most economic activities within the communal territory at the communal level. The communes tried to eliminate transactions between individual producers and consumers, and they also attempted to integrate the rural marketing cooperatives and the local organs of state commerce into communal

[69] See Donnithorne, *China's Economic System,* pp. 151–53.
[70] See *ibid.,* pp. 154–57.
[71] See *ibid.,* p. 288.
[72] *Ibid.*

organs. However, the degree of this integration is in question.[73] And the tendency to centralize was reversed during the course of commune reorganization in commerce as well as in peasant production.

In public finance, the limitation of central administration also is evident, but it is the most difficult to assess. At first, the government had to create a unified budget structure that would give the center effective control over local government revenue and expenditure.[74] There are indications that the center was not completely successful in asserting its authority.[75] The decision of 1957 to abandon the practice of controlling local revenue and expenditure in detail thus might have formalized central inability to review local affairs effectively.[76] On the other hand, the center retained a great deal of control by not splitting all revenues between the central and local organs in fixed proportions. The variation of the local shares in various taxes served to equalize the expenditures of revenue-rich and revenue-poor provinces to some extent. It also enabled the center to limit the total expenditure of any local government. The extra-budgetary revenue of the local governments, which increased notably after 1957 and was restricted again in 1961, could reduce the effectiveness of such limitations. But these additional revenues also had to meet added local expenditures.[77] And they could be taken into consideration in negotiations between central and local authorities. In any case, provincial capital formation remained to be covered by central grants and thus continued to be subject to central scrutiny.[78]

The redefinition of central and local fiscal authority was only part of a more complex fiscal reform. The socialist transformation made it necessary to change the tax paying units. In particular, the obligation to pay agriculture tax shifted from the individual first to the Agricultural Producers Cooperative and then to the rural People's Commune. In 1959, it shifted back to the agricultural production

[73] Note that according to *Lao-tung* (Labor), No. 6 (1959), p. 20, marketing cadres of rural People's Communes in Hupeh continued to be paid by the state rather than the commune.

[74] Note that the Nationalist government had not been able to create such a structure.

[75] For instance, although the government abolished all local surtaxes on the agriculture tax in 1952, such taxes apparently continued to be collected, and surtaxes were reintroduced formally in 1956. See Ecklund, *Financing the Chinese Government Budget*, p. 50.

[76] See Donnithorne, *China's Economic System*, pp. 393–400, for a somewhat different opinion.

[77] See *ibid.*, p. 391, and Ecklund, *Financing the Chinese Government Budget*, pp. 82–83.

[78] See Donnithorne, *China's Economic System*, p. 397.

brigade.[79] Moreover, the socialization of most industrial and commercial enterprises made it possible to simplify the system of taxation and of tax administration. The replacement of five more specific taxes by a unified industrial and commercial tax in 1958 had these effects.[80] Last, the formation and subsequent reorganization of the communes appears to have been associated with a process of delegation and of subsequent resumption of fiscal authority by the provinces.[81]

## LIMITATIONS TO PLANNING

The ability of the government to coordinate—centrally or locally—the activities of large numbers of enterprises in detail on the basis of a forecast of their performances was even more limited than its ability to administer them in a more traditional form. In 1949, the government had to make do with an administrative apparatus which was basically incapable of planning. In an assessment of the heritage, Choh-ming Li holds that for political as well as technical reasons, "the collection of statistical data by central government agencies and provincial governments was perfunctory. There was no demand, and indeed no need, for accuracy and adequate coverage. . . ." [82] The government did not and probably could not do much to improve this situation in the short run. But it began to lay the foundations for future central planning in the state and joint state-private sectors. It formed the Central Financial and Economic Planning Bureau under the Financial and Economic Commission. And it introduced Soviet practices in accounting and statistics, at first in construction, industry, and transportation, and eventually in commerce.[83] Of course, the institution of these techniques took time. And the rest of the economy reported in a nonstandardized form which was of limited use for central planning.[84] As a result:

Although the first five-year plan was scheduled to start in 1953, there was actually no plan, for the only serviceable national data available to Peiping authorities pertained to the industrial output of major state and joint enterprises. If central planning was to be effected, a state statistical system had to be established promptly.[85]

[79] See Ecklund, *Financing the Chinese Government Budget*, pp. 51–52.
[80] See *ibid.*, p. 67.
[81] See Donnithorne, *China's Economic System*, p. 399.
[82] See Li, *The Statistical System*, p. 5.
[83] *Ibid.*, p. 8, and Donnithorne, *China's Economic System*, pp. 26, 276, 457–58.
[84] See Li, *The Statistical System*, pp. 8–9.
[85] *Ibid.*, p. 9.

The institutional innovations were made on the eve of the first five-year plan period, in the fall of 1952, when the State Statistical Bureau and the State Planning Commission were established. Once again it took time to create the organizational structures. The planning apparatus became more complex at the center in 1954, with the formation of the State Construction Commission. With Soviet aid, it produced the first five-year plan soon afterward. The apparatus proliferated again in 1956, when the State Economic Commission, the General Bureau for the Supply of Raw Materials, and the State Technological Commission were created.[86] But it did not develop commensurately at the provincial level. And it was just beginning the tremendous task of establishing itself organizationally below the district level when the socialist high tide occurred.[87] It therefore could not effectively incorporate the large numbers of newly formed collective and joint state-private enterprises into a central plan. Indeed, it still faced difficulties in dealing with the existing state sector in this manner.[88]

If the government's ability to plan effectively did not extend beyond its ability to administer economic activities, there was reason to decentralize the planning along with the administration of such activities. This change occurred in 1958. The central planners now were limited to allocating interprovincial transfers, as well as most of the surplus of the economy.[89] By delegating most other planning functions fully or in part to provincial or lower local organs, the center may have given up some of its authority in some instances. In other cases, however, the center may have reduced its influence in name only. That is to say, in planning as in administration the center simply may have institutionalized a limitation which could not be overcome with the available resources.[90]

The decentralization measures and the emphasis on local development during 1958–59 tended to accelerate the development of planning organs at all local levels and notably below the *hsien* level.[91] However,

[86] See Donnithorne, *China's Economic System,* p. 458.

[87] See Li, *The Statistical System,* p. 19.

[88] *Ibid.,* pp. 63–65.

[89] See Donnithorne, *China's Economic System,* p. 462, for a list of the centrally planned variables.

[90] See *ibid.,* p. 461: "The decision to decentralize appears, at least in part, to have been a belated recognition that highly centralized control was impossible and that in fact local authorities had already taken over some of the functions supposedly reserved for the centre."

[91] See Li, *The Statistical System,* pp. 79–80.

they also tended to have the opposite effect on the central planning organs.[92] Moreover, the politicizing of planning and statistics during the Great Leap Forward and the hectic formation and reformation of People's Communes rendered much planning meaningless, especially at the local level. After the failure of these policies became evident, planning as well as statistical work once again improved. Most of the institutions that had been impaired previously were reconstituted, rehabilitated, and even expanded to a considerable extent. Yet such advances apparently did not lead to a change in the division between central and local planning which had been formalized in 1958.[93]

## LIMITATIONS TO CONTROL

Limitations to the government's ability to plan and direct economic activities centrally or locally had to effect the form of control. Audrey Donnithorne makes this point much more strongly:

China's economic planning has been restricted mainly to the setting of targets, to drawing up lists of resolutions. It does not attempt to effect close integration of different economic sectors, nor is it much concerned with optimum allocation of resources. Throughout, and this can scarcely be stressed too much, economic planning in China is constrained by the deficiencies of the information on which it has to work, as well as by weaknesses in the administrative and supervisory organs charged with implementation of plans and with checking this implementation.[94]

In recognition of such constraints, which necessarily leave a considerable degree of freedom of decision making to the managers of the enterprises that are to be controlled,[95] the government did not attempt for long to operate with the Soviet system of control. The formation of control organs along with planning and administrative organs had taken time. By 1953, however, control organs had been introduced at all levels of government down to the *hsien* and in most departments of the state budget sector.[96] The system was unified in 1954 under the

[92] See Donnithorne, *China's Economic System*, pp. 467–68.

[93] See Li, *The Statistical System*, pp. 111 ff.

[94] See Donnithorne, *China's Economic System*, p. 457.

[95] See Barry M. Richman, *A Firsthand Study of Industrial Management in Communist China* (Los Angeles: Graduate School of Business, University of California, 1967), pp. 16–19, for a description of the degree of freedom of Chinese managers in comparison with U.S. managers.

[96] See Franz Schurmann, *Ideology and Organization in Communist China* (Berkeley and Los Angeles: University of California Press, 1966), pp. 323–24.

People's Supervisory Commission, which subsequently became the Ministry of Supervision.[97] The process of decentralization and localization of control began earlier than elsewhere on the eve of the socialist high tide, and the system of comprehensive control was soon changed.[98] Managers once again were supervised in particular respects by organs of the business affairs ministries as well as by the Ministry of Finance and the state banking system.[99] The Ministry of State Control itself was abolished in 1959. At issue is the degree to which the system of control had ever functioned. In the words of Franz Schurmann: ". . . because of the necessary flexibility in day-to-day operations, any investigation, before-the-fact or after-the-fact, would come up with so many irregularities that, under strict interpretation of the laws, all management would march off to prison. . . . Thus to get things done 'illegality' had to be tolerated." [100]

Because constraints to the government's ability to control enterprises left the managers fairly free to act, additional extragovernmental controls had to be used in order to assure that managers would act "correctly." In principle, such controls were inherent in the pattern of contractual relations between banks and businesses, manufacturers and merchants, and employers and employees, due to the interest of at least one party in each instance in holding the other party to the contract. Yet the effectiveness of these controls depended also on the other party's ability and willingness to meet the terms of the contract. If it were common for enterprises not to fulfill their obligations, this system of control could not work.

Terms which enterprises were able and willing to meet could be determined by the market mechanism. Markets remained expedient control devices for the residual individual sector, for transactions of commodities of tertiary importance, and for direct sales by producers to consumers. But they could not be accepted as permanent solutions to the control problem even for this limited sphere, as the extreme restrictions on the individual sideline occupations of peasants during

---

[97] *Ibid.*, p. 328.

[98] *Ibid.*, pp. 346–47.

[99] See Ecklund, *Financing the Chinese Government Budget*, pp. 33–36, for a discussion of the extraordinary functions of tax offices and bank offices. In summary, "The bank has, in fact, provided a closer degree of control and a more stringent check on operating efficiency of state firms than have the tax offices. The latter seem to operate more as an auxiliary management service, designed to be helpful whenever their peculiar knowledge can make a definite contribution" (reference omitted).

[100] See Schurmann, *Ideology and Organization*, p. 349.

the socialist high tide and again during the Great Leap Forward made clear. Moreover, for practical as well as for ideological reasons,[101] markets were basically unacceptable for the socialist and semi-socialist sectors of the economy. This position, which already had affected China's response to the Yugoslav managerial reforms of the early 1950's, was restated repeatedly in recent times, most forcefully in the criticism of Sun Yeh-fang during the early phase of the Great Proletarian Cultural Revolution.[102]

Alternatively, control could be exercised politically through the Party in either of two ways. On the one hand, it seemed possible to operate with the residual ideological and organizational components of the Soviet system, namely the inculcation of an expert ethos on the managers [103] and the institution of political control in the form of the managerial triangle.[104] Characteristic of the expert ethos was that it raised the specter of "high hats" in a new form. Characteristic of the triangular system of control was that each of the three participants— manager, Party secretary, union secretary—represented a bureaucratic organization at its lowest level. The effectiveness of control through such a system depended decisively on the bureaucratic adequacy of the extragovernmental organizations, and notably of the Party, espe-

---

[101] Conceptually, the market functions when (1) many units are (2) formally free to (3) compete rather than cooperate, that is, to pursue separate rather than joint interests. To which extent were these conditions existent and acceptable after the socialist high tide? With respect to (1), the large number of units, which had operated originally in every locality and branch, continued to operate at most times only in rural subsidiary production. Everywhere else, the state trade monopoly faced substantially smaller numbers of contractual partners because of the socialist transformation of the economy. These could not be dominated as easily *ceteris paribus,* and problems of group egoism, therefore, could be expected to become more significant. With respect to (2), the formal freedom to contract was principally incompatible with the methods of price determination which the government had instituted in the state sector. It thus contained an implicit threat to the state trade monopoly which the government had eliminated originally by instituting planned and unified marketing of the more important products. With respect to (3), competitive behavior, that is, the psychologically unrestrained pursuit of self-interest (notably profit) by units, was incompatible with the utopia. The transition to socialism was to be a transition to cooperative behavior. Enterprises had been socialized so that the behavioral change could occur. The provision of material incentives was to be reduced everywhere accordingly for the same reason, whether they were collective or individual in scope. For a description of the managerial incentive system, see Richman, *A Firsthand Study,* pp. 39–45.

[102] See "On Sun Yeh-fang's Reactionary Political and Economic Program," *Hung Ch'i* (Red Flag), No. 10 (1966), as translated in K. H. Fan (ed.), *The Chinese Cultural Revolution: Selected Documents* (New York: Grove Press, 1968), pp. 141–58.

[103] See Schurmann, *Ideology and Organization,* pp. 280 ff. Note the analogous cultivation of a "business ethic" in the American setting.

[104] See *ibid.*

cially under conditions of inadequate administrative subordination of the manager.

In most Chinese enterprises, control through parallel bureaucracies, all of them permeated by the Party organization, could not be practiced easily or well. In the cooperative enterprises in particular, which accounted for the vast majority of enterprise units in the economy, labor and management were not—and could not be—organized separately. Moreover, even the creation of one structure in addition to that of the Party was problematic in the absence of adequate numbers of qualified cadres.[105] Such problems had to effect the many local state and joint state-private enterprises, too. Enterprises in this category usually were unionized. But they were too small to employ full-time trade union functionaries. And the primary trade union committees which they formed did not add much to the control exercised by the primary Party units.[106] Control through the managerial triangle thus appeared to be a workable solution merely for the larger and more modern enterprises, many of which were administered centrally. Yet the system had its shortcomings here, too. While it could keep managers and functionaries from colluding with each other at the enterprise level, it would force them to become more similar to each other as well as more "separate from the masses." The Soviet system of control in this sense posed the problem of "high hats" everywhere. And it thereby obstructed the "democratization" of management which in Maoist perspective was essential to progress on the road toward socialism.

The Party thus had practical as well as ideological reasons when in 1956 it substituted for managerial ethos and the managerial triangle a system of managerial responsibility, first in combination with and then under the collective leadership of the Party committee.[107] Of course, the institution of Party domination over management did not have to lead to mass participation in all decision making processes and

---

[105] See note 61.

[106] The Trade Union Law of the People's Republic of China specifies in Article 13 organizers for enterprises which employ less than twenty-five persons and primary trade union committees for enterprises which employ twenty-five or more persons. Article 15 prescribes a minimum of two hundred employed persons per enterprise for a full-time trade union functionary. See *Labor Laws and Regulations of the People's Republic of China* (Peking: Foreign Languages Press, 1956), pp. 10–11. The average number of employed persons per industrial enterprise increased from 24 in 1949 to 132 in 1956. See note 52.

[107] See Schurmann, *Ideology and Organization,* pp. 284 ff., and Donnithorne, *China's Economic System,* pp. 196–97.

to mass control through such participation. The "mass line" and "democratic management" became themes during the Great Leap Forward, when the Party committee and the workers took over the functions of management and sent management to work in production. In consequence of these changes, which assumed a very extreme form in the collective sector where the subordination of management to state administrative organs was lacking or still was extremely limited, problems of management and of control developed to an extraordinary degree. The breakdown of the system of control is most clearly evident in the statistical failure of 1958–59. Controls became effective once again in 1961 when managers were rehabilitated and when their spheres of authority and responsibility were more clearly delineated.[108] But the necessary limitation of worker participation in management and of managerial participation in work also posed the problem of whether collective leadership by the Party committee was a meaningful alternative to the Soviet system of control.[109] The introduction of political work organs during the socialist education campaign seemed to indicate that the Party committees themselves were considered to be insufficiently red and excessively expert oriented.[110]

## IMPACT OF THE GREAT PROLETARIAN CULTURAL REVOLUTION

On the eve of the Cultural Revolution, the Chinese economy could be and—if the findings of Barry Richman[111] and of Shahid Javed Burki[112] are taken as indications—was managed at least as well as ever before. The number of persons prepared to become accountants, administrators, economists, managers, planners, statisticians, and so on had increased greatly because the expansion of the school system during the 1950's began to show substantial results by the early 1960's. The instruments of planning, direction, and control, which had been

---

[108] See Donnithorne, *China's Economic System*, p. 198.

[109] See Richman, *A Firsthand Study*, p. 44, for the following observation: "As of the spring of 1966, worker participation in management did not seem to be hindering productive efficiency very seriously at the majority of the enterprises surveyed, and it may well have been playing a positive role at many. It is interesting to note that at a majority of the enterprises visited there were no workers on the enterprise party committee, and at all of the others workers constituted only a relatively small proportion of the Committee's membership."

[110] See Schurmann, *Ideology and Organization*, pp. 303 ff., and Donnithorne, *China's Economic System*, p. 199. Note that Schurmann's attribution of administrative significance to the political departments may be dated.

[111] See Richman, *A Firsthand Study*, pp. 29–35. Note that Richman's specific assessments tend to conflict with his general evaluation.

[112] See Burki, *A Study*, especially pp. 8–49. Note that Burki as a rule does not generalize on the basis of his experiences in thirteen communes in 1965.

much impaired during the Great Leap Forward, appeared to be re-habilitated and improved on the decentralized pattern envisaged in 1957, with a more clearly defined managerial position subject to Party control and limited mass participation. Moreover, the lessons of the Great Leap Forward were still fresh in the minds of most people to such a degree that, with reference to the proposals of E. G. Liberman, even more comprehensive changes in the direction of market socialism could be propagated by Sun Yeh-fang and others.

All of these developments appear to have contributed to the events of 1966–68. In reverse order, Sun's call for a form of market socialism in China was attacked as reactionary, capitalist thought.[113] Of course, his challenge of the institutional status quo as such was quite unrealistic, even if he stood with Liu Shao-ch'i and others in making it. But it indicated the extent of the resurrection of managerial ideology which made itself felt much more immediately and importantly, for instance, in the neglect of the mass line by managers and Party committees. Such a consequence of ideological aberration was to be rectified by an attack on its strategic organizational locus, the Party committee and the Party organization in general. To support such an attack, it was possible to muster the young intelligentsia who were destined to become management in the future but who faced employment problems under the existing system.[114] Moreover, by inducing students to attack functionaries in the spirit of the Great Proletarian Cultural Revolution, it seemed feasible to reconstruct both groups ideologically.[115] Yet the memories of the Great Leap Forward seem also to have affected revolutionary tactics. The struggle was to be limited so that it would not interfere with production to a significant degree.

The indications are that such restrictions were reasonably effective at first but that they did give way in part eventually.[116] Nevertheless, the collective sector, and agriculture in particular, where management was less professionalized, where the Party was more dominant, and

---

113 See Fan (ed.), *The Chinese Cultural Revolution,* pp. 141 ff.

114 See Edwin F. Jones, "The Emerging Pattern of China's Economic Revolution," in Joint Economic Committee, Congress of the United States, *An Economic Profile of Mainland China,* I (Washington, D.C.: U.S. Government Printing Office, 1967), 79 ff., for an emphasis of this factor.

115 Note that by the late 1950's the principal employment opportunities for additional managerial personnel were located in the rural areas. These appeared unattractive to the educated youth, in China as well as elsewhere. The Great Proletarian Cultural Revolution ended in a call to move to the countryside.

116 For an estimate of the impact, see Dwight H. Perkins, "Economic Growth in China and the Cultural Revolution (1960–April 1967)," *CQ,* No. 30 (April–June, 1967), pp. 33 ff., especially 46–48.

where the Great Leap Forward had done more damage than elsewhere, seemed to remain largely unaffected by the events. In any case, this impact on current performance must be distinguished from the effects on the organizational structure. It seems that the Great Proletarian Cultural Revolution challenged not the pattern of organization which had been formulated at the time of the socialist high tide or soon thereafter, but the spirit in which it was being implemented during the 1960's. On such a premise, it was necessary to change the organizers rather than the pattern of organization in either of two ways: by rehabilitation or by replacement.

The intended consequence—action which is more red and less expert oriented—is likely to give rise once more to some of the problems of 1958–59.[117] But the attempt to change the organizers ideologically may be futile, for reasons which Donnithorne has stated admirably in her assessment of the future of the political work organs:

Doubt may be permitted on whether these political work organs in their turn, may not go the same way as the Party committees. As long as the main task of Party organs in economic sectors is to produce certain economic results, so long must the leading elements in these Party organs concentrate their energies on economic matters. Even if their tasks are expressed in political terms, success in these may be measured by the degree of subsequent economic success—i.e. the attainment of targets is the most easily ascertainable proof of ideological zeal. This inevitably involves taking sides on economic issues, for example which method of production to prefer in a given instance. Before long these problems engross the group which has to decide them and mould it rather than the group moulding the economic matters with which it deals. That the group in question continues to repeat the approved political slogans may disguise rather than demonstrate its chief preoccupations. This trend may be hastened, if, as often seemed to occur, new industrial recruits to the Party have been chosen in great measure for their competence in their jobs, and whose interests may therefore be more professional than political.[118]

[117] See Richman, *A Firsthand Study*, p. 44: "Since I left China it is possible that workers have come to play greater or even dominant management roles at numerous enterprises. If this is so, economic efficiency and industrial progress are no doubt suffering substantially in many instances."

[118] See Donnithorne, *China's Economic System*, pp. 199–200 (note 4 omitted).

❦❦❦❦❦❦❦❦❦❦❦❦❦❦❦❦❦❦❦❦❦❦❦❦❦❦❦❦❦❦❦❦❦❦❦❦❦❦❦❦❦

*VICTOR H. LI*

# The Evolution and Development of the Chinese Legal System

## Two Models of Law

During the past twenty years, the Communist Chinese have used two separate models of law, each having its own rationale and objectives. Depending on the period, one model or the other has been dominant, but on the whole, they have existed side by side in a combination of harmony and competition.

The first model (for convenience, I will call it the "external model") is based upon the establishment of a formal, detailed, and usually written set of rules, that is, a legal code which defines permissible and impermissible conduct. A governmental organization enforces compliance with these rules, resolves ambiguities, and settles disputes. This organization in turn has regulations of its own that specify the manner in which it should operate and that provide means for members of the public to obtain redress against improper official actions. Generally, the legal system and the rules of law tend to be complicated and difficult to understand. Trained specialists are required to manage the legal bureaucracy and to act as legal advisors to the public.

This model of law is similar to and derives mainly from the Western legal concepts that were introduced into China at the beginning of this century, and reinfused into Chinese life with the adoption of Soviet legal institutions, methods, and thinking after Liberation in 1949. To a lesser degree, this model also is influenced by traditional Chinese legal practices. Some of the early legalist philosophers (*fa-*

*chia*) had similar attitudes toward the role and function of law.[1] More important, in spite of the Confucian disdain for formal coercive law, China has had for many centuries an active and complex legal system, complete with codes, courts, and the like.[2] Thus, as part of their cultural heritage, the Communists possessed some familiarity with a formal legal system and with centralized bureaucratic government.

The adoption of the external model of law provides many advantages for the Chinese. For one thing, it makes the Chinese legal system more recognizable, and consequently more acceptable, to the West and to the Soviet Union. China's past difficulties with Western criticism of the Chinese legal system and with extraterritoriality make this an important consideration. The external model also provides a clear and rationalized system of government and administration to nation builders who are seeking clarity and rationality; and it strengthens central control. Through the establishment of legal rules and procedures, higher level authorities not only can provide guidance for lower level officials, but also can restrict the scope of their discretionary powers. Moreover, through the medium of law, the public can know when an official is acting improperly and can inform the higher level authorities through the various complaint and appeal procedures. The legal system also is an effective means of controlling the public. In addition to maintaining a degree of public order, law can be used to publicize and to enforce new social policies, as well as to monitor the implementation of and response to these policies.

The second model of law (I will call it the "internal model") is quite different. Proper modes of behavior are taught not through written laws, but rather through a lengthy and continuing educational process whereby a person first learns and then internalizes the socially accepted values and norms. Compliance is obtained not through fear of governmental punishment, but from a genuine understanding and acceptance of the proper rules of conduct. Where such self-control fails, social pressure arises spontaneously to correct and to control the deviant. The coercive power of the state is used for enforcement only in

---

[1] T'ung-tsu Ch'ü, *Law and Society in Traditional China* (The Hague: Mouton, 1961); *The Book of Lord Shang,* trans. J. J. L. Duyvendak (London: Arthur Probsthain, 1928); *The Complete Works of Han Fei,* trans. W. K. Liao (London: Arthur Probsthain, 1939 and 1959).

[2] See generally, Derk Bodde and Clarence Morris, *Law in Imperial China: Exemplified by 190 Ch'ing Dynasty Cases* (Cambridge, Mass.: Harvard University Press, 1967); T'ung-tsu Ch'ü, *Local Government Under the Ch'ing* (Cambridge, Mass.: Harvard University Press, 1962); Sybille van der Sprenkel, *Legal Institutions in Manchu China* (London: Athlone Press, 1962).

the most serious cases in which the deviant is particularly recalcitrant or depraved. Since each individual is deeply involved in the legal process, law must be simple and must be capable of being applied without the help of skilled specialists. And, since enforcement is handled to a great extent by the community at large, the role of the state in legal administration is limited and the size of the legal bureaucracy is small.

This model seems to include many traditional Chinese ideas and practices. Especially striking is its similarity to the concept of *li*.[3] Both rely heavily upon persuasion and education rather than force, and upon the use of social pressure rather than governmental power. Both also stress the importance of internalizing the rules of conduct and point out the ineffectiveness of using fear of punishment to make people behave. Indeed, if one substitutes the term "socialist morality" for "Confucian morality" and the term "comrade" for *"chün-tzu"* (gentleman), one can use some of the Chinese classics to describe this model of law.

While the traditional influences certainly are present, other factors are no less important. Communist Chinese ideology, for example, calls for the participation and involvement of the masses in all aspects of government, including law.[4] Some degree of decision making and of sanctioning power also is granted to the masses, or at least to a local social group. Ideological commitment to the mass line is reinforced by some practical considerations. To begin with, internalization of the socially accepted values and norms is a more effective means of controlling conduct than the use of coercive force, and self-policing is much cheaper than the employment of a vast state police apparatus. Because of problems such as the size and variety of Chinese society, the difficulties of communication, and the limited amount of available resources, Peking can exercise direct and strict control over local administration only in the most important matters. For routine items, including much of the administration of the legal system, it is more

[3] See Benjamin Schwartz, "On Attitudes Toward Law in China," in Milton Katz (ed.), *Government Under Law and the Individual* (Washington, D.C.: American Council of Learned Societies, 1957), reprinted in Jerome A. Cohen, *The Criminal Process in the People's Republic of China, 1949–1963: An Introduction* (Cambridge, Mass.: Harvard University Press, 1968), for an enlightening discussion of the meanings and functions of *li* and *fa*.

[4] See, generally, James R. Townsend, *Political Participation in Communist China* (Berkeley and Los Angeles: University of California Press, 1967). For a discussion of the relation of the mass line to legal work, see Stanley Lubman, "Mao and Mediation: Politics and Dispute Resolution in Communist China," *California Law Review*, No. 55 (November, 1967), p. 1284.

efficient and effective to permit a substantial degree of local autonomy. Furthermore, the Communists have a distrust of and a dislike for bureaucrats and bureaucratism. This results in part from a reaction against the isolation and abuses of power by the traditional and the Nationalist powerholders, and in part from a fear that an entrenched bureaucracy will not heed Party direction. As a result, the Communists use the masses as a check on official actions and as a counterbalance to official power.

Other aspects of the internal model also reflect a combination of traditional and nontraditional influences. For example, the traditional practice of having members of the community handle most dispute settlement and control most deviant conduct prepared the way for the contemporary belief that legal administration does not require the services of skilled specialists. This traditional influence is reinforced by the Communists' own experiences. In the border and the liberated areas which they occupied before 1949, there was little functional specialization in the government or in the legal system. Cadres tended to be jacks-of-all-trades. This worked fairly well since the areas were small, the societies they contained were simple, and the cadres and the masses were highly motivated by the concerns of revolution and war. In addition, almost no legal specialists were available, even if one wanted to use them. This personnel problem was not alleviated after Liberation, even though the law schools and the holdovers from the Nationalist regime provided a small supply of legally trained persons. Consequently, legal theory and practice had to be adjusted to enable generalists to operate the legal system.

There are a number of areas where the external and internal models of law conflict or, at least, pull in opposite directions. For example, the internal model stresses local initiative and decision-making power, and tolerates considerable variations in norms, methods, and results from area to area. This runs counter to the external model's desire for clarity and certainty and its emphasis on strong central government. The external model's reliance upon a professional bureaucracy and skilled specialists to administer the legal system in an efficient and rationalized manner conflicts with the internal model's commitment to simplicity and mass participation. The internal model also lacks the clear appeal procedures and channels of the external model, and must therefore find very different means to protect a person from arbitrary actions by officials or by members of his peer group.

While the two models are quite dissimilar, some of their differences are more apparent in theory than in practice. Often the two models complement each other, with the external model handling serious matters and the internal model dealing with more routine affairs. Furthermore, the existence of the external model usually does not preclude the simultaneous existence of the internal model. In general, a person does not learn what he can and cannot do by studying or even by referring to the legal codes. Most notions concerning proper and improper conduct are learned as part of the socialization process, a process whose concepts and practices greatly resemble those of the internal model.

By the same token, over a period of time the internal model tends to evolve into the external model. In the ideal internal model, general patterns of proper conduct are truly internalized so that one "knows" what to do in each case. In many instances, however, this general understanding consists of or soon turns into a list of specific precepts. These may be called *li*, rules of propriety and morality, or any other legal or nonlegal name, but in due course they come to have much the same effect as the rules of law in the external model. Both the precepts and the rules of law tell one what to do in a particular situation; failure to comply results in sure and unpleasant consequences, although in the internal model, these may be social or economic sanctions rather than forty blows of the heavy bamboo. In a similar manner, the informal style of the internal model tends to ossify and to become rigid and formalized. With continued development and refinement, the legal system increases in complexity, and legal specialists are needed more and more to operate the system. At the same time, despite the emphasis on self-policing and on community action, the legal bureaucracy tends to grow and the state comes to play a larger role in legal work.

## THE DEVELOPMENT AND EVOLUTION OF THE CHINESE LEGAL SYSTEM

### THE INITIAL ASCENDANCY OF THE EXTERNAL MODEL

Although there were many changes and shifts as the Chinese experimented with both models of law, until 1957 the Chinese legal system generally developed along the lines of the external model. One of the first orders of business after Liberation was the establishment of a legal system.[5] The Chinese leaders seemed to have accepted a priori the principle that a state must have law. It probably did not occur to anyone at this time that law might be dispensed with entirely, as some legal writers suggested after 1957. A viable legal system was regarded as an important prerequisite to claims of legitimacy and to hopes for acceptance at home and abroad. It also facilitated the managing of the government and the society by establishing lines of control and communication, by maintaining public order, and by publicizing and enforcing the new social policies.

Even before Liberation, of course, the Communists had worked with law and had established a fledgling legal system.[6] In the border and the liberated areas, a series of laws and regulations had been promulgated which defined the organization and manner of operation of the government, and which set forth the new policies and norms. Many of the laws issued after Liberation—such as the Land Reform Law, the Marriage Law, the various labor laws, and the organic laws of legal and quasi-legal bodies such as the court and the mediation committee —had their origins in the pre-Liberation period.

The Common Program was passed by the Chinese People's Political Consultative Conference immediately after Liberation. This document stated the fundamental principles of the new regime and established the basic governmental structures. Article 17 abolished "(a) ll laws, decrees and judicial systems of the Kuomintang reactionary government which oppress the people."[7] Despite the possible ambiguity in wording, this provision was understood to have abrogated all Kuomintang (KMT) laws. Its practical effect, however, was more limited. Many of the KMT judicial and police organs were retained by the Communists with little change. These organs were useful and necessary instruments of administration. They were politically neutral

---

[5] On land reform, see William Hinton, *Fanshen: A Documentary of Revolution in a Chinese Village* (New York and London: Monthly Review Press, 1966); Ezra Vogel, "Land Reform in Kwangtung 1951–1953: Central Control and Localism," *CQ*, No. 38 (April–June, 1969), p. 27; Kuang-tung sheng t'u-ti kai-ko wei-yüan-hui (Kwangtung Province Land Reform Committee) (ed.), *Kuang-tung sheng t'u-ti kai-ko fa-kuei hui-pien* (Kwangtung Province Land Reform Laws and Regulations Compendium) (Hsin-hua shu-tien, 1950). I feel that this period is characterized by special problems and unique circumstances, and should be treated separately. See Victor H. Li, reviews of Cohen, *Criminal Process,* and of Bodde and Morris, *Law in Imperial China,* in *Michigan Law Review,* No. 67 (November, 1968), pp. 179, 184.

[6] Shao-chuan Leng, *Justice in Communist China: A Survey of the Judicial System of the Chinese People's Republic* (Dobbs Ferry, N.Y.: Oceana Publications, 1967), pp. 1–26.

[7] Albert P. Blaustein (ed.), *Fundamental Legal Documents of Communist China* (South Hackensack, N.J.: Fred B. Rothman & Co., 1962), p. 41.

in and of themselves, and could be converted with relative ease to serve the goals of the new regime. In Peking, for example, the KMT court system was retained virtually intact after Liberation, except that it was now called the "people's court." [8] Two former public security cadres (from Kwangtung and Chekiang, respectively) who were interviewed said that the only change in police organization that they were aware of was the replacement of the term *ching-ch'a* (police) by the term *kung-an* (public security) on the nameplates in front of the police stations.

Even some KMT laws which had no obvious political or class character, such as traffic regulations or laws concerning the common crimes, continued to be applied. Taken literally, Article 17 of the Common Program created a legal vacuum in the large areas where the new regime had not yet passed any laws. When dealing with problems in these areas, the administrators of the legal system often looked to the *Complete Book of the Six Laws,* which was the KMT code, for guidance. This was especially true of the former KMT officials who were retained by the Communists after Liberation.

This group of retained personnel constituted one of the most important links between the old regime and the new. They usually were officials who were not politically offensive, and who possessed the technical skills and specialized knowledge (which the Communist cadres usually did not have) that were needed to operate the political-legal system. The percentage of retained personnel was highest in the judiciary, which was an area where the Communists had almost no qualified cadres of their own at the time of Liberation. As revealed in the documents of the 1952 judicial reform campaign and of the 1957 antirightist campaign, this percentage varied from 50 per cent to as high as 90 per cent of the total number of judges in a court system.[9] The number of retained personnel in the public security was consider-

[8] Pei-ching shih jen-min fa-yüan mi-shu-ch'u (Secretariat of the Peking City People's Court) (ed.), *Pei-ching shih jen-min fa-yüan kung-tso kai-kuang* (The General Work of the Peking City People's Court) (Peking: Hsin-hua shu-tien, date unknown).

[9] Hsiao Hung, "Can We Let the Old Law Viewpoints Come Back to Life? Refute the Rightists' Derogation of Judicial Reform," *Kuang-ming Jih-pao* (hereafter *KMJP*), October 6, 1957. See also, Ch'en Su-fang, *Chung-kung ti ssu-fa kai-ko* (The Judicial Reform of Communist China) (Hong Kong: Yu-lien ch'u-pan-she, 1953); "Fan-tui chiu fa kuan-tien; kai-tsao ho cheng-tun ssu-fa chi-kuan" (Oppose Old Law Viewpoints; Reform and Improve the Judicial Organs), *CFJP*, August 21, 1952; Li Kuang-lin and Li Chien-fei, "Su-ch'ing fan jen-min ti chiu fa kuan-tien" (Eradicate the Anti-people Old Law Viewpoints), *JMJP*, August 22, 1952. A campaign similar to the judicial reform campaign was conducted within the public security. See, for example, "Kuang-k'ai fan-tui chiu ching-ch'a tso-feng yün-tung" (Open the Campaign Against the Old Police Work Style), *NFJP*, October 1, 1952.

ably smaller; the coercive nature of police work would tend to make a policeman more disliked by the Communist "bandits," and a substantial part of police activity can be handled by Communist cadres after only a little training. Despite this, however, many KMT policemen were retained after Liberation. The two public security cadres mentioned above estimated that about one-third of the household patrolmen engaged in the early household registration work were retained personnel.

As more Communist cadres entered political-legal work and as these cadres began to acquire the necessary technical skills, the retained personnel were replaced. The public security removed virtually all retained personnel by 1953. The better ones were transferred to less sensitive work or were forced into retirement. The others were purged in the three anti and five anti campaigns and in the 1952 police rectification (*cheng-ching*) campaign. Many former KMT judges also were removed in the three anti and five anti campaigns and in the judicial reform campaign. It appears, however, that the judges either were more difficult to replace than policemen or were cleverer in convincing the regime of their loyalty, since a substantial number survived until the antirightist campaign of 1957, and perhaps even beyond.

On the basis of the Common Program, the Communists took rapid steps to set up the governmental structure, including the legal system. Beginning in 1950 and culminating in the constitutional and organic enactments of 1954, they established a judiciary and procuracy that were patterned closely after the Soviet model.[10] In addition, a series of regulations issued in 1954 redefined the organization and operation of the police station (*p'ai-ch'u-so*), the street office (*chieh-tao pan-shih-ch'u*), the residents' committee (*chü-min wei-yüan-hui*), and the mediation committee (*t'iao-chieh wei-yüan-hui*).[11] A large number of substantive laws and regulations also were promulgated. Some, such as the Land Reform Law and the Marriage Law, were of a revolutionary nature, and some, such as the Labor Law and the Labor Insurance Law, were of a propagandist nature. There also were sev-

[10] For a description of the formal legal system, see Cohen, *Criminal Process;* Leng, *Justice in Communist China,* pp. 27–178; and Tao-tai Hsia, *Guide to Selected Legal Sources of Mainland China* (Washington, D.C.: Library of Congress, 1967), pp. 1–76. See also three articles by George Ginsburgs and Arthur Stahnke, "The Genesis of the People's Procuratorate in Communist China: 1949–51," *CQ,* No. 20 (October–December, 1964), p. 1; "The People's Procuratorate in Communist China: The Period of Maturation: 1951–1954," *CQ,* No. 24 (October–December, 1965), p. 53; and "The People's Procuratorate in Communist China: The Institution in the Ascendant: 1954–1957," No. 34 (April–June, 1968), p. 82.

[11] Cohen, *Criminal Process,* pp. 106, 109, 110, 124.

eral statutes dealing with the suppression of corruption, counterrevolution, and other criminal activities, and there was a large body of economic regulations.[12]

Efforts to strengthen the formal legal system continued through the mid-1950's. Internal directives were issued to control police practices and to regularize judicial procedures. Work was begun on a criminal code, and a draft of this code was circulated for study at the 1956 Party Congress. A code of criminal procedure and a civil code also were promised. Law schools were operating again, and legal publications were appearing in increasing numbers. The work of the people's lawyers, and to a lesser extent the notarial offices, received great publicity and praise.[13] Civil litigation, while still not popular, was gaining in acceptance,[14] in part because of the airing of pre-Liberation grievances against the former privileged groups. Equally important, however, was the fact that people felt greater confidence in the courts and were beginning to accept the idea that the courts were proper places for resolving personal problems. Women in particular turned to the courts to obtain redress against oppressive husbands and parents-in-law.

The promulgation of laws and the establishment of legal organs were accompanied by a drive to urge strict adherence to the rules of law. A large number of articles and pamphlets were published which stressed the importance of *shou-fa* (observing the law) by all citizens and officials.[15] In the 1956 Party Congress, Tung Pi-wu, the president of the Supreme People's Court, said:

> The Party's Central Committee calls on all public security organs, procuratorates, law courts and all other state organs to conduct their affairs according to

[12] Many of these laws are translated in Blaustein, *Fundamental Legal Documents,* and in Cohen, *Criminal Process.*

[13] See Leng, *Justice in Communist China,* pp. 127–46; Huang Yüan (ed.), *Wo-kuo jen-min lü-shih chih-tu* (My Country's System of People's Lawyers) (Canton: Kuang-tung jen-min ch'u-pan-she, 1956). On the notarial offices, see "Ch'üan-kuo hsü-to ch'eng-shih chan-k'ai kung-cheng kung-tso" (Many Cities in the Entire Country Developing Notarial Work), *KMJP,* June 18, 1955; and "Ko-ti chi-chi chan-k'ai kung-cheng kung-tso" (Notarial Work Actively Developed in Many Places), *KMJP,* November 26, 1956.

[14] See, for example, "Hei-lung-chiang kao-chi fa-yüan kung-tso pao-kao" (Work Report of the Heilungkiang High Level People's Court), *Hei-lung-chiang Jih-pao, September 27, 1957.* See also, "Pin-yang jen-min chien-ch'a-yüan chung-shih jen-min lai-fang kung-tso" (The People's Procuracy of Pin-yang Seriously Regards the Work of Receiving People's Visits), *Kuang-hsi Jih-pao,* June 11, 1957, which attributes the increase in complaints made to this procuracy to the fact that the masses are satisfied with its work.

[15] For example, Ch'en Fou, *T'an-t'an shou-fa* (Discussions on Observing the Law) (Tientsin: Jen-min ch'u-pan-she, 1956).

law. I believe that doing everything according to law is a most important link in the forging of a sounder and stronger people's democratic legal system.

To do things according to law has two aspects:

First, there must be laws to go by. This means that we must quickly promulgate, in a complete form, several important laws and regulations of the state which are not in existence. . . . In my opinion, the drafts [of the criminal code and the code of criminal procedure] can soon be completed. . . .

Second, laws must be complied with. All laws and regulations, once enacted, must be strictly enforced and complied with. All judicial organs, in particular, should strictly abide by them and are absolutely forbidden to violate them. . . .

To further strengthen the people's democratic legal system, the Party must pay attention to ideological education on the legal system so that Party members will know that the law of the state and Party discipline must both be observed and cannot be violated; that adherence to the state law is an intrinsic part of adherence to Party discipline and that violation of the state law is a violation of Party discipline.[16]

Thus, as of early 1957, the Chinese appeared to have adopted the external model of law. They had established courts, procuracies, and other legal organs familiar to Western and Soviet lawyers, and they were training specialists to operate the legal system. A constitution and a number of other laws had been promulgated, and a complete and detailed code defining the rights and duties of individuals and officials was promised. Even though there were many requirements of the external model which had not been met, these deficiencies were attributed to inexperience and to incomplete implementation of the legal system. As the system developed further, the deficiencies would decrease and then would disappear.

## THE DEVELOPMENT OF THE INTERNAL MODEL
### DURING THE EARLY YEARS

While the external model of law flourished, the internal model also was making important gains, though to a smaller degree and in a less apparent manner. So long as the formal legal system was not complete, much of the work of correcting and controlling deviant conduct was handled by local groups. Until full legal codes were promulgated, many social norms and rules of behavior had to be fixed locally, with great variation from area to area and even from case to case.

The internal model was regarded, however, as much more than a mere stopgap measure to be discarded when the formal legal system

16 "Speech by Comrade Tung Pi-wu," *Eighth National Congress of the Communist Party of China* (Peking: Foreign Languages Press, 1956), II, 94–96. See also the speeches by Teng Hsiao-p'ing and Chou En-lai at the same congress, in *ibid.*, I, 169, 261.

became fully implemented. The Communists had deep and abiding commitments to many of the principles and methods of this model. They favored, for example, a simple and flexible legal system, in part because of their familiarity with an informal style of legal work from their pre-Liberation experiences, and in part because of the inability of the new Communist cadres to operate a complex and specialized legal system. More important, however, the Communists believed that law *ought* to be simple. The masses should be able to understand and to utilize the law fully; law must not be so complex that it becomes the private domain of a few specialists or a tool by which officials can oppress the masses.

Much effort was expended to educate the masses about law. Legal cadres continually made speeches, arranged exhibits, wrote articles, and led discussions about various aspects of law.[17] Legal language was kept simple and straightforward, with a minimum of technical terms and jargon.[18] The promulgation of each new statute or regulation was accompanied by extensive campaigns to explain its content and rationale to the masses.[19] Texts of the law were circulated, together with commentaries and illustrations. Newspapers published articles about the law and over a period of time reported on its implementation. All these materials were used as the bases of small group discussions, during which the law was examined in detail, particularly as it applied in the lives of the discussants.

At the same time, there was an informalization of the legal work

[17] Chuang Shih-min, *et al.*, "Cheng-ch'üeh ch'u-li jen-min nei-pu ti chiu-fen" (Properly Handle the Disputes Among the People), *Cheng-fa yen-chiu* (Political-Legal Research (hereafter *CFYC*), No. 4, 1959.

[18] "Properly Launch the Judicial Reform Campaign," *KMJP*, August 27, 1952; "Tsui-kao jen-min fa-yüan tsai 'san fan' hou chien-hua-le hsü-to wen-tu shou-hsü" (The Supreme People's Court Simplifies Many Secretariat Procedures After the "Three-Anti"), *JMJP*, July 24, 1952; "Ying-kai yen-su ti t'ai-tu lai hsieh p'an-chüeh-shu" (A Serious Attitude Should Be Adopted When Writing a Judgment Document), *KMJP*, January 20, 1957.

[19] For example, when the Security Administration Punishment Act (SAPA) was promulgated, Lo Jui-ch'ing, then minister of public security, said in an accompanying speech:

It should be explained repeatedly that thoroughly putting into effect the SAPA adopted by our country, like putting into effect other laws and decrees or government administrative orders, requires passing through [a period of] thorough propaganda-education. If the reasons are not clearly explained to the people to obtain their adherence and support, and if it is not founded on the basis of self-awareness and voluntarism of the vast [number of] people, but rather, coercion is simply understood to mean crude oppression that does not require any educating, it will be completely incorrect, and it will definitely get nowhere.

Lo Jui-ch'ing, "Explanations of the Draft SAPA of the PRC," cited in Cohen, *Criminal Process*, p. 203.

style.[20] Judicial and administrative procedures, which probably comprise the area of law that laymen find most abstruse and annoying, were drastically simplified. The imposing of penalties for failure to meet procedural requirements was criticized as bureaucratism. Mass line concepts, which fitted in well with the internal model's emphasis on individual involvement, also were applied to legal work. Cadres were instructed to "penetrate the masses" and to "rely on the masses." This meant not only asking the masses for information and assistance when conducting investigations, but also seeking their advice on how cases should be decided. In turn, the masses on their own initiative were supposed to help in any way possible. They also could comment on the manner in which the cadres carried out their work. In addition, the introduction of the practice of "people's reception" gave the masses access to all officials, thus enabling them to bypass procedural obstacles and to overcome bureaucratic indifference and tyranny.[21] In like manner, an individual could air a grievance and could obtain redress without resorting to the legal system by appealing directly to the Party and, to a lesser extent, to the Ministry of Supervision and the newspapers.[22]

These changes in legal work were not due entirely to a commitment to the internal model of law. Another important factor was that most of the new Communist cadres who replaced the purged Nationalist

[20] Sung I, "Su-sung-shu hao nan hsieh!" (How Difficult It Is to Write a Complaint!), *KMJP*, September 8, 1956; "Properly Launch the Judicial Reform Campaign," *KMJP*, August 27, 1952.

[21] See generally, "Chung-yang jen-min cheng-fu cheng-wu-yüan kuan-yü ch'u-li jen-min lai-hsin ho chieh-chien jen-min kung-tso ti chüeh-ting" (Decision of the Government Affairs Council of the Central People's Government Concerning the Work of Handling People's Letters and Receiving the People), *CFJP*, June 9, 1951; "Pi chung-shih ch'u-li jen-min lai-hsin ti kung-tso" (The Work of Handling People's Letters Must Be Regarded Seriously), *JMJP*, December 4, 1955; "Kuo-wu-yüan kuan-yü chia-ch'iang ch'u-li jen-min lai-hsin ho chieh-tai jen-min lai-fang kung-tso ti chih-shih" (Directive of the State Council Concerning the Strengthening of the Work of Handling People's Letters and Receiving People's Inquiries), *JMJP*, November 25, 1957. See also note 29.

[22] During 1954, the *NFJP* conducted a campaign to have readers send in complaints to the newspaper. "Pan-yüeh tu-che lai-hsin ch'u-li ch'ing-k'uang" (The Situation of Handling Letters From Readers During the Past Half Month), *NFJP*, August 5, 1954, states that 2,158 letters were received in a two-week period. Even in the absence of such a campaign, all newspapers receive a steady stream of letters. On the work of the Ministry of Supervision, see Franz Schurmann, *Ideology and Organization in Communist China* (Berkeley and Los Angeles: University of California Press, 1966), pp. 309–64. Is the "control correspondent" discussed by Schurmann the same as the "procuratorial correspondent"? See, for example, "Ch'üan-kuo chien-ch'a t'ung-hsin-yüan tao chiu-wan-ssu-ch'ien-to ming; t'ung wei-fa fan-tsui fen-tzu tso tou-cheng ch'i-le hen-to tso-yung" (The Number of Procuratorial Correspondents in the Country Reach 94,000; Very Useful in the Struggle Against Illegal Elements), *JMJP*, September 5, 1956.

judges or who were later added to political-legal work had little legal training or experience.[23] As might be expected, the retained personnel and the new cadres had very different understandings of the nature of legal work. There was considerable conflict between the two groups over professional and personal styles. It is not difficult to imagine the differences and problems a former guerrilla squad leader would have in working with a colleague who is an Oxford or Sorbonne trained lawyer.

More generally, the conflict was between the legal specialists (consisting of the retained personnel and some of the recent law school graduates) who were well trained in law and who held Western ideas concerning the role of law and the structure of the legal system, and the new cadres who were appointed to political-legal work for their ideological correctness and not for their legal expertise. The specialists occupied most of the positions on law faculties, codification commissions, and editorial boards of legal journals. They also were active in the middle and upper level judiciary. Their influence can be seen in the adoption of the constitution and the Soviet model of law in 1954. It seems to me, however, that their influence, while considerable, may have appeared to Western analysts to be greater than it actually was. These cadres dominated the area of legal writings and publications, and therefore were the only persons visible to the West.

The new cadres held most of the positions in the public security and in the lower and middle level judiciary. Not being scholars, they wrote almost nothing for the legal journals. Indeed, where their work was discussed in scholarly writings, it usually was being disparaged by a specialist. Nevertheless, through holding positions concerned with the actual implementation of the legal process, they played an important role in determining the new political-legal work style. Their influence was enhanced by the fact that they were in greater political favor than the specialists, and therefore could count on the support of the political cadres in most disputes.

The conflict between the two groups existed in every aspect of

[23] See Li, book reviews, p. 189; "Chuang-chia-jen tang fa-kuan" (Peasants Become Judges), *KMJP*, March 4, 1955; "Pen-shih i p'i you-hsiu t'iao-chieh wei-yüan pei-hsüan-fa ts'an-chia fa-yüan kung-tso" (A Group of Superior Mediation Committee Members Selected to Enter Judicial Work in This City), *Fu-chien Jih-pao*, November 26, 1952. See also, "Ssu-fa-pu chih-ting p'ei-yang kan-pu, k'ai-chan fa-hsüeh yen-chiu kung-tso ti chi-hua" (The Ministry of Justice Determines the Plan for Developing Cadres and Expanding Legal Research), *KMJP*, June 8, 1956. The plan was that after twelve years of correspondence courses, 30 per cent of the judicial cadres would have the equivalent of a "high level" legal education, and the rest would have the equivalent of two years of legal training.

political-legal work, but was most intense or, at least, most visible in the judiciary, since large numbers of both groups worked in that organ. For example, after Liberation there was a drive to clear up the cases which had accumulated on the court dockets during the past several years. As part of this drive, judicial personnel were urged to work harder and faster. Some of the new cadres took this urging quite to heart. My best calculations indicate that the judges of the Peking city court dealt with about one case every ten minutes, a rate not unlike our traffic courts. While we feel embarrassed about the "justice mills" of our system, the Chinese praised the Peking judges, hailing their work as an excellent example of the new revolutionary justice.[24]

Not all of the consequences of using untrained cadres in political-legal work were counterproductive or ludicrous. The new cadres also had many positive and lasting effects on the legal system. In large part because of their efforts, law was kept simple and easy to understand. They constantly resisted the adoption of complicated rules or a complex legal system. To a certain extent, their attitude was a rationalization for their own lack of technical knowledge and skill. It also reflected, however, a belief that as law increases in complexity, it becomes alienated from the masses and becomes their master rather than their servant.

The new cadres were particularly unhappy with the cumbersome and stylized rules of procedure, especially judicial procedure, which the legal specialists had copied from continental and Soviet law. One writer complained:

In handling a case from beginning to end, there are thirty procedural steps, and one delay may last from several months to two or three years. It results in the infliction of great injuries on the people. The people sigh and say: "In the Kuomintang courts one needed a lot of money to try a case. Now one needs a long life."[25]

Beginning with the judicial reform campaign, the new cadres pressed for the reduction of the number of procedural rules and for the adoption of an informal and flexible style of legal work. Cadres were urged to allow a case to "bloom."[26] That is, whatever the original subject

---

24 "Jen-min fa-yüan chi-chi ch'ing-le chi-an; wu-jih nei chieh-an wu-pai-ssu-shih chien" (The People's Court Actively Clears Up Accumulated Cases; 540 Cases Concluded Within Five Days), *JMJP*, May 22, 1950; Pei-ching shih jen-min fa-yüan mi-shu-ch'u (ed.), *Pei-ching shih jen-min fa yüan*.

25 "Properly Launch the Judicial Reform Campaign," *KMJP*, August 27, 1952.

26 *Ibid.*

matter or the cause of action, a cadre was supposed to look into and to resolve any matters that might arise during the handling of a case. Judges also were admonished not to "sit in court and handle cases." [27] Rather than rely only on the evidence presented by the parties, a judge should personally go out and investigate the facts. Neither should a cadre wait for a complaint to be filed before taking action on a matter.[28] A good cadre should penetrate the masses and should take the initiative in seeking wrongs to rectify. Harking back to pre-Liberation practices, a judge was asked to act not only as an adjudicator, but also as a policeman and a public guardian.

The new cadres also were influential in introducing many substantive innovations and changes into the legal system. The practice of people's reception whereby formal procedural rules and bureaucratic red tape could be bypassed has been mentioned earlier. In the courts, people's reception at first involved only the operating of a reception office to handle matters such as accepting complaints, issuing summonses, and controlling the court calendar. Gradually the functions of this office expanded, especially after the judges were directed to "receive the masses" in person. The office began to help parties write their pleadings; soon it also gave opinions on the merits of the claims, and even investigated factual allegations and mediated disputes. Thus, the masses were able to get authoritative legal advice from the same persons who would act as judges if a formal suit were filed, without having to go through any of the regular court procedures or incurring any expense.[29]

One of the most interesting consequences of using untrained cadres

[27] "Hsi-pei chin-hsing ssu-fa kai-ko" (Northwest Carries Out Judicial Reform), *KMJP*, August 24, 1952; "Ta-tiao tso-t'ang wen-an ti kuan-feng" (Overthrow the Bureaucratic Attitude of Sitting in Court to Hear Cases), *Pei-ching Jih-pao*, June 25, 1958.

[28] *Ibid.*

[29] This conclusion is supported by interviews. See Victor H. Li, "The Use of Survey Interviewing in Research on Chinese Law,'" in Jerome A. Cohen (ed.), *Contemporary Chinese Law: Research Problems and Perspectives* (Cambridge, Mass.: Harvard University Press, 1970), p. 118. See also, Yüan Kuang, "Jen-min fa-yüan ti jen-min chieh-tai-shih" (The People's Reception Office of the People's Court), *JMJP*, December 2, 1953; Ssu Hsüan, "Jen-min fa-yüan jen-min chieh-tai-shih kung-tso chung ti chi-ko wen-t'i" (Several Problems in the Work of the People's Reception Office of the People's Court), *JMJP*, July 21, 1954. On "people's reception" by other organs, see "Shih kung-an-chü ch'u-li jen-min lai-hsin lai-fang kung-tso ti ching-yen" (The Experiences of the City Public Security Bureau in Handling the Work of People's Letters and People's Inquiries), *Kuang-chou Jih-pao*, November 29, 1953; "Kan-su sheng tang cheng chi-kuan jen-chen tui-tai lai-hsin lai-fang; ken-chu ch'ün-chung p'i-p'ing chien-i ch'ieh-shih kai-chin kung-tso" (Party and Government Organs in Kansu Province Sincerely Accept Letters and Inquiries; Definitely Improve Their Work on the Bases of the Criticisms and Suggestions of the Masses), *JMJP*, January 9, 1962. See also note 21.

was that law did not develop as fully as it might have into an effective means by which the central authorities could control the actions of lower level administrators. Many of the laws and regulations issued by the central authorities were drafted in a very unlawyerlike fashion, which probably reflected the influence of the new cadres. These laws usually contained a broad statement of purpose and direction (for example, "All counterrevolutionary criminals whose goal is to overthrow the people's democratic regime or to undermine the undertaking of the people's democracy shall be punished in accordance with this Act." [30]), which was followed by a series of rules dealing with detailed and specific situations, such as "struggling to be first to board a ferry, in disregard of an order to stop, or coercing a ferry pilot to overload in the course of providing ferry service." [31] They would end with a catch-all provision such as the following: "Those who, with a counterrevolutionary purpose, commit crimes not covered by the provisions of this Act may be given punishments prescribed for crimes enumerated in this Act which are comparable to the crimes commited." [32] The phrasing of the laws often was ambiguous, and there seemed to be a reluctance or inability to define terms. What, for example, is meant by "those who behave like hooligans" [33] or by "conducting counterrevolutionary agitation and propaganda"? [34] Between the vagueness of the wording and the failure to state rules in a generalized form that would still be easy to apply in concrete cases, the laws did not provide much guidance for or restraints upon the local administrator. In many instances, the laws merely indicated broad policy concerns and cited examples of the application of these policies, but otherwise, they left the local administrator free to do as he wished.[35]

[30] Article 2, "Act of the PRC for the Punishment of Counterrevolution," in Cohen, *Criminal Process,* p. 300.

[31] Article 9(8), "SAPA," in *ibid.,* p. 217. The imperial codes also used very specific and narrow statutory language. For example, "If a knavish fellow from outside [the capital], with a yellow banner planted upon his head, and accusations issuing from his mouth, rushes into a government office in order to exercise coercion upon the officials there . . ." cited in Bodde and Morris, *Law in Imperial China,* p. 68.

[32] Article 16, "Act of the PRC for the Punishment of Counterrevolution," in Cohen, *Criminal Process,* p. 302. The use of analogy also has roots in traditional law. Analogy was allowed under the imperial code whenever "there is no precisely applicable statute or sub-statute." In such cases, the sentence together with an explanation of the case must be submitted to the emperor for review. Bodde and Morris, *Law in Imperial China,* pp. 117, 175-78.

[33] Article 1(1), "Decision of the State Council of the PRC Relating to Problems of Rehabilitation Through Labor," in Cohen, *Criminal Process,* p. 249.

[34] Article 10(3), "Act of the PRC for the Punishment of Counterrevolution," in *ibid.,* p. 301.

[35] On problems of granting discretionary power to local level administrators, see

Even where there was a clear and explicit statutory rule which obviously applied in a particular situation, this rule still might be ignored. Jerome A. Cohen's book contains numerous examples of such violations.[36] While Western lawyers would be quite upset by this practice, the Chinese did not appear to be especially bothered. Perhaps the Chinese, or at least the new cadres, felt that it was not possible to draft laws which did more than merely state general policies and positions, leaving great discretionary powers in the hands of the administrator. Even Tung Pi-wu in his 1956 Party Congress speech said: "Of course, the state affairs we are engaged in are concrete and varied, while the law is general and fixed and so it is impossible to prescribe everything by law." [37] For the same reason, it also would be incorrect to require strict adherence to all rules of law. Thus, in discussing the Security Administration Punishment Act, Lo Jui-ch'ing, then minister of public security, said: "[T]he Act cannot be executed in a mechanical and inflexible way. Naturally it would be wrong to apply it uniformly and without inquiring into specific circumstances." [38]

Another area where the internal model of law was thoroughly implemented before 1957 was at the lowest levels of social organization and interaction. The basic neighborhood unit in urban areas, for example, was a group of several hundred to several thousand residents who were formed into a large number of small groups, which in turn constituted one or more residents' committees and street offices.[39] To a considerable extent, these units, under the leadership of the local public security station and the household patrolmen, were self-governing. They usually received only general policy guidelines from the higher level authorities and had to formulate their own implementing directives and plans. These units also reflected a high degree of participatory democracy; all persons were encouraged to take part in the decision making processes. In addition, most officials were elected, and they served for little or no monetary compensation. This granting of local autonomy and the reliance upon local personnel were partly

Victor H. Li, "The Public Security Bureau of Hui-yang *Hsien*," in John W. Lewis (ed.), *The City in Communist China* (forthcoming).

[36] See, for example, items 56, 90C, and 91, in Cohen, *Criminal Process*. See also *ibid.*, items 57, 71A, 78C, and 89.

[37] "Speech by Comrade Tung Pi-wu," p. 95.

[38] Lo, "Explanations."

[39] See Cohen, *Criminal Process,* pp. 97-170; Lubman, "Mao and Mediation," pp. 1309–25; Henry Lethbridge, *China's Urban Communes* (Hong Kong: Dragonfly Books, 1961); Janet Salaff, "The Urban Communes and Anti-city Experiment in Communist China," *CQ,* No. 29 (January–March, 1967), p. 82.

due to the state's lack of sufficient material and human resources to penetrate completely the lowest levels of society. Far more important, however, was the belief, which was supported both by ideology and by the Communists' pre-Liberation experiences, that local people *ought* to manage their own affairs and to solve their own problems.

A neighborhood unit handled a wide variety of matters, ranging from the preservation of public order and the mediation of disputes, to the operation of educational and medical facilities and the management of affairs relating to the public welfare of the residents. Each unit played a particularly important role in molding and controlling the conduct of its members. Through the endless study sessions, the limits of permissible and impermissible behavior and thinking were explored in detail, using each discussant's actions as concrete examples. However cynical one may be about the therapeutic and "thought reform" effects of these sessions, they certainly served at least to inform each person of the nature and probable consequences of his acts.[40]

The control of conduct was not limited merely to discussions and explanations. Each person was supposed to act as his brother's keeper and to correct any improper behavior of his neighbors. Few secrets were possible in this small and close social unit where busybodyism was regarded as a virtue. Whenever a person's actions or thoughts began to deviate from the accepted norms and patterns, a variety of social pressures would arise spontaneously to steer him back to the correct path. At first, these pressures would consist of persuasion and light criticism. If the errors remained uncorrected or became worse, increasingly severe sanctions would be imposed. At some point, the deviations might be so substantial or the deviant might appear to be so recalcitrant and incapable of being reformed that the coercive power of the state must be applied. The neighborhood unit would then turn the matter over to the appropriate official, who was usually the local household patrolman.

THE ENHANCEMENT OF THE INTERNAL MODEL AFTER 1957

A fundamental change in attitude toward law and legal work occurred around 1957. There was no official declaration of this change,

[40] For a description of a study session, see A. Doak Barnett, *Communist China: The Early Years, 1949–55* (New York: Frederick A. Praeger, 1964), pp. 89–103. See also, *ibid.*, pp. 104–15; Allyn Rickett and Adele Rickett, *Prisoners of Liberation* (New York: Cameron Association, 1957); Robert Lifton, *Thought Reform and the Psychology of Totalism* (New York: Norton, 1961); Harriet Mills, "Thought Reform: Ideological Remoulding in China," *Atlantic Monthly* (December, 1959), p. 71.

but with the antirightist campaign, the activity and prestige of almost all the legal organs fell sharply. Many judicial functions were reassigned to other organs, particularly to the public security. The procuracy, which had been established with great fanfare only a few years earlier, ceased to be developed. A large number of judicial and procuratorial cadres were transferred out of political-legal work and were not replaced. The people's lawyers came under attack for "tailism," apparently for serving their clients too well. Legal advisor offices no longer functioned, although the name was retained and a lawyer occasionally was hired to act as defense counsel in a public trial. Law schools, called political-legal institutes, continued to operate, but they taught more politics than law. Publications of legal materials also declined both in quantity and in quality. Of the political-legal organs, only the public security grew in size and importance after 1957. Over the years, it had been assigned the most reliable and capable personnel. When the other political-legal organs were attacked and began to lose their power and influence, the public security moved in to fill the vacuum. In due course, it completely dominated the court and the procuracy, and also took over almost all criminal law work. And, at least at the local levels, it played an increasingly important role in all aspects of political and administrative work. Public security organs often were placed in charge of matters that had only indirect bearing to public security work, such as famine relief or the reform of backward areas.[41]

As the court and other legal organs declined, many writers began to argue against having legal codes or even a formal set of laws.[42] Some believed that while laws were clearer and more precise after being written down, they also became more difficult to change. This stabilizing quality was thought to be undesirable at a time when China was engaged in a revolution in which enormous social, political, and economic changes were taking place continually, and in which a rule that might be appropriate one day might no longer be suitable the next. In such a situation, the desire for clarity was outweighed by

[41] For a detailed discussion of the work of the public security, see Li, "The Public Security Bureau"; Cohen, *Criminal Process,* pp. 104–31, 200–95, 368–405; Kuo Shou-hua (ed.), *Kung-fei kung-an chu-chi yü jen-min ching-ch'a chih yen-chiu* (Studies on the Public Security Organization and the People's Police of the Communist Bandits) (Taipei: Yang Ming-shan Institute, 1957).

[42] A fine article on the changing Chinese attitude toward codification is Arthur Stahnke, "The Background and Evolution of Party Policy on the Drafting of Legal Codes in Communist China," *American Journal of Comparative Law,* No. 15 (1966–67), p. 506.

the need to keep the revolution moving ahead. Other writers said that the articulation and promulgation of rules of law tended to make people litigious and loophole-happy. More laws did not make men behave better. On the contrary, the larger the set of laws, the less likely that men would forego their own "rights" and work unselfishly for the greater social good.[43] A few writers contended that codification simply was impossible. No set of general principles or specific rules could be devised which could deal satisfactorily with every situation and circumstance in the vast gamut of human experiences. At any rate, the draft codes disappeared, and no more was heard about them. The entire legal system moved toward increased informality, with emphasis placed on handling cases "according to the concrete circumstances" rather than "according to law."

Part of the change of attitude toward law was due to the fact that the lawyers, particularly the highly trained and skilled specialists, were among the most vociferous critics of the regime during the Hundred Flowers period.[44] When the reaction set in, not only were these critics personally attacked and branded as rightist, but the positions that they advocated—such as the codification of the law and the development of a strong legal system operated by trained specialists—also were attacked and were declared to be wrong. In a similar manner, the things criticized by the rightists, such as the low level of legal training for most cadres and the failure to establish and to follow procedural rules, were considered assets of the Chinese legal system. Having in effect

---

[43] Cf. the reaction of a sixth century B.C. Confucian scholar on hearing that a rudimentary criminal code had been promulgated:

The ancient kings . . . did not make [general] laws of punishment, fearing lest it should give rise to a contentious spirit among the people. . . . When the people know what the exact laws are, they do not stand in awe of their superiors. They also come to have a contentious spirit, and make their appeal to the express words, hoping peradventure to be successful. . . . When once the people know the ground for contention, they will cast propriety away, and make their appeal to your descriptions. They will all be contending about a matter as small as the point of an awl or a knife. Disorderly litigations will multiply, and bribes will walk abroad.

"Tso Chuan," in *The Chinese Classics* . . . , trans. James Legge, V, 609.

[44] See Roderick MacFarquhar (ed.), *The Hundred Flowers Campaign and the Chinese Intellectuals* (New York: Praeger, 1960), pp. 122–24; "T'an-t'an yu-kuan chia-ch'iang fa-chih chi-ko jen-shih wen-t'i" (Talks on the Understanding of Several Problems Concerning the Strengthening of the Rule of Law), *KMJP*, January 22, 1957; "Tang-wai lü-shih ch'ang-t'an tui ssu-fa pu-men ti i-chien" (Non-Party Lawyers Have a Pleasant Discussion of Opinions About the Judicial Departments), *Kuei-lin Jih-pao*, May 30, 1957. See also, "Grave Struggle Still Exists on Political and Legal Front," *JMJP*, October 9, 1957, in *SCMP*, No. 1636 (October 23, 1957); "Overcome the Two Deviations in Political and Legal Work," *JMJP*, October 14, 1957, in *SCMP*, No. 1638 (October 25, 1957); "Political and Law Departments Must Be Thoroughly Reorganized," *JMJP*, December 20, 1957, in *SCMP*, No. 1687 (January 9, 1958).

rejected many of the basic premises of the 1949–57 legal system, the Communists returned to concepts and practices with which they were more familiar and more comfortable. Heavily influenced by their pre-Liberation experiences with legal work, the Communists moved to de-emphasize the role of the formal legal system and to promote the principle of local management of local affairs. The new system was an extension of the methods described above for the neighborhood unit. Disagreements and conflicts within a group would be resolved by its members through informal and enlightened discussions. Improper conduct would be corrected and controlled by social pressure, and the coercive power of the state would be called in only in the most serious cases. Decisions would be made, not on the bases of fixed written rules, but rather through consideration of what course would yield the best results for all.

In addition to the reaction against the rightists, a number of other factors came together at this time to accelerate the decline of the formal legal system. In response to a variety of domestic and international stimuli, the Chinese proceeded into the commune movement and the Great Leap Forward. One consequence of this was that law, which had represented stability and regularity and had acted as a buffer against too rapid change, became incompatible with the frenzied dynamism and the search for new methods of the Great Leap. At the same time, the "reds" prevailed over the "experts," including the legal specialists. In part, this was an assertion of authority by the Party over the bureaucracy in general and the legal cadres in particular. It also reflected the belief that law was really a simple matter and that specialists were not required to handle legal work. This belief was vital to a society which, after purging most of its legal specialists, lacked the facilities for training more within a short period of time. On a more theoretical level, the informalization of law might be regarded as an indication of the withering away of law as Chinese society moved closer to the ultimate communist state.

More fundamentally, the decline of law is attributable in large measure to a lack of understanding about the nature and the function of law by both the new Communist cadres and the leaders of the regime. As discussed earlier, a legal system was adopted after Liberation because of a desire for legitimacy and because no alternative courses of action had occurred to anyone. The Chinese leaders were not committed to the rule of law and did not fully appreciate the utility of law. They often paid lip service to law and legality, but they were never comfortable working or thinking in a legal context. Even before 1957, the legal system and rules of law often were ignored or rejected when they got in the way or during crises. For example, during the rectification campaigns separate rules and organs were established to handle the cases and to impose sanctions.[45] When they were attacked by the supporters of a more formalized legal system in 1957, the Chinese leaders did not hesitate to give up this puzzling and troublesome institution and to replace it with concepts and techniques with which they felt more at ease.

The Communists' lack of familiarity with law is not surprising. As far as I know, none of the top leaders were trained in law.[46] While the Communists did gain a great deal of practical experience in government before Liberation, they did not develop a large core of legal cadres. The border and liberated areas were sufficiently simple and ideological indoctrination was sufficiently thorough that legal administration was not a major concern.

The nonlegal background of the Communists was reinforced by the traditional attitude of de-emphasizing law. Although a formal legal system had existed in China for many centuries, whenever possible people avoided resorting to it.[47] Law suits were costly, judicial procedure was harsh, the rules of law often were unknown to the litigants, and the magistrate was of a totally different cultural world than the vast majority of the people he ruled. Perhaps more important, in the

[45] During land reform, a people's tribunal was set up "to try and punish, according to law . . . all such persons who resist or violate the provisions of the Agrarian Reform Law and decrees." Article 32, "Agrarian Reform Law," in Blaustein (ed.), *Fundamental Legal Documents,* p. 288. Separate courts were established during the three anti and five anti campaigns. "Kuan-yü san-fan yün-tung chung ch'eng-li jen-min fa-t'ing ti kuei-ting" (Regulations on the Setting Up of People's Tribunals During the Three-anti Campaign), *JMJP,* March 31, 1952. See also pp. 247–54 for a discussion of the tribunals established during the Cultural Revolution. In other campaigns, a variety of sanctions also were meted out without the involvement of the courts. See generally, Cohen, *Criminal Process,* pp. 238–95.

[46] For example, Shen Chün-ju, the first president of the Supreme Court, had extensive legal training and experience, but he was not a Party member or an influential member of the government. The same is true for Shih Liang, the minister of justice during 1954–59. Tung Pi-wu, the chairman of the Political-Legal Affairs Committee in 1949 and president of the Supreme Court during 1954–59, studied law in Japan in 1916; but thereafter he was engaged primarily in Party work and not in legal work. *Who's Who in Communist China* (Hong Kong: Union Research Institute, 1966), pp. 498–500, 508–10, 586–88. In contrast, many of the early leaders of the Soviet Union, including Lenin, were trained in law.

[47] Van der Sprenkel, *Legal Institutions,* pp. 80–130; Wejen Chang, "The Traditional Chinese Fear of Litigation: Its Causes and Effects" (unpublished). A strong challenge to this view is presented in David C. Buxbaum, "Some Aspects of Civil Procedure at the Trial Level During Ch'ing Times in Tanshui and  Hsinchu from 1789–1885" (unpublished).

simple and immobile society of traditional China (and indeed, of China today) the parties to a dispute knew that they must continue to live and to deal with each other regardless of the outcome. Hence, they tried to resolve their differences in such a way as to preserve the over-all relationship, even if this entailed accepting an unsatisfactory compromise. Only in the most unusual situations would they risk destroying the over-all relationship by turning to a court of law for an acrimonious and costly struggle and an all-or-nothing decision.

The traditional attitudes probably were not much affected by the Nationalist law reforms and codifications of the 1920's and 1930's. Because of the disruption from civil and foreign wars, preoccupation with more pressing political and economic problems, and the peculiar temperaments of the law reformers, little effort was made to educate the people about the new law. Outside of government circles and the urban commercial centers, the new law probably had little real impact.[48]

While the internal model of law occupied the dominant position after 1957, it encountered many difficulties, just as the external model did in earlier years, in trying to translate ideals and principles into practice. For example, in the internal model the individual must be very involved in the operation of society and must be committed to the social goals. I do not doubt that in the early years after Liberation, many people were genuinely motivated to create a "New China" which would be proud and powerful and free from the injustices of the past. This attitude probably changed over the years. For one thing, it was not possible to maintain a high degree of enthusiasm for a long period of time, especially the active and strident enthusiasm demanded by the Communists. Even with the pauses between campaigns, people grew tired. Some also began to lose faith as the Communists made more mistakes and lost their aura of infallibility. Even the strongest adherents must have been shaken by the Hundred Flowers episode, the antirightist campaign, the Great Leap Forward, and the several years of agricultural disaster. The Cultural Revolution must have been a particularly severe blow, since it vividly pointed out the fact that the new god, the Party, also had feet of clay. With the loss of faith, cynicism and selfishness increased. People began to look out

[48] Very little work has been done in English on the Nationalist efforts at modernization and reform of the legal system. Some of the studies are: Marinus Meijer, *The Introduction of Modern Criminal Law in China* (Batavia: Koninklijke Drukkerij de Unie, 1950); Mark van der Valk, *Conservatism in Modern Chinese Family Law* (Leiden: E. J. Brill, 1956). See also F. T. Cheng, "A Sketch of the History, Philosophy, and Reform of Chinese Law," in *Studies in the Law of the Far East and Southeast Asia* (Washington, D.C.: Washington Foreign Law Society, 1956), p. 19.

only for their own interests. Many years of experience in dealing with the system had enabled them to develop sophistication in appearing socially aware and concerned while actually thinking only of their own position and comfort.[49]

Implementation of the internal model also was limited and distorted by conditions in Chinese society. For example, whether local social groups could successfully carry out the many duties and functions that were assigned them depended in large measure on the quality of the community leadership. Able leaders would have the skill and the knowledge needed to handle this work, as well as the stature to command the respect and the cooperation of the members of the community. Inept leaders, on the other hand, would be able to accomplish little.

On the whole, the Communists had difficulty finding able community leaders. When the residents' committees first were established, many Party members, cadres, enterprise managers, teachers, and other persons of high status and ability were elected as officials,[50] but this situation quickly changed. These persons were too valuable in their regular work to be allowed to spend much time on neighborhood work. In addition, they often did not like neighborhood work, since it required great effort and yielded little material, professional, or psychic reward. In due course, residents' committee officials consisted, with only slight exaggeration, of the old, the lame, the infirm, and the female, especially the female.[51] Only these persons had the necessary

---

[49] See Li, "The Public Security Bureau." See also, Ezra Vogel, "The Regularisation of Cadres," *CQ,* No. 29 (January–March, 1967), p. 36.

[50] While it is difficult to obtain firm data in this area, interviews suggest that the neighborhood officials elected in the early years were such higher status persons. See also Article 4(1), "Provisional Act of the PRC for the Organization of Security Defense Committees," and Article 5, "Provisional General Rules of the PRC for the Organization of People's Mediation Committees," in Cohen, *Criminal Process,* pp. 115, 124, which describe the qualifications needed to become a neighborhood official.

[51] "Chin-shih hsü-to t'ui-hsiu lao-kung-jen pei t'ui-hsüan ch'u-lai ts'an-chia-le chieh-tao kung-tso" (Many Retired Elderly Workers Are Elected to Take Part in Street Work in Tientsin), *T'ien-chin Jih-pao,* July 10, 1956. Another article in the same paper indicates that housewives make up as high as 90 per cent of the total number of elected neighborhood officials. "Chin-shih ko-chieh p'u-p'ien chin-hsing k'ai-hsüan chü-min wei-yüan-hui kung-tso" (All Streets in Tientsin Carry Out the Work of Electing Residents Committees), *ibid.* And in Canton, "of the activists in street level work, a majority are housewives and another substantial portion are unemployed persons." The writer also complains that due to the low status of these persons, some cadres are not sufficiently respectful. Speech of Huang Hsiu-chüan, "Chieh-tao kung-tso ti yao-ch'iu" (The Requirements of Street Level Work), *Kuang-chou Jih-pao,* December 5, 1956. On the busybodyism of neighborhood officials, see "I wei 'yang-yang-kuan' ti chü-min hsiao-chu-chang" (An 'Involved in Everything' Residents' Small Group Chief), *Shanghai hsin-min wan-pao,* October 29, 1964; Lubman, "Mao and Mediation."

time and were expendable from other work. Worse yet, many fishwives became officials; their busybody nature inclined them toward this line of work and qualified them as activists. As a result of this personnel problem, most neighborhood work was not satisfactory. The better residents' committee officials acted as neighborhood work details, but they were unable to mobilize the rest of the community. The worse ones merely fussed and harangued, but they were ignored as much as possible by their neighbors.

THE EXTERNAL MODEL AFTER 1957

As discussed earlier, even before 1957 the new Communist cadres had developed concepts of law and styles of legal work which differed considerably from those of the legal specialists. These differences decreased somewhat as the two groups worked together for a longer time, but the new cadres continued to maintain their distinctive views. During this period, the specialists occupied the dominant position, and their theories and practices were incorporated into the constitution and the constitutional model of the legal system. At the same time, however, the new cadres also were influential. They held many of the middle and lower positions in the legal bureaucracy, and were able to impose their stamp on the work of the lower level legal organs. Thus, the removal of the legal specialists and the change in attitude toward law in 1957 were not abrupt and complete reversals, but rather shifts in the relative positions of two competing concepts of law and styles of legal work.

With this shift, the external model of law declined in importance, but it was by no means discarded. Although the level of activity of many legal organs diminished, the organs themselves were retained. In major or notorious criminal cases, for example, public show trials that followed the constitutional model still were conducted, complete with procurator, defense counsel, and all the procedural trimmings. Law schools and legal publications also continued to operate, although their emphasis changed from law to politics.

Two aspects of the external model which continued to be important after 1957 were the emphasis on providing clear and detailed rules to cover every situation, and the insistence upon strict adherence to these rules. In past years, as the bureaucracy became more entrenched, and as increased discretionary powers were granted to middle and lower level cadres, geographical and departmental feudalities began to form. Their development and growth were further enhanced by the decentralization moves of the late 1950's, and by the breakdown of lines of communication and control during the Great Leap Forward. These feudalities essentially were self-contained units operating with relative freedom from effective control by the upper level departmental organs, the Party, or both, although at various times they attempted to curb the feudalities' independence. This often was done by issuing extensive and detailed rules to define what should be done in every situation and requiring strict adherence to these rules.

For example, the public security of Hui-yang *hsien* (county) in Kwangtung had a history of resisting controls imposed by the Party and by upper level public security authorities.[52] The cadres also protected each other and avoided reporting either professional or political errors committed by their colleagues. During and immediately after the antirightist campaign, efforts were made to bring this unit under firmer control. Several public security cadres were removed, and a *hsien* level Party organ—the political-legal staff office—was created to co-ordinate and oversee legal work. The legal rules governing public security work were increased and improved, which is most interesting from a lawyer's point of view. Several new regulations, including the People's Police Act of the People's Republic of China (CPR), the Security Administration Punishment Act of the CPR, and the Decision of the State Council of the CPR Relating to Problems of Rehabilitation through Labor, were issued by the central government in middle and late 1957.[53] In addition, the political-legal staff office was ordered to review all existing regulations related to public security work, and to make recommendations for annulling contradictory, moot, or inappropriate rules, and for establishing new rules to fill gaps or to improve existing practice. This office also was instructed to make sure that all legal rules were observed. A senior public security cadre was demoted for ordering the detention of a suspect without first obtaining the approval of the bureau chief as required by the Arrest and Detention Act of the CPR.[54] Since such violations had been common and had never drawn censure in the past, this cadre may have been punished as an example to show that legal rules must be followed strictly.

If the quality of the rules and the degree to which they are observed are criteria for determining the rule of law, then the few months be-

---

[52] See Li, "The Public Security Bureau"; Vogel, "Land Reform in Kwangtung."

[53] Cohen, *Criminal Process,* pp. 107–108, 205–37, 249–50.

[54] For a more detailed discussion of this and related problems, see Li, "The Public Security Bureau." For the Arrest and Detention Act, see Cohen, *Criminal Process,* pp. 360–62.

tween the end of the active period of the antirightist campaign in the fall of 1957 and the beginning of the Great Leap Forward in the spring of 1958 was the Golden Age of the rule of law in this *hsien*.

The requirement of strict adherence to established rules also was used as a means of restoring economic stability after the Great Leap Forward. Agricultural producers were urged to sign contracts before planting time which fixed the price and the quantity of goods to be delivered to marketing units after harvest.[55] These contracts helped establish economic order by implementing production quotas and by providing reliable information on expected future production. And through contract enforcement procedures, failures and bottlenecks in the economy could be spotted quickly and easily. Enterprises also were instructed to carry out the exact terms of their contracts. A 1962 directive of the Party Central Committee and the State Council ordered:

All organs of the national economy must strictly implement their economic contracts; all production enterprises must produce in accordance with their contract demands, and guarantee the quality of their products and the time of delivery. Organs ordering goods must accept delivery and make payment in a timely manner, strictly implement the order contract, and not return goods. . . . Where disputes arise in the course of implementing a contract, the economic committees of each area shall arbitrate.[56]

This directive is one of the rare instances in which the Communists call for arbitration (*chung-ts'ai*) rather than mediation (*t'iao-chieh*) of disputes.

THE CULTURAL REVOLUTION AND THE TWO MODELS OF LAW

It is difficult to write with assurance about the Cultural Revolution, since many of the events of that period still are unclear. Nevertheless,

[55] See generally, Richard Pfeffer, "The Institution of Contracts in the Chinese People's Republic," *CQ*, No. 14 (April–June, 1963), p. 153, and No. 15 (July–September, 1963), p. 115; Richard Pfeffer, "Contracts in China Revisited, With a Focus on Agriculture 1949–1963," *CQ*, No. 28 (October–December, 1966), p. 106; Gene Hsiao, "The Role of Economic Contracts in Communist China," *California Law Review*, No. 53 (October, 1965), p. 1029. See also, Sung Chi-shan, "A Brief Discussion of the Nature and Function of Economic Contracts in Industry," *Ching-chi yen-chiu* (Economic Research), No. 2 (February, 1965), p. 38, in *JPRS* (July 12, 1965), No. 31033, p. 57.

[56] "Chung-kung chung-yang, kuo-wu-yüan kuan-yü yen-ko shih-hsing chi-pen chien-she ch'eng-hsü, yen-ko shih-hsing ching-chi ho-t'ung ti t'ung-chih" (Communique of the Central Committee of the Communist Party and the State Council Concerning the Strict Implementation of Basic Level Construction Procedures and the Strict Implementation of Economic Contracts), *Chung-hua jen-min kung-ho-kuo fa-kuei hui-pien* (Compendium of the Laws and Regulations of the CPR), No. 13 (January, 1962–December, 1963), p. 62, trans. in Whitmore Gray and Victor H. Li, *Communist Law Materials* (unpublished) III, 833.

in the area of political-legal work several broad patterns of development can be seen, although there are variations, which sometimes are considerable, from one part of the country to another. To a large degree, these patterns reflect the continuing interplay of the external and internal models of law.

The initial stage of the Cultural Revolution was characterized by a drastic decline in the position of the formal legal system. Beginning in the summer of 1966, many Red Guard groups entered into, and in some instances even took over, political-legal work. They conducted investigations of their political enemies, carried out arrests, and through a variety of tribunals and mass meetings, adjudicated cases and imposed sanctions.[57] The Red Guards sometimes worked in conjunction with the public security and the court, but often they acted independently without reference to the formal legal organs.[58] This bypassing of the formal legal system had occurred in past campaigns, of course, but never to such an extent nor in a manner so disorganized and so free from central control.

The Cultural Revolution differed from past campaigns in one major respect: whereas the entire political-legal system again was criticized, the public security for the first time became the primary target of the attacks. These attacks came from several different directions. At the central level, the leaders of the Cultural Revolution accused the public security of being the stronghold of the anti-Mao group. Lin Piao said:

Public security work had been under the control of P'eng Chen, Lo Jui-ch'ing, Lu Ting-i, and Yang Shang-k'un—especially P'eng Chen and Lo Jui-ch'ing— for seventeen years. They did not of course carry out all things according to Mao Tse-tung's thought. . . . The thought of Chairman Mao has not yet established its dominance and absolute authority in the public security and judicial systems.[59]

Hsieh Fu-chih, the vice-premier and minister of public security, admitted:

[57] "Report on an Investigation into the Facts of the Persecution of the Aug. 1 Combat Corps," Kang pa i (Steel August 1), October 15, 1967, in SCMP, No. 4096 (January 10, 1968), p. 1.

[58] See "Resolutely Defending the Dictatorship of the Proletariat, Checking the Evil Wind of Fighting, Smashing and Looting," Pei-ching Kung-jen, May 17, 1967, in SCMP, No. 3966 (June 23, 1967), p. 13; "Brief Introduction to the Three Big Factions in Shenyang," Liao-lien chan-pao (Liao-lien Combat Bulletin), September 6, 1967, in SCMP, No. 4091 (January 13, 1968), p. 7; "Death Sentence Levied on Four at Canton Rally," Canton, Kwangtung Provincial Service, 1000 GMT, November 10, 1967; "US Agents Sentenced in Peking," NCNA, Peking, September 27, 1967, in SCMP, No. 4031 (September 29, 1967), p. 18.

[59] "Chairman Mao and Central Committee Leaders on Public Security Organs, Procuratorates and Law Courts," Fan P'eng Lo hei hsien (Resist the P'eng-Lo Black Line), No. 2 (July, 1968), in SCMM, No. 625 (September 3, 1968), p. 15.

Our great leader Chairman Mao has told me on eight to ten occasions that thoroughgoing revolution must be carried out in the public security organs, procuratorates, and law courts, because the things copied from the Kuomintang and the Soviet revisionists have deep-rooted influence and P'eng Chen and Lo Jui-ch'ing had controlled them for more than ten years.[60]

Chiang Ch'ing told of how she and Chairman Mao were shadowed, how their letters were censored, and how listening devices were installed in their residence. She demanded that "the public security organs, procuratorates and law courts must be completely smashed." [61] The distrust of the entire public security system was reflected in one of Chairman Mao's "latest instructions" which provided:

Public security organs are a knife in the hands of the proletariat. If properly grasped, they can be used to attack the enemy and protect the people; if not, they can easily be used against us. If they are taken away by the enemy, there will be even greater danger. Hence public security work can only be under the direct leadership of the Party Committee and *cannot be under the vertical leadership* of the relevant government department. [Emphasis added.] [62]

Some of the attacks on the public security on the local level followed similar lines. Red Guard groups recognized early in the Cultural Revolution that the support of the public security was needed if the reactionary powerholders were to be overthrown. One successful Red Guard group in Heilungkiang felt that they could "instruct the rest of China how to do it," and suggested that "[b]efore seizing the power of the leadership of the provincial Party Committee, the newspapers and radio, as the voice of the proletarian revolution, and the Public Security Bureau, as an organ of the dictatorship, should first be seized." [63] In many areas, however, the public security sided with the existing powerholders against the Red Guards or, at least, in trying to preserve public order and to prevent violence, inhibited the actions of the Red Guards. The public security was attacked for its reactionary stance. The attacks quickly expanded to accusing the public security of always having been reactionary and of having been the tool by which leftist revolutionaries had been suppressed for more than ten years.[64] This organ also was criticized for having been too lenient with

---

[60] *Ibid.*, p. 16.

[61] *Ibid.*

[62] "Chairman Mao's Latest Instructions," *Wen-ko t'ung-hsin* (Cultural Revolution Bulletin), No. 1 (October 6, 1967), in *SCMP*, No. 4060 (November 15, 1967), p. 1.

[63] "Experience of Heilungkiang Red Rebels in Seizing Power," NCNA, Peking, February 10, 1967, in *SCMP*, No. 3880 (February 15, 1967), p. 1.

[64] See, for example, "Consolidate the Victory of the Struggle Launched by Revolutionaries to Seize Power," *JMJP*, February 13, 1967, in *SCMP*, No. 3999 (February 28,

class enemies. Following the Liu-P'eng-Lo line that class struggle was over, the public security adopted the erroneous position that "everyone is equal before the law," and thus failed to distinguish between the enemy and the people. Therefore, it became not a weapon of the working class in the class struggle, but rather a means by which reactionary persons could be protected.[65]

In addition to attacks on its political position, the public security also was criticized for having a bad work style. Many of these criticisms repeat the charges which were leveled against the judiciary and the external model of law in 1952 and 1957. For example, the public security was accused of not respecting the masses and of failing to implement the mass line.[66] That is, as the public security cadres developed more professional expertise, they began to feel that the participation of the masses in public security work only contributed confusion and inefficiency. They believed instead that "cases must be handled by a small number of technically proficient experts, and the masses of the people can do nothing in this respect." [67] This reliance upon specialists and upon specialized techniques separated the public security from the people, and rendered it difficult or impossible for

1967), p. 1; "Down With Chiang Hua," *Wen ko t'ung-hsin*, No. 16 (July, 1968), in *SCMP*, No. 4230 (August 1, 1968), p. 1. See also, "Another Criminal Proof of 'Canton Repudiate T'ao Joint Committee's Attempt to Seize Power From the Army," *San chün lien-wei chan-pao* (Services Joint Committee Combat Bulletin), No. 10 (September 13, 1968), in *SCMP*, No. 4275 (October 10, 1968), p. 1. Hsieh Fu-chih estimated that fully 80 per cent of the *hsien* level public security organs supported the conservatives. "Comrade Hsieh Fu-chih's Important Speech," *Chiu P'eng Lo chan pao* (Drag-out P'eng-Lo Combat Bulletin), No. 3 (February, 1968), in *SCMP*, No. 4139 (March 15, 1968), p. 5. It is anomalous that Hsieh, who has been the minister of public security since 1959, was able to blame all the wrongdoings within his department on his predecessor Lo Jui-ch'ing and on P'eng Chen. Hsieh suggested that the higher level public security officials, including himself, were estranged from the lower level cadres, and did not know what was happening. *Ibid.* Chou En-lai tried to excuse Hsieh by saying: "Although Comrade Hsieh Fu-chih is a very good minister, yet because he went there late and because he is a man of discipline in work, he did not think it fit to change the original personnel without good reasons. Because of this, the influence of P'eng Chen and Lo Jui-ch'ing was still very great." "Chairman Mao and Central Committee Leaders," p. 16.

[65] "Completely Smash the Feudal, Capitalist and Revisionist Legal Systems," *Fan P'eng Lo hei hsien*, No. 2 (July, 1968), in *SCMM*, No. 625 (September 3, 1968), p. 23; "Down With P'eng Chen, the Sworn Enemy of Proletarian Dictatorship," *JMJP*, October 15, 1967, in *SCMP*, No. 4051 (October 31, 1967), p. 1.

[66] "Suppression of the Masses Is Bourgeois Dictatorship," *Wen-hui Pao*, June 5, 1968, in *SCMP*, No. 4210 (July 3, 1968), p. 1.

[67] *Ibid.*, p. 4. See also, Ts'un Min *et al.*, "Overthrow the Rule of the Bourgeois 'Scholar Tyrants,'" *JMJP*, June 6, 1966, in *SCMP*, No. 3722 (June 21, 1966), p. 12, in which Peking Law School's emphasis on professional proficiency rather than Chairman Mao's thought was criticized.

the Party and the masses to supervise public security work. It also made public security cadres feel that they were somehow "special" and superior to the common people. All these factors contributed to the formation of an independent-kingdom mentality within the public security.

Reminiscent of some of the criticisms made against the retained Nationalist judges in the early 1950's, the personal style of the cadres again was attacked. "The capitalist roaders of the judicial organs also worshipped things of foreign and ancient origin. They abolished the revolutionary work style, and advocated that lawyers should attend court in European dress and pointed shoes, and assumed the airs of bourgeois lords." [68]

More generally, the entire external model of law came under criticism.[69] The development of political-legal organs and the push for "strengthening the legal system" were called attempts to adopt wholesale the feudal, capitalist, and revisionist legal systems. Legal procedure once again was charged with causing undue confusion and with being a ruse by which justice could be thwarted. The use of lawyers also was denounced, since this led only to endless battles of words rather than to concrete results.

The very role of and need for law was called into question. To begin with, since the Liu-P'eng-Lo group controlled the political-legal system, many if not most of the laws could be presumed to further the reactionary cause and to "provide legal grounds for those turncoats to hide themselves." [70] Through the ruse of requiring strict adherence to law, this group "attempted to fetter with law the instruments of dictatorship hand and foot, and prevent the masses of the people from daring to interfere with counter-revolutionary activities." [71] On a deeper level, the "bourgeois" position that law should be the ultimate guide for action was strongly criticized. Under this theory, the masses would take orders not from the Party, but from the law. The masses also would look to the law rather than to Chairman Mao's thoughts for guidance and inspiration.[72] There was a re-

[68] "Completely Smash the Feudal, Capitalist and Revisionist Legal Systems," p. 25.
[69] *Ibid.*
[70] "Shanghai Struggle Rally Raps Local Plotters," Shanghai City Service, 2300 GMT, November 29, 1967.
[71] "Completely Smash the Feudal, Capitalist and Revisionist Legal Systems," p. 23. See also, "China's Khrushchev Book on Strategy Criticized," NCNA Domestic Service, 1252 GMT, November 13, 1967.
[72] *Ibid.*

newed demand for fewer laws, and there was even a call for "law-lessness." [73]

The transformation of the political-legal organs was accomplished in part by a revolt of the leftist elements within these organs and in part by the entry of revolutionary mass organizations into political-legal work. The most important factor, however, was the decision "to impose military control on all organs of dictatorship"—that is, on all political-legal organs.[74] Three-way alliances were formed, consisting of members of the People's Liberation Army (PLA), revolutionary cadres, and the masses. In the public security, military control com-mittees of the PLA were placed over each organ.[75] In addition, many public security cadres were purged and were replaced with demobilized PLA men.[76] In some areas, PLA soldiers were stationed within the public security organs.[77]

As the Cultural Revolution ran its course, a gradual effort was made to restore order and to re-establish lines of communication and con-trol. Sometime around late 1967 or early 1968, the desire to smash the political-legal system began to give way to an attempt to strengthen this system and to rebuild it according to correct Maoist principles.[78] Political-legal cadres were barred from joining mass organizations or

[73] "In Praise of 'Lawlessness,'" *JMJP*, January 31, 1967, in *SCMP*, No. 3879 (February 14, 1967), p. 13.

[74] "Vice Premier Hsieh Fu-chih's Talk at the Supreme People's Court" (excerpts), *Hung tien hsün* (Red Telegraph Dispatch), No. 3 (March 27, 1968), in *SCMP*, No. 4157 (April 11, 1968), p. 4. In the same talk, Hsieh rejected the suggestion that the Supreme Court be merged with the ministry of public security, but he left the question open with respect to the procuracy. He also called for a reduction in the staffs of the political-legal organs.

[75] See, for example, "PLA's Great Role in Seizure of Power in Shansi Reviewed," NCNA, Peking, February 28, 1967, in *SCMP*, No. 3891 (March 3, 1967), p. 11; "Shanghai Moves Against Hoodlums, Delinquents," Shanghai City Service, 1300 GMT, December 26, 1967; "Kiangsi Trial Convicts Counterrevolutionaries," Nan-ch'ang, Kiangsi Provincial Service, 2340 GMT, February 6, 1968; "Rally Sentences Counter-revolutionaries," Harbin, Heilungkiang Provincial Service, 1130 GMT, March 3, 1968; "Wuhan Rally Sentences Incorrigibles to Death," Wuhan, Hupeh Provincial Service, 1130 GMT, April 30, 1968.

[76] "Important Speeches by Central Leaders on March 15" (Chinese source unknown), in *SCMP*, No. 4181 (May 20, 1968), p. 1; "Important Speeches by Central Leaders on March 18," Red Guard tabloid dated April 13, 1968, and produced by the "Red Rebel Corps" of Yingte Middle School, Kwangtung, in *SCMP*, No. 4182 (May 21, 1968), p. 1.

[77] "Comrade Hsiao Ssu-ming, Commander of X Army and Vice Chairman of Tientsin Municipal Revolutionary Committee, Relays Speeches Made by Central Leaders at Reception," *Wen ko t'ung-hsin*, No. 14 (April, 1968), in *SCMP*, No. 4172 (May 7, 1968), p. 17.

[78] "Shanghai Revolutionary Committee Adopts Resolution Strengthening Dictatorship of the Proletariat," NCNA, Peking, June 8, 1967, in *SCMP*, No. 3958 (June 13, 1967), p. 1; "Vice Premier Hsieh Fu-chih's Talk at the Supreme People's Court," p. 4.

from participating in political demonstrations, and were ordered to be strictly subordinate to the local revolutionary committee.[79] Mass organizations were urged to support the public security in its work, but they also were warned by Chou En-lai not to interfere in its internal rectification.[80] At the same time, the central authorities tried to re-establish their control. The term "according to law" appeared once again in many directives,[81] and strict compliance with central regulations was urged.[82] The mass line also was toned down somewhat, on the theory that to let the masses decide everything would be "tailism" and would indicate a lack of leadership.[83]

It is difficult to assess the present position of the political-legal system. The formal legal organs continue to operate, but they appear to share their powers with a variety of informal bodies. For example, one can find reports telling that the court still functions, but one can also find reports describing how other nonjudicial tribunals adjudicate cases and impose sanctions.[84] The most far-reaching change has been

[79] "The Premier's Speech," *Hung-ch'i t'ung-hsin* (Red Flag Bulletin), No. 1 (Mid-June, 1968), in *SCMP*, No. 4212 (July 8, 1968), p. 1; "Accusations by Victimized Passengers of No. 606 Special Train," *Liu-ling-liu tz'u t'e-pieh lieh-ch'e shih-chien chuan-k'an* (Special Issue of Incident of Special Train No. 606) (July 12, 1968), in *SCMP*, No. 4230 (August 1, 1968), p. 12.

[80] "Premier Chou's Talk With Five Representatives of Proletariat Revolutionary Rebels of Canton," *Kuang yin hung ch'i* (Bright Red Flag), October 29, 1967, in *SCMP*, No. 4091 (January 3, 1968), p. 1. A related item appears in *SCMM*, No. 611 (January 22, 1968), p. 12.

[81] In the "six articles on the public security" (*kung an liu t'iao*), the term "according to law" appears five times. "Certain Regulations Concerning the Strengthening of Public Security Work in the Great Proletarian Cultural Revolution," *Kuan-yü ch'ing li chieh chi tui wu tzu liao chuan chi* (Special Collection of Materials Concerning the Clearing Up of Class Ranks) (July, 1968), in *SCMP*, No. 4235 (August 9, 1968), p. 1. See also, "Public Notice No. 1 of Tsinghai Provincial Revolutionary Committee," NCNA, Peking, August 12, 1967, in *SCMP*, No. 4008 (August 24, 1967), p. 1; "Message from Party Central Committee and Other Central Organs to Revolutionary Masses and PLA Commanders and Fighters in Wuhan," *Chung-ta hung-ch'i* (Red Flag of Chung-shan University), in *SCMP*, No. 4041 (October 26, 1967), p. 8; "Check This Gust of Evil Wind," *Ching kang shan*, No. 47 (May 16, 1967), in *SCMP*, No. 4078 (December 12, 1967), p. 15.

[82] See, for example, "Opinions Concerning Cleaning Up of Teachers' Ranks," *Tung-fang hung tien-hsün* (The East Is Red Telegraphic Bulletin), No. 2 (July, 1968), in *SCMP*, No. 4227 (July 29, 1968), p. 4.

[83] "Execute Proletarian Policy," Kweiyang, Kweichow Provincial Service, 1300 GMT, January 17, 1969. Cf. "Exposed Class Enemies Subject to Mass Trials," Shanghai City Service, 0330 GMT, December 13, 1968.

[84] On the court continuing to function, see, for example, "Current News," *Kung-jen chan-pao*, December 1, 1967, in *SCMP*, No. 4122 (February 20, 1968), p. 6; "Nanking Public Trial, Rally Sentences 18," Nanking, Kiangsi Provincial Service, 1030 GMT, April 19, 1968. On nonjudicial organs adjudicating cases, see, for example, "A Serious Statement," *Hsüeh an chuan k'an* (Special Issue on the November 29 Bloody Incident) (December 8, 1967), in *SCMP*, No. 4117 (February 13, 1968), p. 1; "US-Chiang Agents

the replacement of a large number of cadres who have considerable professional expertise and departmental ties, with a new group of cadres who have little experience in political-legal work or little loyalty to the political-legal system. Perhaps, like the early years after Liberation, there will be another period where functional lines are blurred and the work style is loose and informal.

## THE CHINESE LEGAL SYSTEM IN COMPARATIVE PERSPECTIVE

It is clear that the existence of and interaction between the external and internal models of law are by no means unique to China or unknown to the West. One of the most striking differences between the Chinese and Western legal systems, however, concerns the respective attitudes toward the internal model of law. Although the Western legal system does rely on the internalization of the rules of conduct and does use social pressure to control deviant behavior and to control disputes, the West tends to downgrade the internal model, associating it with the less important aspects of law or even regarding it somehow as "non-law." The West also is a little embarrassed by the presence of this model in its legal system. The goal of legal development is the perfection of the external model, with protection for the individual based upon a well drafted code enforced by an efficient bureaucracy.

The Chinese, on the other hand, greatly admire the internal model of law. It supports their ideological commitment to have every individual participate in the political-legal process, to implement the mass line, and to emphasize the collective way of life. It also is consistent with traditional concepts of law and legal work, concepts which were reinforced by the Communists' own experiences prior to Liberation. Finally, this model is well suited to conditions in Chinese society. It required few legal specialists, a commodity which China did not have. It also provided a rationalization for granting large amounts of local decision making power for a country which may be too vast and too diverse to be tightly controlled by the center. Indeed, the internal model was so well suited for China during this period that the Chinese leaders were able to take that most difficult step of disagreeing with the "established fact" that the goal of legal development is the perfection of the external model of law.

The external model still retains importance in China. It was a

Sentenced at Public Trial," Hangchow, Chekiang Provincial Service, 1000 GMT, August 17, 1968.

major political and social instrument during times when an effort was being made to regularize the political-legal system or to implement stronger central controls. Thus, it played a large role during the time between Liberation and the Great Leap Forward, in the recovery period of the early 1960's, and to a lesser extent, in the retrenchment stages of the latter part of the Cultural Revolution.

Many ideological, political, and other influences will determine how the external and internal models of law will interact in the future. If the upper level leadership wishes to try to establish strong central controls, it will issue directives defining permissible and impermissible conduct and restricting local discretionary powers. It also will try to enforce these directives strictly, possibly by using the political-legal bureaucracy.

Another question which must be considered is whether the internal model is compatible with modernization. That is, do the personal, flexible, and even amorphous requirements of this model obstruct the industrialization of the Chinese economy? Does the running of a complex industrial society demand clear and explicit rules which are carefully enforced by skilled professionals? I would guess that as time goes by, the body of economic regulations and "contract law" will grow in size and complexity. Indeed, this may have occurred already, and merely have escaped the attention of Western scholars. It does not necessarily follow, however, that a similar development must take place outside the economic area. The prime contribution of the Chinese to legal thinking may well be that in matters affecting personal conduct and interpersonal relationships, the internal model is both more desirable and more effective than the external model.

In thinking about the future of the Chinese legal system, one important factor to bear in mind is that all developments must take place within the context of the available pool of political-legal cadres. As in 1949, the Chinese lack a large group of legally trained personnel. Thus, they will be unable fully to implement the external model, even if they wish to do so. This problem cannot be quickly solved. To build a corps of law teachers may take many years, not to mention a corps of cadres to administer the political-legal system. Until this is achieved, we can expect that the Chinese and Western systems will be very different.

DONALD J. MUNRO

# Egalitarian Ideal and Educational Fact in Communist China

## INTRODUCTION

Egalitarianism is one element at the core of Mao's revolutionary dream. Two aspects of it must be distinguished. One pertains to distribution of income and wealth, and here we must speak of modified egalitarianism. As early as 1929 Mao waged an ideological struggle in the Red Army against "absolute equalitarianism," saying that it is wrong to seek completely equal distribution of goods.[1] Although he still accepts this position (intellectuals are often accused of the sin of "absolute equalitarianism"), he has favored policies that come closer to absolute equalitarianism than those found in other socialist states. For example, in a factory in Communist China wage differentials exist, but the difference between the highest and the lowest paid worker is much smaller than in other Communist countries. He clearly meant it when he said that the distribution of goods in the Red Army should be "as equal as possible." A radically more equitable distribution of the wealth has consistently been a principal Maoist aim.[2]

[1] Mao Tse-tung, *On the Rectification of Incorrect Ideas in the Party* (Peking: Foreign Languages Press, 1953), pp. 10–15.

[2] Charles Hoffmann, *Work Incentive Practices and Policies in the People's Republic of China, 1953–65* (Albany: State University of New York Press, 1967), pp. 18–22. In a poor country there are special economic considerations that suggest the desirability of reducing the income of the educated and thus minimizing the differentials between high-paid and low-paid workers. W. A. Lewis points to the problem in Africa:

The main limitation on the absorption of the educated in poor countries is their high price, relative to average national output. In a country where most people are illiterate, the primary school graduate, whose only skills are reading and writing,

The other aspect of the egalitarian ideal is even more important to Mao: breaking down the barriers that separate people from each other (class, type of occupation, region). In China the main barrier today is said to be between elitist "mental aristocrats" who "work with their minds" and others who "work with their hands." The second aspect of egalitarianism (breaking barriers) is especially pronounced in the ancient Confucian vision of an Age of Great Harmony (*ta-t'ung*) in which "all men are brothers" and the barriers of family and clan are not present. In 1949 Mao used the term *"ta-t'ung"* to refer to a Communist society.[3] Socialism has drawn strength in China from this legacy. The communes were the first instrument of social organization intended to realize the egalitarian ideal. Khrushchev accused the Chinese of seeking "equalitarian communism" through the communes.[4] Of course, even the Maoist approach to status egalitarianism permits certain individuals (such as model soldiers, peasants, or workers) to occupy a position above that of the ordinary citizen. The distance between the Party member and the citizen is reduced, not eliminated, in Maoism.

The egalitarian ideal is not treated as an abstraction. Mao is especially sensitive to the political utility of eliminating status barriers. It facilitates governing by reducing the inevitable gap between officials or occupational supervisors and other people. In his 1965 interview with André Malraux, Mao spoke of equality as something that emerges naturally when the right relations exist between cadres and people: "Equality is not important in itself; it is important because it is natural to those who have not lost contact with the masses."[5] One

commands a wage much higher than a farmer's income. A university graduate who, in a rich country, commences at a salary about equal to a miner's wage, in a poor country will receive five times a miner's wage. In consequence, all production or provision of services which depend on using educated people are much more expensive, in relation to national income, in poor than in rich countries. The poor countries may need the educated more than the rich, but they can even less afford to pay for or absorb large numbers.

W. A. Lewis, "Education in Economic Development," *Social and Economic Studies*, X, No. 2 (June, 1961), quoted in Richard Jolly, *Planning Education for African Development* (Kampala, Uganda: Makerere Institute of Social Research, 1969), p. 139.

[3] See *Selected Works of Mao Tse-tung*, Vol. IV: *On the People's Democratic Dictatorship* (Peking: Foreign Languages Press, 1961), pp. 412, 414, and 423, n. 1. The note makes the following comment about the world of Great Harmony, "It refers to a society based on public ownership, free from class exploitation and oppression—a lofty ideal long cherished by the Chinese people. Here the realm of Great Harmony means communist society."

[4] See *The Origin and Development of the Differences Between the Leadership of the CPSU and Ourselves* (Peking: Foreign Languages Press, 1963), p. 27.

[5] André Malraux, *Anti-Memoirs*, trans. Terence Kilmartin (New York: Bantam Books, 1968), p. 464.

motive for realizing the ideal may be this utilitarian consideration, but this does not diminish its importance. As Mao makes clear in his "Sixty Points on Work Methods," the goal of achieving status equality is a continuing policy guideline. "The attitude of true equality must be adopted toward cadres and the masses. It is necessary to make people feel that mutual relationships between people are really based on equality and that one has bared his heart to them." [6]

Twenty years ago the leaders of Communist China faced two problems: how to transform egalitarianism from a cardinal ideal into reality, and how to transform manpower requirements from a modernization blueprint into fact. This study examines the role of the educational system in China's pursuit of these aims. More precisely, it deals (among other things) with the eventual conflict between the two aims that brought in its wake a fundamental dispute over what the manpower requirements are. The study concludes with the judgment that the existence of quality education, which is necessary to produce high-level scientific and technical skills, is impossible without some serious abuse of the egalitarian ideal. The leadership is left with a choice of minimizing the need for quality education while pushing closer to the ideal; it must then reassess manpower needs. Or it can ignore more and more the utopian social vision. Each of these choices in turn matches a position on the most desirable locus of educational control: the local organization (commune, production brigade, and so on) or the central Ministry of Education. This matter will be examined also.

China's problems are in some ways common to those of most developing nations, and, to some degree, they even have counterparts in a country like the United States. The group that was favored by the existing educational institutions in China in 1949 and, in spite of certain corrective measures, for seventeen years thereafter, was the same group that is favored in Nigeria, Brazil, France, the USSR, and the United States: an urban segment, including the leading educationalists, that is separated in a number of ways from the rural citizenry and the urban poor.

Julius Nyerere has pointed to the problem in Tanzania:

The education now provided is designed for the few who are intellectually stronger than their fellows; it induces among those who succeed a feeling of superiority, and leaves a majority of the others hankering after something they

6 Mao Tse-tung, "Sixty Points on Work Method," *Collection of Statements by Mao Tse-tung (1956–1967)*, CB, No. 892 (October 21, 1969), p. 8. Translation slightly revised.

will never obtain. It induces a feeling of inferiority among the majority, and can thus not produce either the egalitarian society we should build nor the attitudes of mind conducive to an egalitarian society. On the contrary, it induced the growth of a class structure in our country.[7]

Another writer explains the African situation like this:

One of the major shortcomings of government in Africa since independence is its failure to adapt a metropolitan type of government to the needs of the country-side. . . . The modern elites have institutionalized the wide gap between the modern and traditional sectors and between towns and the countryside. This has made it much more difficult to achieve effective integration between the different societies; it intensifies the competition between them, and has undermined the post-independence political system which, while invariably laying stress on egali-tarianism, has in fact widened the gap. . . . Educationalists and academics, who form a strong pressure group within the modern elites, have shown themselves committed to maintaining their own values (mainly western values) within the educational institutions. In many countries these values conflict with those estab-lished at the national level.[8]

The gaping inequity that education can perpetuate or ameliorate exists between rural and urban areas.

Among the most blatant of many practices that favor the urban elite in various countries are school admissions examinations and as-sorted promotion criteria. They test the kind of knowledge most readily available to a certain sector of the society. A recent visitor to Brazil has written:

This obsolete social order maintains itself with the help of an archaic educational system. A good education is reserved for a minute segment of the youthful population, and every attempt is made to recruit the future elite from those circles which are already in power. . . . Instead of expending the necessary efforts in the field of education, Brazil tries to keep a growing number of young people from obtaining a higher education by making crucial examinations constantly more difficult.[9]

In July, 1968, M. Edgar Faure, France's new education minister, vowed to democratize France's education by changing the university admissions system which, he stated, acts as a barrier to the children

---

[7] Julius Nyerere, "Education For Self-Reliance," quoted in Colin Legum, "Africa on the Rebound," *Africa Report* (December, 1967), p. 26.

[8] Colin Legum, "Africa on the Rebound," *Africa Report* (December, 1967), p. 26.

[9] Leonard Singer, "Brazil Restricts College to the Few," Toronto Telegram News Service feature, *Ann Arbor News,* January 30, 1969.

of workers. The *Wall Street Journal* recently described attempts to face the same problem in the United States:

Schools are having to make difficult readjustments in their curriculums and methods to accommodate the new arrivals whose backgrounds differ markedly from those of their predominantly middle-class student bodies. And some colleges that have eased admissions policies for the poor now find themselves the target of heated and possibly damaging criticism from alumni, townspeople, and legislators.[10]

Mao Tse-tung may have taken some time developing the opinion, but it is clear that he now faults the Soviet educational system for perpetuating an elite class. A 1967 article states:

Under the Soviet educational system, it is obvious that treatment as between the poor and the rich differs vastly and an extreme inequality prevails. On the one hand are the sons and daughters of the bourgeois strata who enjoy every kind of favorable treatment and on the other are the sons and daughters of the workers, peasants and other working people who are discriminated against and always get unfair treatment.[11]

The rhetoric aside, Khrushchev himself said, "We still have a sharp distinction drawn between mental and manual labor," and he referred to the pre-1958 Soviet educational system as doing little to inhibit it.

Thus, one of China's fundamental problems was and is: How can the educational system be used to help institutionalize the egalitarian ideal of the revolution? Needless to say, we have here a question of values. But the pursuit of this ideal is also a means for achieving the political power necessary to realize other policy ends. Peasant loyalty, which was won through increasing the educational possibilities of their children, is an important source of that power.

China's second problem has been to determine how best to introduce congruity between educational practices and manpower needs. The problem is related to the previous one. If the Chinese lay relatively strong stress on the need for a number of highly trained scientists and technicians, they will be very concerned about quality in students and about providing special schools for the bright ones (especially college preparatory middle schools). If they are especially concerned with the egalitarian ideal, they may argue against special schools as being elitist and also as being nonessential in terms of manpower needs.

10 *Wall Street Journal,* January 24, 1969.
11 "Going All Out With a Revisionist Line in Education," *Peking Review,* No. 45 (November 3, 1967), p. 34.

They will be less concerned with the quality of schools than with making easy access to schools available to all—quantity over quality. A course that is ideologically sound often may involve procedures that are also functionally sound. This is the case with the second option. In many modernizing states the manpower problem has a special feature: Professional educators assume that the kind of heavy academic burden in the arts and sciences that will ultimately prepare students to enter a college or university is right for many students. Thus, a large share of the educational budget may go to ordinary middle schools that turn out too many graduates for the colleges and the job market to absorb. Concurrently, educators will be doing far less than they could in the teaching of new, basic level skills that must exist to meet the ever changing problems of the developing economy. Khrushchev addressed himself to this matter in 1958. Arguing that there was something wrong in the Soviet educational system that was giving an expensive education to many students as if they were going to college (when in fact few were), the Soviet government temporarily switched to a less academic approach and to more emphasis on work-training in polytechnical and vocational schools.[12] (The Soviet leadership has since ceased to regard the issue as Khrushchev did, and the work-training element in polytechnical education has been drastically watered down.) The Tanganyika government decided in 1962 to close down a number of residential public schools with excellent equipment, although Africans had been integrated well in them. The reason was the expense of staffing and maintaining the facilities, as well as the fear that the graduates would evolve into a privileged elite.[13] The Maoist position on regular middle schools in China is similar: "They were turned into preparatory schools for colleges, and their main task was to send students to colleges instead of training up ordinary workers with both socialist conscience and culture." [14]

The debate in China over the relative desirability of a centralized or decentralized school system, which is our third problem, was colored from the start by the Soviet model, which was very centralized. In Mao's eyes, the resolution of the debate on the side of decentralization gradually took on signs of urgency because he eventually regarded it as bound up with the issues of egalitarianism and manpower needs.

[12] Nigel Grant, *Soviet Education* (Baltimore: Penguin Books, 1964), pp. 100–101.

[13] Guy Hunter, *Education For a Developing Region: A Study in East Africa* (London: Allen and Unwin, 1963), p. 17.

[14] " 'Indigenous Experts' and the Revolution in Agricultural Education," *Peking Review*, No. 51 (December 21, 1968), p. 4.

The initial reason for decentralization was largely economic. The argument was that unless decentralization occurred, local areas would wait for the central government to provide money for schools and to send teachers. A poor central government that spends much of its funds on quality education in cities will provide little. Decentralization shifts the financial and the training burden to the local areas, releasing untapped physical and motivational resources. From the standpoint of the egalitarian ideal, there is a payoff: More schools blossoming forth mean more places for children of peasant families. In manpower terms, more technicians are educated, and the schools which they attend have a curriculum geared to local production needs, unlike those provided by Peking.

A number of incidents beginning in September, 1967, in New York City "exposed the deep fears and hostility that existed between the white, middle-class educational establishment and the black community." [15] The issue was "community control" of the schools. In order to understand the Chinese problem, an American might analogize and might substitute "Ministry of Education" for "New York City Board of Education." For local footdragging over the implementation of federal school desegregation orders, he might substitute footdragging in China over the admission into middle schools and universities of children of worker and peasant background. Both the Maoist decentralization program and the Ford Foundation community control plan ("Bundy Report") have been criticized by educators for their attacks on "professionalism." The analogy would break down somewhat on the matter of the constitution of local authority. But it would not break down on the basic assumption underlying the decentralization argument in both places. As Jason Epstein has characterized it in New York City: " Both the Bundy Plan and the Regent's proposal are content to assume that once the present bureaucracy is out of the way, talents and energies which heretofore have languished will awaken and find their way through the presumably enlightened local boards into the schools." [16] Mao would certainly agree. In both New York City and Peking there has been more romantic confidence in the miracles of decentralized control than clear thinking about the concrete form that it should take (or might take in time if it were im-

15 *The Burden of Blame: A Report on the Ocean Hill-Brownsville School Controversy* (New York: New York Civil Liberties Union, 1968).
16 Jason Epstein, "The Politics of School Decentralization," *New York Review of Books* (June 6, 1968), p. 28.

plemented). A recent Chinese Communist study on the educational revolution in rural China makes the following point:

The poor and lower-middle peasants change their former viewpoint on the schools when they really exercise power over education. The former relationship between the school and the production brigade was: "I do my teaching, you do your farm work." When speaking of a school, the poor and lower middle peasants often said, "your school. . . ." Now they always talk about "our school." [17]

The assumption is that only when they talk about "our school" will the schools really begin to serve China's new goals. Those who share confidence in decentralization have yet to direct their attention to two problems. First, can controls be established to insure that membership in local governing boards will not simply find itself moving into the hands of a new elite? Furthermore, what guarantees are there that local boards will not opt for quality education and special schools (for their own children, or to increase the number of high-level technicians locally available)? Second, if local areas not only have self-management but also provide a substantial amount of their own financing, does this mean that poor areas will provide educational facilities inferior to those of prosperous areas and, thus, that the problem of equity will not be solved after all? [18]

The efficacy of the educational system in helping to realize any revolutionary goals since 1949 has been seriously hampered by one brute fact: in the brief twenty-year period, four traumatic shifts in educational policy have occurred. From 1949 until the late fall of 1951 (in some areas, until 1953) many middle schools and institutions of higher learning still followed the Anglo-American model, that is, a liberal arts approach with teachers and students using many English and American texts (translated or in the original). From 1952 until 1958 China emulated the Soviet educational example with a heavy stress on engineering and science, a preference for the specialized and technical college, a stress on the quality of the students rather than on their quantity, the professional ideal, the use of Soviet texts, the highly centralized control over all schools, and a heavy academic burden on students. But beginning in early 1957 there was a reduction in the growth rate of higher institutions and a debate on the kind

[17] "*Jen-min Jih-pao* and *Hung ch'i* Investigation Report on Education Revolution in Countryside," NCNA, Peking, September 15, 1968, in *SCMP* No. 4261 (September 19, 1968).

[18] Professor Michel C. Oksenberg brought this to my attention.

of education appropriate for Chinese students at all levels. This occurred in the general *hsia fang* climate in which teachers were often sent to rural areas to perform labor. Matters crystallized between 1958 and 1961 when Mao, inspired by the Yenan experience, sought to apply to China at peace a model that in part was derived from guerrilla days. This meant combining education and productive labor, a stress on the quantity of students enrolled rather than on their quality, the reduced importance of academic study, the use of locally prepared Chinese texts, and decentralization. After the failure of the Great Leap, from roughly 1961 to 1964 (especially until September, 1962), there was a return to a liberalized version of the Soviet model—one more permissive of reading and discussing previously taboo subjects and foreign writings, which gave more authority to senior teachers in running the school. In 1964 Mao began his attempt once more to control the destiny of the educational system, an attempt that reached its climax during the Cultural Revolution. The Chinese People's Resist-Japan Military and Political University (*K'ang ta*), of which Lin Piao was once the director, again became the model school.

It hardly needs stating that such frequent, all-embracing shifts have had a deleterious effect on students, teachers, and administrators. The activities of these three groups are so interrelated that any change in one educational sector affects the others. For example, in 1958 when the key word was "simplify" and teachers were working to simplify texts, there was also a call to "simplify administration," and in response the Ministry of Higher Education was abolished. When popularly controlled schools with local autonomy were set up in 1958, most universities were returned to local control. Decentralization meant increasing student license to speak out on educational matters, and many teachers were subjected to substantial abuse. A return to centralization would mean taking away the students' new sense of participation, while changes in the teaching materials would mean an increase in the teacher's burden of work, which would cause teacher alienation.

## CENTRALIZATION OR DECENTRALIZATION

Those who view the educational system as a key instrument for realizing the egalitarian ideal have a preference for decentralization. The economic dimension of the problem of expanding educational opportunity was only partially recognized in the first years of the regime in the pious slogan "work industriously and be thrifty in educational expenditure" (*ch'in-kung chien hsüeh*). Not until 1958 did the dim recognition emerge as national policy with the directive that locally funded and managed schools were to become the rule. The group who advocated the reduction of quality control and of standards supervised by the Ministry of Education (through admissions policies, examinations, and uniform curriculum) thought this would make it possible to admit many more students into extant schools and to allow them to go farther up the ladder. And new "irregular" schools (a pejorative term used by professionals) with irregular standards could be opened. Education, including upper level education, would no longer be open only to a select group. Quantity would dominate over quality. In contrast, those whose primary concern has been with quality education in order to train high-level scientific and technical skills and who have not been troubled by the abuse of the egalitarian ideal that this entailed, have advocated centralization.

The question of locus of control is also important in the debate over manpower needs that stems from the "quantity versus quality" dispute. Decentralization is the vehicle for cultivating on a large scale basic level skills geared to local production needs. There will be more students, and a local character can be given to the curriculum. For example, in a chemistry course in an agricultural area, students might study chemistry only as it relates to chemical fertilizers. In fact, national reforms in teaching method and curriculum content in order to make education more functional, were expected to follow from the decentralization. In contrast, when there is a stress on schools that offer a solid grounding in fundamental mathematics and scientific theory (and on middle schools serving a college preparatory function), centralized control is viewed as the most effective guarantee that they will all fill this role.

The centralization/decentralization issue has two dimensions: the relative power balance in school policy between the ministry and the local organization (commune, production brigade, and so on), and the locus of authority within any given institution. Mao has assumed that when local people have substantial control, they can be relied upon to carry out the national policy of placing quantity over quality in admissions and promotion policies, and that they will opt for a curriculum with courses that relate closely to China's production demands.

Initial efforts at decentralized control were rather low key. In 1951 government encouragement was given to independently run primary schools (*min-pan hsiao-hsüeh*). Such schools, which might operate in abandoned temples, were financed and managed by organizations at the village or multivillage level. They received little or no financial aid and minimal supervision from authorities in the chain of command of the Ministry of Education. The basic operational unit in that official chain was the county (*hsien*) or city Bureau of Culture and Education (*wen-chiao-chü*). It received its directives from the ministry via the provincial Department of Culture and Education (*wen-chiao-t'ing*). Cultural Revolution documents assert that the policy of encouraging independently run schools had begun to pay off by the fall of 1956. Not only had the number of primary school students increased considerably, but many of the locally controlled primary schools had added middle school grades, which increased the number of middle school students. The independence of these schools was not welcomed by officials in the ministry, who also objected to the absence of "quality control" over them. They issued a directive on November 15, 1952, stating that there would be a three-year moratorium on establishing more independently run schools. In effect, this was the first step in a policy of limiting the growth of popular control.[19] Mao's own position was made publicly explicit in 1953, when he said that "independently run primary schools are permitted." [20] In 1957 some areas like Shanghai again encouraged the schools. As Christopher Howe has shown, factories used them to keep the unemployed occupied.

One dimension of the centralization/decentralization issue concerns whether the ministry or the local district has the dominant voice in deciding on school policy. The Soviet educational system, which was inherited from the czarist era, is highly centralized. During the period of intensive borrowing from the Soviet Union in the 1950's, officials in the Chinese Ministry of Education reinforced the argument for centralization by appeal to the Soviet model. Thus, before and after the period 1958–60, the ministry determined nationwide policy on school administration and organization, curriculum, textbooks, and teaching method.[21]

It was not until 1958 that Mao began the effective implementation of an educational revolution, a major feature of which was local con-

19 "Tsai ko-ming ti ta p'i-p'an chung shen-ju k'ai-chan hsüeh-hsiao tou-cheng p'i-kai" (In the Great Decisions of the Revolution, Wholeheartedly Begin the Struggle to Correct the Schools), *Chiao-yü ko-ming* (Educational revolution), No. 4 (May 6, 1967), p. 2 (University of Michigan, Asia Library call number: DS/777.55/.W355/IXXII-1-3).
20 *Ibid.*, p. 3.
21 Leo Orleans, *Professional Manpower and Education in Communist China* (Washington, D.C.: U.S. Government Printing Office, 1961), p. 13.

trol. His slogan was "control by the entire party and all the people." [22] The chief instruments for turning slogan into fact were the half-work (farming), half-study schools, most of which were directly managed by the brigade or production team in the communes. The state provided little or no financing and had minimal control over admission policies, teaching plans, course contents, and so forth. One source of the financing was the payment for productive labor done by students, which was used to support the school rather than being given as remuneration to the students. At the elementary level, it is difficult to distinguish between newly *reinstituted* independently run primary schools and half-farming, half-study primary schools. Such schools were to be the key to the expansion of educational opportunity.

Although the work-study school or popularly controlled school was the prototype of a locally managed school, we can examine the dramatic effect of decentralization by looking at ordinary schools. Institutions of higher learning make an interesting case study of the effect of the two policy alternatives in revolutionary China. The Ministry of Education falls under the Office of Culture and Education (*wen-chiao pan-kung-shih*) of the State Council (after 1954). By November, 1952, in addition to the Ministry of Education, the Ministry of Higher Education had been established. Among other things, this mushrooming of the bureaucracy was intended to provide the machinery whereby uniform control could be exercised over the following matters in all schools of higher learning: admissions requirements (with some exceptions), financial plans, personnel (hiring and transferring teachers), teaching plans, and the establishment of new departments in colleges.[23] In 1958, however, the Ministry of Higher Education was abolished, and its functions were absorbed by the Ministry of Education. The consequence for decentralization was immediate. Thirty-nine of the fifty-three schools of higher learning directly controlled by the Ministry of Higher Education were returned to provincial and city control.[24] Of forty-seven schools under the authority of various central

[22] *Kung-fei ti hsüeh-hsiao chiao-yü* (School Education in Communist China) (Taipei, 1966), p. 55. Note: This work was prepared for internal distribution by a governmental office in Taiwan. Information within is frequently documented. References are made to standard newspapers and journals, regional newspapers, and radio broadcasts. The authors also give evidence of relying on other non-public sources such as interviews. Evaluation is kept somewhat to a minimum. The work is basically descriptive.

[23] *Kung-fei ti hsüeh-hsiao*, pp. 15–16.

[24] The Ministry retained control of Chinese People's University, Peking University, Tsinghua University, Szechwan University, Peking Normal University, Peking Russian Language College, Peking Foreign Languages College, and a few other institutions.

special ministries, twenty-one were returned to local control. In sum, of 227 schools of higher learning, the Ministry of Education and the central specialized ministries were to have authority over 40, and the other 187 were to be returned to local control.[25] At this time, the uniform, nationwide admissions system was replaced by a system whereby each school either established its own admission procedures or entered into some cooperative arrangement with other schools. Local provincial or city conditions would dictate different policies for different places.[26] "Local control" meant not just a significant policy voice for the regional authorities, but more authority for the individual university administration with the aim of encouraging educational creativity and particularity.[27]

Mao watched the gradual erosion of his 1958 educational revolution. After 1960 many of the work-study schools simply ceased to function. For example, in early 1964 there were only eight left in Tientsin as compared to thirty-five the year before, which was itself a significant drop from 1960. In 1959, the focal universities (chung-tien kao-teng hsüeh-hsiao) such as Peking University, Tsinghua University, and others controlled directly by the ministry, reinstituted a unified national admissions policy and turned away from the 1958 spirit. The Ministry of Higher Education was re-established in 1964. Significantly, Yang Hsiu-feng, who was appointed minister, was among the first educational officials purged during the Cultural Revolution.

The other dimension to the problem concerns the decision making process within schools. Let us speak now about students. One must always attempt to differentiate representative bodies that exist primarily to enable a leadership group to implement its policies on a large scale from those bodies that exist, among other things, to solicit ideas and to solidify the sense of identification between an organization and its members. During the first few years after 1949 there were student bodies. In most ordinary middle schools and universities, for example, there would be an All School Students Society (ch'üan-hsiao hsüeh-sheng hui), a Class Association (pan hsüeh-sheng hui), and individual Students Sections (hsüeh-sheng hsiao-tsu).[28] The All School Students

---

[25] Kung-fei ti hsüeh-hsiao, p. 17.

[26] Ibid., p. 39.

[27] Yang Hsiu-feng, "Ch'üan-kuo jen-min tai-piao ta-hui ch'ang-wu wei-yüan-hui chü-hsing k'uo-ta hui-i chien-ch'a cheng-fu kung-tso" (Standing Committee of the National People's Congress Arranges Expanded Meeting to Investigate the Government's Tasks), Hsin-hua pan-yüeh-k'an (New China Fortnightly) (hereafter HHPYK), No. 11 (109) (1957), p. 42.

[28] "Kuan-yü chung-hsüeh-hsiao chiao-tao kung-tso ti ch'u-pu i-chien" (Some Initial

Society would be run by seven to fifteen students chosen from the entire student body to form a Student Committee (*hsüeh-sheng wei-yuan-hui*) with a chairman and several vice-chairmen. It would break into operational sections, concerned with physical education, hygiene, military affairs, culture and recreation, propaganda, and so forth. The Class Association, under the leadership of a class president (*pan-chang*), was the direct action arm of the All Student Society, receiving guidance both from that society and from the teacher who served as class supervisor (*pan chu-jen*).[29] In 1950 it was said that these organizations were to help students develop a "democratic mentality" by offering them a forum in which they could speak out.[30] In fact, such groups, which continued to exist until the Cultural Revolution, seem to have served the almost exclusive function of enabling those in charge to implement authorized school policies more efficiently, and, in this connection, they were the vehicle for organizing students for various officially encouraged group activities.

In contrast, the establishment in 1958 of the Three-in-One groups in charge of running schools and departments was intended, among other things, to solidify the sense of identification between the organization and its members by soliciting their ideas on educational matters. The group in charge of a given department would be composed of Party members, certain teachers, and students; the Party members always were supposed to have the "leading role." The experience of the physics department at Nan-k'ai University is typical of the kind of topic on which student opinion was solicited. Its Three-in-One section (*san chieh-ho hsiao-tsu*) decided on what courses should be offered, the content of those courses, the kinds of teaching materials to be used, and the method of instruction.[31]

A number of issues that had caused widespread student discontent —such as the minimal control one had over his job assignment after graduation, the low mobility rate from middle school to higher institution and from university to graduate school, and student stipends, which could be reduced suddenly or eliminated entirely by central authorities—were not open for student opinion. The discussions in which student participation was permitted were limited to curriculum,

Ideas on the Work of Teaching and Leading in Middle Schools), in *Hsin-chiao-yü ts'an-k'ao tzu-liao* (Reference Material on New Education) (Canton: Hsin-hua shu-tien, 1950), pp. 84–86.

[29] *Kung-fei ti hsüeh-hsiao*, p. 89.

[30] *Hsin-chiao-yü ts'an-k'ao tzu liao*, p. 84.

[31] *Kuang-ming Jih-pao* (hereafter *KMJP*), June 27, 1960. See also *Chiao-yü ko-ming*, p. 5.

teaching materials, and teaching method. But these are not trivial matters; they are of vital concern to students of all countries. The relative nonexistence of previous student participation in these decisions demonstrates the significance of this aspect of the Maoist innovation in local control, in spite of the limitations on topics open for opinion in the new bodies. The changes in curriculum and teaching materials were expected to bring the content of education more in line with the actual skills that graduates would be required to demonstrate.

An indirect but positive consequence of the decentralization spirit in individual schools might have been the reform of teaching methods in order to develop the students' ability to solve problems in the technical sphere. Essentially, rote memorization was to be terminated as much as possible, and in its stead the active involvement of the student in the learning process was to be substituted. This applied to lower schools and to institutions of higher learning. Administrative changes that formalized student participation in decisions about course content, examinations, and teaching method were expected to entail an alteration of the classroom teacher-student relationship as well. The work-study model was expected to have an additional favorable effect. However, teacher discipline often broke down as the bounds within which student participation was to be exercised were transgressed.[32] The academic orientation of the reforms was often submerged in generalized attacks on teachers as representatives of the "mental aristocracy," with substantial intimidation and purposeless disrespect. Student leverage was not merely theoretical; the governing body in a school had the authority to transfer a teacher, and the recommendation of students that a teacher should be transferred carried weight.[33]

Mao has continually argued for the changes in teaching method. In July, 1964, at the time of his second major attempt to force a revolution in education, he stated in a directive that one must "concentrate on cultivating and training the ability to analyze problems and solve them; one must end the constraint of having to run after teacher." Official publications often note that students cannot cease the reflexive response to antecedent blueprint and develop independent judgment unless the traditional domineering posture of the teacher is changed.[34]

---

32 *KMJP*, July 19, 1961.
33 Wen Shih, "Ch'ing-nien hsüeh-sheng ju-ho keng-hao ti hsüeh-hsi ho lao-tung" (How Youthful Students Can Study and Labor Even Better), *HHPYK*, No. 424 (5) (1959), p. 7.
34 *KMJP*, March 29, 1956 and November 16, 1961.

"Equalize the relation between students and teachers in institutions of higher learning," was one slogan.[35] Problem solving in class, open book examinations, and a host of other techniques were called for. Another aspect of the teaching reform was to reduce the amount of academic work that students must do, both the number of courses required and the amount of material covered in individual courses. The argument is that excessive absorption of facts or memorization of abstract theory does not leave time for students to think things out for themselves or to take part in activities where they can apply what they have absorbed.

The rote approach is traditional in China, and like the heavy academic burden, it is also characteristic of the Soviet model. These faults with the Chinese educational system were recognized early (actually in the 1920's, by Hu Shih and his Society for Chinese Educational Reform). Year after year in Communist China journals echoed the plea to get on with the reforms, and individual universities claimed to have implemented them.[36] But, symbolically, the provincial educational journal *Anhui chiao-yü* (Education in Anhui) still complained in 1966 that teachers are simply not aware of the significance of letting students figure out by themselves the answers to questions posed by the teacher.[37] The work-study school introduced in 1958 and again in 1964 was designed to embody in its very structure one of Mao's solutions to the dilemma. The close liaison between teaching unit and production unit was believed to insure the rapid transition from theoretical study to concrete application. Learning would not depend on rote memorization. The immediacy of the economic demands of the production unit would inhibit the inclusion in courses of material that was not relevant to production needs. Hence, the mushrooming academic burden on students would be reduced. But the work-study schools were aborted, and the Maoist demand for radical reforms in ordinary schools ran into the cautionary wall of the educational authorities. Lu Ting-i is reported as having attacked the Maoist approach in April, 1964, saying that all of China's reforms such as land reform had been carried through after a certain amount of experiment and experience,

---

[35] *KMJP*, February 18, 1959.

[36] *T'ou-k'ao ta-hsüeh shou-ts'e* (Handbook on Reporting for University Examinations) (Shanghai: *Wen hui pao*, 1951), pp. 2–4. Ts'ao Chao-lun, "T'i-kao kao-teng chiao-yü ti chih-liang" (Elevate the Quality of Higher Education), *HHPYK*, No. 8 (106) (1957), p. 113.

[37] Liu Ch'ao-jan, "K'o-t'ang t'i-wen shih ch'i-fa shih ma?" (Is Posing Questions in Class a Way of Instructing?), *An-hui chiao-yü* (Education in An-hui), No. 2 (1966), p. 25.

and that the same holds for changes in teaching method, examination method, and course content. The previous month he had blocked a plan to cut class time in half.[38] Ho Wei drafted a document on "reducing the students' burden and protecting their health." But instead of cutting down the academic work, he favored reducing the political activity, militia training, and productive labor of students.[39] Lin Piao alone applied Maoist principles (to army schools) on the slogan, "less [academic material] but finer, shorter and fewer [courses]."

After 1960, in individual courses the teacher's position once more became dominant with respect to homework, course examinations, and other details.[40] There was peace in the schools, but no reform of teaching methods. As for the school itself, the Party committee again took over exclusively the decision making function. There is one important qualification to this, however. Old teachers, especially in institutions of higher learning, were given a greater local voice than they had had since the early 1950's. They expressed it through the Committee on College Affairs, which in some cases exercised more authority than the Party committee.

Decentralization, which was aborted in its various dimensions after 1960, had been intended among other things to help resolve the conflict that arose between the egalitarian ideal and actual educational practices. Let us return to this matter.

### EGALITARIANISM AND QUALITY EDUCATION

During the period 1952–57, leading educational officials hoped eventually to provide a uniform, common core primary and middle school education of high academic quality for all students. The nation-wide uniformity of curriculum content and quality was expected to be conducive to realization of the egalitarian ideal—equalization through a common educational experience. Each student was to develop into the identical type of "all-round man," fully developed in the spheres of general academic knowledge of all kinds—knowledge of production, technology, morality, aesthetics, and physical education.[41] Actually, general academic knowledge of all kinds became the central feature of all-around development during this period. As opponents of the

---

38 *Chiao-yü ko-ming*, p. 8.
39 *Ibid.*
40 *KMJP*, July 19, 1961, and August 2, 1961.
41 Tu Ch'ing-hua, "T'an kao-teng kung-yeh-chiao-yü ti fang-chen" (A Discussion of the Guidelines For Industrial Education in Institutions of Higher Learning), *HHPYK*, No. 6 (104) (1957), p. 79. See also *KMJP*, September 24, 1955, and *Chiao-yü ko-ming*, p. 2.

policy were quick to point out, teachers would make no attempt to take account of individual differences in capability or interests.[42] Certain highly placed officials and teachers struggled against excessive homogeneity and favored "teaching according to the student's abilities" (*yin ts'ai shih chiao*). But to overemphasize individual differences between students made one liable to the charge of resurrecting the pedagogical principles of John Dewey and Hu Shih.[43] Thus, academic uniformity emerged as the policy in the 1950's.

The conflict between these educational practices entailed by the egalitarian ideal and the actual qualitative differences between students (resulting from differing backgrounds or innate factors), broke to the surface. Institutionally, the conflict showed itself in the increasing appearance of tracks within certain schools separating the backward students from the others, and, in 1962, in the formal maintenance of special schools for more qualified students. But from the broadest perspective, the approach through homogeneity simply did not deal with the essential barrier to egalitarianism in China: the imbalance between rural areas (poor and heavily populated) and the cities (more prosperous and with a fraction of the population). Quite simply, the ministry policy of emphasizing quality education meant that there were too few schools, and in those that existed, the admissions practices and internal standards impeded the mobility of children of peasants and workers.

The term "quality education" refers to a system with at least three characteristics. First, the ordinary schools offer preparation for a higher rung on the educational ladder rather than feeding directly into the manpower pool through providing vocational training (for example, the middle school curriculum is college preparatory). Second, at the middle school and university level there is a stress on basic theory and fundamentals (for example, in mathematics and the sciences) that may have no direct and immediate practical application. Third, there is a certain selectivity in enrollments, and not all who are admitted survive the competition. Quality education by definition posed a threat to the egalitarian ideal. The Maoist response to that threat was to

---

[42] Chang Yeh-ming, "Ho Chiang Nan-hsiang t'ung-chih shang-ch'üeh chiao-yü fang-chen wen-t'i" (Discussing Some Questions About Educational Guidelines With Comrade Chiang Nan-hsiang), *HHPYK*, No. 3 (101) (1957), p. 77.

[43] Ch'en Yu-sung, "Chien-ch'a Hu Shih tsai chiao-yü fang-mien ti fan-tung ying-hsiang ho Hu Shih ssu-hsiang tui-wo ti ying-hsiang" (An Examination of Hu Shih's Reactionary Influence in the Educational Sector and the Influence of Hu Shih's Thought), in *Tzu-ch'an-chieh-chi chiao-yü p'i-p'an* (A Critique of Capitalist Education) (Peking: Wen-hua chiao-yü ch'u-pan she, 1955), pp. 193–97. Also *KMJP*, May 15, 1956.

tamper with the procedures that insure superior quality in an educational system, to insist on substantial productive labor for all students (intended to help break the barrier that exists between mental and manual laborers, and between students in ordinary schools and those in work-study schools), and to inject political indoctrination of a special kind in the schools. Purely academic study was downgraded.

ELIMINATING QUALITY CONTROL

In October, 1951, the government issued a "Decision Concerning the Reform of the Educational System." Its major point was that "education will be used to open the door to workers in industry and agriculture.[44] In Shanghai during the same year, it was announced that preferential consideration would be given in colleges and universities to the following categories of people: (1) high school graduates of peasant or worker families, (2) cadres of peasant and worker origin who had devoted three or more years to revolution, (3) cadres not of peasant or worker origin who had devoted themselves to revolution for five or more years, and (4) 1949 high school graduates who had involved themselves in revolutionary work after graduation.[45] A 1956 statement for universities all over China adds other categories to the list.[46] Such students often received full scholarship and, occasionally, permission to ignore the foreign language requirement.[47] Such improvement in the situation was achieved without a major institutional change in general admissions procedures, which were by examination. Note the statistics on increases in peasant and worker students in the student body given in Table 25.

TABLE 25
PERCENTAGE OF PEASANT AND WORKER STUDENTS IN THE STUDENT BODY

| Type of school | 1950 * | 1958 * | 1962 † | 1964 ‡ |
|---|---|---|---|---|
| Schools of higher learning | 19.3% | 48% | 67% | xxx |
| Specialized middle schools | 56.6% | 77% | xxx | xxx |
| Ordinary middle schools | 51.3% | 75.2% | xxx | 75% |

   * *Kung-fei ti hsüeh-hsiao,* p. 4.
   † Cheng, *Scientific and Engineering Manpower,* p. 88.
   ‡ Stewart Fraser, *Chinese Communist Education* (Nashville, Tenn.: Vanderbilt University Press, 1965), p. 17.

44 *Kung-fei ti hsüeh-hsiao,* p. 21.
45 *T'ou-k'ao ta-hsüeh shou-ts'e,* p. 35.
46 *KMJP,* July 4, 1956.
47 Cheng Chu-yüan, *Scientific and Engineering Manpower in Communist China, 1949–1963* (Washington, D.C.: National Science Foundation, 1965), p. 58.

The figures may be exaggerated. They also reflect the enrollment situation in new institutions of uneven quality that catered especially to students of worker and peasant background. Thus, in 1958 at Peking University, such students comprised only 19.5 per cent of the student body, as compared with the 48 per cent figure for the country as a whole.[48] In any case, the pace up to 1958 was not rapid enough for Mao, and the education revolution of 1958–60 included policies aimed at correcting the situation: schools of higher learning were ordered to establish fixed ratios for students of peasant and worker background, supplementary classes were organized for academically unqualified students of peasant and worker background prior to or after their formal admission, and there was some decentralization of nationwide admissions procedures.[49] In addition, classroom places were increased by sending many students of bourgeois background down to the countryside. Although these measures were helpful in dealing with the problem in schools of higher learning, they did not constitute a solution. The real bottleneck, which was noticed during 1958–60, was not identified as being crucial until the mid-1960's. This was the policy of holding entrance examinations, over which the Ministry of Education had exercised some control in many instances. Token loopholes were established in 1958. For example, in the city of Kweiyang, schools of higher learning permitted each *hsien* to send one or two applicants to a school without their taking the examination, and teacher training middle schools could send 5 per cent of their top graduates to normal universities without examination.[50] But this was a drop-in-the-bucket approach. (Not until the Cultural Revolution were steps taken to eliminate the examinations.) Nationwide entrance requirements were spelled out in detail in 1959. They specified that with one exception all applicants must pass the joint entrance examination. The exception was that a given ratio of workers, peasants, worker and peasant cadres, and senior cadres could bypass the joint entrance examination on recommendation of their organizations; however, the recommending agency must give an examination.[51]

[48] Chiang Lung-chi, "Hsing-wu mieh-tzu hung-t'ou chuan-shen, wei chien-she kung-ch'an-chu-i ti hsin Pei-ching ta-hsüeh erh tou-cheng" (Raise Up the Proletariat, Annihilate the Capitalist; Be Red Through and Through and Highly Qualified; Fight to Establish a Communist New Peking University), *Pei-ching ta-hsüeh hsüeh-pao* (Journal of Peking University), No. 3 (1958), pp. 32–33.

[49] *KMJP*, January 1, 1958 and May 15, 1958. Also *Kung-fei ti hsüeh-hsiao*, p. 39.

[50] *KMJP*, May 15, 1958.

[51] *Ibid.*, June 11, 1959. The other general entry requirements were: (1) be under thirty years of age, (2) be a graduate of an upper middle school or its equivalent, (3) if

Successful implementation of the policy of preferential consideration for workers and peasants was impeded by the nature of the examinations themselves. Even if preferential treatment is given to children of worker and peasant background in the group who pass the examination (and only when they score the same as children of bourgeois backgrounds), a larger number of such youths is eliminated by the examination itself. The problem is the same one that American test makers have encountered with blacks: since the test makers and many of the test takers have different respective backgrounds and experiences, the validity of the tests is open to question. And in 1962, during the attack against Mao's educational revolution, even the practice of preferential treatment may have been abandoned.[52] A statement of entry requirements in 1963 not only does not mention the practice,[53] it states that those who pass the initial entry examinations must go on to take a second examination to qualify (*fu shih*).[54] Schools that instituted radical admissions policies were not the ordinary schools, but rather were the institutions blessed by Mao that catered especially to peasants and workers. For example, a work-study university in Kiangsi required no written examination, only an oral test for both high school graduates and candidates coming from factories. The latter, in addition, had to demonstrate a knowledge of machine operation.[55] There was a good bit of remedial course work in such schools for students inadequately prepared. Spare-time schools of higher learning required only good class background, a high degree of political consciousness, and good physical health.[56] Soon after the victory, Mao had backed an irregular primary school and middle school system for workers and peasants that also bypassed normal examination, entry, and promotion procedures. These were called "workers and peasants accelerated primary/middle schools" (*kung-nung su-ch'eng chung/hsiao-hsüeh*). The primary school program was for two or three years instead of the normal five, and the middle

one is a cadre, be recommended to the Joint Entrance Examination Committee by Party organs, industrial agencies, administrative agencies, or other civic organizations, and (4) preferential consideration for workers, peasants, veterans, and on-the-job training cadres.

[52] *Chiao-yü ko-ming*, p. 7.

[53] The only exception to this is the following token loophole: candidates for graduate school who come not from a university but from some occupation will be selected over a regular university graduate only if they make the same examination score as the graduate. See *JMJP*, October 14, 1963.

[54] *JMJP*, May 31, 1963.

[55] *Chiang-hsi Jih-pao*, February 20, 1960.

[56] *KMJP*, March 6, 1958.

school was for three or four years instead of the normal six. But the accelerated schools were ordered by the Ministry of Education to cease admitting students in July, 1955, because of the "irregular standards" they employed. The number of work-study schools declined drastically after 1960, and many were attacked on the same grounds. A recent report citing incomplete statistics of 1962 states that the abortion of the 1958–60 educational reform drastically reduced the number of new students accommodated in these schools that were less quality conscious. For example, by 1962 the number of agricultural middle schools had dropped from 22,600 with 2,030,000 students to 3,715 schools with 266,000 students.[57] This is consistent with the thrust of a 1960 report.[58] In sum, this attempt to increase quantity at the expense of quality in order to come closer to the egalitarian ideal was unsuccessful.

Within certain universities the Maoist egalitarian ideal was further shattered by the existence of two streams, one for regular students and one for those of worker or peasant background who were unable to compete with the others. Tsinghua University reported in 1957 that most of the students in its classes for those who were deficient in background were graduates of "worker/peasant accelerated middle schools." [59] A short story written at the time describes the difficulties faced by cadres coming to school directly from their jobs when they had to compete with regular students.[60]

In addition to its admissions procedures, the Ministry of Education fostered elitism in two other ways. One was to permit the existence of special schools for children of high officials. Such, for example, were the Capability Cultivating School (*yü-ts'ai hsüeh-hsiao*) for children of high Party cadres in Peking and the August 1 School (*pa-i hsüeh-hsiao*) for children of high officers in the People's Liberation Army (PLA). They were criticized during the Hundred Flowers Campaign for inhibiting contact between the children and the masses.[61]

It should be noted that school alumni associations, which were subdivided into associations for graduates of given years, were

[57] Fei-ch'ing yen-chiu tsa-chih-she (Institute for the Study of Chinese Communist Problems), *I-chiu-liu-pa fei-ch'ing nien-pao* (1968 Yearbook on Chinese Communism) (Taipei: Fei-ch'ing yen-chiu tsa-chih she, 1968), p. 194. See also *JMJP*, July 18 and 19, 1967.
[58] *KMJP*, June 6, 1960.
[59] *KMJP*, September 25, 1957.
[60] Hsiung Pei-yüan, "Ta-hsüeh li fa-sheng ti shih-ch'ing" (What Happened in the University), *CKCN*, No. 8 (1957), pp. 13–19, and No. 9 (1957), pp. 15–18.
[61] *KMJP*, May 23, 1957.

forcibly disbanded.[62] These were interest groups that could lobby for special treatment for given schools.

The educational authorities also permitted certain primary and middle schools and institutions of higher learning to be officially recognized as having special status because of the high percentage of their graduates who passed the admissions examination for higher schools. One basis for this practice was a 1954 Ministry of Education plan that worked out a method for determining a teacher's work load and salary based on the success of his students in qualifying for higher rungs on the educational ladder.[63] The formal institutionalization of the situation occurred in December, 1962, when the Ministry of Education instructed all provinces and municipalities to select a number of "key schools" at each level.[64] They became known as "little treasure pagodas" (*hsiao pao-t'a*), that is, buildings housing treasured students who could rise farther and farther up the educational ladder. In urban areas, municipal Party committees had some special control over these key schools. They received special personnel and material resources, and they had special regulations regarding admissions. In the "little treasure pagodas" at the primary and middle school level, the academic plan was different from that at the rest of the full-time schools. In the former, formal instruction was to last not less than nine and one-half months in primary school and nine months in middle school. The labor requirement (one-half month a year for primary students, one month for middle school pupils) could be worked off cleaning up the school grounds. The teaching plan was very different in the other schools; the duration of academic instruction was one month less per year and the requirements were lower (for example, sometimes no foreign language).

In addition to this clear-cut institutionalization of elitism through the establishment of key schools, the same effect was in fact achieved as a result of two other kinds of prestige distinction between schools. One was between full-time schools and work-study schools. The other (sometimes related) was between those financed and controlled by the state and those financed and controlled largely by the collective.

Lu Ting-i is quoted as having said in 1961: "Speak less of universal-

62 *KMJP*, March 15, 1967.

63 *Chiao-yü ko-ming*, p. 3.

64 *JMJP*, December 17, 1967; "Be Successors to the Proletariat," *Peking Review*, No. 32 (August 9, 1968), p. 11. In Shantung, for example, in the first selection 25 per cent of full-time secondary schools were so designated, as were 31 per cent of the primary schools; the number was then further narrowed down. In Peking, middle schools No. 4 and No. 31 were among the key schools.

ization and more of raising quality. We must energetically raise the standard of key schools. In the categories of university, middle school, and primary school, the key school kind must all be run well. Stress raising quality." [65] The trend after the Great Leap was clearly in the direction of quality over quantity in education.

In sum, the situation during the early 1960's was generally this. Many middle schools and universities had not institutionalized admissions procedures that would genuinely open their doors to students of peasant background. The examination hurdle remained in most ordinary schools. The elite status of a school was actually measured not in terms of the number of its students of worker or peasant background, but in terms of how many of its graduates were able to go on to more advanced prestigious schools.

COMBINING EDUCATION AND LABOR

The typical Maoist approach to breaking the status barrier has been to transform the occupants of one position into the other: "Workers and peasants must be intellectualized; intellectuals must be transformed into workers and peasants." [66] In his "Sixty Points on Work Method" of January 31, 1958, Mao laid out the concrete policy direction for realization of this goal. In essence he said that where possible universities and urban middle schools should establish alliances with factories, technical middle schools should try running factories or farms, students in agricultural middle schools should do labor on their own farms and on those of the cooperative as well as send their teachers down to do labor, students in rural village primary and middle schools should do farm labor for the cooperative, and so forth. [67] The educational guideline was pinpointed in the maxim, "education must be combined with productive labor," which was contained in the State Council "Directive Concerning Educational Work" of September 19, 1958. Work-study schools blossomed forth. In ordinary middle schools labor was treated as a standard course.

In addition to the educational value of labor, from a Maoist perspective there are very important economic reasons for combining educa-

[65] *JMJP*, December 17, 1967.

[66] Quoted, among other places, in Ch'en Po-ta, "Tsai Mao Tse-tung t'ung-chih ti ch'i-chih hsia" (Under the Banner of Comrade Mao), *Pei-ching ta-hsüeh hsüeh-pao*, No. 3 (1958), p. 21.

[67] *Chiao-yü ko-ming*, pp. 4–5. In 1957 the Ministry of Education had directed that a course in the fundamentals of agriculture should be offered in elementary schools, that a manual labor course should be offered in some elementary schools and lower middle schools, and that a course in productive labor should be given in all middle schools.

tion and labor, especially in rural areas. It is a way of rapidly spreading education without the state having to bear the financial burden. Students often build their own buildings. And the money they earn through their labor goes to support the school.

In the educational sector, high level opposition to Mao's policies seems to have emerged well before the failure of the Great Leap had become obvious. Lu Ting-i, Lin Feng, Ch'en Tseng-ku, and others are now reported to have criticized many aspects of the educational revolution during 1958 and 1959. At the school level itself, some teachers and students were aghast at the probable lowering of educational standards when ordinary schools were transformed into work-study schools.[68] One report frankly says that when the program was first launched, only 20–25 per cent of the students were enthusiastic about it. Student stipends were removed in order to force the students to earn their keep.[69]

In 1958, Mao portrayed China as needing to cease the slavish imitation of the Soviet method and to go her own way.[70] In this connection, it was necessary to end the exclusively academic orientation of education. This is curious, to say the least, because in 1958 the Soviet Union carried out its own sweeping educational reform (which was later somewhat aborted), and the most striking characteristic of the new approach was manual labor for all students. One recent writer, describing the 1958 Soviet reforms, says that the important matter was: "The retreat from the overwhelmingly academic character of the old ten-year school, and the much greater emphasis on polytechnical and vocational training of all types . . . the stress on practical work for all is the keynote of the 1958 reform." [71] The basic motive was ideological. Khrushchev stated: "We still have a sharp distinction between mental and manual work. . . . This is fundamentally wrong and runs counter to our teaching and aspirations. As a rule, boys and girls who have finished secondary school consider that the only acceptable path in life for them is to continue their education at higher schools. . . . Some of them even consider [work] beneath their dignity." [72] As a result of the 1958 reform, Russian middle school students who did not attend "Secondary Specialized Schools" (about

---

68 *Chi-so pan-kung pan-tu ti hsüeh-hsiao* (The Half-Work, Half-Study Schools in Various Places) (Shanghai: Shanghai chiao-yü ch'u-pan she, 1958), p. 2.

69 *Ibid.*, p. 3.

70 *Chiao-yü ko-ming*, pp. 4–5.

71 Quoted in Grant, *Soviet Education*, p. 99.

72 *Ibid.*, p. 102.

twice as much vocational element as general academic), Vocational Technical Schools (trade schools), or part-time schools, were to attend three-year "Secondary Polytechnical Schools." In these, one-third of the time was to be spent on the theory and application of work-study material, with the application being done in a local factory with which the school had an arrangement.[73] The third year of school had been added for this purpose. They were to graduate prepared either for industrial or academic work. In this same spirit, university admissions boards were to give preferential treatment to secondary school graduates who had spent at least two years doing productive labor after graduation (except for students in mathematics and physics).[74] In actual fact, major aspects of Khrushchev's plan have been largely abandoned in the Soviet Union. Liaisons with factories often did not succeed. His successors never provided sufficient funds to schools to make much work-training possible. The extra year of secondary school was eliminated in 1964, and "shop-work" has become an extracurricular activity rather than a part of the curriculum's core. However, educators in the USSR are still greatly concerned with changing educational methods in order to decrease formalism and verbalism and to increase "the tie of education with life." The irony is that on the labor issue, Mao himself is more in tune with the spirit of the 1958 Soviet model, while his opponents, who were accused of Khrushchevian revisionism, stood opposed to it.

The Ministry of Education took formal steps to return to the pre-1957 educational system, eliminating the labor requirement, between July, 1961, and August, 1962. Lu Ting-i played a major role in formulating the new policy. Alliances between factories and schools were terminated, as were many of the 1958 work-study schools.

Since the beginning of Mao's 1958 education revolution, much of the distrust and eventual open conflict over the labor question between him and his opponents has centered on the work-study system. There is no doubt that the system was blessed by Mao at the start. In September, 1958, at Wuhan University, he said, "It is a good thing for students consciously to seek to implement a half-work, half-study system. It is a necessary trend if schools are to run factories on a large scale. We can approve this kind of demand and in addition, we

---

[73] Polytechnical education is rejected by Maoists because the emphasis is on learning the theory of production processes (hence the *poly*technical stress). Maoists emphasize more heavily labor as a "great furnace" for molding men's attitudes, and thus a single production activity suffices.

[74] Grant, *Soviet Education*, p. 118.

should give them our support and encouragement." [75] Among other things, the tremendous importance of the work-study idea lies in the fact that some people in China treat it as part of Maoist educational "theory" (*li-lun*, not *ssu-hsiang*), a great contribution to Marxist-Leninist "theory" (*li-lun*).[76]

The potential for conflict lay in the fact that the function of the work-study system in society was open to various interpretations. People like Liu Shao-ch'i and Lu Ting-i clearly interpreted the function differently from the way Mao did. Most important, Liu and Lu wanted two completely different educational systems in the country: work-study for future skilled workers, technicians, plant supervisors, and the like, and ordinary schools for other people. That is, they failed to regard the ideological purpose of labor as all important. The idea that labor is essential for the proper political education of the youth leads rather to the Maoist position that eventually there should be one system, not two, with labor for everyone, even if it is not necessarily half labor. In other words, in Mao's view, it was not so much the "*half*" labor" that was important as the fact that there was substantial labor required in those schools. This guaranteed graduates equipped with a "labor viewpoint." Such schools should serve as models for ordinary institutions, which should gradually change their structure to permit a considerable amount of labor as a standard part of the curriculum. At the beginning of the 1958 revolution, Lu Ting-i had made it clear that "ordinary schools do not need to run on a half-half system." [77]

Today Liu Shao-ch'i stands accused, first, of stealing Mao's idea of the work-study school, of linking himself with Marx, Engels, Lenin, and Stalin as a great theoretician, and of proceeding to present the idea as his own.[78] He is said to have done this both in May, 1958, and in May, 1964; both times he presented his views under the theme, "The Two Kinds of Educational System and the Two Kinds of Labor System." Second, he is charged with emasculating the idea. He failed to regard the "labor" element as essential to all education, as shown by his desire to perpetuate ordinary schools in which labor is kept to a minimum. And it was this emasculated version that was peddled all

[75] *Chiao-yü ko-ming*, p. 5. This is only one of many such references.
[76] *Ibid.*, p. 8.
[77] *Ibid.*, p. 5.
[78] *Ibid.*, p. 8. Liu is said to claim that he first outlined the idea at Tientsin University in 1958. Mao is recorded as referring to it in a speech on January 31, 1958.

over the country by Ho Wei, who became Minister of Education in October, 1964.[79]

In 1964 when Mao attempted once more to revitalize the education revolution, the work-study concept had not yet been irreparably soiled by the special understanding that Liu Shao-ch'i and Lu Ting-i had of it. Their special interpretation would be made evident during the two years 1964 and 1965.[80] Thus, in December, 1964, at the First Session of the Third National People's Congress, Chou En-lai still stated, "Half work and half study along with half-farming and half-study schools are schools of a new type which integrate education with labor. . . . These schools provide the direction for long range development of socialist and communist education."[81] This is basically the same line that was adopted in 1958.[82] In other words, uniformity through labor for all was the Maoist approach to the egalitarian ideal at both times.

POLITICAL INDOCTRINATION

Among other things, political education aims to create in students a selfless attitude that prevents the quest for personal privilege that characterizes the elites. There was a hiatus in political education which lasted from 1953 to the end of 1957. In imitation of the Soviets, by 1956 the only remaining course for many middle school students was a meeting for one hour a week on "The Constitution" for students in the final year. In September, 1957, university Party committees for the first time established "Committees on Education in Socialist Thought," and each department was required to establish a "Section on Education in Socialist Thought."[83] The Maoist approach to political education in the school is threefold. First, it emphasizes making the lessons concrete and avoiding a theoretical approach where possible. Thus, the teaching is often by model emulation with "selfless" Party

[79] *Kung-fei ti hsüeh-hsiao*, p. 7.

[80] Mao formally attempted to revitalize the educational revolution at a Central Committee meeting on February 13, 1964. See Donald J. Munro, "Maxims and Realities in China's Educational Policy," *Asian Survey*, IV (April, 1967), 254–72. Also, *Chiao-yü ko-ming*, p. 7.

[81] *JMJP*, December 31, 1964.

[82] Explicitly stated by Vice-Minister of Education Tung Ch'un-ts'ai, "Chia-ch'iang ssu-chiao-yü, lao-tung-chiao-yü, t'i-ch'ang ch'ün-chung pan hsüeh, ch'in-chien pan hsüeh" (Strengthen Thought and Labor Education, Promote the Masses Running Schools, and the Diligent and Frugal Management of Schools), *She-hui-chu-i chiao-yü chien-she kao-ch'ao* (High Tide in the Establishment of Socialist Education) (Peking: Jen-min chiao-yü ch'u-pan-she, 1958), pp. 4–5.

[83] *KMJP*, August 22, 1957.

cadres (in the late 1950's), PLA men, and old workers or peasants (in the 1960's) doing the instruction rather than academicians. Symbolically, in 1958 at Peking and Tsinghua Universities, the strongest opponents of attempts to strengthen political indoctrination of students came from the heads of "The Offices for Research in Education in Political Theory" (*cheng-chih li-lun k'o-chiao yen shih*).[84] Second, not only are political courses incorporated into the formal curriculum (for example, "History of the Chinese Revolution"), but also ordinary language, natural science, and mathematics materials are saturated with political examples. Last, there is a tendency to substitute the writings of Mao for Marxist classics and scholarly treatises on dialectical materialism. Signs of the times were the organization in the spring of 1958 in Peking of a "Society for the Study of the Philosophical Works of Comrade Mao Tse-tung," [85] the claims in 1959 that Mao is "the most outstanding contemporary revolutionary, statesman and theoretician of Marxism-Leninism," [86] and the publication of the fourth volume of his *Selected Works* in 1960. Middle school students studied his "On the Correct Handling of Contradictions Among the People." University students studied his other essays. The Department of Chinese Literature at Peking University introduced "Courses on Literary Theory," the purpose of which was to indoctrinate students in Mao's literary thought.[87] In 1964 and 1965, the Chinese media baffled foreign readers with a violent attack on the popular philosopher Feng Ting. Recent documents indicate why. After the Great Leap, officials in the Ministry of Education opposed using Mao's works as basic teaching materials in middle school political courses, and in May, 1963, Feng Ting was chosen as editor-in-chief of the work *Dialectical Materialism* that was to take their place.[88]

[84] "Ma-k'o-ssu-chu-i li-lun chiao-hsüeh ti i ko chung-ta wen-t'i" (An Important Question on Education in Marxist Theory), *Hsüeh-hsi* (Academic Studies), No. 2 (1958), pp. 17–18.

[85] *JMJP*, April 26, 1958. Reference is made to this in D. W. Fokkema, *Literary Doctrine in China and Soviet Influence* (The Hague: Mouton, 1965), p. 194.

[86] *JMJP*, September 28, 1959, quoted in Philip Bridgham, "Mao's 'Cultural Revolution': Origin and Development," *CQ*, No. 29 (January–March, 1967), p. 3. It is interesting that Liu Shao-ch'i was the first to refer publicly to the role of Mao's thought in guiding the Chinese Communist Party (CCP). In 1945 he stated: "The General Programme of the Party Constitution provides that the Chinese Communist Party guides all its work by Mao Tse-tung's theory of the Chinese revolution. . . ."

[87] *KMJP*, December 24, 1960.

[88] *Chiao-yü ko-ming*, p. 7.

CONCLUSION

After the Great Leap, the labor and political education that were instruments especially designed to realize the egalitarian ideal were reduced or eliminated. They were accused of taking time from academic study. Yang Hsiu-feng and others worked out a new plan for primary and middle schools. Lin Feng and others were charged with drafting a new plan for higher education to emphasize academic work; the plan is contained in the "Sixty Points on Higher Education" (*kao-chiao liu-shih t'iao*). In 1961, the Youth League in some places changed its chief function from the political to the stimulation of enthusiasm for academic pursuits.[89] In essence, as the conflict between the egalitarian ideal and the practices needed to insure quality education became manifest, many educators ignored the conflict by ignoring the ideal.

If the conflict required an ostrich attitude toward the egalitarian ideal on one side, it required on the other side that Mao Tse-tung reassess China's manpower needs to justify playing down the special concern with quality education.

MANPOWER NEEDS AND THE EGALITARIAN IDEAL

In quantitative terms, the government's attempts to increase rapidly the number of engineers, scientists, and others with high level skills has been successful. After the revolution, education in general received a much larger budget (for example, 1 per cent in 1948 versus 7.28 per cent in 1956).[90] The number of institutions of higher learning increased significantly between 1949 and 1962: 205 in 1949, 841 in 1960 (including many rapidly organized schools of uncertain quality as a part of the Great Leap), and 400 at the end of 1962 after the disbanding of some Great Leap schools. In 1949 some 117,000 students were in colleges and universities; by September, 1962, there were 820,000.[91] With the adoption of the policy of emulating the Soviet model, a special stress was placed on engineering colleges and on strengthening natural science departments in comprehensive universities.[92] According to figures compiled by Cheng Chu-yüan, during the period 1949–63, 671,000

---

[89] *KMJP*, November 29, 1961.

[90] "Hsin-chung-kuo chiao-yü shih-yeh ti fa-chan kai-k'uang" (The General Situation in the Development of New China's Educational Enterprise), *HHPYK*, No. 1 (123) (1958), p. 138.

[91] Cheng, *Scientific and Engineering Manpower*, pp. 73, 84; *Kung-fei ti hsüeh-hsiao*, pp. 36–37; *KMJP*, February 5, 1960.

[92] Cheng, *Scientific and Engineering Manpower*, p. 37.

students graduated from colleges and universities in the categories of engineering, natural science, agriculture and forestry, and medicine, compared with only 70,000 in the 1928–48 period.[93]

A first glance at the statistics gives an impressive picture of middle school education since 1949 as well, but the figures may hide a serious problem.

Ordinary middle schools have a curriculum that includes: Chinese language and literature, mathematics, physics, chemistry, biology (broken into three subdivisions), geography (since 1953, divided into some six subdivisions), history, general study of politics, general study of the science of society (as of 1955), the constitution (introduced in 1955), foreign language (removed from many schools in the 1960's), physical education, music, fine arts (changed to drawing), fundamentals of agriculture, current events and policy (abandoned in 1953 and reintroduced in 1957), and productive labor (added as a formal course in 1958). In essence, the curriculum is college preparatory. There were only 2,536 such schools in all China in 1949 (excepting the Southwest); by 1956, the number had risen to 6,715, giving a middle school education to 4,196,000 students as compared to only 1,039,000 seven years earlier.[94] In addition to the ordinary middle schools, there is a variety of specialized middle schools: technical schools (industrial, agricultural, communication, transportation, and so on) and normal teacher training middle schools.

Now the problem. In 1956 the number of Chinese youths in the middle school age bracket (twelve to seventeen years inclusive) was approximately sixty-three million. Of these, only 4,196,000 were in middle school. In 1966, the number in the age bracket was about seventy-three million of whom only fifteen million were in middle school (ten million in ordinary schools and the other five million in specialized schools).[95] Sizable funds were being spent to give ten million youths a middle school education that was essentially college preparatory. The college preparatory curriculum dictated by the ministry and the extreme concern with quality control from the center were both aspects of the Soviet model. In terms of China's immediate

[93] *Ibid.*, p. 269.

[94] *Kung-fei ti hsüeh-hsiao*, p. 51.

[95] The number of youths in the twelve to seventeen years age bracket is roughly 10 per cent of the population. The population according to the 1953 census was 580,000,000. The 1966 population is crudely estimated at 730,000,000. The number of students in middle schools in the 1960's is based in part on figures (and inferences from figures) given to the chancellor of Toronto University when he visited China in 1962. See *Kung-fei ti hsüeh-hsiao*, pp. 51, 55.

manpower needs there are two related questions: (1) Should there be less college preparatory education and more stress on gearing the curriculum to locally needed agricultural and industrial skills? (2) In spite of the impressive growth since 1949, is the number of students in middle schools (especially in lower middle schools) really enough (or as many as possible)? Mao's own answer to (1) was "yes," to (2) "no." His response was to encourage the liaison of schools with production organizations in 1957–58, which meant decreasing the amount of academic material covered in order to increase time for learning production skills. The work-study schools were established as Mao's answer to the question of whether or not the number of students was really sufficient.[96] Statistics on enrollment increases as a result of his 1958 educational reform were cited above. The whole approach rested on decentralization. A local character for the curriculm is more possible under decentralization, and, it is believed, so is a surge in enrollment (through the blossoming of work-study schools that could not previously meet ministry standards). The Maoist answer is dictated in part by his primary commitment to the egalitarian ideal (ordinary middle schools are elitist, catering to a select number of "future mental aristocrats" who look down on manual labor and on work-study schools). But the rationality of his answer must be evaluated on its own terms.

The aim of increasing training in locally needed production skills is reflected most clearly in Mao's directives regarding preparation of teaching materials for institutions of higher learning and middle schools. One of the major responsibilities of the Three-in-One combinations that took charge of schools and school departments in 1958 was outlined in the following order of the State Council, dated August, 1958: "Teaching materials should be compiled according to the Three-in-One principle, through the cooperation of students and teachers, under the leadership of the party committee."[97] Mao argued that new teaching materials should have a local character. His own model would be those used in schools in areas controlled by the Communists prior to 1949. Local areas were still to follow central educational guidelines, and to submit their teaching plans and texts to county authorities for approval. But the local bodies were for the first time actively en-

---

[96] Work-study schools at the lower middle school level predominated. They were especially common in the fields of agriculture, forestry, fishing, and so forth. Rural children often began to acquire on-the-job skills at the primary level in so-called "ploughing-study primary schools" (*keng-tu hsiao-hsüeh*).

[97] *KMJP*, February 18, 1959.

couraged to tackle the text and teaching program problems themselves. Where formerly they would have waited for the central government to provide the financial and personnel means and the final teaching products, they were now to rely more on their own resources. In the rural areas, the central government frequently had provided neither or, when it did, what was provided was not appropriate to local production needs. Many extant texts were suspect, first, because they were translations of Soviet works [98] (meaning that their relevance to specific Chinese problems was open to question) and, second, because they were edited by people associated with the old regime. But the major problem was that texts used in rural areas often reflected an urban orientation by the author, both in vocabulary used and in the subject matter presented.

The attack on the Maoist educational revolution that followed the Great Leap failure affected the policy of locally determined teaching materials. In February, 1961, Lu Ting-i, Teng Hsiao-p'ing, and others, in the name of the Central Secretariat, placed Chou Yang in over-all charge of the editing of liberal arts materials for higher level schools, while Yang Hsiu-feng (Vice-Minister of Higher Education during 1952–54 and Minister of Higher Education 1964–65) and Chiang Nan-hsiang (Vice-Minister of Education of 1960–64 and Minister of Higher Education 1965–66) were to supervise the editing of natural science and engineering works. Three academicians—the philosophers Feng Ting and Fung Yu-lan, and the historian Chien Po-tsan—were placed in direct charge of the editing of the liberal arts materials. (Feng came under severe attack in 1964 and Chien in 1965, when Mao began his attempt to reassert control over educational policy.) New teaching plans and materials began to issue from the central Ministry of Education once again. The newly adopted materials of the early 1960's are now criticized as too theoretical and ponderous, increasing the burden of students and teachers.

Any extensive evaluation of the above approach to introducing congruity between China's education and manpower needs is beyond the scope of this study. But a few facts are suggestive. First, there is no question about the fact that the ministry policy was turning out large numbers of upper middle school graduates in cities every year

---

[98] In July, 1953, the Ministry of Education put out a teaching program for middle schools in China based completely on that of the USSR. During the next year huge quantities of teaching materials, instruction plans for over three hundred specialized fields, and between three thousand and four thousand course outlines (all for institutions of higher learning) were translated from the Russian.

who had college hopes that were shattered because they could not be admitted. They were also generally untrained to enter production and were often sent (again untrained) to agricultural areas. Their frustration constituted a serious political problem. It is perfectly true that keeping the upper middle school youths in school was a means of alleviating the unemployment problem. But equally significant is the fact that the content of their education was largely unrelated to the rural or urban production tasks in which they would have to be employed in the long run. Second, in the USSR, where the Khrushchev reforms were aborted, a serious shortage of blue collar workers and technicians is already being felt, and the projection is for the shortage to increase. The cause lies in an insufficiency of specialized secondary schools. Officials are seriously questioning whether too many engineers are being turned out.[99]

Third, the most impressive evidence in any evaluation is the tested experience of other countries that share significant characteristics with China that have implemented similar policies. Tanzania (formerly Tanganyika) is a case in point. Tanzanian educational policy has differed in one way from the Maoist. The government has purposively impeded the growth of primary education beyond that needed to keep the present level at pace with population rise. Until the economy generates more funds, it prefers to invest in secondary and high level manpower training and agricultural extension. Because the country is so short on highly trained skills, secondary school graduates face no unemployment problem. Thus village "self-help" primary schools have been positively discouraged.[100] The egalitarian ideal in China would not permit this policy of aborting, even temporarily, the universalization of low level education.

But the Tanzanians have been inspired, in part by Maoist models in the late 1950's, to implement two policies that institutionalize the rural perspective.[101] The correctness of the policies has been affirmed by UNESCO and English specialists as well as by the Tanzanians themselves. First, it has been recognized that attitudinal questions

[99] See Ann S. Goodman and Murray Feshbach, *Estimates and Projections of Educational Attainment in the U.S.S.R. 1950–1985* (Washington, D.C.: U.S. Bureau of the Census, 1967). Also see *New York Times*, July 29, 1969.

[100] Guy Hunter, *Manpower, Employment, and Education in the Rural Economy of Tanzania* (UNESCO: International Institute for Educational Planning, 1966), p. 37, and George Skorov, *Integration of Education and Economic Planning in Tanzania* (Paris: UNESCO International Institute for Educational Planning, 1966), p. 44.

[101] Hunter, *Manpower, Employment, and Education*, pp. 30–33, and Skorov, *Integration of Education*, pp. 60–61.

regarding rural life are fundamental to any educational changes. This means that a substantial amount of political education of students, teachers, and parents must occur to facilitate their acceptance of (1) changes in the schools, and (2) the desirability of the students' returning to a modernizing rural life. This makes it necessary, among other things, to change the primary school syllabus itself so that it concretely demonstrates to student and teacher what can be done in a transformed countryside. In other words, it is not enough just to maintain schools. This must be accomplished by a battery of procedures (societal, economic, and educational) to help make the agricultural life appear more attractive; otherwise the investment in rural schools will be lost as graduates flock to pools of unemployed in the cities, increasing the imbalance of town and country. And one of these procedures is to correct the improper portrayal of rural life in the previous educational materials prepared by city intellectuals. Second, the textbooks and curriculum in the traditional Tanzanian schools prepared students for a higher rung on the educational ladder and ultimately supplied them with skills for the British style civil service. It was essential to reverse this trend and to teach in rural schools a subject matter that could be understood and utilized in a rural economy. The identification of these issues as vital in Tanzania and the indications of success of policies put forth to cope with them is serious evidence that certain Maoist educational guidelines are on the right track.

## THE CULTURAL REVOLUTION

The following remarks indicate what the character of the educational system is likely to be if the Maoist guidelines of the Cultural Revolution prevail. Obviously, the situation in education is no less fluid than in other sectors of Chinese society today. The following brief discussion is intended simply to show the continuity in the Maoist use of the educational system as a vehicle for realizing the egalitarian ideal, and the implications of this goal for questions about locus of control and manpower needs.

### DECENTRALIZATION OR CENTRALIZATION?

Teachers and administrators are viewed as having been previously responsible to superiors in a bureaucratic hierarchy (to which they themselves belonged) rather than to the parents and students themselves; this was conducive to perpetuation of the gap between "mental aristocrats" and others:

> For the sake of upholding and meeting the old concept of education, the revisionist educational system has set up a large set of bureaucratic organizations divorced from the masses. They are not only divorced from politics and the masses, but also have widened the gap between the teachers and students.[102]

The continuing assumption is that, "when the peasants really exercise control over education" and talk about "our school" and not "your school," then they will choose the right curriculum and will terminate the divorce of teachers from themselves and their children.[103]

In the past, the ministry formulated policy and relied on the county Bureau of Culture and Education to implement it in individual rural schools.[104] The new authority structure for rural areas will involve commune management of most middle schools and brigade management of primary schools and of seven-year combination primary-lower middle schools. The control unit will be the Three-in-One committee of various mixtures of activist peasants, commune and brigade cadres, and teachers and students (according to Mao's March 7, 1967, directive). The close liaison between production units and schools, which was intended among other things to terminate the aloofness of mental from manual workers, is achieved by having heads or vice-heads of school committees and brigade committees sit on each other's boards.[105] Of course, the central government supposedly always holds the final lever in all schools, in that "revolutionary cadres" retain the "leading role" in the committees.

ELITES

Teachers in most schools are automatically suspect as real or potential mental aristocrats. In addition to the requirement that they participate in productive labor, a new method of payment is intended to

---

102 "Be Explorers in the Revolution in Education Under the Guidance of Mao Tse-tung's Thought," *JMJP*, October 28, 1967, in *CB*, No. 846 (February 28, 1968).

103 "*Jen-min Jih-pao* and *Hung ch'i* Investigation Report." Also "Suggestion for Revolutionizing Rural Education Widely Supported by Revolutionary Masses," *SCMP*, No. 4302 (November 20, 1968). Also, "Schools in Rural Areas Must Be Managed by Poor and Lower-Middle Peasants," *KMJP*, September 2, 1968, in *SCMP*, No. 4269 (October 1, 1968).

104 *SCMP*, No. 4261 (September 19, 1968); "Nation's Revolutionary People Discuss Revolution in Rural Education," *Peking Review*, No. 51 (December 20, 1968), pp. 7–8.

105 "*Jen-min Jih-pao* and *Hung ch'i* Investigation Report"; also *SCMP*, No. 4269 (October 1, 1968).

help undercut their elite status. Wherever possible, teachers will be paid by the production brigade according to the work-point system rather than being paid a salary by the state. A certain number of increments of teaching will be worth a certain number of work-points. This brings them under the same payment schedule as ordinary farm workers, and the method also has the economic attraction of saving the state the financial burden of paying the teachers.[106]

A favorite Maoist technique for breaking a barrier between two types of people is to attempt to turn each into the other. Students, workers, and peasants are encouraged periodically to change places with the teacher and to take charge of the class, to conduct discussions, to give lectures, and so forth. A Yenan principle is cited to argue for the Maoist technique, "officers teach soldiers, soldiers teach officers, and soldiers teach each other." [107]

The system of designating some institutions as "key schools" that exist to prepare students for entry into the better institutions of higher learning is to be abolished. The second antiegalitarian division that is to be modified, though not abolished, is between ordinary full-time schools and work-study schools. Most likely, the work-study system never again will be heralded as "providing the direction for the long-range development of socialist and communist education." Nevertheless, one continues to find favorable reference to particular schools run on a work-study basis today, especially in rural areas.[108] Among other things, the economic advantage of saving the state the expense of running the schools is singled out. But many of the alliances between schools and factories were extremely artificial, and they have withered.[109] Where the system has worked, it is apparently being perpetuated.[110] The important thing to Mao is the "work," not the "half." The problem of a division between the two tracks is lessened by requiring all students to do a substantial amount of labor, though not half-labor. Something on the order of ninety to one hundred days

[106] "Vigorous Educational Revolution Develops in China's Countryside," *SCMP*, No. 4290 (November 1, 1968). Also *SCMP*, No. 4302 (November 20, 1968). Also, "The Road to Rural Education as Seen Through the Development of People-Run Education," *KMJP*, November 19, 1968, in *SCMP*, No. 4312 (December 5, 1968).

[107] "Workers Mao Tse-tung Thought Propaganda Team Leads Teachers and Students in Revolutionary Struggle," *SCMP*, No. 4296 (November 12, 1968).

[108] "Working Class Must Supervise Education," *Wen-hui-pao*, Shanghai, August 17, 1968, in *SCMP*, No. 4254 (September 10, 1968); "A New Type Agricultural Labor School Run by Poor and Lower-Middle Peasants," *SCMP*, No. 4288 (October 29, 1968); *SCMP*, No. 4312 (December 5, 1968); *Peking Review*, No. 44 (November 1, 1968), p. 8.

[109] *SCMP*, No. 4252 (September 10, 1968).

[110] *SCMP*, No. 4290 (November 1, 1968).

of labor a year for middle school students (and seventy to eighty for teachers) seems to be in the wind for students in rural areas.[111] It may be less for primary school students, but they are not exempt, even in the cities.

The major Maoist thrust in pursuit of the egalitarian ideal is directed at the obstacles that prevented large numbers of children from entering schools of various kinds or from climbing up the educational ladder from one level to another, including university. Contrary to the view which is frequently encountered among foreigners that China has virtually achieved its goal of universalization of lower education, numerous Cultural Revolution materials state that in rural areas significant proportions of children do not attend primary school.[112] The major complaint, however, seems to be about the small proportion able to attend lower middle school.[113]

Four obstacles to student entry and mobility up the school ladder are to be removed. The first is the method of entrance examinations, end-of-term examinations, and graduation examinations.[114] Red Guard students at a former "little treasure pagoda" school (Peking No. 4 Middle School) reflected the Maoist position when they said, "What we are out to smash is not just an examination system but the cultural shackles imposed on the people for thousands of years, the breeding ground in which intellectual aristocrats and high-salaried strata are matured, the stepping stone to modern revisionism." [115] "The method of combining recommendation and selection" (*t'ui-chien ho hsüan-pa hsiang chieh-ho*) will take the place of entrance examinations for upper middle school and university. Moral (that is, political), intellectual, and physical qualifications are to be considered (especially the first two). Thus, intellectual qualifications are not ignored, as some critics maintain; they merely take their place as one of three, being treated as equally important with political factors.[116] In rural areas

111 "Revolution in Education in Three People's Communes in Shantung," *SCMP*, No. 4257 (September 13, 1968); "Schools in Rural Areas"; "Running the School For Training Successors to the Revolutionary Cause of the Proletariat," *Peking Review*, No. 47 (November 22, 1968), p. 28.

112 For example, see *SCMP*, No. 4312 (December 5, 1968).

113 For example, see *SCMP*, No. 4269 (October 1, 1968).

114 "Schools Managed By the Poor and Lower-Middle Peasants," *Peking Review*, No. 45 (November 8, 1968), p. 16; "Peasant-College Student-Peasant," *Peking Review*, No. 44 (November 1, 1968), p. 9; "Workers' Mao Tse-tung's Thought Propaganda Teams Lead Proletarian Revolution in Education," *Peking Review*, No. 50 (December 13, 1968), p. 21.

115 "*Jen-min Jih-pao* on Transforming the Educational System," *CB*, No. 846 (February 28, 1968).

116 *Ibid.*

the production brigade is to do the selecting and the commune is to do the recommending.[117] The fact that leaders of production brigades are being encouraged to sit on the committees that run schools is expected to contribute to informed judgment concerning which students to select.

The idea of advancement by recommendation rather than by examination has roots in utopian Confucianism and in scholarly debate in T'ang and Sung times. David Nivison has examined the attempts by Neo-Confucianists to resurrect in part the idealized Chou practice in which the best men are supposedly spotted and directly recommended to the court.[118] These Sung scholars opposed the use of written examinations on two grounds, using arguments that have a definite echo today. First, the examinations test only memorization and do not adequately test the student's ability to understand or to apply his knowledge to the serious problems facing the state. Second, the examinations cause students to compete for personal gain and fame, rather than to be concerned for their character. In the words of Chu Hsi, when officials were recruited by direct recommendation rather than by examination, "men's minds were composed and they had no distracting desires. Night and day they were diligent, fearing only lest they be wanting in virtue, and not caring whether rank and salary came their way." [119]

Some adjustments are also to be made in end-of-term and pre-graduation examinations. In addition to the considerations just mentioned, these are faulted for causing large numbers of peasant children to have to repeat grades or to drop out of school. Among the injustices cited are the facts that students of worker or peasant background often have not had exposure to the kinds of words that are part of the working vocabulary of bourgeois intellectuals, and that instead of having parents who can tutor them, they have parents who require their labor.[120] There does not seem to be any plan to eliminate examinations altogether but rather, where it is feasible, to experiment with new forms.

Flexibility in setting class locations and meeting times is permitted

117 *SCMP*, No. 4288 (October 29, 1968).

118 David S. Nivison, "The Criteria of Excellence," in Johanna M. Menzel (ed.), *The Chinese Civil Service* (Boston: D. C. Heath, 1963), pp. 92–106.

119 *Ibid.*, p. 99.

120 "The Revolution in Education in Colleges of Science and Engineering as Reflected in the Struggle Between the Two Lines at the Shanghai Institute of Mechanical Engineering," *Peking Review*, No. 37 (September 13, 1968), p. 15; "It Is Essential to Rely on the Poor and Lower-Middle Peasants in the Educational Revolution in the Countryside," *Peking Review*, No. 39 (September 27, 1968), p. 20.

by decentralization and is an aid in attempts at universalization. Students' failure to attend middle school is often attributed to the school's distance from their homes. Production brigades are being encouraged to deal with the problem by extending existing primary schools through the lower middle school years wherever possible.[121]

Other hurdles facing worker or peasant offspring have been school age limits (for example, age thirty for regular universities) and difficulties in the way of lateral movement from job or spare-time school into a regular school. In the future, greater emphasis will be placed on recruiting from these ranks of workers and peasants, students who have several years of practical experience in production. This is especially true for entry into technically specialized institutions of higher learning.[122]

Measures being taken to realign educational practice with the Maoist perception of China's manpower needs include: (1) gearing the content of middle school and university education to China's immediate production and human service needs, and (2) shortening the number of years students must spend at each level and reducing the number of courses they must take.

Many of the humanities and social science type courses will be dropped, and "irrelevant theoretical content" will be eliminated wherever possible. In contrast to the ministry's policy, there will be a definite local character to the curriculum in each school. This would mean, for example, that courses mainly concerning agriculture would predominate in middle schools in rural areas, and that the content of every other course would be made relevant wherever possible to the production problems (for example, in the mathematics course, focus would be on how to use an abacus, how to measure land, how to calculate the volume of grain stocks, and so on). An example of a human service training that was not regarded as pertinent to China's present needs was medical education. Some of the schools had an eight-year course, and many of the texts were Russian. It was felt that graduates were unprepared to deal with rural medical problems in the particular circumstances in which they are found. ("How do you treat severe burns when you do not have a germ-free room and ultraviolet rays?" "How can you be expected to diagnose tracoma, which is frequently encountered, when the 'foreign' medical texts never mention it?") [123]

121 *SCMP,* No. 4269 (October 1, 1968).
122 *SCMP,* No. 4254 (September 10, 1968).
123 "Medical Education Must Follow the Road of Thorough Revolution," *JMJP,* August 24, 1968, in *SCMP,* No. 4254 (September 10, 1968).

The curriculum is to be changed so that graduates are equipped to deal with such problems better than in the past.

Shortening the length of the educational period is seen as a way of bringing students who are equipped with basic skills into the manpower pool much earlier.[124] Primary schools will be reduced from six to five years, and middle schools from six to four years.[125] Thus, a combined primary–junior middle school of seven years and a senior middle school of two years. This is intended to bring the youth into the manpower pool at the age of fifteen or sixteen rather than at seventeen or eighteen. The number of courses within each year is also reduced. The same situation holds for universities. Shanghai's T'ung-chi University reports cutting the number of required courses in half (from thirty) and shortening the duration from five to three years.[126]

By keeping the schools closed for so long during the Cultural Revolution in order to restructure the student body and the educational system, Chairman Mao has also had to pay a price that can only be measured in manpower terms. A recent estimate from the Soviet Academy of Science indicates that about 150,000 engineers, 100,000 teachers, and 50,000 physicians who ordinarily would have entered the manpower pool during this period (to the middle of 1969), have gone without training.

## EVALUATION

Revolutionary China's educational system presents a picture of tragedy and glory. Periodic violent shifts from one model to another since 1949 could not but take their toll in psychic scars on teachers and students, and diminish the system's effectiveness in cultivating the skills needed by a modernizing country. From the Anglo-American to the Soviet model, from the Soviet to the Maoist, from the Maoist to a liberalized Soviet pattern, and from that back to the Maoist style, there were new teaching materials to be adopted, new course syllabi, new masterplans for the curriculum as a whole, new teaching methods to be tried, and new relations to exist between teachers and students or between teachers, students, and administration. The eminent social scientist, Fei Hsiao-t'ung, described the first transition as he experienced it:

---

124 *JMJP*, July 12, 1966.
125 *SCMP*, No. 4269 (October 1, 1968).
126 "Nationwide Effort to Run Great Schools of Mao Tse-tung's Thought," *Peking Review*, No. 20 (May 17, 1968), p. 12.

In the early stage of educational reform, teachers went through a period of great tension. Because it was necessary to learn from the Soviet Union, they had to prepare new teaching materials. Furthermore, as a result of the thought reform movement, they had to discard what they had studied, but they had not been able to establish a new system to take the place of the old. The task of rushing to produce Russian or translated syllabi, kept them extremely busy. . . . Books from England and America merely took up room on the bookcases; they were sold as scrap paper. There was no time to study Russian, and so the teachers had to be satisfied with the small translated editions they could buy. When they wrote articles or lectured in class, all that they needed to do was to cite passages from the works of the approved authorities, and to pick out a few British or American scholars to criticize and revile. This was not difficult to do, and it was exactly what many scholars did.[127]

The most frequently mentioned effect of this recurrent instability has been "passivity."[128] Many administrators and teachers have often been loath to do more than meet the minimal professional requirements, mindful that today's right approach is tomorrow's wrong one. Without question the periodic permissiveness, which allowed students to struggle against teachers, has contributed to this. Many reports in the early 1960's speak of teachers in previous years neglecting (through fear) to enforce academic standards by insisting that assigned work be completed or by grading strictly.[129] There is every evidence that the same passivity will be a by-product of the Cultural Revolution in education.[130]

It would be far too simple to explain the absence of any steady march toward educational utopia in terms of good guys being thwarted by bad guys. There has been both right and wrong on the side of Mao's opponents and on his own side. When a person begins to evaluate the attempts of China's leaders to institutionalize the revolution in the educational sector, he is faced with a very mixed bag.

IN PRAISE OF MAO

The trouble with Lu Ting-i and officials in the Ministry of Education is that they seem to have been devoid of much willingness to experiment—to test a policy, to examine its merit critically, and then to retain or to reject it. They adopted the Soviet model for most schools

---

127 Quoted in Theodore Chen, *Thought Reform of the Chinese Intellectuals* (Hong Kong: Hong Kong University Press, 1960), p. 96.

128 "Another Discourse on What to Do in Scientific and Technical Circles," *Wen-hui-pao,* Shanghai, August 4, 1968, in *SCMP,* No. 4250.

129 *KMJP,* June 24, 1961.

130 A number of provincial radio broadcasts in 1967 suggest this.

and then mindlessly continued to keep to the blueprint without relating it to China's actual needs. The *raison d'être* for the curriculum was that the Russians do it this way, not that China's special manpower needs are satisfied best this way. A ludicrous example is the introduction of ballroom dancing into the physical training course at Shanghai Institute of Mechanical Engineering, because that is the way things work in the USSR. Other examples are more serious. The unreasonably heavy academic burden, the archaic teaching methods (both recognized as faults very early), and the college preparatory nature of the education received by so many middle school students are also characteristic of the Soviet model. At a 1960 conference, a distinguished Soviet scientist had the following comment on the Russian situation:

The worst feature is that such a youth feels himself a schoolboy at college too. He is expected to read textbooks, pass tests, attend compulsory lectures, and least of all, to show independence. He is thus taught so much that he leaves college like a stuffed fish. People may have different ideas about its content, but one thing is certain: it cannot swim.[131]

The Chinese Ministry of Education was simply unwilling to take the radical steps away from the Soviet model to try to deal with these issues, and so the problems remained uncorrected right up to the Cultural Revolution.[132] This is not to deny that they gave oral recognition to the existence of these problems. One can hardly blame Mao for wishing to tamper with the Soviet model when the Russians have been finding many problems with it themselves. Khrushchev once remarked, "Owing to the fact that the secondary school curriculum is divorced from life, these boys and girls have absolutely no knowledge of production, and society does not know how best to utilize these young and vigorous people," and his 1958 reforms sought to readjust the curriculum to correct the problem. Only within the past few years has the Academy of Educational Sciences in Moscow (A.P.N.) seriously come to grips with the problem of reforming teaching method.

Khrushchev also recognized the role of the Russian schools in perpetuating an elite. The 1958 Soviet reforms were supposed to deal with this situation through the work-training emphasis. In view of this fact and of the fact that Marx and Lenin both had argued for the combination of study and productive labor, Mao's 1958 maxim that

---

131 Quoted in Grant, *Soviet Education*, p. 122.
132 *Chiao-yü ko-ming*, p. 7.

"Education must be combined with productive labor" is not original. But Mao's originality is that he, far more than the Russians or the Chinese ministry officials, has attempted to live up to the spirit of the ideal of eliminating the "sharp distinction between mental and manual labor." This he has tried to do through the requirement of substantial labor for all students, as well as through eliminating the entrance examinations and other hurdles that continued to deny mobility to those of disadvantaged backgrounds. The egalitarian ideal may be a distant dream, but there is no reason the Chinese cannot come closer to it than the Russians have.

A final example of bureaucratic reticence and Maoist initiative is in the matter of decentralization, which ran contrary to the Soviet model. It is customary to look on the year of liberalization after the Great Leap failure as a golden age of reason in educational policy. There is something to be said for this, but it was also a time in which a rather exciting experiment in local control over curriculum, staffing, and school administration was scrapped.

IN PRAISE OF THE MINISTRY

On the positive side, Lu Ting-i and the ministry officials had a broader conception of China's manpower needs. One can grant the desirability of drastically increasing enrollments by more equitable adjustments of quality control standards. But this does not mean that one must be as cavalier about the teaching of fundamental theoretical information as Mao has often been. At least one ill effect is suggested in the following complaint by a former vice-president of Harbin Polytechnic University:

Many students say, "fundamental knowledge is important but has no practical application." They one-sidedly interpret the principle of "learning for the sake of application." They want to learn what they can immediately and directly apply and consider it useless to learn anything else. This attitude betrays their narrowmindedness.[133]

Technical innovations required by a dynamic economy depend on men who are firmly grounded in the theory that Mao is often so quick to disdain. High level technical skills can only be produced in institutions that are bound to seem to outsiders to have special privileges. The professional educators have not been so naïve about the possibility of the egalitarian ideal remaining untarnished. They saw the danger

[133] Quoted in Cheng, *Scientific and Engineering Manpower*, p. 96.

of diluting all education with excessive political education and labor. Their conception is broader also in not being so restricted to people trained in "science and technology." (One of Mao's Cultural Revolution directives begins: "It is still necessary to have universities; here I refer mainly to colleges of science and engineering.") A willingness to curtail drastically the training in the social sciences and the humanities tells us something about the quality of the society that was envisioned by Mao—a quality of questionable congeniality to many people. Furthermore, these professionals have not been as blindly utopian as Mao has been about sustaining control over educational standards. Workable substitutes for grades, examinations, and the teacher's freedom from intimidation have yet to be demonstrated. Nor have they been as utopian about the ease with which schools can establish liaisons with factories and farms (or vice versa); the facts in both the Soviet Union and in China have proved them right.

A dangerous character of the Maoist approach has been the suddenness of change to policies of untested worth. In reaction to a system that placed a heavy academic burden on the student, the Maoist approach is to cut the number of courses in half overnight. Where rote learning was an acknowledged evil, the Maoist solution is suddenly to try to teach everything by the "case method." He has had his model, just as the ministry had theirs. His is Yenan, and too often there has been the facile assumption that what worked for that rural community in a military situation, can work for the country as a whole in peacetime. Indeed, there have been overt statements during the Cultural Revolution that the Maoist educational revolution seems more applicable to rural than to urban areas.[134]

A certain ethnocentrism shines a bit too clearly through the harping on the "experience of the old liberated areas." It manifests itself in attacks on Liu Shao-ch'i for saying that China could learn from some of the achievements in Western Europe, England, America, France, and Japan.[135] The praises for experimentalism should certainly go to Mao. It is he who pushed in 1958 for experiments with "ten year schools," "nine year schools," "the five year middle school," "the two year lower and two year upper middle school." It is he who has at least faced the problems in curricula and teaching method. The very idea of "decentralization" suggests openness to variation. Yet one wonders

---

[134] "A New School That Integrates Theory with Practice," *Hung-ch'i* (Red Flag), No. 4 (October 14, 1968), in *SCMM*, No. 634 (November 12, 1968).

[135] *JMJP*, July 19, 1967.

whether the Maoist condemnation of those who "slavishly imitate the foreign [that is, Russian] way" is likely to generalize itself into a reflexive unwillingness to give any non-Chinese approach a fair hearing.

## CONCLUSION

In the final analysis the Maoist approach reflects a concern to bring about a convergence between local needs and the content of curriculum and the structure of schools. This means Chinese ways rather than Russian ways. In particular, it demands a rural rather than an urban perspective in texts and programs for schools in the countryside. In addition, the Maoist approach reveals a combination of dedication to specific values and concern with political power. To forget values and to think only of power is to understand only half of the situation. The value concern is reflected in the essence of the entire conflict between Maoist and ministry policies: the Maoist insistence that *all* educational materials and practices be judged in ethical terms, that is, by whether or not they actively cultivate "revolutionary successors" who are dedicated to the realization of an egalitarian society in which men are "in the service of the people" rather than in the service of themselves. But the loyalty of the peasant masses, which was secured by increasing the educational mobility of their children, is a parallel consideration. The political strength that thus was afforded eventually will permit the leader to pursue economic modernization in his own way, that is, with determination but without the degree of abuse to socialist values that has characterized it in other countries. This, at any rate, is the pious assumption.

PART IV

*China and the World:*
*The Subordination of Foreign Affairs to Domestic Politics*

DONALD W. KLEIN

# The Management of Foreign Affairs in Communist China

## INTRODUCTION

This paper deals with the management of foreign affairs in Communist China. It makes no attempt to cover foreign policy per se, a subject already dealt with by A. Doak Barnett, Donald Zagoria, Harold Hinton, and others, and it assumes a broad familiarity with the Bandung period, the Sino-Soviet dispute, and the other landmarks of Chinese foreign policy. The central focus is on the institutionalization of the foreign affairs apparatus, principally in the Foreign Ministry, but also in the many other organizations which have responsibilities in international relations. In this sense the paper can be viewed as a study of a "system" (*hsi-t'ung*), which as Barnett has noted can also be translated as "network" or "organizational sector."

## THE EARLY YEARS AND THE KIANGSI PERIOD

The early years of the Chinese Communist movement were focused on domestic affairs. The major concern of the Chinese Communist Party (CCP), which as late as 1925 had fewer than one thousand members, was with recruitment and organizational work in urban areas. It is true that the early Party leaders had a keen awareness of foreign affairs, which often was the result of study abroad or training in China's major urban centers where the foreign impact was greatest. But their view of foreign affairs tended to be essentially a version of the century-long quest for the political instruments that would make China strong and prosperous. They believed that they had found this in the Leninist model of a disciplined political party which would provide the strength to gain control of the Chinese political system and to eradicate imperialism.

The CCP became affiliated with the Comintern in 1922, but there is little suggestion that these ties were regarded in institutional terms by the early CCP leaders, and the documents from the period give no hint that a foreign affairs apparatus was beginning to evolve within the Party structure. The near total destruction of the urban base of the Party in 1927 by Chiang Kai-shek naturally mitigated against the development of such an apparatus. However, in a curious footnote to history, we find that the first Chinese Communist "foreign ministry" traces back to the Canton Commune of December, 1927. Reflecting the usage in the Soviet Union, Communist China's first "foreign minister" was known as the Commissar of Foreign Affairs.[1] Nothing further need be said about this situation or about Commissar Huang P'ing, because the commune was crushed within two and a half days, and Huang and his colleagues fled.[2]

Another effort to establish a foreign affairs apparatus took place during the Kiangsi period. The First All-China Congress of Soviets, held in late 1931, established the Council of People's Commissars. One of the ten subordinate organs under the council was the People's Commissariat for Foreign Affairs, headed by People's Commissar Wang Chia-hsiang. Eighteen years later Wang became Peking's first ambassador to the Soviet Union, but during the embattled years of the Kiangsi period he held other and more important posts in the Red Army, and there is little to indicate that Wang's commissariat was more than a paper organization. The constitution[3] adopted then makes mention of foreign affairs, but the tone is more polemical than institutional (for example, Article 8 pledged to free China from the "yoke of imperialism"). If there was any sense of external affairs, it was mainly in connection with Japan, which from the time it invaded Manchuria in 1931 was the foreign nation that concerned all thinking Chinese. The Kiangsi Communists went as far as declaring war on

[1] Trotsky was the Soviet Union's first foreign commissar for a brief time, after which G. V. Chicherin held the post until 1930.

[2] Huang was later a delegate to the Comintern and took part in Li Li-san's "trial" in late 1930. He was arrested in China in 1932 and, according to Harold Isaacs, he defected to the KMT.

[3] The constitution is printed in Conrad Brandt, Benjamin Schwartz, and John K. Fairbank, *A Documentary History of Chinese Communism* (Cambridge, Mass.: 1952), pp. 220–24.

Japan in 1932, and while we need not doubt their sincerity, we surely can question their expectations about the effectiveness of such declarations. In short, from the establishment of the Chinese Soviet Republic in 1931 through the end of the Long March in late 1935, a government apparatus for foreign affairs was largely irrelevant.

## A Foreign Affairs Apparatus Begins to Emerge— the Yenan Period

By the end of the Long March, a new situation had emerged. Responding to the rising menace of Hitler and the Japanese militarists, the Seventh Comintern Congress of mid-1935 issued a call for an international united front against fascism. But it is one thing to pass formal declarations and another to set them into motion by means of new organizations or institutions, or by the allocation of significant amounts of financial and personnel resources. As usual in a revolutionary situation, the Chinese Communists found themselves reacting largely to their immediate need to survive. Thus, the early Yenan period was devoted to efforts to consolidate the new base, to refurbish supplies, and to get new recruits for the Red Army and the CCP (both of which had received devastating blows during the Long March). Edgar Snow, on the basis of his 1936 visit to north Shensi, speaks of a "foreign office," but he does so in quotation marks.[4] Although he is not specific, one surmises that the apparatus was more of an intelligence operation than a foreign ministry.

Another major turning point took place in the period between the Sian incident (December, 1936) and the outbreak of the Sino-Japanese War (July, 1937). Briefly put, the continuous Japanese incursions upon Chinese sovereignty provided the momentum which culminated in a reasonably viable Kuomintang (KMT)-CCP alliance during the early war years. Even though we are three decades removed from this period, it was then that the broad outline of the present-day foreign affairs apparatus began to emerge. Then, as now, it centered around the person of the ubiquitous Chou En-lai, who led a small liaison group to Hankow and, after that city fell in 1938, to the new temporary capital at Chungking. It is doubtful, of course, if Chou and his colleagues saw themselves as foreign emissaries. They had not been sent there, after all, to deal with foreigners; the prime task was to coordinate the war effort against Japan. Moreover, they did not know

4 Edgar Snow, *Red Star over China* (New York: 1938), p. 50.

how long they would be in Hankow (and then Chungking), nor did they know how effectively they could operate in the heart of Nationalist territory. Why, since Chungking was on Chinese territory, should the Chou mission be regarded as a nascent foreign ministry group? The answer is that for the first time since 1927 the CCP was able to operate legally in a locality which provided some access to the outside world. Equally important, the early period of wartime cooperation with the KMT soon gave way to an adversary relationship, and this in turn forced the members of the mission to deal with the KMT more in the fashion of a foreign state than of a coalition government.

Chou's "mission," a term used here in a broad sense, initially included some of the major luminaries of the CCP: Ch'en Shao-yü (Wang Ming), Ch'in Pang-hsien (Po Ku), Lin Po-ch'ü, Wu Yü-chang, Tung Pi-wu, and Teng Ying-ch'ao (Chou's wife). The last two remained with Chou almost continuously throughout the war, but the others soon returned to Yenan. More important for our discussion here is the group of second and third echelon leaders who worked for Chou. This group, which was composed of political unknowns, included Wang Ping-nan, Ch'en Chia-k'ang, and Chang Han-fu, all of whom became key figures in Peking's Foreign Ministry fifteen years later. Apart from the mission's normal contacts with the Nationalist government, it also had informal contacts with the large Soviet embassy in Chungking, as well as with American and British diplomats. Chou's group also published two of the Communists' most important wartime organs: *Hsin-hua Jih-pao* (New China Daily) and *Ch'ün-chung* (The Masses).

The Chungking group served as the nerve center for two satellite missions, one in Kweilin and the other in Hong Kong. Li K'o-nung headed the Kweilin operation which, among other things, housed a branch office of the *Hsin-hua Jih-pao* and published an international news service which purportedly reached a large overseas Chinese audience. Li is best known as an intelligence operative, but he is familiar to students of Chinese Communist affairs as a latter-day vice-minister of foreign affairs (1949–54) under Chou. The Hong Kong apparatus was under the direction of Liao Ch'eng-chih, who became one of Peking's most important "unofficial" diplomats in the post-1949 period. A top aide to Liao in Hong Kong was Ch'iao Kuan-hua (Ch'iao Mu), who was still another diplomat of note in later years. Aside from its obvious function as a window on the outside world for the Communists,

Hong Kong was also a haven for many members of the Chinese intelligentsia and, thus, a major publishing center. Many of these intellectuals were of leftist persuasions, and as the war progressed a number of them became closely identified with the Communist cause. Furthermore, many of them had past ties with the West which they were able to use to get war relief funds and supplies, particularly from the United States. (It should be noted, however, that most of these funds and supplies found their way into Nationalist rather than Communist hands.)

Both the Kweilin and Hong Kong operations were abruptly halted in 1941. Kweilin was closed down by the Nationalists in the wake of the New Fourth Army Incident of January, 1941, and the Hong Kong operation was closed when the Japanese captured the city soon after Pearl Harbor. From the New Fourth Army Incident until late in the war, Chou's mission in Chungking operated under the handicap of increasing harassments and surveillance, but in terms of personnel it was augmented by a number of highly talented persons from the Kweilin and Hong Kong missions. The best known among those who went to Chungking after 1941 was Ch'iao Kuan-hua. The able Kung P'eng, who later married Ch'iao, was also then in Chungking, where she had already established a wide range of contacts with foreigners in her capacity as an assistant to Chou En-lai.

By late in the war Chou's team in Chungking had become a well-recognized foreign policy "interest group"—if not in the political science sense of the term, then certainly in the eyes of the many American diplomatic and military personnel. Developments in 1944 quickly brought to light still another echelon of persons who would later play a major role in foreign affairs. The situation came about as a result of continual efforts by American diplomats to bring the Communists and the Nationalists together in hopes that renewed cooperation would make China a more effective ally against Japan. Such endeavors were also abetted by the persistent demands of foreign correspondents (especially Americans) to visit the then mysterious Communist capital at Yenan. Permission for the United States Army to set up an observers' mission in Yenan and for foreign newsmen to visit there was finally worked out in mid-1944. The Communists, who obviously were eager to put their best foot forward, were very cooperative. Extensive briefings were arranged and liaison officials were assigned to help the visitors in other ways (for example, escorting them to Communist-held guerrilla bases in North China). Among those who now gained their first intensive experience in dealing with foreigners were Huang Hua and K'o Pai-nien.[5]

## THE MARSHALL MISSION

American involvement in Chinese affairs in the immediate postwar days led, ironically, to the unveiling of still another foreign affairs group, which had its origins in General George C. Marshall's famous mission to China. The American general-diplomat quickly arranged for a truce between Communist and Nationalist forces (January, 1946). Operating first out of Chungking and then from the spring of 1946 in Nanking and Shanghai, Chou was once again in charge of the Communist side in these protracted negotiations. To implement the truce arrangements, the Peiping Executive Headquarters was set up, and it in turn supervised approximately forty truce teams which were located at various places in North China and Manchuria. Both the headquarters and the truce teams consisted of American, Nationalist, and Communist representatives. No reliable figures are available, but the Communists assigned something on the order of two hundred men to these quasi-diplomatic posts. Some familiar faces re-emerged at the Peiping headquarters: Li K'o-nung headed the staff office, K'o Pai-nien directed the Communists' publications and translations section, and Huang Hua was in charge of the information section.

Many of the Communist representatives returned to the battlefields when the truce collapsed in the latter half of 1946 and early 1947, but a remarkable number were assigned to the Foreign Ministry in the post-1949 period. Still others took up assignments which involved them in one aspect or another of foreign affairs. The details regarding the men and their posts are given in Appendixes A through E, but we can observe here that the Marshall Mission "group" probably contributed more men to the foreign affairs apparatus than any other clustering of personnel with origins in the pre-1949 period.

[5] Huang was Peking's ambassador in Ghana from 1960 to 1966 and is now ambassador in Cairo. He was Edgar Snow's interpreter in Shensi when Snow was gathering material for his classic *Red Star over China*. In 1949, when Huang was director of the Alien Affairs Office in Nanking, he held informal talks with J. Leighton Stuart, then American ambassador to Nationalist China, regarding the possibility of United States diplomatic recognition of the Communists. Ironically, Huang had been a student at Yenching University in 1935 when Stuart was president of the school. In 1953, Huang was the chief Chinese negotiator at Panmunjom in Korea, where he engaged in sharp verbal duels with his American counterpart, Arthur H. Dean.

K'o Pai-nien was ambassador to Rumania from 1955 to 1959 and to Denmark from 1963 to 1966.

Our image of the period from 1946 to 1949 is that of another return by the Communists to the rural hinterlands. In general, this is true. However, a number of important Communists were traveling back and forth to Europe to take part in meetings of the various Soviet-inspired international front organizations as the first stage of the Cold War began to emerge. If we can date the beginnings of the Foreign Ministry apparatus back to the early Sino-Japanese War years, then we can find in the early Cold War period the institutional origins of the group that has played a major role in international liaison on the semi-official level. We will return to this subject later, but for the moment noteworthy examples of the personnel involved include Ts'ai Ch'ang (in the Women's International Democratic Federation) and Liu Ning-i (in the World Federation of Trade Unions). In these same years from 1946 to 1949 the Hong Kong operation was resuscitated as an informal but highly active base of international liaison. The importance attached to Hong Kong by the Communists can be judged in part from the fact that Chang Han-fu, Ch'iao Kuan-hua, and Kung P'eng were assigned there.

## ESTABLISHMENT OF THE FOREIGN MINISTRY

The more formal processes of institutionalization, beginning with the Ministry of Foreign Affairs (MFA) and Peking's establishment of inter-state relations, took place in the weeks following the formation of the People's Republic of China (CPR), when the initial personnel appointments were made in the MFA. With few exceptions, the men were drawn from Chou's coterie, and the organization of the ministry paralleled most foreign offices throughout the world. The structure of the ministry, with a comparison for 1969, is outlined in Table 26.

In the years after 1949 the Foreign Ministry departments grew in size as their responsibilities increased. Working under Foreign Minister Chou and Vice-Ministers Li and Chang, most of the best talent was kept in Peking to put the Foreign Ministry into operation. A diplomatic mission, headed by Ambassador Wang Chia-hsiang (concurrently the third vice-minister), was immediately sent to Moscow, but it was not until the latter half of 1950 that embassies were established in the other Communist nations. As the diplomatic service evolved over the next decade, it became apparent that the essential core of the talent lay in the group of directors and deputy directors of the various

## TABLE 26
### MINISTRY OF FOREIGN AFFAIRS

| 1949 | 1969 * |
|---|---|
| *Functional Departments* | |
| Staff Office | Staff Office |
| Information Department | Information Department |
| International Affairs Department | International Affairs Department |
| Personnel Department | Personnel Department |
| Protocol Department | Protocol Department |
| Foreign Policy Committee | |
| Treaty Committee | Treaty and Law Department |
| | General Services Department |
| | Training (or Education; *chiao-yü*) Department |
| | Consular Affairs Department |
| | Translation Department |
| *Geographic Departments* | |
| American-Australasian Department | American-Australasian Department |
| Asian Department | 1st Asian Department (non-Communist) |
| | 2nd Asian Department (Communist nations, plus Laos and Cambodia) |
| USSR-East European Department | USSR-East European Department |
| West European and African Department | West European Department |
| | West Asian-North African Department |
| | African Department (sub-Sahara) |

* All these departments existed in 1966 on the eve of the Cultural Revolution; some of them were identified in 1969 and presumably all of them still exist. Prior to the Cultural Revolution the departments were mentioned with great regularity, but since then MFA officials have often been referred to in generic terms, for example, "responsible personnel from the foreign ministry. . . ."

Foreign Ministry departments.[6] This group, for example, has provided the largest single source for ambassadorial appointments: thirty-three of the one hundred men who have held ambassadorial posts [7]

[6] I was told by one Asian diplomat with several years' experience in Peking that the department deputy director level was the lowest echelon of real authority. He gained the impression that the directors could make at least some decisions of importance without referring them to higher authority, but he noted further that the deputy director level was the place where the "real work was done." These comments should not be construed to mean that *basic policy-level decisions* are made at these levels—such decisions are made higher up the chain of command.

[7] For the sake of convenience I have used the term "ambassador" to include all heads of mission. In the strictest sense of the term four men were not ambassadors: Ch'ai Ch'eng-wen, the minister in Denmark; Hsieh Li, the chargé d'affaires of the Office of the Chargé d'Affaires in the Netherlands; and Hsiung Hsiang-hui and Huan Hsiang, both of whom have headed the Office of the Chargé d'Affaires in Great Britain.

served as a director or deputy director of a Foreign Ministry department before becoming an ambassador.

Another testing ground for diplomats is found in an institutional
structure that is not normally characteristic of other foreign offices.
Throughout much of 1949 a number of foreign diplomats were
stranded, so to speak, in Nanking, which was the former capital, and
in such places as Shanghai and Tientsin where there were also many
businessmen and other foreign nationals. The government to which
the diplomats were accredited had fled, and the Communists had not
yet established a national government. In response to this situation,
the Communists posted key diplomatic figures such as Chang Han-fu
and Huang Hua in these cities. By the early 1950's this practice had
become institutionalized, and over the ensuing years provincial and
municipal "Foreign Affairs Offices" (sometimes translated as "Alien
Affairs Offices") were established. In general these offices fit into an
easily defined pattern: there is one in every province with a foreign
border.[8] In addition, there are offices in Shantung, Hopeh, Honan,
and Hupeh (possibly to service the rather frequent foreign visitors to
Tsingtao, Tientsin, Chengchow, and Wuhan), as well as Peking and
Shanghai.[9] The offices are officially subordinate to provincial or municipal governments, but it is clear that they have close ties with the
Foreign Ministry and, to a lesser degree, with the Foreign Trade
Ministry.[10] A number of the office directors have moved into the
Foreign Ministry; the most notable example is Yang Kung-su who,
after spending several years with the office in Tibet, became ambassa-
dor to Nepal.

Reliable figures on the size of the MFA in terms of personnel are
difficult to find, but some rough estimates can be made. We know of
approximately twenty professional-level appointments that were made
within the Foreign Ministry by the end of 1949. Presumably another
fifty or so persons were engaged in technical work (interpreters and
so on) or were working in the embassy in Moscow. Later, as new

[8] Heilungkiang, Kirin, Liaoning, Inner Mongolia, Sinkiang, Tibet, Yunnan, Kwangsi,
and Kwangtung (which only recently lost its contiguous border with Vietnam). The
one minor exception in Kansu, which has a very short border with Mongolia in a
sparsely populated area.

[9] Offices existed in Mukden, Harbin, Port Arthur-Dairen, Tientsin, and Canton in the
early 1950's, but by the mid-1950's they seem to have been absorbed by provincial-level
offices.

[10] Donnithorne has noted that by 1955 every province had established a bureau of
foreign trade, and that these are jointly supervised by the Ministry of Foreign Trade
and the local authorities concerned. Audrey Donnithorne, *China's Economic System*
(New York: Frederick A. Praeger, 1967), p. 322.

embassies were established abroad, somewhat more accurate estimates can be made. These figures, which do not include technical specialists, are given in Table 27.

TABLE 27
PERSONNEL IN MFA AND ABROAD *

| Group | 1953 | 1960 | 1963 | 1966 |
|---|---|---|---|---|
| MFA personnel in Peking † | 32 | 54 | 76 | 75 |
| Personnel in missions abroad ‡ | 154 | 351 | 411 | 582 |
| Totals | 186 | 405 | 487 | 657 |

* Lists of personnel are taken from United States government directories for the years indicated. The list for 1966 was published on the eve of the Cultural Revolution.

† These figures consist of the various directors and deputy directors of the departments listed in Table 26, in addition to the minister, vice-ministers, and assistant ministers.

‡ These figures include accredited diplomats, but not "housekeeping" personnel.

This expansion of personnel derives mainly from the large increase in the number of foreign missions, which have averaged about forty-five since the mid-1960's. In fact, the number of professional diplomats assigned abroad has remained quite constant in relation to the number of missions, as Table 28 indicates.

TABLE 28
PERSONNEL IN MISSIONS ABROAD

| | 1953 | 1960 | 1963 | 1966 |
|---|---|---|---|---|
| Number of missions | 17 | 33 | 42 | 48 |
| Average per mission | 9 | 11 | 10 | 12 |

TRAINING

We have thus far emphasized the recruitment of personnel from men who had, in effect, received on-the-job training, but a few words are required about the more formal training programs for younger personnel. The Chinese apparently decided against establishing a single institute to train all of their foreign affairs specialists. Rather, a number of institutes have contributed to the flow of new personnel into the foreign affairs apparatus. Among these are the Shanghai Foreign Languages College, the Russian Language School, the Number 1 and Number 2 Institutes of Foreign Languages in Peking, the Institute of Foreign Affairs, and the Academy of Sciences' Institute of International Relations. In addition, a number of the larger universities have diplomacy and language courses. One participant in the 1954 Geneva Conference on Indochina and the 1961–62 Geneva Conference on Laos was impressed by the large number of youthful Chinese who were not among the "official" delegates to these meetings, and he concluded that they had been brought along to gain firsthand experience in major diplomatic negotiations.

DIPLOMATIC MISSIONS ABROAD

In a discussion of Chinese missions abroad, we will begin with a "when-and-where" listing (Table 29), which is annotated to highlight international events which either have impeded or have hastened the establishment of diplomatic relations between China and other countries.

TABLE 29
NATIONS HAVING DIPLOMATIC RELATIONS WITH PEKING (1969) *

*1949* †

1. USSR
2. Bulgaria
3. Rumania
4. Hungary
5. Korea
6. Czechoslovakia
7. Poland
8. Mongolia
9. Germany
10. Albania

*1950*

11. Vietnam
12. India
13. Sweden
14. Denmark
15. Burma
16. Indonesia
(Korean War begins)
17. Switzerland
(Chinese Army enters Korea)
18. Finland

*1951*

19. Pakistan

*1952*

None

*1953*

None
(Korean War ends)

*1954*

20. U.K.
21. Norway
22. Netherlands

*1955*

23. Yugoslavia
(Bandung Conference)
24. Afghanistan
25. Nepal

*1956*

26. Egypt
27. Syria
28. Yemen

*1957*

29. Ceylon

*1958*

(Total reduced to 28 with merger of Egypt and Syria into UAR)
29. Cambodia
30. Iraq
31. Morocco
32. Sudan

TABLE 29 (*Continued*)
NATIONS HAVING DIPLOMATIC RELATIONS WITH PEKING (1969)

*1959*

33. Guinea

*1960*

34. Ghana
(16 African nations gain independence)
35. Cuba
36. Mali
37. Somalia ‡

*1961*

38. Syria (Syria splits away from the UAR)
39. Tanganyika
40. Laos

*1962*

41. Algeria
42. Uganda ‡

*1963*

43. Zanzibar
44. Kenya
45. Burundi ‡

*1964*

46. Tunisia ‡
47. France

48. Congo (Brazzaville)
(Total reduced to 47 with merger of Tanganyika and Zanzibar into Tanzania)
48. Central African Republic
49. Zambia
50. Dahomey ‡

*1965*

(Total reduced to 49 with break in relations with Burundi, January, 1965)
50. Mauritania

*1966*

(Total reduced to 47 following break in relations with the Central African Republic [January], Dahomey [January], and Ghana [October])

*1967*

(Total reduced to 45 following break in relations with Tunisia in September and with Indonesia in October)

*1968*

46. Southern Yemen (Chinese embassy established in 1969)

*1969*

(No change)

 * China has an embassy in all of these nations, except in the United Kingdom and the Netherlands where there is an Office of the Chargé d'Affaires.
 † The year indicates the date when formal relations were established.
 ‡ These nations do *not* have a mission in China—all others have such a mission.

Broadly speaking, Chinese missions are similar to those of most nations. The key diplomats are the ambassador, the counselor, the commercial counselor, the cultural counselor, and the military attaché. This was the general pattern until 1964 when a new post, the economic counselor, was added to the foreign service. For the most part, common sense has governed the size of the embassy: large and important nations house large staffs, and small, unimportant countries have small staffs. Thus, the larger embassies contain several posts beyond those mentioned above—for example, trade and cultural attachés, press attachés, and sometimes several first, second, and third secretaries, in addition to a number of attachés with no specific functional designation. Where it has been warranted, Peking has also posted religious attachés and student consuls abroad. As with most nations, the Chinese have adjusted the size of their missions in accordance with political conditions, and therefore, it is not surprising that the large embassies in Moscow and New Delhi during the 1950's dwindled sharply in size during the 1960's.

The ambassador, of course, is the key figure in Chinese embassies. Aside from the normal protocol functions, it is not easy to make generalizations which are lasting for different areas (both political and geographic) and for different periods. In the early years of the CPR, Chinese diplomacy was conducted under the shadow of Stalin. As a consequence, Chinese ambassadors, half of whom were in Communist nations, were seldom heard from. However, the pace of their work stepped up markedly during the Bandung era; not only did direct contacts increase with persons in the host nations, but the typical ambassador found himself deeply engaged in the activities of the countless delegations that were sent abroad from Peking. This generalization continued to be valid until the Cultural Revolution in regard to the non-Communist world, especially the so-called Third World. But the splintering of the Communist Bloc in the early sixties produced sharply varying effects. In some Communist nations (for example, Albania and Rumania) the ambassador became increasingly active, and in others (for example, Bulgaria) his work was curtailed as contacts with Peking diminished.

Because one hundred different men have served as ambassadors, some reasonably firm generalizations can be made about them and about personnel practices in the Foreign Ministry. Understandably, some of the initial ambassadorial appointments were marginal in terms of previous diplomatic or quasi-diplomatic experience. These men were quickly weeded out and given domestic assignments quite divorced from foreign affairs. But the overriding trend was the development within a decade of a core of experienced ambassadors who, as in most diplomatic services, began to rotate between Peking and posts abroad. Suggestive of this trend is the fact that fifteen of the one hundred ambassadors served as *both* a director (or deputy director) of a Foreign Ministry department and as a counselor of an embassy *before* assuming an ambassadorial appointment. Another twenty-seven ambassadors served as embassy counselors *or* as MFA department directors (or deputy directors) before becoming ambassadors.

Viewing this process of professionalization in another fashion, we find that twenty-two of the ambassadors have been ambassadors in two different countries, and another nine have served in three or more nations.[11] For a period from about 1961 to 1965, it appeared from ambassadorial appointments that the foreign service was being eroded by the introduction of a number of "amateur" diplomats. In particular, several ambassadors were drawn from the CCP apparatus, and a few more were drawn from the public security system and the People's Liberation Army (PLA). This may have been a reflection of the domestic situation in China during the post-Great Leap Forward period when many Party, public security, and PLA figures were transferred into posts for which they had little technical experience. Whether this actually represented a new trend in the foreign service is open to question; in any event, post-1965 ambassadorial appointments clearly demonstrated a return to the process of selection that was based chiefly on diplomatic experience.

Another personnel practice noted in many instances is that new ambassadors will disappear from the public scene for many months prior to their official appointment. It is tempting to hypothesize that they were undergoing an intensive training program, but there is little firm evidence to support this. It has been Peking's general practice, prior to the Cultural Revolution, to keep its ambassadors overseas for three to four years, apparently with little or no vacation. In general, they will accompany the highest national leaders on state visits to China, and often the ambassador will remain in Peking after the national leader has returned home (presumably for further consultations). Only on the rarest occasions are more than two or three ambassadors called back to Peking at the same time; perhaps the best known instance was in the late spring and early summer of 1958 when eight of them were back in China. This may have been in relation to the second session of the Eighth Party Congress, or perhaps to the grave Middle East crisis which saw the landing of American and British troops in Lebanon and Jordan.

The number two man in the embassy, the counselor (ts'an-tsan), often fills in for the ambassador at lesser functions in the host country, and in the ambassador's absence he serves as chargé d'affaires ad interim. In career mobility terms, this is an exceptionally important post. Of the one hundred different men who are or have been ambassadors, almost one-fourth served at least one tour abroad as a counselor before receiving an ambassadorial appointment. In sharp contrast, no

[11] In terms of accreditation to different countries, the three leading ambassadors are Keng Piao (Sweden, Denmark, Finland, Pakistan, Burma, and Albania), Wang Yup'ing (Rumania, Norway, Cambodia, Cuba, and Vietnam), and P'an Tzu-li (Korea, India, Nepal, and the USSR).

commercial or cultural counselor has become an ambassador. Most of the counselors remain in the foreign service, and they often serve as director or deputy director of one of the Foreign Ministry departments in Peking. Even when counselors leave the foreign service, it is usually to assume an assignment in a "mass" organization with strong foreign affairs interests or in one of the institutes of higher learning that is devoted specifically to international relations (for example, the Foreign Affairs Institute).

The commercial counselors (*shang-wu ts'an-tsan*) are frequently in the news for the simple reason that trade is a major function of many embassies. They normally take part in the top-level trade negotiations and are sometimes the signatories of the agreements which result. On occasions they serve as the chargé ad interim. However, in career terms the pattern differs markedly when it is compared with that of the counselor. Many of the commercial counselors have worked in the Foreign Trade Ministry, and it is not unusual for them to return to this ministry after a tour abroad as a commercial counselor.[12] It is also common practice for the commercial counselors to be reassigned to one of the many national corporations, for instance, the China National Import-Export Corporation.[13]

The post of cultural counselor was introduced in the mid-1950's, the timing of which suggests a relationship with the Bandung period when the activities of the embassies were considerably broadened. Like the commercial counselors, the cultural counselors are often in the news, particularly in the Third World countries to which Peking has sent so many culturally oriented delegations. They are probably in close contact with the many New China News Agency (NCNA) correspondents abroad,[14] and they appear to be a major link with the

[12] Two men, Tu Yü-yun and Li Cho-chih, rose to the assistant minister level. Tu had been commercial counselor in India, and Li held this post in Czechoslovakia, Yugoslavia, and Great Britain.

[13] A brief sketch of the career of Chang Hua-tung is suggestive of the latitude of assignments in connection with foreign trade specialists. In the early years of the CPR, Chang was deputy director of the Foreign Trade Department under the Northeast People's Government and, concurrently, director of the central government's Northeast Customs Control Bureau. In early 1950 he was in Moscow with Mao and Chou for the important negotiations which led to the Sino-Soviet Treaty of Alliance and several trade agreements. He later worked in Peking as head of the Import Department in the Foreign Trade Ministry. After this, from 1957 to 1962, he was commercial counselor in Moscow. Returning home, he was made a vice-chairman of the important China Committee for the Promotion of International Trade, and in this capacity he led delegations in 1964 to Japan and North Korea to set up trade and industrial exhibitions.

[14] The subject of the overseas NCNA correspondents deserves further study. By the nature of their profession, the Chinese newsmen have roamed far and wide. The following places where they have been reported at different times during the 1960's is almost

numerous "friendship" associations abroad, especially those in other Asian nations.[15] Few of the cultural counselors have returned home to assume higher echelon posts in the Foreign Ministry. However, many have gravitated to the internationally oriented "mass" organizations, especially the friendship associations. Others have worked in the Chinese People's Association for Cultural Relations and Friendship with Foreign Countries or its governmental counterpart, the Commission for Cultural Relations with Foreign Countries. In fact, a former official of this commission claims that "cultural cadres" that were assigned to embassies "were chosen from an elite group" within the commission.[16] This may be an overstatement, but a clear pattern of personnel assignments suggests that the informal core of former cultural counselors provides an important link, at the working level, between the Foreign Ministry and many other organs concerned with foreign affairs.

The most recently created (*circa* 1964) high-level embassy post is the economic counselor (*ching-chi ts'an-tsan*). Unlike the commercial counselor, who is concerned with trade, the economic counselor deals with China's aid programs. On the eve of the Cultural Revolution, there were ten economic counselors working in nations where China has major aid programs: Albania, Burma, Mali, Cambodia, Nepal, Indonesia, Algeria, Congo (B), Korea, and Ghana.[17] (The men in Indonesia and Ghana were withdrawn when these nations broke with Peking.) The official in Albania had previously served there as the commercial counselor, and the man in Korea is a member of the

certainly not complete, but nonetheless suggestive. *Communist nations:* USSR, Bulgaria, Czechoslovakia, Yugoslavia, Rumania, Hungary, Poland, East Germany, Albania, North Korea, Mongolia, North Vietnam, and Cuba. *South and Southeast Asia:* Pakistan, India, Ceylon, Afghanistan, Nepal, Indonesia, Cambodia, Laos, Hong Kong, and Macao. *Japan. Middle East and Africa:* The United Arab Republic, Yemen, Iraq, Kuwait, Syria, Ethiopia, the Sudan, Tanzania, Somalia, Guinea, Ghana, Mali, the Congo (B), Senegal, Tunisia, and Algeria. *West Europe:* Great Britain, Norway, Sweden, Finland, Denmark, France, Italy, and Switzerland. *The Americas:* Canada, Mexico, Brazil, and Chile. One might logically assume that many NCNA foreign correspondents had served at one time or another in the foreign service, but I have seen little evidence to support this.

[15] The numerous "friendship" or "cultural" associations abroad seem to range from full-fledged and highly active organizations to small groups of maverick Sinophiles. I have compiled a list of forty-six countries where such exist, and no doubt there are others.

[16] Tung Chi-ping and Humphrey Evans, *The Thought Revolution* (New York: Coward-McCann, 1966), p. 218.

[17] Peking has also had an economic representative in Vietnam since the mid-1950's, and in Tanzania since July, 1965. Vietnam is obviously a special case, and it long predated the creation of the post of economic counselor. However, it is unclear why the man in Tanzania is known as an economic representative (*ching-chi tai-piao*) rather than an economic counselor.

State Council's Commission for Economic Relations with Foreign Countries. However, rather oddly, there is no background information on the other eight economic counselors.

In terms of institutional practices, ambassadors are appointed by the chairman of the CPR, but the counselors, commercial counselors, cultural counselors, and economic counselors are appointed by the State Council. The lesser officials mentioned above are presumably appointed directly by the Foreign Ministry. However, it is probable that military attachés are assigned by the Defense Ministry or by PLA headquarters. At the beginning of the Cultural Revolution they were posted in twenty-six nations, and the pattern of their posts is obviously no accident. First, with the unusual exception of Mongolia, military attachés are assigned to all nations bordering on China. Second, attachés are in all the East European Communist countries (including, for a short while in the mid-1950's, Yugoslavia) and in Cuba. Still others are in nations with high-level military technology (Sweden, Switzerland, France, and Denmark), and a final category consists of nations where China has high priority revolutionary interests (for example, the United Arab Republic). A list of the military attachés is given in Appendix F.

The military attachés range in rank from major to major general,[18] although it appears that general officers have been assigned only to Moscow. Because of their relatively low rank in the PLA, rather little is known about the approximately eighty men who have served as military attachés. Twenty-one of them have served in more than one nation, but most, presumably, return to PLA assignments in China after a tour abroad—a practice that is common in many nations. The most important exception to this general practice is Chang T'ung who, after being the military attaché for several years in Denmark and India, was the chargé d'affaires in the Congo—not in Brazzaville or Leopoldville, but in Stanleyville, where for six weeks in 1961 the Chinese had an "embassy" during the short life of the abortive Gizenga government. Chang later headed the Foreign Ministry's First Asian Affairs Department, and in 1969 he was appointed ambassador to Pakistan.

The Chinese have also established a number of consulates general and consulates. Not surprisingly, these have been set up in large cities

[18] Military ranks existed throughout the PLA only from 1955 to 1965. Prior to 1955 Chinese military attachés held simulated ranks. However, since ranks were abolished in 1965, the officers abroad have been referred to simply by their titles (for example, Military Attaché Wang, but not Colonel Wang).

or towns which are a long distance from the national capital (for example, Dacca and Medan); others are in the "special interest" category such as the one in Phong Saly, which is not far from the Chinese border in Laos, and the one in Gdansk, Poland, which is there to service Chinese shipping interests. (Peking has reciprocated, and at one time or another there have been many consulates in China, mainly in Shanghai, Canton, and Tientsin. The Soviet Union had several consulates throughout China, but they were all closed down by 1962. Special interests have also played a role in the establishment of foreign consulates, as they did in the case of Nepal's mission in Lhasa and Vietnam's in Kunming.) As a group, the Chinese consuls general can be likened to the counselors. They tend to remain in the foreign service, and three of their number went on to become ambassadors.

## SPECIAL MISSIONS ABROAD

Part of the conventional wisdom about China is that the "two Chinas" agree on only one issue: There is but one China. In fact, however, both Peking and Taipei have demonstrated considerable flexibility when it suited their interests. In mid-1955, following up on the contacts made at the Bandung Conference, the Chinese Communists began a series of diplomatic maneuvers in the Middle East, which was an area where their contacts had been almost nil. In August they signed an agreement with Egypt which provided for the establishment of "commercial representatives' offices" in Cairo and Peking. From Peking's view, there was nothing unofficial about this agreement: it was signed by the Chinese foreign trade minister, it was duly ratified by the State Council, and the two Chinese "representatives" to the commercial office were officially appointed by the State Council. The two men took up their duties in Cairo in January, 1956, but it was not until several weeks later that relations were severed between Cairo and Taipei (the initiative in this case was taken by the Egyptians, not the Nationalists). In the meantime, beginning in August, 1955, an important Chinese Communist trade official led a delegation to the Middle East. In Syria in November and in Lebanon in December, agreements were reached for the establishment of two more commercial offices. Once again these were completely official on the Chinese side, and the trade representatives arrived in Syria and Lebanon in July and September, 1956, respectively. Syria joined Egypt in establishing diplomatic relations with Peking, but the Chinese Nationalists "tolerated" the Communist mission in Lebanon and eventually the Communists withdrew. A basically similar set of events took place in Cambodia in 1956, and from then until July, 1958, when Cambodia extended *de jure* recognition, the Communist commercial office served, in effect, as its diplomatic mission in Pnom Penh. The Nationalists, in the meantime, maintained a consulate in Pnom Penh until October, 1958.

Having viewed the embassies principally in terms of the individual posts, we can now move to a broader consideration of their collective functions. There are many pitfalls in such an endeavor; among them is the high level of secrecy that is maintained by the Chinese in the conduct of their affairs. However, thanks to a landmark volume by D. M. Johnston and Hungdah Chiu on the approximately twenty-three hundred agreements signed between 1949 and 1967,[19] we are now in a position to discern some interesting patterns. The Johnston-Chiu definition of an "agreement" is extremely broad and ranges from the most important treaties of alliance and long-term trade pacts to relatively innocuous joint communiques pledging lasting friendship. However, the very breadth of the definition provides a better operational view of Peking's foreign policy than would a narrow definition which dealt only with high-level, government-to-government treaties. Our focus for the moment is on the activities of Chinese diplomats abroad, but first we should see where the action has been. This is given in Table 30.

The figures in Table 30 demonstrate, not surprisingly, a sharp *percentage* drop in diplomatic and quasi-diplomatic contacts between China and the other Communist nations. However, the actual number of agreements signed in the 1960's is still about double the number signed during the early 1950's. Moreover, the figures for the Communist nations conceal the fact that agreements between China and Albania, Rumania, and North Vietnam have risen markedly. Between 1949 and 1967 China concluded some fourteen hundred agreements with Communist countries, and about five hundred of these were signed abroad.[20] At first glance one would suspect that Chinese diplomats had signed the majority of those concluded abroad, but in fact

---

[19] Douglas M. Johnston and Hungdah Chiu (eds.), *Agreements of the People's Republic of China, 1949–1967: A Calendar* (Cambridge, Mass.: Harvard University Press, 1968).

[20] There is about a 5 per cent error factor in the locality of the signing of agreements, because this information was sometimes not published. The figure of five hundred may, therefore, be low.

the figure is about 20 per cent. The situation is broadly similar in Asia, Africa, and the Middle East, where the diplomats have signed only about a third of all agreements that were concluded abroad. In Western Europe, Peking's diplomats have signed only an insignificant handful of agreements. Japan, which does not have diplomatic ties with Peking, is a special case; all but one of the ostensibly unofficial forty-four agreements between China and Japan were concluded in Peking.

## DIPLOMACY BY DELEGATION

The reason why Peking's diplomats have signed a relatively small percentage of these agreements is suggestive of a major operational principle in the management of China's foreign policy: most agree-

TABLE 30
AGREEMENTS SIGNED BY CHINA

| | Nation | October, 1949–September, 1954 | | October, 1954–September, 1960 | | October, 1960–September, 1967 | |
|---|---|---|---|---|---|---|---|
| | | Number | Per cent * | Number | Per cent * | Number | Per cent * |
| Communist | USSR | 46 | 17% | 101 | 11% | 61 | 5% |
| | Eastern Europe | 124 | 46% | 346 | 38% | 289 | 26% |
| | Asian Communist | 47 | 17% | 188 | 20.6% | 184 | 17% |
| | Cuba | 0 | | 4 | 00.4% | 47 | 4% |
| | Totals | 217 | 80% | 639 | 70% | 581 | 52% |
| Non-Communist | Western Europe | 21 | 8% | 28 | 3.1% | 32 | 2.88% |
| | Japan | 3 | 1% | 23 | 2.5% | 18 | 1.62% |
| | USA | 0 | | 1 | 00.1% | 2 | 00.18% |
| | Subtotals | 24 | 9% | 52 | 6% | 52 | 5% |
| | South-Southeast Asia | 29 | 10.7% | 140 | 15.4% | 234 | 21.06% |
| | Africa | 0 | | 19 | 2.1% | 190 | 17.10% |
| | Middle East | 0 | | 58 | 6.4% | 52 | 4.68% |
| | South and Central America | 1 | 00.3% | 1 | 00.1% | 2 | 00.18% |
| | Subtotals | 30 | 11% | 218 | 24% | 478 | 43% |
| | Totals | 54 | 20% | 270 | 30% | 530 | 48% |

* Percentage of agreements signed with all nations. The percentages for subtotals and totals have been rounded. The three time periods are not of equal length; the first is for five years, the second for six years, and the third for seven years. The first period covers the takeover and consolidation years, and ends with the adoption of the Constitution in September, 1954. The second period deals with the rapid expansion of Chinese contacts with both Communist and "Third World" nations, and ends with the withdrawal of Soviet technicians and the subsequent deterioration of Chinese relations with the Soviet Union and several of the Eastern European Communist nations. The third period begins with the fragmentation of the Communist Bloc; it is terminated in 1967 in accordance with the last entries in the Johnston-Chiu volume.

ments signed abroad, and especially the important ones, are negotiated by delegations sent from Peking. How does this work? First, of all agreements, those concerning trade constitute about one-quarter. Of those government-to-government trade agreements signed abroad, many have been concluded by delegations led by the foreign trade minister or one of his several vice-ministers. (It is difficult to find a group in Peking which has been abroad more frequently than the top officials of the Foreign Trade Ministry.) The field of science and technology provides a category which is almost the exclusive domain of the nondiplomats. For example, diplomats have signed only four of sixty-eight agreements providing for cooperation between the Chinese Academy of Sciences and counterpart academies abroad. Another example is found in the "joint commissions for scientific and technological cooperation" which were set up between Peking and the other Communist countries in the mid-1950's. These bodies meet once or twice a year, and with a few exceptions the 120-odd agreements have been signed by nondiplomats.

Are we to conclude from these figures that Chinese diplomats are little more than messengers for the bureaucracy in Peking? No doubt this is true in some cases, but there are other factors which suggest a negative answer. As a developing nation which is constantly seeking to advance her technological capacities, many of China's overseas ventures are of necessity beyond the abilities of foreign service personnel. Moreover, because the CPR controls almost all enterprises in China, many technical and business contracts would in a Western setting be negotiated by private firms which have personnel with skills unmatched in any diplomatic service. Much the same can be said about the innumerable cultural agreements; a Sino-Rumanian cultural cooperation agreement might be roughly parallel to an agreement concluded between a Broadway producer and a London theatrical company. In brief, it is doubtful if a satisfactory answer can be supplied until comparative government specialists produce more work on the diplomatic missions of the other Communist or developing nations.

## MASS ORGANIZATIONS

We have concentrated thus far on Peking's state relations. But even casual observers of Chinese foreign policy are aware that a vast amount of China's foreign relations is conducted on what purports to be an unofficial basis. The subject is much too large to deal with in detail in this essay, but some of the broad guidelines can be given.

Peking's "unofficial" relations are conducted by a complex network of "mass" or "people's" organizations. As might be expected, in the two-decade life of the CPR there have been wide variations in the work of those mass organizations whose major focus is on foreign affairs. In what might be called the Stalinist period, or perhaps more appropriately the Korean War period, Peking's reach out into the world was rather sharply confined to the Communist nations. There were, of course, limited contacts with some Asian nations, but the now familiar forays into Africa and the Middle East were almost nil. The major thrust was toward the international peace movement which, decoded, meant an effort to rally support for China and its ally North Korea in the Korean War. On a broader level, a good case can be made that the work of the Chinese mass organizations in international affairs was essentially an adjunct of Moscow's foreign policy.

In organizational terms, the most important Chinese mass organizations maintained steady contact in the early 1950's with the various international Communist front organizations that had headquarters in Moscow or in one of the Eastern European countries. Thus, the China Peace Committee was affiliated with the World Peace Council, the All-China Federation of Labor with the World Federation of Trade Unions, and the All-China Federation of Democratic Youth with the World Federation of Democratic Youth. These and similar international bodies held scores of congresses and special meetings which were regularly attended by Chinese delegations. Such important Chinese Communist leaders as Liu Ch'ang-sheng, Liu Ning-i, Liao Ch'eng-chih, and Ts'ai Ch'ang spent a good deal of their time abroad during those years. In retrospect, however, there was a barrenness to their activities; Moscow's tight control over Communist Bloc nations in those years had the effect of stifling the hopes which the Chinese presumably entertained to move into the world at large. Peking maintained its ties with the international front organizations into the early 1960's. However, by that time the Chinese were attending meetings mainly to gain a forum from which to denounce the Soviet Union as "revisionists" or worse. To this day Peking retains these ties, but in the middle and late 1960's they had become nominal.

Another and far more useful device to manage foreign affairs by mass organizations is found in the field of foreign trade. The first major move in this direction began at the Soviet-sponsored International Economic Conference, which was held in the spring of 1952 in

Moscow. Moscow as well as Peking was then attempting to maneuver around the United States–sponsored embargo which had been set up during the Korean War. The Chinese concluded a number of ostensibly unofficial trade contracts with Western European business groups, and although they were of minor importance in themselves, they set the pattern for the years ahead. For organizational purposes, Peking immediately established the China Committee for the Promotion of International Trade. This organization has been utilized mainly to negotiate trade contracts with countries that do not have diplomatic relations with Peking. It was already very active by the mid-fifties, and by the mid-sixties it was negotiating something on the order of half of China's foreign trade. Not surprisingly, many of the committee's key officials hold concurrent posts within the Foreign Trade Ministry. Under the auspices of the committee, the Chinese also established "unofficial" commercial offices in Japan, Italy, Austria, and Chile in the mid-1960's. (Taiwan has diplomatic relations with Japan, Italy, and Chile, but neither China has formal diplomatic ties with Austria.)

Mass organizations have also been adroitly utilized for more selective, short-term goals. In the post-Korean War period, for example, Peking apparently decided upon a more activist policy vis-à-vis Japan. The thousands of Japanese who were stranded in China after the Sino-Japanese War were of considerable concern to the Japanese government and people. Seizing upon this situation, the Chinese conducted a series of repatriation talks in both Japan and China. Under normal circumstances, such negotiations would have been conducted by the respective foreign ministries, but in this instance they were managed by the Chinese Red Cross Society. The principal figure on the Chinese side was Liao Ch'eng-chih, who was born and bred in Japan, and who was perhaps Peking's most important "unofficial" diplomat until the Cultural Revolution. A similar situation regarding fishing rights, which are of vital importance to Japan, was worked out in like fashion. The head of the Chinese Fishery Association, a little-known man named Yang Yü, led the negotiations which resulted in several agreements regarding fishing rights in the East China and Yellow seas.

These selected cases could be duplicated many times, but this is not to suggest that they were all as successful as those involving Japan. Charles Neuhauser, for example, has demonstrated the essential failures of the Afro-Asian "solidarity movement" in which Peking invested countless man-hours and large sums of money in the late 1950's and 1960's. [21]

## OTHER INSTRUMENTS OF FOREIGN AFFAIRS

In addition to the MFA, the Foreign Trade Ministry, and the mass organizations, there are several other government organs with obvious foreign interests and responsibilities. The Commission for Cultural Relations with Foreign Countries, which was set up in 1958, has taken a more active role in negotiating cultural agreements. Peking's aid program was institutionalized in 1961 with the establishment of the Bureau for Economic Relations with Foreign Countries. Led by Fang I, who was the chief aid administrator in Vietnam for many years, the bureau was raised to the commission level in 1964. The Overseas Chinese Affairs Commission has been another active body. Liao Ch'eng-chih has been the key figure in this work since 1949. In the 1950's the commission was instrumental in setting up a number of special schools for overseas Chinese and in inducing overseas Chinese students to return to the motherland from South and Southeast Asia. Other significant State Council organs include the People's Bank of China, which maintains several overseas branches, and the Foreign Experts Bureau, which tended to the interests of the thousands of foreign advisers until most of them were withdrawn in 1960 and after. There is also the Foreign Language Publications and Distribution Bureau, which handles the output of the Foreign Languages Press, and Radio Peking, which is under the jurisdiction of the State Council's Broadcasting Administrative Bureau.

## THE FLOW OF INFORMATION

We should explore briefly the question of the information available to the foreign affairs apparatus and the ability of the apparatus to communicate this information up and down the hierarchy.[22] Some of our knowledge of these processes is quite firm, but other aspects remain largely in the realm of speculation. We know, for example, that Peking receives a very wide range of foreign political journals, both

[21] Charles Neuhauser, *Third World Politics: China and the Afro-Asian People's Solidarity Organization, 1957–1967* (Cambridge, Mass.: East Asian Research Center, Harvard University, 1968).

[22] The remarks in this and succeeding paragraphs have been culled from Tung and Evans, *The Thought Revolution;* Henry G. Schwarz, "The *Ts'an-k'ao Hsiao-hsi:* How Well Informed Are Chinese Officials about the Outside World?" *CQ*, No. 27 (July–September, 1966), pp. 54–83; and from several interviews with Asian and Western diplomats who have negotiated with Chinese officials.

popular and professional. All the major world press services are monitored, and much of this information is published in *Ts'an-k'ao Hsiao-hsi* (Reference Information). This cannot be regarded as a Chinese version of *The New York Times,* but one careful analysis of its contents indicates a concerted effort to provide information from non-Communist news sources. The *Ts'an-k'ao Hsiao-hsi* is a restricted publication, but it reaches a rather wide range of officials. Furthermore, we know that diplomats about to go abroad receive intensive briefings and that at least some of the briefing materials are collated from this publication.

Still another input of information comes from embassy dispatches to Peking. There are conflicting judgments about the value of this reporting, and we are ignorant of most of the details. Some diplomats who have dealt with their Chinese counterparts have been impressed by their knowledge of the country to which they were accredited and, rightly or wrongly, assume that much of this information is transmitted back to Peking. Others hold the opposite view and feel that embassy reporting leaves much to be desired. In any case, it is safe to assume fluctuations in the quality: reporting is probably cautious, and it may be distorted during periods of high political tension in Peking.

NCNA, of course, provides another source of information. We have already indicated the far-flung overseas NCNA network, but here again the question of quality is pertinent. Setting aside the real possibility that NCNA correspondents file separate reports for a privileged group in Peking, we can take a fleeting look at the "open" dispatches of these newsmen. Each reader will have his own impression of NCNA reports on foreign countries, and in recent years he can point to gross vilifications of, say, the USSR or to equally gross glorifications of Albania. On the other hand, there have been periods when NCNA coverage has been quite good. For instance, from roughly mid-1955 to the end of 1957 some outstanding dispatches were filed from Yugoslavia (during the relatively brief "honeymoon" period of Sino-Yugoslav relations). In general, however, considering the twenty-year span of the CPR, one surmises that NCNA dispatches have been less useful than *Ts'an-k'ao Hsiao-hsi* for the working diplomat.

Intelligence reporting is presumably another information "input" in Peking, and one can further assume an intimate relationship between intelligence personnel and the embassy and NCNA networks. Beyond such unsatisfactory assumptions, however, the subject is outside the competence of academicians to investigate. However, from diplomats who have dealt with Chinese officials, we do have one useful measuring rod for evaluating the information flow into Peking. Despite some practices which often annoy foreigners, such as extreme aloofness, diplomats uniformly attest to the fact that when the Chinese come to the conference table to deal with a specific matter, they come with a good command of the subject matter at hand. The frequent negotiations for the huge grain sales to China during the past decade are a case in point.

Assuming that the above paragraphs paint a roughly accurate picture of the information input, and assuming further that this information is coordinated by the State Council's Staff Office for Foreign Affairs and the CCP's "foreign section," we are still left with the tantalizing question of how information is transmitted to the highest policy making levels. The uncertainties involved in speculating on this question are obvious. Few of the Politburo members since 1949 have had much concern with foreign affairs on a continuing basis; Chou En-lai and Ch'en I (until the Cultural Revolution) are the obvious exceptions. Perhaps Chou's long-term relationship to Mao has served well enough to "clear" the highest priority policy questions with the Chairman. And, at a notch below Chou, the extraordinary continuity of foreign affairs apparatus personnel provides at least another intimately familiar echelon to Mao and his immediate colleagues. Nonetheless, in considering the flow of information to the highest-level policy makers and the decisions which result after the information has been absorbed and evaluated, a central fact remains: the over-all foreign affairs apparatus has a minuscule "constituency," if only in contrast to many other sectors of the society. Moreover, even the presumed advocates of foreign affairs "interests"—most notably Chou—must balance and weigh the allocation of resources, both human and material, with other demands of state.

## ORGANIZATION AND HIERARCHY

All of these government organs and mass organizations have required some instrument for coordination. Unfortunately, we have little specific information on how this works in practice. A reasonable guess, made on the basis of both timing and personnel, would place the center of coordination in the State Council's Staff Office for Foreign Affairs (*wai-shih pan-kung-shih*). The office was established in early 1958, when most of the various components of the foreign affairs apparatus had been set up. In institutional terms, the time had come for this burgeoning bureaucracy to be placed under central direction.

Foreign Minister Ch'en I was placed in charge of the office. Even more revealing than Ch'en's appointment was the selection of the four deputy directors: Liao Ch'eng-chih, Liu Ning-i, K'ung Yuan, and Chang Yen. We have already indicated the breadth of Liao's foreign activities (ranging from the youth and peace movements to overseas Chinese affairs to his special background in Japanese affairs). Liu brought to the office an extensive background in the international trade union and peace movements. K'ung was a foreign trade expert, and Chang Yen, an administrative generalist, had worked directly under Chou in the State Council for several years. Moreover, all of these men ranked fairly high in the Party hierarchy. At the time of their appointment to the Foreign Affairs Office, Ch'en, Liao, and Liu were already Central Committee members, and a few weeks later K'ung was elected as an alternate. In 1961 Central Committee alternate Fang I was added as a deputy director. Here again the man and the timing seem significant; on the same day that Fang became a deputy director, he also became head of the newly established government body to coordinate the foreign aid program.

The hierarchical structure for the foreign affairs apparatus within the government and the mass organizations can be pieced together with a measure of confidence. But the task takes on many uncertainties when we turn to the CCP. Prior to the Cultural Revolution most writers on China's foreign affairs assumed that the CCP hierarchy maintained over-all direction of foreign policy. There is, doubtless, a large measure of truth in this assumption, but it is difficult to compile the supporting evidence. For example, our knowledge about the proceedings of the Politburo is scanty at best, and even the bare fragments that we have suggest a much greater concern with domestic affairs. Much the same can be said about the infrequent plenums of the Party Central Committee. Indeed, it was not until 1959 that a Polish news agency specifically mentioned the existence of a "foreign section" under the Central Committee. However, thanks to the punctiliousness of Chinese news media, it is possible to reconstruct a rather select group of men who, time and again, have taken part in the discussions with the foreign Communist Party leaders who visited Peking so often in the late 1950's and early 1960's. Tracing these threads over the years, one is consistently led to the Party Secretariat which, until the Cultural Revolution, was usually rated as second only to the Politburo Standing Committee as the center of political power in

China. The Secretariat, under the 1956 Party Constitution, was charged with the day-to-day implementation of Politburo policies, and thus it is logical to assume that this body may have been the heart of Party control over foreign affairs—subject only to the over-all guidance of the Politburo and the Politburo Standing Committee. The Secretariat, of course, had more domestic than foreign responsibilities, and it may have delegated considerable authority to the Party-dominated Staff Office for Foreign Affairs. This, however, is a supposition and not a demonstrated fact.

In addition to the question of Party direction or coordination of foreign affairs in general, we need to explore the sectors of foreign affairs which the CCP has pre-empted for itself. The answer is the obvious one of Party-to-Party relations and, in a broader sense, the relationship of the CCP to the entire world Communist movement. Because the Sino-Soviet ideological dispute has attracted so much of our attention for a decade, it is easy to forget Chinese preoccupation with domestic affairs in the formative years of the CPR, not to mention the vast energies that were expended on the Korean War. In any event, as in the case of the mass organizations, the towering figure of Stalin seems to have overshadowed any pretensions the Chinese might have had to exert their will on the world Communist movement. One means by which we might measure the level of Chinese activity—or the lack of it—on the international Communist scene is to examine the congresses of fraternal Communist parties. In the first place, relatively few national Party congresses were held in or out of the Communist bloc in the years just before Stalin's death. The Chinese never sent a representative to a congress outside the bloc during this period, and their presence at a congress in Czechoslovakia in 1949 and at ones held in Germany in 1950 and 1952 were not noteworthy. In none of these three cases did they send a group from Peking: A Youth League leader who was touring the Eastern European nations attended the 1949 meeting in Prague; the Chinese ambassador in Moscow attended the 1950 meeting in Germany; and the Chinese ambassador posted to Germany attended the 1952 conference there. In fact, Peking's first important representation at a foreign Party congress took place in October, 1952, when Liu Shao-ch'i led a delegation to the Nineteenth Congress of the Communist Party of the Soviet Union (CPSU), which was the last before Stalin's death five months later. The broad outline of Peking's participation in foreign Communist Party congresses is contained in Table 31.

TABLE 31

CCP DELEGATIONS TO FOREIGN COMMUNIST PARTY CONGRESSES
(AND CONFERENCES) AND THE "WORLD CONGRESSES" (WC)
OF COMMUNIST PARTIES *

| Country | 1949 | 50 | 51 | 52 | 53 | 54 | 55 | 56 | 57 | 58 | 59 | 60 | 61 | 62 | 63 | 64 | 65 | 66 | 67 | 68 | 69 |
|---|---|---|---|---|---|---|---|---|---|---|---|---|---|---|---|---|---|---|---|---|---|
| USSR | | | | X | | | | X | WC | | X | WC | X | | | | | O | | | ● |
| Bulgaria | | | | | | O | | | | X | | | | X | | | | O | | O | |
| Poland | | | | | | O | | | | | | | | | | O | | | | O | |
| Czechoslovakia | X | | | | | X | | X | | X | | | | X | | | | O | | O | |
| Hungary | | | O | | | O | | | | | X | | | X | | | | O | | | |
| Germany | | X | | X | | X | | X | | X | | | | | X | | | | O | | |
| Rumania | | | | | | | X | | | | | X | | | | | X | | | | O |
| Albania | | | | O | | | | X | | X | | | X | | | | | X | | | |
| Korea | | | | | | | | X | | | | | X | | | | | | | | |
| Vietnam | | | | | | | | | | | | X | | | | | | | | | |
| Mongolia | | | | | | X | | | | X | | | X | | | | | O | | | |
| Cuba | | | | | | | | | | | | X | | | | | | | | | |
| U.K. | O | | | O | | O | | O | O | | O | | | | O | | O | | O | O | |
| Italy | | | O | | | | X | X | | X | | | | X | | | | O | | | O |

| Country | 1949 | 50 | 51 | 52 | 53 | 54 | 55 | 56 | 57 | 58 | 59 | 60 | 61 | 62 | 63 | 64 | 65 | 66 | 67 | 68 | 69 |
|---|---|---|---|---|---|---|---|---|---|---|---|---|---|---|---|---|---|---|---|---|---|
| Finland | | X | O | | | O | O | | X | | | X | X | | O | | | O | | | O |
| Sweden | | | O | | O | | O | | X | | | | X | | | O | | | O | | |
| Denmark | O | | | O | | O | | | O | X | | O | | | | | O | | | | |
| Norway | O | O | | | | | | | | | | | X | | | | O | | | O | |
| Belgium | | | O | | | O | | | X | | | X | | | O | O | O | O | O | O | |
| Austria | | | O | | | O | | | O | | | | X | | | O | | | | | O |
| New Zealand | | | | | | | | | | | | X | | | X | | | O | | | |
| Totals | 1 | 1 | 0 | 2 | 0 | 3 | 2 | 5 | 5 | 5 | 4 | 8 | 8 | 4 | 2 | 0 | 1 | 1 | 0 | 0 | 0 |

Total number of delegations: 52

*Key:*   X—CCP attendance
       O—Non-attendance by CCP delegation
       WC—"World Congresses" of Communist parties attended by a CCP delegation
       ●—"World Congresses" of Communist parties not attended by a CCP delegation

* This table does not purport to be a listing of Communist congresses in *all* countries since 1949. It merely lists those countries in which CCP delegations attended at least one congress. The Chinese also named P'eng Chen to lead delegations to congresses of the Communist Party of Japan in 1961 and 1964, and Ulanfu to lead another delegation to a congress in France in 1961. In each instance, the nation in question refused to allow the Chinese delegation to enter the country.

Beginning with Liu Shao-ch'i's delegation in 1952, the standard pattern was for Peking to send about three delegates to each congress, and in most cases the ambassador on the scene was also named to the official delegation. (Outside the bloc nations, the general practice has been to send only one delegate.) All told, fifty-one different men (excluding the ambassadors) have attended either these congresses or the two critically important Communist "summit" meetings held in Moscow in 1957 and 1960. More pertinent is the fact that ten men attended four or more of these meetings: Wu Hsiu-ch'üan (ten); K'ang Sheng (eight); Chao I-min, Liu Ning-i, Teng Hsiao-p'ing, and Wang Chia-hsiang (five); and Liu Ch'ang-sheng, P'eng Chen, Tseng Shan, and Hsiung Fu (four).[23] Except for Hsiung, an ideologue who only came to prominence in the 1960's, the other names are familiar to students of Peking's foreign policy and, particularly, of the Sino-Soviet ideological dispute. And this is the same core group which met on scores of occasions with foreign Communist leaders who were visiting Peking in the late fifties and early sixties when Peking was actively dueling with Moscow for primacy in the Communist world.

As Table 31 indicates, the heyday of Chinese participation was the period from 1956 to 1962. As we now know, the CCP delegates did not attend as meek followers of Moscow-dictated policies. Until 1960 China was willing for the sake of bloc unity to sign harmonious sounding communiques, but from that year onward they displayed an increased willingness to challenge Moscow openly. And, at the four congresses in late 1962 and the one in early 1963, the Sino-Soviet dispute was on the table for all to see. It is no accident that Peking has only attended bloc congresses in Rumania and Albania since that time. In terms of the management of foreign affairs, the Sino-Soviet dispute had the effect of transferring many sectors of what had been state relations with Communist nations, as well as the ties with the international Communist front organizations, to the realm of the CCP apparatus. With the obvious exception of Albania and Rumania, Peking simply stopped sending top-level "state" delegations to Moscow and the Eastern European nations. This was strikingly illustrated in July, 1963, when Teng Hsiao-p'ing led a group of top-flight Party leaders in the last attempt (and a very reluctant one at that) to resolve policy differences between the CCP and the CPSU. Of course,

[23] The importance of the Party's Secretariat in Party-to-Party relations was also demonstrated in the case of these congresses. Prior to the Cultural Revolution, the Secretariat consisted of ten full and three alternate members. With the single exception of Lo Jui-ch'ing, all the others attended at least one of these meetings.

it was a meeting of Party leaders, but given the well-known interlocking directorate of state and Party leaders in China, it would not have been unreasonable to expect that at least one representative from the Chinese Foreign Ministry (for example, Foreign Minister Ch'en I or ex-Foreign Minister Chou) would be included. In fact, the Foreign Ministry was not represented at this fateful encounter. It is worth repeating that it was during exactly this same period that a number of ambassadors were being appointed from outside the foreign service, and that most of these nondiplomats came from the ranks of the CCP apparatus.

## THE CULTURAL REVOLUTION

The domestic turmoil caused by the Cultural Revolution was quickly reflected in Chinese foreign relations. Embassy officials abroad clearly overreacted in several situations—presumably on the assumption that it was politically safer to be more rather than less "red." For example, the virtual kidnaping of a defecting Chinese technician from a Dutch hospital in 1966 or the escalation of a simple auto accident into a "political murder" in East Germany in 1967 were cases which would certainly have been handled more judiciously prior to the Cultural Revolution. We need labor neither the dreary list of ugly incidents abroad which made headlines in the world press, nor the sacking of the British mission and the harassment of scores of diplomats in Peking. Perhaps we should be more surprised that, in spite of the tumult, certain sectors of foreign affairs were sheltered from the worst extremes of the Cultural Revolution. In particular, foreign trade declined less than a reasonable person might have expected, and some scientific and technological contacts were maintained. In institutional terms, the Foreign Ministry seems to have fought a daily rearguard action to remain even vaguely viable. The turmoil within the ministry was most evident in the late summer of 1967 when it appeared that the hitherto obscure, third-level diplomat Yao Teng-shan might become China's foreign minister.[24]

We also witnessed the withdrawal of every ambassador abroad save Huang Hua in Cairo. Why Huang was exempted remains a mystery; surely the embassy in Cairo is no more important than, say, the one in Hanoi. But again, what happened may have been less important

---

[24] For a survey of these events, see Melvin Gurtov, "The Foreign Ministry and Foreign Affairs during the Cultural Revolution," CQ, No. 40 (October–December, 1969), pp. 65–102.

than what did not. Except for the disputes which led to the closure of embassies in Ghana, Tunisia, and Indonesia, all the other missions were kept open. However, most of the front-rank talent was withdrawn—the ambassadors and most of the other key diplomats. After returning home, few of the ambassadors and almost none of the lesser diplomats were mentioned in the press. In contrast, the top personnel working in the Foreign Ministry in Peking were subject to numerous attacks, and it appears that the Cultural Revolution ended the careers of such outstanding specialists as Chang Han-fu and Wang Ping-nan. More important was the fall of most of the CCP figures who had played such vital roles in the management of inter-Party affairs: Liu Shao-ch'i, Teng Hsiao-p'ing, and P'eng Chen, to mention only a few.

The Ninth Party Congress in the spring of 1969 gave further testimony to the decline and fall of many of the figures who had conducted Peking's foreign relations for two decades. The two vice-ministers of Foreign Affairs who had been alternate members of the Eighth Central Committee (Chang Han-fu and Lo Kuei-po [25]) were both dropped. Also dropped were all the former ambassadors who had been full or alternate members of the Eighth Central Committee: Wang Chia-hsiang, Chang Wen-t'ien, Wu Hsiu-ch'üan, Liu Hsiao, P'an Tzu-li, and the above-mentioned Lo Kuei-po. Among other things, this had the effect of removing *all* former ambassadors to Moscow: Wang, Chang, Liu, and P'an.[26] On the new Central Committee, foreign affairs experts did poorly. Ex-Foreign Minister Chou En-lai and Foreign Minister Ch'en I were elected, as were ambassadors Huang Chen and Keng Piao. Hsieh Hsueh-kung, a former vice-minister of Foreign Trade, was elected to Central Committee membership, and foreign aid and trade expert Fang I was re-elected to alternate membership. But insult was added to injury when the new Central Committee failed to re-elect Ch'en I to the Politburo. The Party Secretariat was simply dropped as an organization, but it is more likely that this was because of domestic rather than foreign affairs.

In the immediate wake of the Ninth Congress, the situation looked bleak indeed for the foreign affairs apparatus. Chou—always the exception—remained as the single experienced voice for foreign affairs

[25] Although Lo was dropped from the Central Committee, he continued to appear regularly after the Ninth Congress in his capacity as a vice-minister of foreign affairs.

[26] This is a nice point to score for those who wish to demonstrate Sino-Soviet hostility. In fact, however, prior to 1969 only six ambassadors had been Central Committee members, and four of them were posted in Moscow. Moreover, Chang Wen-t'ien and Wang Chia-hsiang had disappeared from the political scene long before the Cultural Revolution.

in the Politburo. There were only a handful of internationally oriented persons on the much enlarged Central Committee, and most of the other top diplomatic personnel seemed to have disappeared from the scene. However, from the latter part of 1968 there had been some faint signs that Peking wished to normalize its foreign relations. Decisions to this effect must have been made during the Ninth Congress, because within a few weeks a series of ambassadorial appointments were made. The sequence of nations to which they were appointed, especially the first few, is in itself suggestive: Albania, France, Vietnam, Cambodia, Pakistan, Tanzania, Zambia, Guinea, the Congo (B), Syria, Rumania, Sweden, Nepal, Mauritania, Afghanistan, Algeria, and Yemen. But of greater importance is the fact that all of these seventeen new ambassadors were drawn strictly from the foreign service. Thirteen of them had previously been ambassadors, and the other four had lengthy diplomatic experience at lesser posts.[27] Put in other terms, more than one-third of Peking's embassies were staffed with experienced personnel within a brief period, and the regularity of these appointments suggested that most of the other vacant ambassadorial posts would be filled in the near future. In fact, however, after this spate of appointments within a two-month period, no further appointments were made through the fall of 1969. Almost all of the new appointees had been unreported in the Chinese press for about two years, so it should not be surprising if others are brought back to resume their careers. But even if most of the old foreign affairs specialists are resuscitated, they will resume their careers in a new political atmosphere. Almost all political leaders in China have undergone a three-year psychological, and in some instances a physical, ordeal that is bound to leave its imprint. We have already suggested a foreign affairs apparatus that possesses only a minor constituency, and with the Cultural Revolution so close at hand, it is difficult to estimate future attitudes about foreign policies and their management. Perhaps, to use Morton Halperin's phrase, the Chinese are "turning in" and during the years ahead foreign relations will receive a low priority. But, as we have tried to demonstrate, if they choose to move out again into the international arena, they have available an experienced core of men and an institutional framework which could be revitalized.[28]

[27] Still another man with lengthy diplomatic service was dispatched in July, 1969, as the chargé d'affaires ad interim to open a new embassy in the People's Republic of Southern Yemen.

[28] For valuable assistance in preparing this paper, I would like to thank Lois B. Hager, Jane L. Lieberthal, and Susan Horsey.

## APPENDIX A

PARTICIPANTS IN MARSHALL MISSION WHO LATER BECAME
MINISTERS, VICE-MINISTERS, OR ASSISTANT MINISTERS
OF FOREIGN AFFAIRS

Minister:
  Chou En-lai, 1949–58
Vice-Ministers:
  Li K'o-nung, 1949–54
  Wu Hsiu-ch'üan, 1950–55
  Keng Piao, 1960–63
  Huang Chen, 1961–64
  Wang Ping-nan, 1964–?
  Han Nien-lung, 1964–
Assistant Ministers:
  Wang Ping-nan, 1954–55
  Han Nien-lung, 1958–64
  Tung Yueh-ch'ien, 1964–

## APPENDIX B

PARTICIPANTS IN MARSHALL MISSION WHO LATER
BECAME AMBASSADORS (OR HEADS OF MISSIONS)
(Nations italicized indicate that the man in question
was the first head of mission in that nation.)

| | |
|---|---|
| Huang Chen | *Hungary,* 1950–54 |
| | Indonesia, 1954–61 |
| | *France,* 1964– |
| Keng Piao | *Sweden,* 1950–56 |
| | *Denmark,* 1950–55 (Minister—concurrent) |
| | *Finland,* 1951–54 (Minister—concurrent) |
| | Pakistan, 1956–59 |
| | Burma, 1963–66 |
| | Albania, 1969– |
| Feng Hsuan | *Switzerland,* 1950–59 (Minister, 1950–56; Ambassador, 1956–59) |
| Han Nien-lung | *Pakistan,* 1951–56 |
| | Sweden, 1956–58 |
| Wu Hsiu-ch'üan | *Yugoslavia,* 1955–58 |
| Wang Ping-nan | Poland, 1955–64 (concurrently the representative to the Sino-American ambassadorial-level talks in Geneva and then Warsaw, 1955–64) |
| K'o Pai-nien | Rumania, 1954–59 |
| | Denmark, 1963–66 |

| Tung Yueh-ch'ien | Sweden, 1958–64 |
| --- | --- |
| Huang Hua | *Ghana,* 1960–66 |
| | United Arab Republic, 1966–69 |
| Ch'en Shu-liang | Cambodia, 1962–67 |

# APPENDIX C

### PARTICIPANTS IN MARSHALL MISSION WHO LATER BECAME DEPARTMENT OFFICIALS WITHIN THE FOREIGN MINISTRY

| Wu Hsiu-ch'üan | Director, Soviet Union-East European Affairs Department, 1949–52 |
| --- | --- |
| Wang Ping-nan | Director, Staff Office, 1949–55 |
| Tung Yueh-ch'ien | Deputy Director, Staff Office, 1949–52 |
| | Director, International Affairs Department, 1949–58 |
| | Director, Staff Office, 1965– |
| K'o Pai-nien | Director, American-Australasian Department, 1950–54 |
| Ch'en Shu-liang | Assistant Director, Asian Affairs Department, 1952 |
| | Deputy Director, Asian Affairs Department, 1955–59 |
| | Director, 2nd Asian Affairs Department, 1959–62 |
| Huang Hua | Director, West European-African Affairs Department, 1954–56 |
| Fu Hao | Assistant Director, Asian Affairs Department, 1954–55 |
| Han Nien-lung | Director, Staff Office, 1959–60 |
| Chang Lin-sheng | Assistant Director, Information Department, 1961– |
| Li Hui-ch'uan | Deputy Director, Soviet Union-East European Affairs Department, 1956–61 |

# APPENDIX D

### PARTICIPANTS IN MARSHALL MISSION WHO LATER HELD LESS THAN CHIEF OF MISSION POSTS ABROAD

| Ch'ai Chün-wu | Counselor in North Korea, 1950–? |
| --- | --- |
| Fu Hao | Counselor in Mongolia, 1950–? |
| | Counselor in India, 1955–62 |
| Chu Kuang | Military Attaché in North Korea, 1950–? |
| Hao T'ing | Counselor in Sweden, 1950–? |
| | Counselor in Denmark, 1950–? (concurrent) |
| P'eng Hua | Counselor in Switzerland, 1951–57 |
| Ch'en Shu-liang | Counselor in Indonesia, 1952–54 |
| Chiang K'o-ting | Military Attaché in Burma, 1956–61 |
| | Military Attaché in Pakistan, 1964–66 |
| Wang P'ing | Cultural Counselor in East Germany, 1960–? |
| | Counselor in France, 1964– |

Li Hui-ch'uan    Counselor in USSR, 1955–56
    (Participated in Sino-American ambassadorial-level talks in Geneva, 1955, as assistant to Wang Ping-nan)

## APPENDIX E

### Participants in Marshall Mission Who Later Took Part in Quasi-Diplomatic Work (Selected List)

Li Ch'u-li    Director, Staff and Liaison Offices, Overseas Chinese Affairs Commission; member, Board of Directors, Chinese People's Institute of Foreign Affairs.

Chang Hsing-yen    Deputy Director, Foreign Experts Bureau, State Council.

Lei Ying-fu    Adviser to delegations to Geneva Conferences on Indochina (1954) and Laos (1961); adviser to delegation at Warsaw Pact meeting, 1955; member of military delegation to Indonesia, 1959.

Lu Ts'ui    (Mme. Jao Shu-shih) Member, Board of Directors, Chinese People's Institute of Foreign Affairs; director, International Liaison Department, All-China Federation of Democratic Women; member of five delegations to East and West Europe concerning Communist-front organizations for peace and women, 1950–54.

Kuang Jen-nung    Director, Civil Aviation Administration. Has signed civil aviation agreements with several nations; led civil aviation delegations to Indonesia and Pakistan, 1965.

Wu Yun-fu    Member, Chinese People's Association for Cultural Relations with Foreign Countries; member, Commission for Cultural Relations with Foreign Countries; participant in Red Cross and relief delegations to Japan in 1954 and 1961.

Lai Tsu-lieh    Deputy Director, Foreign Experts Bureau, State Council.

Yü Kuang-sheng    Chairman, Chinese Changchun Railway Company (managed jointly with USSR).

Chang Hsiang-shan    Observer at Third All-African People's Conference, Cairo, 1961; council member, Asia-Africa Society of China; member of delegation to Third Afro-Asian People's Solidarity Conference, Tanganyika, 1963; member, China-Japan Friendship Association.

# APPENDIX F

## MILITARY ATTACHÉS
### (by order of first identification)

| | |
|---|---|
| USSR | January, 1950 |
| Korea | January, 1950 |
| Poland | July, 1950 |
| Indonesia | August, 1950 |
| India | September, 1950 |
| Burma | September, 1950 |
| Bulgaria | October, 1950 |
| Sweden | October, 1950 |
| Switzerland | December, 1950 |
| Czechoslovakia | January, 1951 |
| Hungary | January, 1951 |
| Rumania | March, 1952 |
| Denmark | August, 1952 |
| Nepal | July, 1956 |
| Yugoslavia | September, 1956 |
| Vietnam | August, 1957 |
| UAR | August, 1957 |
| Germany | September, 1957 |
| Iraq | August, 1960 |
| Albania | July, 1961 |
| Pakistan | August, 1961 |
| Afghanistan | August, 1961 |
| Cuba | August, 1962 |
| Algeria | February, 1963 |
| Laos | August, 1963 |
| Syria | August, 1963 |
| France | July, 1965 |

ELLIS JOFFE

# The Chinese Army Under Lin Piao: Prelude to Political Intervention

"Political power," Mao Tse-tung observed in a much-quoted statement, "grows out of the barrel of the gun. Our principle is that the Party commands the gun and the gun shall never be allowed to command the Party." [1] The cataclysmic events which effectively convulsed China under the name of the Great Proletarian Cultural Revolution [2] have dramatically demonstrated the correctness of the first part of Mao's statement; but they have also cast serious doubt on the validity of the second part.

Political power gravitated to the People's Liberation Army (PLA) as a result of the role which it was called upon to play in the Cultural Revolution. From the start of this great upheaval Mao Tse-tung turned to the military leadership for support in his attempt to push through his policies and to purge his opponents in the Party. Subsequently, the PLA was pulled more and more deeply into the political maelstrom until it emerged as the central force in China's power structure, especially in the provinces.

The growth of the army's power, however, has been accompanied by an erosion of political control over it. The very events which cast the PLA into the political arena and which catapulted it to a position of power also seriously undermined the authority of the Party, as represented by Mao and his supporters, over the military. While the PLA has remained basically committed to the concept of political

---

[1] Mao Tse-tung, *Selected Military Writings* (Peking: Foreign Languages Press, 1963), p. 272.

[2] For my general interpretation of these events, see *Collier's Year Book, 1967, 1968, 1969* (New York: Crowell-Collier, 1968, 1969, 1970).

supremacy over the military and to the desire for national unity, in practice local commanders have frequently taken advantage of their new power to contradict the principle that "the Party commands the gun."

The events of the past few years, in short, have wrought momentous changes both in the role of the army and in its relations with the Party.[3] These changes started with Mao's reliance on the military leadership in his power struggle with top leaders in the Party which began to surface toward the end of 1965, and, more specifically, with the army's active intervention in January, 1967, in the nationwide conflict which erupted with the launching of the Cultural Revolution. The roots of these changes, however, go back several years, when developments in the Party as well as in the PLA set the stage for such an intervention. These developments form an essential background to an understanding of the army's involvement in politics during the Cultural Revolution. A preliminary examination of this background is the purpose of this article.

## FROM THE PARTY TO THE PLA

Although many of the complex moves and maneuvers surrounding the PLA's intervention in politics have yet to be disentangled, this much can be stated with certainty: In this era of military coups and takeovers, the Chinese army arrived at a position of political power by a different route. In the first place, the PLA did not intervene in politics against the wish of the political leadership, but rather was brought into the political arena by this leadership, albeit with unforeseen consequences. Second, the PLA did not carry out a coup, but rather moved into politics gradually in the course of a complicated process, which was determined by developments outside the army at least as much as by its own initiative. The most decisive and dramatic of these developments was Mao's growing distrust of the Party as the instrument for implementing his revolutionary policies. As this distrust deepened, Mao turned away from the Party and began to rely more and more on the army.

[3] Although I am well aware that the Chinese army was never monolithic, for the purpose of this analysis, the Party and the PLA will be treated as distinct hierarchies. It should be noted, however, that there were both intra-PLA tensions and probably a considerable convergence of views between certain segments of the army and the Party (for example, between the professional officers and the more moderate Party leaders). Nonetheless, prior to the collapse of the unity of the Party leadership these were undercurrents in an over-all pattern within which it is possible to speak of a Party-PLA dichotomy.

The immediate roots of Mao's disaffection from the Party can be traced back to the aftermath of the Great Leap Forward. Conceived mainly by Mao,[4] this euphoric effort in rapid development through mass mobilization resulted, as is well known, in catastrophic consequences. Confronted with a dangerous economic crisis and widespread demoralization, the leadership decided on a radical shift of course, which was sanctioned by the Ninth Plenum of the Central Committee in January, 1961.[5] This shift was most pronounced in the economic field, but it encompassed virtually every sphere of Chinese life.[6] As the Maoist interpretation of this period put it in retrospect:

From 1960 through 1962, due to natural calamities and the sabotage of the Soviet revisionists, China encountered temporary economic difficulties. Our great leader Chairman Mao adopted a series of effective measures to lead the whole Party and the people of the whole country to fight against natural calamities and the class enemies.[7]

The hallmark of these "effective measures" was that they were governed primarily by pragmatic and materialistic considerations rather than by politics and ideology.

Propelled by these considerations, Chinese society began to move in a direction which, in terms of the goals and techniques of the Great Leap Forward, amounted to nothing short of a great retreat. Arching over the various concrete manifestations of this retreat was the dominant fact that it was squarely opposed to the very core of Mao's thought: his belief that the subjective "human element"—human will as fashioned by the human spirit—is more important than objective material elements in determining the outcome of the revolutionary struggle, be it the struggle against opposing forces or against the forces of nature. Inseparably connected with this belief is the notion that the virtually boundless revolutionary potentialities inherent in the "human element" can be released and realized only if the masses are subjected to an ongoing spiritual transformation, which will inculcate them with the Maoist revolutionary ethic. Since political and ideological factors

[4] See, for example, "Mao Tse-tung's Speech at the 8th Plenary Session of the CCP 8th Central Committee," *The Case of P'eng Teh-huai, 1959–1968* (Hong Kong: Union Research Institute, 1968), p. 25.

[5] "Communique of the Ninth Plenary Session of the Eighth Central Committee of the Communist Party of China," *Peking Review*, No. 4 (January 27, 1961), 5–9.

[6] See, for example, Franz Schurmann, "China's 'New Economic Policy'—Transition or Beginning," *CQ*, No. 17 (January–March, 1964), pp. 65–91.

[7] *Outline of the Struggle Between the Two Lines From the Eve of the Founding of the People's Republic of China Through the 11th Plenum of the 8th CCP Committee,* undated pamphlet reproduced from *CFJP*, in *CB*, No. 884 (July 18, 1967), p. 18.

are crucial in effecting such a transformation, they should take precedence over all other considerations. During the period of retreat, however, it was precisely nonpolitical considerations which in general were given precedence.

There can be little doubt that Mao viewed these developments with deep disdain. For his overriding, almost mystical, faith in the "human element" and in the supreme importance of putting "politics in command," was not noticeably diminished by the failure of the Great Leap Forward. Mao, in fact, evidently did not view the Great Leap as a failure. Although he admitted that some mistakes were made,[8] he obviously remained convinced that only by applying the maxims and methods that underlaid it, could China develop without compromising its revolutionary character. From his vantage point, therefore, the post-Great Leap Forward relaxation represented a dire threat to the Chinese revolution—a threat underscored by his growing preoccupation with the deteriorating Sino-Soviet relations, and by his belief that the Soviet Union had already succumbed to "revisionism" and had betrayed the revolution. As the Maoists put it during the Cultural Revolution:

If things had developed according to . . . [the] counterrevolutionary revisionist line, drastic class differentiation would have occurred in the countryside; new bourgeois elements would have appeared in great numbers in the cities; the masses of workers and poor and lower-middle peasants would have had a second dose of suffering and sunk back into the miserable life of slaves and beasts of burden; our country's socialist economic base would have been utterly destroyed; a complete change would have taken place in the nature of our proletarian state power and history would have been turned back on to the old road leading to a semi-colonial, semi-feudal society.[9]

Nevertheless, for some two years after the Great Leap, Mao apparently acquiesced in the retreat. This, however, must be attributed to one of two reasons (or a combination of both): either Mao realized the need for a relaxation, or this relaxation was forced upon him by his colleagues. Be that as it may, it is clear that Mao accepted the retrenchment grudgingly and only as a tactical measure. And indeed, as soon as it became apparent that China had weathered the worst features of the crisis,[10] Mao decided to put an end to the retreat and to

[8] See Mao's speech to the Tenth Plenum of the Central Committee which was published in a Red Guard wall poster. *Mainichi* (Tokyo: March 9, 1957).

[9] *Along the Socialist or the Capitalist Road?* (Peking: Foreign Languages Press, 1968), pp. 36–37.

[10] This point was made by Mao in his speech to the Tenth Plenum. See Note 8.

revitalize the Chinese revolution. At a conference of the Central Committee in August, 1962, and at its Tenth Plenum in September, Mao pressed for a reversal of the post-Great Leap trend:

Socialist society covers a fairly long historical period. In the historical period of socialism, there are still classes, class contradictions and class struggle, there is the struggle between the socialist road and the capitalist road, and there is the danger of capitalist restoration. We must recognize the protracted and complex nature of this struggle. We must heighten our vigilance. We must conduct socialist education. . . . Otherwise a socialist country like ours will turn its opposite and degenerate, and a capitalist restoration will take place. . . .[11]

Thus, Mao issued his now-famous clarion call: "Never forget class struggle."

This, however, was precisely what some of his top colleagues wanted to do. To them, the Great Leap was a traumatic and sobering experience, one from which they obviously emerged with new perspectives. Whether or not they had fully supported Mao's plan to launch the Great Leap, there can be little doubt that its collapse convinced them of the futility of Mao's extreme methods for modernizing China. As Liu Shao-ch'i reportedly said at a Central Committee conference in January, 1962:

How did such a difficult situation appear? Why was it that production of food, cloth, and consumer goods was not increased but decreased? What is the reason? One is natural disasters. . . . The other is that since 1958 we have had shortcomings and mistakes in our work. I went to a place in Hunan. There the peasants said that 30 percent of the difficulties were brought about by natural calamities while 70 percent were caused by man-made factors. This you have to admit. . . .[12]

Not only were these leaders disillusioned with Mao's methods, but the success of the more moderate post-Great Leap policies in pulling China out of the crisis must have strengthened their determination not to reverse these policies, even if they ran counter to Mao's revolutionary principles. "Any cat that can catch mice is a good cat," Teng Hsiao-p'ing is supposed to have said, "be it white or black."[13] And

[11] "Lin Piao's Report to the Ninth National Congress of the Communist Party of China," April 1, 1969, *Peking Review,* Special Issue (April 28, 1969), p. 15.

[12] *Selected Edition on Liu Shao-ch'i's Counter-Revolutionary Crimes,* in *SCMM,* No. 652 (April 28, 1969), p. 25. This is a Red Guard pamphlet that was published in April, 1967. Without going into the question of the authenticity of the precise wording, there is no reason to doubt that the general thrust of these remarks was in accord with Liu's views.

[13] This phrase has been attributed numerous times to Teng. See, for example, *Thirty-three "Leading Counterrevolutionary Revisionists,"* in *CB,* No. 874 (March 17, 1969), p. 6. This is a Red Guard pamphlet published in March, 1968.

here were sown the seeds which were to bear such bitter fruit in the Cultural Revolution. From this point on, the leadership became increasingly and irreparably divided over fundamental policy differences, which blended into a power struggle and at last exploded in the Cultural Revolution.

At the heart of these differences lay no less than the question of the future of the Chinese revolution. Without attempting to go into specific issues and the shades of opinion which separated individual leaders over these issues, in retrospect it is clear that following the Tenth Plenum the leadership tended to polarize into two main groups. And in the swirl of crosscurrents there was a sharp dividing line. On one side of this line stood Mao and his supporters, demanding, with mounting urgency, a return to Mao's revolutionary principles as the sole safeguard against the "revisionist" pitfalls and pressures of the post-revolutionary era. Ranged against them were some of Mao's top colleagues, who maintained that Mao's revolutionary principles were no longer fully applicable to a modernizing society, and who were prepared to depart from these principles in the direction of economic rationality, technical specialization, bureaucratic routinization, and administrative institutionalization.[14]

The most outspoken of the opposition leaders was the former Minister of Defense, P'eng Teh-huai, who denounced the Great Leap on the eve of, and during, the critical Lushan Plenum of the Central Committee in July–August, 1959.[15] But P'eng went further than that; he violated Party discipline by lining up backstage support for his views in opposition to the Party leadership and, what was probably more serious, by maintaining some sort of contact with the Soviets.[16] Other top Party leaders did not support P'eng at Lushan, but this seemed to be because he had blatantly contravened the rules of the political game and not because they disagreed with the substance of his opinions. As Liu Shao-ch'i reportedly said in January, 1962:

Some comrades have also made speeches which more or less resemble those made by P'eng Teh-huai. For example, the loss involved in the large-scale refining of iron and steel was greater than the gain; the mess halls were no good; the free

[14] This, of course, is clear from numerous articles and pamphlets, both official and nonofficial, that were published during the Cultural Revolution and that denounced Mao's opponents.

[15] For a collection of P'eng's statements, see *CB*, No. 851 (April 26, 1958), and *The Case of P'eng Teh-huai*. See also, David A. Charles, "The Dismissal of Marshal P'eng Teh-huai," *CQ*, No. 8 (October–December, 1961), pp. 63–76.

[16] See, for example, *The Case of P'eng Teh-huai*, pp. 36, 179–80.

supply system was bad; the people's communes were premature, etc. However, these comrades are different from P'eng Teh-huai in that, uttering these words, they had not organized an anti-Party clique or wanted to usurp the Party.[17]

One striking but subtle measure of the attitudes prevailing at the top level of the Party hierarchy during this period was the devastating criticism directed at Mao and his policies by leading Peking intellectuals, especially Wu Han and Teng T'o. Employing the time-honored device of historical allegories and allusions, these intellectuals condemned the dismissal of P'eng Teh-huai and launched scathing personal attacks on Mao and his programs.[18] Such blasphemy cannot be attributed to the freer intellectual atmosphere of 1960–62, since the bounds of this relative liberalization certainly did not extend to such attacks on the Chairman's programs, let alone on the Chairman himself.[19] Since the writings of these intellectuals could hardly have escaped the attention of top Party leaders,[20] their boldness can only be explained by the supposition that they knew or assumed that their views were shared by powerful personalities in the Party on whom they could rely for protection. The facts that they were able to carry on their attacks in such a sustained manner and that they did not have to pay for them until Mao launched his all-out onslaught on the Party, appear to bear out this supposition.

Policy differences alone, however, cannot explain why Mao became so disaffected from the Party that he found it necessary to turn away from it and then to assault it with such unbridled fury. Such differences, after all, are nothing new to the Chinese leadership. In fact, it can be safely assumed that every major decision of the regime was accompanied by differences of opinion and by heated debates within the ruling group.[21] Nevertheless, it seems that once a major decision was reached, the leadership closed ranks behind Mao and continued to maintain its remarkable cohesion. Leaders who opposed the de-

[17] *Selected Edition,* p. 30.

[18] See, for example, the collection of articles in *The Great Socialist Cultural Revolution in China* (Peking: Foreign Languages Press, 1966) II. See also Merle Goldman, "The Unique 'Blooming and Contending' of 1961–1962," *CQ,* No. 37 (January–March, 1969), pp. 54–83.

[19] The memory of the Hundred Flowers affair alone would certainly have been enough to remind the intellectuals of the limits of criticism.

[20] Mao himself clearly referred to these writings in his speech to the Tenth Plenum. See "Lin Piao's Report," p. 16.

[21] See, for example, Franz Schurmann, *Ideology and Organization in Communist China* (Berkeley and Los Angeles: University of Cailfornia Press, 1966), pp. 55–56. Evidence of conflicts within the top ruling group has, of course, come forth in abundance during the Cultural Revolution.

cision either went along with it [22] or dropped out of the ruling group while this decision governed national policy; [23] in the rare cases that a leader overstepped the bounds of legitimate disagreement and opposition, he was removed.[24] The over-all unity of the ruling, however, was preserved.

Why then did this unity begin to disintegrate after the Tenth Plenum with such gathering force that it soon lay shattered in the shambles of the Cultural Revolution? The main reason can only be this: During this period the disputes among China's rulers became so bound up with questions of power that they could not be resolved without a colossal struggle at the top of the political pyramid. And questions of power entered the picture because Mao's opponents at the highest level of the Party, and almost the entire Party bureaucracy, not only disagreed with Mao's views, but were able and willing to resist their implementation. Policy differences, in short, were transformed into organizational resistance.

This resistance must have become apparent to Mao soon after he issued his call to revive the revolutionary momentum of Chinese society. In order to put this call into effect, Mao and his supporters launched a wide-ranging and many-faceted "socialist education" movement, which Mao viewed as "a struggle that calls for the re-education of man . . . a struggle for reorganizing the revolutionary class armies for a confrontation with the forces of feudalism and capitalism which are now feverishly attacking us." [25] This movement encompassed several related campaigns: the campaign to cultivate "revolutionary successors," [26] the effort to eliminate "spontaneous tendencies to capitalism" in the countryside,[27] the campaign to rectify the Party organization (the "four clean-ups" [28]) and to purify it of unorthodox ideological tendencies (the campaign against Yang Hsien-chen [29]), and

22 Chou En-lai seems to be a good example of this type.
23 Ch'en Yun would appear to fall into this category.
24 P'eng Teh-huai, of course, is the most notable example.
25 "Draft Resolution of the Central Committee of the Chinese Communist Party on Some Problems in Current Rural Work (The First Ten Points)," in Richard Baum and Frederick J. Teiwes, *Ssu-ch'ing: The Socialist Education Movement of 1962–1966* (Berkeley: Center for Chinese Studies, University of California, 1968), p. 70.
26 See, for example, "Training Millions of Successors to Proletarian Revolution," *Peking Review,* No. 32 (August 7, 1964), pp. 12–15.
27 See, for example, Philip Bridgham, "Mao's 'Cultural Revolution': Origin and Development," *CQ,* No. 29 (January–March, 1967), pp. 10–11.
28 Baum and Teiwes, *Ssu-ch'ing.*
29 See, for example, Donald J. Munro, "The Yang Hsien-chen Affair," *CQ,* No. 22 (April–June, 1965), pp. 75–82.

the crackdown in literature and the arts.[30] Central to these and other campaigns was the attempt to re-establish Mao's authority in every sphere through a renewed emphasis on the study and implementation of his revolutionary principles.

This, however, was exactly what the Party did not do. Although the various "socialist education" campaigns differed widely in scope and intensity, it seems clear in retrospect that from Mao's viewpoint they failed, on the whole, to achieve their purpose. For instead of mushrooming into important mass movements they tended either to fizzle out unceremoniously or to flicker on as low-keyed and ritualistic affairs.[31] And the main reason was that Mao's demands were resisted by the very organization which was supposed to take the lead in putting them into effect—the Party apparatus.

This resistance was subtle and indirect. Instead of opposing Mao openly, the moderate leaders resorted to the tactic of "waving red flags to oppose red flags"; they complied in theory but resisted in practice.[32] This resistance was not necessarily coordinated, but whether it took the form of ignoring, watering down, distorting, or sabotaging Mao's directives, the result was the same: in his efforts to return China to a revolutionary course Mao found himself balked and blocked by the Party bureaucracy.[33] As Mao increased the pressure, the Party bureaucracy increased its resistance.

This resistance had at least two major organizational sources, which shed much light on why Mao finally had to assault the Party from the outside. The first one lay in the fact that during these years top Party leaders managed to carve out and to consolidate institutional and relatively autonomous bases of power within the Party hierarchy, and within these bases they seem to have had almost a free hand. In part, the growth of such bases, or "independent kingdoms," has been the natural result of inexorable pressures toward the separation of functions and the establishment of entrenched hierarchies, or "systems," within the giant Party organization.[34] These pressures were reinforced as a result of a shift in the power relations which occurred at the top

30 See, for example, "For a More Militant Literature and Art; National Conference of Writers and Artists," *Peking Review*, No. 22 (May 31, 1963), pp. 7–9.

31 See, for example, Charles Neuhauser, "The Chinese Communist Party in the 1960's: Prelude to the Cultural Revolution," *CQ*, No. 32 (October–December, 1967), pp. 19–23.

32 See, for example, *Outline of the Struggle*, pp. 23–24.

33 Cf. Neuhauser, "The Chinese Communist Party."

34 See, for example, A. Doak Barnett, *Cadres, Bureaucracy, and Political Power in Communist China* (New York: Columbia University Press, 1967), pp. 5–6.

level of leadership during the Great Leap Forward. Symbolized by Mao's resignation as chairman of the republic in favor of Liu Shao-ch'i in December, 1958, the concrete consequence of this shift was that Mao relinquished the daily direction of Party affairs and turned it over to Liu and Teng Hsiao-p'ing.[35] Whether Mao did this, as he later claimed, in order to strengthen the authority of his successors, as well as to devote himself to security and Sino-Soviet affairs,[36] or whether he was forced to dilute his power as a result of the Great Leap debacle, the effect was the same: Liu, Teng, and other leaders solidified their "independent kingdoms" and were able to thwart Mao's efforts to impose his demands.[37] Viewed from this angle, the entire period after the Tenth Plenum emerges as an attempt by Mao to reassert personal and direct control over the centers of power in the Party.

The second reason for the Party's recalcitrance can be attributed to the growing rigidity of the bureaucracy and its loss of revolutionary *élan*. In part, this stemmed from normal tendencies toward bureaucratic routinization and from a hardening of the revolutionary arteries in the Party organism. Until the Great Leap, the leadership sought, with a large measure of success, to combat these tendencies with a variety of internal rectification campaigns that were designed to keep the Party apparatus in a state of perpetual movement and tension. During the post-Great Leap Forward relaxation, however, such campaigns were ineffective in stemming the trend toward the ossification of the Party apparatus.[38] This trend was sharply intensified by the demoralization which spread among Party cadres as a result of the failure of the Great Leap.[39] The cadres, who had enthusiastically carried out the leadership's policies, were saddled with much of the blame when these policies collapsed, and after the Great Leap they were ordered to soften their attitude toward the population. When Mao again called for a step-up of political and ideological pressures, the Party bureaucracy was in no mood to comply.[40] And it was able to withstand Mao's demands because, as has been observed, some of

[35] See Mao's statement reportedly made at an Operations Conference of the Party center in October, 1966, and published in a Red Guard poster. *Yomiuri* (Tokyo, January 7, 1967).

[36] *Ibid.*

[37] *Ibid.*

[38] See, for example, Chalmers A. Johnson, "China: The Cultural Revolution in Structural Perspective," *Asian Survey,* VIII (January, 1968), 3–5.

[39] Cf. Neuhauser, "The Chinese Communist Party," pp. 7–9.

[40] See, for example, James MacDonald, "The Performance of the Cadres," in Jack Gray (ed.), *Modern China's Search For a Political Form* (London: Oxford University Press, 1969), pp. 268–98.

the top leaders in the Party were in no mood to comply either. As this became apparent to Mao, he obviously decided that he would have to shake up the Party apparatus before he could proceed with his revolutionary programs.

In sum, following the Tenth Plenum, the efforts of Mao and his supporters to stop China's post-Great Leap Forward drift toward "revisionism" and to refurbish its sagging revolutionary spirit, ran into effective opposition which was centered in the Party bureaucracy and which reached into its uppermost levels. As the depth and dimensions of this opposition became apparent to Mao, he began to turn more and more to the army, and to view it as the main organizational base for the implementation of his revolutionary policies.

Before we try to examine what role the PLA played in these events, it is necessary to ask: why did Mao turn to the army in the first place?

## WHY THE ARMY?

The fact that Mao turned to the army when he encountered resistance in the Party is not surprising, for in doing so he did not, after all, turn to an alien organization, but to one which he himself had built up, and on which he had relied, as much as on the Party, in waging the struggle which brought him to power. These circumstances, as is well known, forged a special and close relationship between Mao and the army, as well as between the Party and the army. To be sure, Mao has always unequivocally insisted on the supremacy of the Party over the army and has regarded the Party as the sole leader of the Chinese revolution. Nevertheless, it was not such a drastic step for him to fall back upon the PLA once he realized that the Party was no longer fulfilling its revolutionary role.

What is surprising, however, in the light of the post-1949 developments in the PLA, is that Mao found the army to be worthy of his reliance. For only several years earlier the PLA had emerged as the main stronghold of opposition to Mao's ideas and had been shot through with the very defects which Mao now began to discern in the Party. How then did the PLA manage to overcome these defects and to turn itself into a reliable revolutionary instrument? The answer lies in the efforts exerted by the army high command under the leadership of Lin Piao.

When Lin Piao assumed command of the PLA in September, 1959, the military establishment had been through several turbulent years of controversy and conflict between the technically oriented, Soviet-influenced professional officer corps and the politically oriented Party leadership. Central to this conflict was the basic question of political and professional priorities: to what extent were the revolutionary-egalitarian principles and practices that were developed by the Chinese Communists during their struggle for power relevant to the modernized army? This conflict ranged over several interrelated issues. How applicable was the "man-over-weapons" doctrine to modern warfare and the modern army, and how far should it dominate the strategy and organization of the PLA? Should the guerrilla traditions of "democracy" and the "mass line" be perpetuated at the expense of strict formal discipline and hierarchy? How should the relations between the garrison army and the population be regulated? To what extent should the army be employed for nonmilitary purposes? Of what value is the mass militia in the era of nuclear warfare? To what degree should the PLA follow the example of the professional Soviet army? [41]

Differences over these questions emerged in the mid-1950's and deepened dramatically during the next few years. As the professional officers began to denounce or to discard Maoist principles and practices, the Party leadership made repeated efforts to crack down on them. However, the very extremity of these efforts, especially during the Great Leap Forward, only hardened the resistance of the officer corps, which was led by Minister of Defense P'eng Teh-huai. By 1959, tension between the Party and the PLA reached a breaking point.[42]

This tension was brought to a head by the opposition of P'eng to the Great Leap Forward and to the growing rift with the Soviet Union. This opposition was rooted in P'eng's fear that a break with the Soviets would seriously harm China's army and nuclear program as well as her strategic posture.[43] For their multi-faceted opposition to the Maoist line, P'eng and his supporters were removed from their posts. Lin Piao was appointed minister of defense and Lo Jui-ch'ing became chief-of-staff.

The task facing the new high command was far from easy. As a result of the conflict, relations between the Party and the PLA had deteriorated drastically. The officer corps was dissatisfied and de-

---

[41] For details, see Ellis Joffe, *Party and Army: Professionalism and Political Control in the Chinese Officer Corps, 1949–1964* (Cambridge, Mass.: East Asian Research Center, Harvard University, 1965), chap. ii. See also John Gittings, *The Role of the Chinese Army* (London: Oxford University Press, 1967), chap. viii.

[42] *Ibid.*

[43] See Charles, "The Dismissal." See also Gittings, *Role of the Chinese Army,* chap. xi.

moralized. Professional viewpoints and practices which were unpalatable to the Maoist leadership were widespread. Political and ideological compaigns were largely ineffective. And Party organizations in the armed forces—the main instrument for ensuring political control and leadership—had fallen into a state of dangerous disarray.[44]

Vast and fast remedial action was required to purify the PLA, to raise its morale and prestige, and to repair its relations with the Party. This Lin managed to achieve with singular success, and in this success lies the major key to the political role which both he and the PLA were to play on the Chinese scene from the early 1960's onward.

This does not necessarily mean, as has been suggested, that Lin launched his efforts in the PLA with cynical and ulterior motives in mind, namely, to ingratiate himself with Mao in order to lay the groundwork for the army's intervention in politics and for his rise to political power. While motives, of course, cannot be determined with any certainty—except perhaps for the assumption that every political leader is inexorably driven by a desire to attain new heights of power —there is no evidence to support this thesis. For one thing, when Lin set his programs in the PLA in motion there was as yet no indication that Mao would bypass the Party, let alone take more drastic steps against it; and since this is what caused him to turn to the army, Lin could not anticipate this development and plan for it. Second, there was an urgent internal PLA reason for strengthening political control and indoctrination: the dangerous demoralization which spread among the troops as a result of the post-Great Leap economic crisis. Third, the seriousness of this demoralization was enhanced by the possibility, which was very real at the height of the economic crisis, that troops would have to be used to put down outbreaks of violence against the regime. Last and most important, there is no ground for doubting that up to a point Lin is a firm believer in Mao's military theories, and that he considered the restrained implementation of these theories as the best way to ensure the political reliability and combat effectiveness of the army. While Lin was obviously prepared to reap the rewards of his success, this does not mean that the efforts which brought him this success were concocted as part of a strategy for achieving political power.

Nor does it mean, as has also been suggested, that Mao and Lin deliberately groomed the army for its subsequent political role as part of a grand design, or that they used it as a testing ground for political

[44] For details, see Joffe, *Party and Army,* chap. ii and pp. 137–39.

and organizational techniques which were later applied to the population at large. Here too, of course, we are in the murky realm of motives, but there seem to be strong grounds for doubting the theory that Mao operated on the basis of a preconceived plan which called for the politization of the PLA in 1960 because he already foresaw its political use several years later. To be sure, the sharp deterioration in Mao's relations with some of the top Party leaders following the collapse of the Great Leap doubtless added an important impetus to his effort to purify the PLA of its professional tendencies in order to ensure its loyalty, especially in view of the ominous fact that the Lushan opposition was led by the army chiefs.

There is no convincing evidence, however, to show that at this stage Mao and his supporters already contemplated the employment of the army in politics, let alone its use as a power base in a struggle with the Party. That this was what eventually happened does not mean that it was predetermined by the Maoists. On the contrary, as has been observed, in the post-Great Leap period, and especially after the Tenth Plenum, the Maoists made every effort to restore the Party's revolutionary qualities in order to make it capable of leading the drive against "revisionism." "The Central Committee believes," it was said in a May, 1963, document which laid down the line for the socialist education movement and which was drafted under Mao's direction, "that among our cadres and Party members efforts should be made through socialist education to rectify the standpoint of the proletariat, overcome the mistakes that cause betrayal of the proletarian standpoint so that our cadres and Party members can correctly provide the leadership for the great majority of the masses in carrying on class struggle between capitalism and socialism." [45] It was only when these efforts began to founder that Mao started to turn to the army; and it was only when they failed completely that he set upon the Party. This, however, was a process which unfolded as opposition to Mao within the Party began to surface in response to his pressures, and on balance it appears that no one, including Mao, had predicted where this process would lead. As for the notion that the PLA was consciously used as a testing ground, this implies that new techniques were tested. Such, however, was not the case. The techniques employed by Lin in the army did not differ in principle from those which the Party had developed during the revolutionary period. What Lin managed to do—

45 Baum and Teiwes, *Ssu-ch'ing*, p. 61.

and what the Party did not—was to revive these techniques and to make sure that they were applied in practice.[46]

When he assumed command, Lin indicated what the main thrust of his efforts would be. He said:

Henceforth, it will still be a fundamental task in the building of our army to strengthen theoretical education in Marxism-Leninism, to strengthen education in socialism and the general line of the Party and to link this closely with the practice of the contemporary revolutionary struggle . . . so as continuously to eliminate from people's minds the vestiges of bourgeois and petty-bourgeois ideology and enhance their socialist consciousness.[47]

The long-range guidelines for the implementation of this "fundamental task" were set down by an enlarged meeting of the Military Affairs Committee, an organ which acquired new power and importance under Lin at the expense of the more professionally oriented Ministry of Defense. This meeting, which lasted from September 14 to October 20, 1960, and which was described as "a new milestone in the progress of our Army," adopted a lengthy and immensely important resolution on "Strengthening Political and Ideological Work in the Army," which called for a concerted consolidation and extension of political control and ideological indoctrination in the armed forces, and which gave detailed instructions for the implementation of its provisions.[48]

The theoretical underpinning for this resolution was enunciated by Lin at this meeting in his famous principle of the "four firsts"—the first and most important of the many slogans which marked the political drives under his leadership, and one which several years later was to have universal applicability in China. This formula postulated that in the relationship between man and weapons, man is primary; in the relationship between political work and other types of work, political work is primary; in the relationship between ideological and routine work, ideological work is primary; and in the relationship between "book learning" and "practical thought," "practical thought" is primary.[49]

With this principle pointing the way, the leadership launched a

[46] Cf. Neuhauser, "The Chinese Communist Party," p. 24.

[47] Lin Piao, *March Ahead Under the Red Flag of the Party's General Line and Mao Tse-tung's Military Thinking* (Peking: Foreign Languages Press, 1959), p. 10.

[48] J. Chester Cheng (ed.), *The Politics of the Chinese Red Army: A Translation of the Bulletin of Activities of the People's Liberation Army* (Standford, Calif.: Hoover Institution, 1966), pp. 66–94.

[49] *Ibid.*, pp. 66–68.

steady stream of parallel and overlapping political and ideological drives in the armed forces. What distinguished these drives from earlier efforts was the leadership's obvious desire to ensure that its directives would be implemented at the basic levels in order to prevent what had happened under the previous high command—the substitution of motion for movement, and of ritualistic compliance for meaningful execution. In retrospect it is clear that this is also precisely what distinguished the activities in the PLA from those in the Party and other organizations during this period.

Before the long-range political campaigns could move into full swing, the high command had to revive and to rebuild the political control apparatus, especially at the grass roots, which had become almost paralyzed under the previous leadership. This task received first priority. Between July, 1960, and February, 1961, Lin completed a rectification campaign of Party organizations in the armed forces, in the course of which reportedly over 80 per cent of the Party organizations at the basic level were reorganized. More important, this campaign was paralleled by a drive to strengthen the Party's presence in the PLA by replenishing its ranks and by establishing Party organizations where none had existed. During 1960, 229,000 new Party members were reportedly recruited in the armed forces, and by early 1961 all the companies had established Party committees.[50]

At the same time, the high command took steps to crack down on the most pronounced manifestations of professionalism among the officers. The principle of collective leadership by Party committees, as opposed to individual leadership by military commanders, was reasserted. A rectification campaign of officers was carried out in the first half of 1961. Party organizations at all levels of the armed forces were directed to strengthen their supervision over the officers. The importance of the political quality and the class background of officers was stressed, and ideological indoctrination in the officer corps was emphasized. The need for practicing "democracy" and for abiding by the "mass line" was reaffirmed. And new military manuals were issued in a major attempt to expurgate Chinese military doctrine of Soviet influence in order to restore the Maoist way of doing things.[51]

After taking these measures, the leadership seems to have left the higher-ranking officers largely alone, and to have directed its efforts to the basic company level of the armed forces. This level remained

50 For details, see Joffe, *Party and Army,* p. 139.
51 For documentation, see *ibid.,* pp. 140, 141–42.

the focus of its attention in the following years, and it is here, first and foremost, that it achieved its success. Several reasons accounted for this concentration on the company. First, this was the level that had been most neglected during the heyday of modernization, and it was here that the paralysis of Party organizations and operations in the PLA was most acute. Second, with the reassertion of Maoist doctrine that was grounded in the "man-over-weapons" concept, emphasis shifted back to the political conditioning of the individual soldier. Third, this emphasis was buttressed by Mao's preoccupation with the problem of "revolutionary successors," and by the fact that the army probably provided the best setting for training such successors. Last, this approach undoubtedly enabled the military leadership to raise the political standards of the troops without arousing substantial opposition among the professional officers.

Supervised by the General Political Department and monitored by almost annual "all-army political work conferences," this multifaceted effort to raise political standards dominated the activities of the PLA during the early 1960's. It was marked by a variety of campaigns, and by the emergence of many model soldiers and units for emulation: the continuous campaign to study and apply Mao's works; [52] the "four-good company" campaign, which was symbolized by the "Good Eighth Company of Nanking Road," the "Tough-Bone Sixth Company," and other outstanding units; [53] the "management and education" campaign; [54] the "five-good soldier" campaign, which was exemplified by such model heroes as Lei Feng, Wang Chieh, and others; [55] the "three-eight work style" movement; [56] the education in

[52] See, for example, "Spur the Fighters of the Whole Army to Greater Efforts in the Study of the Works of Chairman Mao," *CKCNP*, November 17, 1961, in *SCMP*, No. 2631 (December 4, 1961), p. 3.

[53] See, for example, Hsiao Hua, "Basic Experiences of the Past Two Years Concerning the Creation of Four-Good Companies in the Army," *JMJP*, April 1, 1963, in *SCMP*, No. 2971 (May 3, 1963), pp. 1-16. " 'Good Eighth Company on Nanking Road' Lives in Hardship and Frugality, Will Preserve Their Honorable Traditions Forever,"*JMJP*, February 1, 1962, in *SCMP*, No. 2682 (February 20, 1962), pp. 14-15. "The Tough-Bone Sixth Company," *JMJP*, August 14, 1963, in *SCMP*, No. 3057 (September 11, 1963). pp. 1-7.

[54] See, for example, *CB*, No. 732 (May 12, 1964), p. 40.

[55] See, for example, "General Political Department Announces New Conditions For Five-Good Fighters," *Chieh-fang Chün-pao* (Liberation Army Daily) (hereafter *CFCP*), editorial, *CKCN*, November 30, 1961, in *SCMP*, No. 2635 (December 10, 1961), pp. 1-2. "Respond to Chairman Mao's Call to Learn Resolutely from Comrade Lei Feng," *CKCN*, editorial, NCNA Peking, March 5, 1963. "Be Good and Do Good by Learning from Good People and Good Deeds; Look to Wang Chieh for Inspiration," *CFCP*, editorial, November 23, 1965; Peking Radio Domestic Service, November 23, 1965. Cf. Gittings, *Role of the Chinese Army*, pp, 246-54.

[56] See, for example, "PLA Practices 'Three-Eight' Work Style," NCNA, Peking, July 20, 1960, in *SCMP*, No. 2309 (August 3, 1960), p. 2.

revolutionary traditions and the study of revolutionary reminiscences; [57] the movement to "love the soldiers and respect the cadres"; [58] the efforts to foster "revolutionary successors"; [59] and so on. What the leadership tried to do, in essence, was to sustain interest in campaigns that were directed toward the same objective by devising different slogans and approaches which, as in advertising campaigns, seemed to be aimed at popularizing one product by presenting it under new catchwords and by periodic repackaging.

These campaigns found formal expression in three sets of regulations which summed up the various activities and set up guideposts for the future. The "Regulations Governing PLA Management and Education Work at the Company Level," [60] which were promulgated in mid-1961, dealt with methods of leadership and intrarank relations, and stressed the importance of unity and harmony between officers and men. The "Four Sets of Regulations on Political Work in Company-Level Units of the PLA," [61] which were issued in the autumn of 1961, dealt with the role of political commissars, Party branch committees, Youth League branches, and Revolutionary Servicemen's Committees, and amounted to an across-the-board strengthening of political control and education in the companies. But the most cogent and comprehensive reaffirmation of Maoist military principles and practices came in early 1963 with the publication of the "Regulations Governing PLA Political Work," [62] which dealt with doctrine, organization, political work, and leadership methods. As the first such regulations to be issued since the beginning of military modernization,[63] they represented the high point of the political efforts under Lin's leadership and demonstrated that the political reliability and revolutionary character of the PLA had been restored.

The army high command was clearly satisfied with the results of these efforts. In his report to the "all-army political work conference,"

[57] See, for example, Peking Radio Domestic Service, July 25, 1963.

[58] See, for example, "Promote the PLA's Traditional Practice of Respecting Cadres and Loving Enlisted Men," JMJP, July 20, 1961, in SCMP, No. 2551 (August 3, 1961), pp. 1–2.

[59] See, for example, "Anti-Chemical Warfare Company in Canton Trains Successors in Hard and Meticulous Way," JMJP, July 12, 1964, in SCMP, No. 3268 (July 29, 1964), pp. 13–16. "Boldly Promote Really Good Commanders and Fighters to Key Posts of Responsibility," CFCP, editorial, April 19, 1966; Peking Radio Domestic Service, April 19, 1966.

[60] For documentation, see Joffe, Party and Army, pp. 140–41.

[61] Ibid., p. 141.

[62] Ibid., pp. 142–44. Cf. Gittings, Role of the Chinese Army, pp. 250–51.

[63] A draft was apparently drawn up in 1954, but there was no follow-up, presumably because of opposition in the officer corps.

Hsiao Hua, then deputy director of the General Political Department, summed up the PLA's political activities in 1963:

> The work was accomplished with more substantial and concrete results and in a progressive and creative manner, thereby achieving more remarkable successes than in 1962. . . . It can be said that 1963 was a year of a bumper harvest for the movement to create "four good" companies and a year in which political and ideological work, military work, logistic work, and other tasks were carried out more vigorously.[64]

Mao concurred in this assessment. "After Comrade Lin Piao put forward the four firsts and the 3-8 style of work," he said, "the Liberation Army's political-ideological and military work has progressed more significantly than before and has attained a higher concrete as well as theoretical level." [65] As a result, Mao evidently decided that the PLA could begin to play an important political role. In retrospect, it appears that he also began to view Lin as a likely successor, for Lin was turning out to be the most faithful curator of the revolutionary values of which Mao was the creator.

## THE ARMY IN POLITICS

By 1963 the two trends which brought the army into the political arena began to coalesce. On the one hand, Mao's attempts to return China to a revolutionary path started to run into difficulties, which were rooted primarily in the unresponsiveness of the Party apparatus to his demands. On the other hand, the PLA had proved itself to be highly responsive to these demands, and it was implementing the very principles which the Party and other segments of society were not. As a result, Mao began to look upon the army, rather than the Party, as the most revolutionary organization on the national scene and to use it for political purposes.

At the outset, the political role of the PLA was limited in scope and purpose: the Maoists used the army not to replace the Party, and certainly not against it, but to reinvigorate it and other organizations with revolutionary *élan*. The Party bureaucracy, however, refused to be reinvigorated, and in response, Mao intensified the pressure by broadening the role of the army.

The point of departure for the army's move into national politics

---

[64] *JMJP,* January 22, 1964, in *SCMP,* No. 3154 (February 5, 1964), p. 3.

[65] "The Basic Divergence Between the Proletarian Military Line and the Bourgeois Military Line," *JMJP,* September 7, 1967, in *SCMP,* No. 4028 (September 26, 1967), p. 4.

was the setting up of PLA heroes and exemplary units as models for emulation in the context of the socialist education campaign. The first and most famous of these heroes was the young soldier Lei Feng, who was posthumously extolled as having embodied all the revolutionary virtues which Mao wanted to propagate throughout Chinese society: struggle, sacrifice, selflessness, and simplicity. In early 1963, a massive army campaign to "learn from Lei Feng" was extended to the entire nation. Organizations throughout the country were exhorted to follow Lei's example.[66] The essence of this example was total dedication to the cause of the revolution at the expense of personal ambitions and comfort. For example, addressing commercial workers who were dissatisfied with their jobs, the Vice-Minister of Commerce wrote:

From the deeds of Lei Feng . . . we can clearly discern that whether a person has future prospects or not is determined not by the department in which he works or the kind of work he carries out, but whether he puts the interests of the Party and the people above all, by whether he has the aspiration and resolution to serve the people, and by whether he tackles commonplace work with a creative spirit and self-forgetting labor.[67]

The campaign to "learn from Lei Feng" quickly merged into a new one, the campaign to emulate the "Good Eighth Company of Nanking Road." [68] In effect, this exemplary company manifested collectively the same revolutionary qualities which Lei did as an individual. "Their concern is not individual interests at the present moment, but the long-range interests of the people. Moreover, what they are after is not material enjoyment, but a lofty spirit." [69] Like Lei, the soldiers of this company were "hard-working and frugal, self-denying, and loyal to duty. . . ." [70]

An added feature which distinguished this company was its ability to preserve its revolutionary character despite the manifold temptations and corrupting influences of downtown Shanghai, where it was

[66] See, for example, "Carry Forward and Spread Lei Feng's Ordinary But Great Revolutionary Spirit—Campaign to Learn From Lei Feng Intensifies in the Country," *JMJP*, March 16, 1963, in *SCMP*, No. 2952, pp. 2–4.

[67] "Be a Lei Feng-Type Commercial Fighter," *TKP*, July 1, 1963, in *SCMP*, No. 3026, p. 9.

[68] See, for example, "Learn the Political Thinking and Work Experiences of the Good Eighth Company," *KJJP*, editorial, May 11, 1963, in *SCMP*, No. 2991, pp. 19–21.

[69] "Maintain By All Means the Work Style of Fighting Amid Hardship," *CKCN*, editorial, March 30, 1963, in *SCMP*, No. 2965 (April 24, 1963), p. 10.

[70] "An Introduction to the Experience of Political-Ideological Work of the Good Eighth Company of Nanking Road," *KJJP*, May 10, 1963, in *SCMP*, No. 2991 (June 4, 1963), p. 1.

stationed. The soldiers of this company, it was emphasized, had "always . . . guarded against complacency, and maintained and developed the highly valued revolutionary qualities and fine working style of our army" despite the fact that "they not only live in an ordinary peaceful environment but in a . . . big city . . . [where] the reactionary influence of imperialism [and] the ugly and rotten mode of living of the bourgeoisie have remained over a long period. . . ." [71] This, in microcosm, was the problem facing Mao and his supporters: how to perpetuate revolutionary qualities under the eroding conditions of the post-revolutionary era. The army, in Mao's view, succeeded in doing this, and now it was set up as a model for the entire nation.

To this end, a major nationwide campaign to "learn from the PLA," which was begun on a piecemeal basis in 1963, was formally launched on February 1, 1964. [72] For the miltary leadership, this campaign was the payoff for the efforts that had been undertaken during the previous four years. The PLA had come a long way since 1959. Its achievements were praised profusely, and its prestige skyrocketed. Not since the days of Yenan had the army enjoyed such respect, and as in Yenan, it was now called upon to play a role that went far beyond its military functions.

With the launching of the campaign, the entire propaganda apparatus moved into action to publicize the political-ideological achievements of the PLA, and to urge other segments of society to follow in its wake. [73] Only in this way, it was said, could the revolutionary character of Chinese society be maintained: "Facts prove that wherever the method of the PLA is followed . . . revolutionary political work is established, and the Party's leadership is fully realized, true mass movements appear . . . and the leaders and the masses show great revolutionary spirit, not bureaucratism or concern with 'material incentives.' " [74] The purpose of learning from the PLA in every organization, therefore, was "to turn all employees and workers . . . into a revolutionary modern army so that they may prevent the inroad of bourgeois ideas and the influence of modern revisionism, be

---

[71] "K'o Ch'ing-shih's Speech on Good Eighth Company," Peking Radio Domestic Service, May 7, 1963.

[72] "The Whole Country Must Learn From the PLA," *JMJP*, editorial, February 1, 1964, in *CB*, No. 732 (May 12, 1964), pp. 1–7.

[73] See, for example, the collection of articles in *CB*, No. 732 (May 12, 1964). See also Ralph L. Powell, "Commission in the Economy: 'Learn From the PLA,' " *Asian Survey*, V (March, 1965), 125–38; Gittings, *Role of the Chinese Army*, pp. 254–58.

[74] *Political Work: The Lifeline of All Work* (Peking: Foreign Languages Press, 1966), p. 29. This pamphlet consists of a series of articles by Commentator published in *Hung-ch'i* in 1964.

completely revolutionary, and willing to carry out the revolution to the end. . . ." [75]

The most significant feature of the "learn from the army" campaign was its organizational innovations. The leadership did not limit the campaign to publicizing the political techniques of the PLA; it moved to establish a new political apparatus in government and economic organs that was modeled directly on the political control system of the PLA. The purpose of this new apparatus was to ensure that the techniques which the leadership was propagating would be implemented in practice, for by now it must have become apparent that it was precisely in this area that the Party and other organizations were dragging their feet.

The first step was the establishment of political departments for areas such as finance, trade, industry, and transportation, within the Central Committee. These departments, in turn, established political departments within ministries and other organs under their supervision. By June, more than twenty government ministries and bureaus were reported to have established political departments. Subsequently, these departments were extended to provincial and lower levels. [76]

The PLA did not merely provide the model for this political network; army personnel took an active part in setting it up and in running it. For this purpose, political officers were brought in from the PLA to train local cadres in political techniques and to supervise political operations. At the same time, cadres from various organizations were sent to the PLA for training. Although exact figures are unavailable, fragmentary reports give some idea of the scope of the army's infusion into other organizations. For example, it was reported that 32 per cent of the political cadres in the political departments for finance and trade in Heilungkiang and about 40 per cent in Honan were demobilized army men. [77] From Honan it was also reported that in the second half of 1964 fifty leading cadres at the provincial level

[75] "Industry Political Conference Ends," Peking Radio Domestic Service, April 3, 1964.

[76] "Finance and Trade Agencies Set Up Political Departments," *JMJP*, June 7, 1964, in *SCMP*, No. 3249 (June 30, 1964), p. 3. See also reports by Peking Radio Domestic Service, April 3, 1964, and Sinining Radio Domestic Service, May 7, 1964. Cf. Gittings, *Role of the Chinese Army*, pp. 256–57; Powell, "Commissars in the Economy," pp. 130–35.

[77] "Political Work Organs in Finance and Trade Universally Established in Heilungkiang," *TKP*, June 16, 1965, in *SCMP*, No. 3495 (July 13, 1965), p. 6. "Political Work Organs Universally Established in Honan," *TKP*, June 16, 1965, in *SCMP*, No. 3495, p. 7.

were sent to the academy of the PLA for training.[78] Although this infusion of army cadres into other organizations was designed to supplement the Party rather than to supplant it, the rebuke to the Party was clear: it meant that in the view of the Maoist leadership, the Party by itself was incapable of doing the job.

Despite the initial enthusiasm which supposedly greeted the campaign to "learn from the army," it soon became apparent that the new political apparatus was also incapable of doing the job properly. The reason was that it ran into opposition within the departments which it was supposed to revitalize. This opposition was grounded in the notion that the political techniques employed in the army were inapplicable to other organizations. As *Hung-ch'i* (Red Flag) explained it:

Some people think it is understandable that politics take precedence over military affairs, and that military struggle is a means of fulfilling political tasks, because war is "the continuation of politics by other means;" but, they say, after the proletariat has seized political power, politics cannot take first place over economics, because the main task then is economic construction, and, thus, politics must serve the existing economic base. According to these people, therefore, economics should command politics, and not vice-versa.[79]

Because of this resistance, the campaign to "learn from the PLA" could not achieve meaningful results. In the financial and trade departments, for example, the situation more than a year after the launching of the campaign was scarcely encouraging from Mao's point of view:

The foundation for political work has not been properly laid, prominence has not yet been given to politics, the four firsts have not yet been fully implemented, and political work has yet to be placed in the first position. . . . Some units have not yet established political work organs . . . some have not yet been perfected. Particularly in some areas political departments for finance and trade at the *hsien* level have not yet been established, and even fewer political instructors for basic-level enterprises have been assigned. . . .[80]

Thus, it is clear that from Mao's viewpoint the effort to shake up the Party and other segments of society by inculcating them with the

[78] See "Political Work Organs Universally Established." For more details, see Stephen A. Sims, "The New Role of the Military," *Problems of Communism*, XVIII, No. 6 (November–December, 1969), p. 30.

[79] *Political Work*, p. 20.

[80] "Quickly Set Up Political Work Organs in Financial and Trade Departments," *TKP*, June 16, 1965, in *SCMP*, No. 3495 (July 13, 1965), p. 8.

ethos of the PLA and by infusing them with its cadres was, on the whole, unsatisfactory. Stymied in this, as well as other relatively mild attempts to push through his policies, Mao came to the conclusion that far more drastic measures were required. In September, 1965, he began an assault on the power centers of opposition in the Party, sparking a subterranean struggle which several months later exploded in the Cultural Revolution. In this struggle Mao relied squarely on the military leadership for support. Before this, however, it was necessary to eliminate opposition within the army itself, which began to manifest itself during this period.

## POLITICS IN THE ARMY

The nature of this opposition in the PLA and the reason for its emergence at this time can be understood only against the background of the developments within the army under Lin Piao's leadership. The political-ideological efforts which enabled Lin to raise the PLA to such a high revolutionary stature, and which accounted for its move into politics, were only one side of his success. Although it was this side that was most striking, it would be grossly misleading to stop at this point and to assume that Lin managed to turn the PLA into a model of revolutionary virtues simply by feverishly pushing the principle of "politics in command" and by cowing the professional officers into submission. While it is undoubtedly possible to intimidate these officers to some extent, experience has shown that it is impossible to neglect purely military considerations, and to disregard their views, without arousing vocal opposition among the officers. This is due to the character of the Chinese professional officer corps. Its members, it should be stressed, are, by and large, dedicated and loyal Party members who are basically committed to Party leadership and ideology. While their primary orientation has been toward the effective performance of their specialized tasks, they are evidently prepared to accept the "primacy of politics" up to the point where this does not conflict sharply with their sense of professional competence. Once the Party passes this point, as it did with gathering momentum in the 1956–59 period, the stage is set for dissent and conflict. The absence of such conflict from the time of Lin's acceptance of command until the beginning of 1965 indicates that along with his massive political efforts Lin did not disregard the views and requirements of the professional officers.

This is not readily apparent in the Party's statements on military affairs, because the subject of such statements is generally political and because they invariably highlight the supremacy of political over military factors. Nevertheless, although the leadership's pronouncements made no concessions in principle to the professional viewpoints, isolated phrases in such pronouncements suggest that these viewpoints were taken into account. For example, in his first major statement upon assuming command, Lin rejected the views of those officers who wanted to subordinate political to military considerations, but he did not belittle the importance of technology: ". . . we believe that while equipment and technique are important, the human factor is even more so. . . . Men and material must form a unity with men as the leading factor." [81] Addressing a militia conference shortly thereafter, Lin reaffirmed the primary importance of the "human element," but continued: "We must also recognize the important role technology plays in war. We must therefore lose no time in vigorously improving the technical equipment of our forces and in strengthening the modernization of our forces." [82] On other occasions, he stressed the importance of military training,[83] the need for combining "revolutionary enthusiasm with the scientific spirit," and the necessity for maintaining a balance between "democracy" and discipline.[84]

Other military leaders spoke in a similar vein. For example, one of them wrote in 1960 that "stressing the role of man does not at all signify that the role of weapons is no longer important. . . . It is military conservatism to close one's eyes to the development of military techniques or to attach no importance to the role of modern weapons. Conservatism will only make the technical equipment of the army backward. . . ." [85] In his important speeches to the "all-army political work conferences" in 1963 and 1964, Hsiao Hua, who was then deputy director of the General Political Department, said that "political work must ensure the strict enforcement of all war preparation systems," [86] and "political work must guarantee fulfilment of the mission in military training" [87]—formulas which later became heresy.

The most striking statement on this score was contained in an article

[81] Lin, *March Ahead*, p. 17.

[82] NCNA, Peking, April 27, 1960, in *SCMP*, No. 2252 (May 6, 1960), p. 17.

[83] See, for example, *Kung-tso T'ung-hsün* (Bulletin of Activities), No. 1 (January 1, 1960), pp. 9–10.

[84] "Seriously Study and Improve Work Methods," *CFCP*, reprinted in *JMJP*, February 3, 1962, in *SCMP*, No. 2682 (February 20, 1962), pp. 1, 6.

[85] Cited in Gittings, *Role of the Chinese Army*, p. 243.

[86] Hsiao, "Basic Experiences," p. 5.

[87] Hsiao Hua, "Several Questions on the Present Political Work in the Armed Forces," *JMJP*, January 22, 1964, in *SCMP*, No. 3154 (February 5, 1964), p. 12.

published in *Jen-min Jih-pao* (People's Daily) on May 15, 1962. After stressing the importance of strengthening the basic-level units in the armed forces, the author went on to say:

Military training is the army's central task of a routine character in peacetime. . . . It is . . . the most practical and most effective preparation for war. We emphasize the importance of politics assuming command and ideology leading the way, but this definitely does not negate the importance of military strategy and tactics. . . . Apart from possessing a high degree of political consciousness and steadfast will to fight, the whole body of officers and men must expertly master the technique of wiping out the enemy on the battle-field. If military techniques are stressed one-sidedly to the neglect of ideological-political work, the sense of direction will be lost. Conversely, if politics are emphasized in isolation to the neglect of strict military training, the army will be unable to fulfil its own mission. Hence the need to combine politics with military affairs and redness with expertness. . . . In particular the navy, the air force, and units of the special arms have to study assiduously and train intensively before they can handle the complicated technical equipment. . . . Political fervor for military training must be stimulated among the broad masses of officers and men so that they will study diligently, train arduously, and improve their skill constantly. . . .[88]

But the most convincing evidence that professional requirements were not neglected by the high command lies not in what it preached but rather in what it practiced. Some of its most important practices have undoubtedly been in line with the views of the professional officers. First, despite the continuing stress on the doctrine of "people's war," and on the superiority of "man-over-weapons," the leadership has spared no effort to achieve an operational nuclear capability.[89] Second, the conventional military establishment has also been selectively strengthened.[90] Third, the emphasis on the importance of military training found practical expression in the ratio of time that was allocated for military training in relation to political education: 60 to 40 per cent in the regular units, and 70 to 30 per cent in the specialized units.[91] Fourth, the terms of service in the PLA have been extended, evidently in response to the need for specialized personnel.[92] Fifth, the "officers to the ranks" movement has been curtailed and has undergone

---

[88] T'ang P'ing-chu, "On the Basic-Level Construction of the Armed Forces," *JMJP*, May 15, 1962, in *SCMP*, No. 2753 (June 6, 1962), pp. 4–5.

[89] This is evidenced by China's nuclear tests and efforts to develop a missile delivery system.

[90] See, for example, Joffe, *Party and Army*, p. 158.

[91] *Kung-tso T'ung-hsün*, No. 1 (January 1, 1961), p. 10.

[92] Peking Radio Domestic Service, January 29, 1965.

a subtle but significant shift which has undoubtedly made it more acceptable to the officers.[93] Sixth, until 1965 the officers remained largely unaffected by the political and ideological campaigns. Seventh, the militia was rebuilt cautiously and on a limited basis, and in contrast with the 1958–59 period, it was not put on a par with the PLA.[94] Last, despite the lip service paid to the role of the army in nonmilitary activities, these activities declined dramatically every year since 1960: in 1960, the army devoted forty-seven million manpower days to nonmilitary activities; [95] in 1961, twenty-three million; [96] in 1962, at most eight million; [97] in 1963, eight and one-half million; [98] and in 1964, five million.[99]

Lin Piao, in short, managed to raise the political and ideological standards of the PLA in a way which, until 1965, ensured the acquiescence, if not the approval, of the professional officers. His achievement was not simply to make the army "red," for an army exclusively "red" would be rent with dissent, and this would make his achievement hollow; Lin's foremost accomplishment, therefore, and the key to his success was his ability to maintain a delicate balance between "redness" and "expertness," between political and professional requirements. Thus, in contrast with the years 1956–59, when political demands were pushed to what the officers considered senseless and harmful extremes, from 1960 to 1965 the principle of "politics in command" was kept within perimeters that were acceptable to the professional officers. In 1965 these perimeters were overstepped, and the precarious equilibrium between politics and professionalism was upset.

The main reason for this was the Vietnam War. As the war escalated with the initiation of the bombing of North Vietnam by the

---

[93] See Joffe, *Party and Army*, p. 137.

[94] *CFCP*, editorial, January 1, 1966, Peking Radio Domestic Service of same date. Liu Yun-cheng, "The Role of the People's Militia," *Peking Review*, No. 6 (February 5, 1965), p. 20. Cf. Gittings, *Role of the Chinese Army*, pp. 215–24.

[95] "Chinese Armymen Active in Production Work," NCNA-English, January 27, 1961, in *SCMP*, No. 2430 (February 2, 1961), p. 2.

[96] "PLA Renders Great Help to Agricultural Production," NCNA, Peking, February 3, 1964, in *SCMP*, No. 2682 (February 20, 1962), p. 17.

[97] The total figure for the year could not be found, but the Chinese reported that in the first seven months of the year the PLA had contributed two million work days to production work (NCNA-English, July 29, 1962). Even if the bulk of the work was done in the second half of the year, it probably did not amount to more than three times the amount of the first half. Hence, the total figure would not be more than eight million.

[98] Peking Radio Domestic Service, January 30, 1964.

[99] "Chinese Army Carries on Good Work Tradition," NCNA-English, January 30, 1965, in *SCMP*, No. 3391 (February 5, 1965), p. 7.

United States in February, 1965, the Chinese began to consider seriously the possibility that a war might break out between China and the United States. As a result, questions of military strategy and policy, which until now had been submerged, suddenly shot to the surface with a new urgency and had to be settled. In the course of this reassessment, a conflict broke out at the highest level of leadership over contingency plans for a possible war with the United States. The Maoist leadership advocated a low-risk, purely defensive, go-it-alone policy based on the strategy of the "people's war" to meet the American threat. Some professional officers, however, opposed this policy and urged a more conventional strategy, more emphasis on military rather than political preparedness, and some sort of reconciliation with the Soviet Union, presumably in the hope of obtaining the military equipment which such a strategy required. The main spokesman for the opposition was Chief-of-Staff Lo Jui-ch'ing. Lo had been brought in from the public security system in 1959 to eradicate professional viewpoints, but in the course of carrying out his duties he evidently had become converted to these very viewpoints.[100]

Exacerbating this conflict was friction which stemmed from an internal source. In view of the continued emphasis on politics in the PLA, which increased with the broadening of the army's political role, some professional elements headed by Lo apparently concluded by early 1964 that it was necessary to redress the balance between politics and professionalism and to devote more attention to military affairs. To this end, Lo initiated "military competitions," [101] which stressed military skills and achievements—and for which he was later accused of downplaying the importance of politics. Lin, however, took a dim view of these activities, because they reportedly led to the so-called "prominence at two ends" phenomenon,[102] which meant that many units improved their military capabilities at the expense of political

---

[100] For details and interpretations see Donald S. Zagoria, *Vietnam Triangle: Moscow, Peking, Hanoi* (New York: Pegasus, 1967), chap. iii; Alice Langley Hsieh, *Communist China's Military Policies, Doctrine, and Strategy: A Lecture Presented at the National Defense College, Tokyo, September 17, 1968* (Santa Monica, Calif.: The RAND Corporation, October, 1968), pp. 21–39; Uri Ra'anan, "Peking's Foreign Policy 'Debate,' 1965–1966," in Tang Tsou (ed.), *China in Crisis, Vol. 2: China's Policies in Asia and America's Alternatives* (Chicago: University of Chicago Press, 1968), pp. 23–71.

[101] "Big Military Competition Is Big Exposure of Lo Jui-ch'ing's Plot to Usurp Army Leadership and Oppose the Party," *JMJP*, August 28, 1967, in *SCMP*, No. 4022 (September 15, 1967), pp. 1–6. See also, "The Basic Divergence," pp. 4–5.

[102] See, for example, "Acquiring 'Advanced' Techniques Ruins the Foundation," *CFCP*, May 20, 1966, reprinted in *JMJP*, May 21, 1966, in *SCMP*, No. 3708 (May 31, 1966), pp. 4–6. "Is It True of 'Prominence at Two Ends,' One Is Good and the Other Bad?" in *ibid.*, pp. 2–4.

standards. In order to remedy this, at the end of 1964 Lin Piao issued a new directive on "giving prominence to politics."[103]

This directive led to a step-up of political pressures in the PLA, which was clearly reflected in the press. For example, on March 17, 1965, the *Chieh-fang Chün-pao* (Liberation Army Daily) stressed that "it is essential to develop in the whole PLA a new upsurge in the study of Chairman Mao's works. . . ."[104] On July 1, the Canton *Yang-ch'eng Wan-pao* reported that "in accordance with Comrade Lin Piao's directive urging primary attention to politics and intensive study of Chairman Mao's works, the PLA units of Canton since the beginning of this year have whipped an upsurge of a more gigantic and extensive campaign for the study of Chairman Mao's works."[105] On October 13, the army newspaper said that "especially since the placing of emphasis on politics as a leading factor this year, the large-scale effort made by our PLA in tackling living ideas with Mao Tse-tung's thinking as a guide has resulted in political-ideological work becoming more dynamic and brisk . . . more elaborate and practical."[106] And the whole drive was given a new impetus in November, 1965, with the publication of a five-point directive by Lin, the first point of which called on the PLA "to step up even more extensively the study of Chairman Mao's works."[107]

The distinctive feature of this drive was that it was directed not only at the basic level units, but also, if not especially, at high-ranking officers. These officers, as has been noted, had been largely untouched by the political campaigns of the previous years, but now they came under increasing fire for becoming mellow on Maoism. For this reason, "the requirement to study Chairman Mao's works, obey Chairman Mao, follow his instructions, and become his good soldiers is applicable not only to the fighters and basic-level cadres, but even more so to cadres at higher levels. If we are to devote our whole lives to revolu-

[103] See, for example, "Giving Prominence to Politics Is the Foundation For Building Our Army," *CFCP*, editorial, June 11, 1965, in *SCMP*, No. 3487 (June 29, 1965), p. 1.

[104] "Develop More Enthusiastically and Comprehensively the New Upsurge in the Study of Chairman Mao's Works," *CFCP*, editorial, March 17, 1965; Peking Radio Domestic Service, March 17, 1965.

[105] "PLA Units of Canton Achieve Greater Success in Studying Chairman Mao's Works—Leading Cadres Take the Lead in 'Flexible Study and Flexible Application,'" *Yang-ch'eng Wan-pao*, July 1, 1965, in *SCMP*, No. 3507 (July 29, 1965), p. 1.

[106] "Living Ideology Must Be Mastered in Giving Prominence to Politics," *CFCP*, editorial, October 13, 1965, in *SCMP*, No. 3567 (October 28, 1965), p. 1.

[107] See, for example, "Resolutely Carry Out the Five-Point Instruction Given By Comrade Lin Piao, Give Prominence to Politics in an Even More Proper Way, Put the 'Four Good' on a Solid Basis, and Strengthen Combat Readiness," *CFCP*, editorial, November 18, 1965; Peking Radio Domestic Service, November 17, 1965.

tion, we must spend our whole lives studying Chairman Mao's works and reforming our ideology." [108]

This reform of the officers' ideology was one of the major aims of the new effort. "The Party committees of various units," said one report, "are now concentrating their efforts on the study of Mao Tse-tung's works by leading cadres. . . ." [109] According to another report, "leading PLA cadres at and above the army level attained greater results in the creative study and application of Mao Tse-tung's works since the last quarter of 1965 . . . [and] have generally launched a study and rectification campaign." [110] During one such campaign, "many comrades deeply realized that in these past years their improvement had been faster where their work was concerned but their level of mastery of the thought of Mao Tse-tung rose only slowly. They also realized that the longer they remained in circumstances of comparative peace, the weaker would be their idea of class struggle. . . ." [111] In order to remind the officers of this and other egalitarian ideas, the leadership took a major step against professionalism in June, 1965, by abolishing ranks in the PLA.[112]

Thus, the extreme politization of the army at a time when the possibility of a major war was imminent aroused dissent among officers who opposed the "people's war" strategy which could justify such politization. In response, the leadership intensified political pressures, and this, in turn, generated counterpressures in the officer corps. As a result, the "red" and "expert" balance, which had been maintained since Lin's assumption of command, was upset, and a renewed debate over priorities broke out.

The central issue in this debate, which was linked inextricably with the disagreements over strategy, was the relative importance of political and professional tasks. The officers did not deny the need for political work, but they argued that since the principal aim of the army is to maintain its combat capability, political work should be geared to the achievement of this goal. For example, as *Chieh-fang Chün-pao* put it:

108 "Political Work Conference of PLA Appeals to the Whole Army to Hold Higher the Great Red Banner of the Thought of Mao Tse-tung," *JMJP*, January 19, 1966, in *SCMP*, No. 3627 (January 31, 1966), p. 3.

109 Peking Radio Domestic Service, March 18, 1965.

110 *Ibid.*, February 19, 1966.

111 "Leading Cadres of a Certain Unit of Canton Armed Forces Persevere in Ideological Reform, Resolve to Engage in Revolution With Fervor to the End For the Rest of Their Lives," *Yang-ch'eng Wan-pao*, February 20, 1966, in *SCMP*, No. 3650 (March 4, 1966), p. 7.

112 NCNA-English, Peking, May 24, 1965.

Some comrades admit that political work is necessary, but they treat political work as the equivalent of a political and technical guarantee—merely as work for guaranteeing the fulfillment of concrete jobs. They only hope that political work will be done around concrete jobs and confined to such things as mobilization for the fulfillment of a task. . . .[113]

This view was unacceptable to the leadership, who maintained that political work certainly has to ensure the fulfillment of military tasks, but its importance goes way beyond that; political work is of intrinsic and supreme significance in itself. In the words of the army newspaper:

Guaranteeing the fulfillment of jobs is an important aspect of political work. But political work has a more important aspect in that it must guarantee the absolute leadership of the Party over the army, persist in Marxism-Leninism and the thought of Mao Tse-tung, oppose modern revisionism and bourgeois thinking of various shades, and guarantee the extreme proletarianization . . . of our army. In other words, political work must not merely function as a guarantee for other work and jobs; it must exercise the commanding and leading function. . . .[114]

The debate continued to gather momentum until September, 1965, when the publication of Lin's tract, "Long Live the Victory of the People's War," [115] signaled that the views of Lo Jui-ch'ing and his supporters had been conclusively rejected. Some time after November, Lo was removed from his post,[116] and the leadership carried out a mopping-up operation to crack down on those officers who had shared his views.[117] With the elimination of the opposition in the PLA, the

---

[113] "Giving Prominence to Politics," pp. 2–3.

[114] *Ibid.*

[115] Lin Piao, *Long Live the Victory of the People's War* (Peking: Foreign Languages Press, 1966).

[116] There was probably more to the ouster of Lo than policy differences with the Mao-Lin leadership. Numerous articles both in the official press and in Red Guard publications have referred to an anti-Party conspiracy consisting of P'eng Chen, Lo Jui-ch'ing, Lu Ting-i, and Yang Shang-k'un. (See, for example, "The Basic Divergence," p. 2.) Mao himself said in October, 1966, that these four men were "engaged in secret activities which would come to no good." ("Speech at a Report Meeting," in *Long Live Mao Tse-tung's Thought,* a Red Guard pamphlet consisting of speeches reportedly made by Mao, in *CB,* No. 891 [October 8, 1969], p. 72.) Although none of these accusations have furnished any plausible details, they have been made often enough to suggest that there was something behind them. One possible link between these four men was that they were all top-ranking officials in the Party Secretariat, and perhaps in this capacity they were up to something. Precisely what, is a tantalizing question which cannot be answered without more documentation.

[117] See, for example, seven editorials in *CFCP* (no date) transmitted by Radio Peking Domestic Service on February 4, 1966, February 1, 1966, February 14, 1966, February 18, 1966, March 2, 1966, March 23, 1966, and April 5, 1966.

way was cleared for Mao to launch his assault on the Party with the backing of the military leadership. China's Cultural Revolution had begun.[118]

[118] The research from this article was done while I was a research fellow at Harvard University's East Asian Research Center, to which I want to express my gratitude.

# PART V

## China and Comparative Politics

GABRIEL A. ALMOND

# Some Thoughts on
# Chinese Political Studies

I must confess to diffidence in presenting a concluding comment for this volume on governmental aspects of modern China. To an outsider, the size of the country and its population, the difficulty of its language, the antiquity and complexity of its culture, the many strata of its history, and the esoteric aura which surrounds its scholarship, all warn against the amateur intellectual foray, the quick "in and out" approach of the political theorist. What encourages me to add a word is that the wall of Chinese scholarship seems to be in process of being breached from within by an energetic group of Chinese specialists themselves, and this despite the bitter comment of Richard Wilson regarding the continued "qualitative isolation and intellectual barrenness of much of the work in Chinese studies." [1]

Let me orient my comments around two themes: first, the prospects of Chinese political studies, and second, the prospects of Chinese politics. From the point of view of comparative area studies I would have to say that China studies and particularly Chinese political studies are in process of an important move forward in theoretical and methodological sophistication. The most cursory examination of the chapters included in this volume as well as of a growing part of the research and writing on China demonstrate this to be the case. There are strong indications of the importation into the study of Chinese politics of conceptual tools, comparative perspectives, and methodological techniques that have been developed in other branches of poli-

[1] Richard W. Wilson, "Chinese Studies in Crisis," *World Politics,* XXIII, No. 2 (January, 1971), 297.

tical studies, and broadly in the social and behavioral sciences. This penetration is particularly striking to someone, like myself, whose last look at Chinese political studies was taken at a time when the scholarly community concerned with the subject was small, esoteric, ideologically polarized, and, on the whole, conservative. A younger generation of innovative and intellectually aggressive China specialists has taken to the field, and the consequences are evident in many of the pieces included in this volume, and in other recent studies. These achievements are taking place despite the extraordinary difficulties in carrying on research about China. I would suggest that the field of China scholarship is in a position to reap the benefits, and encounter the difficulties, of the "late developer," exploiting the work that has already been done in other areas and in the social sciences as a whole, but having first to adapt these concepts and analytical tools to the Chinese context, and having to work with a thin contemporary data base.

One insurmountable difficulty with China studies, at least in the near future, is the inaccessibility of the country to direct research, and the dependence of our scholarship on newspaper material, radio broadcasts, refugee interviews, and studies of non-mainland Chinese populations. Access to adequate and reliable aggregate data, sample surveys, elite interviews, observational studies are denied us. Thus we may expect improvement only if the knowledge we have or can acquire is more effectively utilized, as a result of the kinds of questions we ask and the kinds of perspectives and analytical tools we can bring to bear.

I have a few comments to offer by way of counsel here. I offer them with hesitation since I have some sense of the problems confronted in China research, the pressures to which the field is subject, and my own vast ignorance. An expert on China these days is very much in the spotlight, very subject to demands for "instant" interpretations. Yet he is not as badly off as were his Russian colleagues back in the 1950s when they had to operate under the intense pressures of the Cold War and McCarthyism. I am not sure how the China specialists experience political pressure these days. The risks of honestly confronting issues concerning China and the prospects of Communist China seem to me to be a good deal lower than was the case for the Russian scholars two decades ago when Russian studies were at about the equivalent stage of development.

In any event there is a serious need to avoid a too-narrow China-watching perspective. The pressures on China scholars to be sucked into the draft of government intelligence operations on the one hand, or publicist-type writing on the other, must be substantial. There may be too much stress on the interpretation of the most recent events, and there may be too much anxiety about sticking one's neck out.

In the course of the past ten or fifteen years a number of theories and hypotheses have been generated out of efforts to explain and predict the course of development in the Third World. Other concepts and analytic approaches are being explored as a result of the current interest in studies of comparative communism. Still other ideas that have emerged in the course of work on American politics have a possible application to the interpretation of the developments in China. A systematic effort at confronting Chinese politics and society by means of these concepts and hypotheses may increase our capacity to interpret the meager data we have.

Some fifteen years ago Barrington Moore, in an imaginative interpretation of conflicting policy tendencies in the Soviet Union, wrote of the "technical-rational," the "traditionalistic," and the ideological-revolutionary currents which were in conflict with one another.[2] He laid out a series of scenarios speculating as to which combination of these three elements was likely to be brought to the fore as a consequence of differing conditions in the international environment of the Soviet Union. In Moore's definition the sector of the Soviet elite characterized by the "technical-rational" tendency would stress organization, institutionalization, and investment to increase the level of economic productivity, and would favor a primarily defensive national security. By "traditionalism" Moore referred to the impulses among the Soviet elite that tended in the direction of reducing risks, and safeguarding and enhancing the existing stratification system in the Soviet Union. The ideological revolutionary current, in the nature of the case, tended in the direction of continued internal mobilization, "ideological purification," and external expansion.

Students of Chinese politics may find this rather simple threefold scheme of some use in the analysis of political trends in contemporary China. It has the advantage over Huntington's [3] institutionalization-mobilization hypothesis of specifying the two forms which institutionalization takes in a modernizing nation. The first tends toward the protection of class and other "sectional interests," either the newer industrial interests, or the persisting interests of peasantry, ethnic-

---

[2] Barrington Moore, Jr., *Terror and Progress USSR: Some Sources of Change and Stability in the Soviet Dictatorship* (Cambridge, Mass.: Harvard University Press, 1954).

[3] Samuel P. Huntington, *Political Order in Changing Societies* (New Haven, Conn.: Yale University Press, 1968), pp. 78ff.

cultural groups, and the like. The second set of institutionalization tendencies are those of the technocratic elites, each one of which presses resource allocation in the direction of its specific professional-functional goals—heavy industry, light industry and consumer goods, national security, and the like.

The burden of Huntington's thesis is that there must be a symmetry between processes of mobilization and processes of organization and institutionalization, if the modernizing system is to develop increasing capacity and stability. The more rapid the mobilization, the higher the probability of instability and breakdown, or the more coercive the institutionalization must be. If mobilization exceeds institutionalization, the cohesion and performance of the system deteriorates. Both of these theories have, at first sight, a considerable amount of explanatory power.

At any rate Soviet and East European studies have long since escaped from the ideological models of the Cold War, in which the positive self-description of the European Communist systems as ideologically cohesive and goal-directed was in a moral sense turned upside down in the monolithic-totalitarian model of Western scholars. The assumption of pluralism—of factional and interest group conflict and their bases and resources—has now thoroughly penetrated studies of European communism. The threefold scheme of Moore has been succeeded by more complicated factional and interest group schemes, such as those of Fleron, Rigby, Barghoorn, and others.[4]

While the polemic on the question of the balance between monolithic and pluralistic tendencies in Soviet politics is still a lively one, it is quite evident that the students of Russian and Eastern European communism have a more confident grasp of the "dynamics" of Communist politics than do the Chinese specialists. And this is only in part due to the relative unavailability of data. While there is evidence in these and other papers of alternative models of Chinese politics, there still would seem to be a tendency to take Chinese Communist self-descriptions at their face value, overlooking structural and cultural limits of the most substantial sort.

Another theory from development literature which may be of use in

[4] Frederic J. Fleron, Jr. (ed.), *Communist Studies and the Social Sciences* (Chicago: University of Chicago Press, 1969); T. Harry Rigby, *Communist Party Membership in the USSR, 1917–1967* (Princeton, N.J.: Princeton University Press, 1967); Frederick Barghoorn, *Politics in the USSR* (Boston, Mass.: Little, Brown, 1971); Gordon Skilling and Franklin Griffiths, *Interest Groups in Soviet Politics* (Princeton, N.J.: Princeton University Press, 1971).

the interpretation of Chinese politics is the "system-development hypothesis" that has been generated out of the comparative examination of European political development. The literature dealing with the political histories of Britain, France, Germany, Italy, and other countries in Europe contains many generalizations and explanations of the different historical paths taken by these countries in the last several hundred years. Thus, historians have "explained" the intensity and violence of German and Italian nationalism in terms of the late arrival of these two countries to nationhood, and the coincidence of these efforts at nation building with the simultaneous "crises" of participation and welfare during the period of industrialization. There was an obvious contrast with the experience of such countries as Britain and France, which had attained settled borders and legitimate national identities long before the onset of the participation and welfare revolutions of the industrial period.

From the perspective of the European history of the last three or four hundred years, it appeared that all of the nations had experienced a set of common problems. Thus, in the age of absolutism, the central institutions of the emerging European states were formed, penetrating the particularistic structures and peripheries of their societies. It was quite evident that the form of this centralizing process had important consequences for the subsequent development of these nations. Thus, centralization and bureaucratization in Prussia were far more thorough-going than they were in Britain. This was presumed to explain the strikingly different experiences with democratization in Germany and Britain. The French pattern of state building differed from both the Prussian and the British patterns, and was similarly assumed to have affected French democratization patterns. A second and related problem had to do with the formation of a sense of national identity. Whether this sense of national identity occurred early or late, whether it spread gradually from upper classes through middle classes to lower classes, or exploded, so to speak, as it did in France during the French Revolution and the Napoleonic period, whether it preceded or came after the Industrial Revolution, whether it encountered or failed to encounter local, religious, or ethnic-linguistic particularism, all had serious consequences for the cohesion of these Western national societies—the structure of their party systems, the commitment to the nation, and the compliance with state authority. During the nineteenth and twentieth centuries the common problems confronting Western European political systems have been those of participation and welfare. Those countries which had more or less resolved their state and nation building problems encountered and solved their participation and welfare problems in a different manner from those nations which entered the nineteenth and twentieth centuries with their state and nation building problems still significantly unresolved.

This "system development theory" was an assertion that in contemporary political systems the relationships between central and local political organs, the homogeneity-heterogeneity of the political culture, the structure of the party and interest group systems, the characteristics of the bureaucracy, and the kinds of public policies produced by the political systems, could be explained in part by the ways in which this common set of environmental challenges had affected the political system historically—the order in which they were experienced, their magnitude and intensity, their separate or simultaneous incidence, and the ways in which elite groups responded to these challenges.[5]

The argument which I would like to advance here is that these various hypotheses and theories of political development have application to the Chinese political experience, but that they have not been thoroughly applied. The principal reason for this failure grows out of the isolation of Chinese studies, and the slow penetration of notions such as these into the study of Chinese politics.

If we apply this system development hypothesis to the Chinese case, we come up with a number of cogent questions. First, in what sense can it be said that China had or has built an effective state apparatus? Second, in what sense have the Chinese attained a sense of national identity? Third, in what way, and to what extent, can the Chinese be said to have experienced a revolution of participation, or better, with what forms of political participation have they historically and culturally been familiar? Fourth, to what extent, if any, have the masses of the Chinese population ever experienced a political and governmental system which deeply and consistently affected their welfare, either through the maintenance of order and justice, or through the provision of positive material benefits?

It is my impression that among the community of students of Chinese development some of these issues are highly controversial. A thorough analysis of Chinese historical experience might give us some

[5] These hypotheses are discussed in greater detail in Leonard Binder et al., Crises in Political Development (Princeton, N.J.: Princeton University Press, 1971), and in a number of my own writings: Gabriel A. Almond, Political Development (Boston, Mass.: Little, Brown, 1970), chap. v, vi, x; Gabriel A. Almond and G. Bingham Powell, Comparative Politics (Boston, Mass.: Little, Brown, 1966), chap. ii, xi.

more solid clues as to the kinds of political material contemporary Chinese political elites have to work with in fashioning their social and political institutions.

Thus, Max Weber and Barrington Moore [6] argue quite persuasively that the Chinese bureaucracy never effectively penetrated the peasantry, and that the sense of Chinese national identity was a rather remote affair shared predominantly by the Chinese officialdom. The burden of these arguments would seem to be that China has come into the twentieth century, and even into modern decades, without having fully developed the penetrative institutions of a regulatory state and the patterns of popular compliance associated with it, or a genuine and deep sense of popular national identity.

From another point of view, it would appear that China has never really had a thoroughgoing revolution of participation. Village and clan affairs in traditional China were dominated by Confucian standards of patriarchal order and propriety. The nationalist revolution did not develop a stable associational and political party life.[7] Finally, taking into account the recent decades under Chinese communism, it would appear that the first experience of the Chinese masses with a governmental and political system concerned with popular welfare has been in the last decades.

These basic questions having to do with Chinese historical and contemporary experience are the kinds of questions which can profitably engage the attention of historians and social theorists concerned with Chinese prospects. More confident answers to these questions should give us clear indications of the structural and cultural limitations on the immediate prospects for political and social change in China. It may be that we have gravely exaggerated the "maturity" of Chinese civilization and failed to pay sufficient attention to the comments of recent Chinese modernizers, including Sun Yat Sen, who spoke of the Chinese as resembling a "heap of loose sand." If what Barrington Moore has to say about peasant rebellions in China is correct, the analogy of sand may not be sufficiently strong; the sand was not passive but was actually alienated from the central and overt institutions of Chinese society. Answers to these questions might give us a better grasp of what seems to be taking place in the contemporary China of

[6] Max Weber, *The Religion of China,* ed. and trans. by Hans H. Gerth (Glencoe, Ill.: The Free Press, 1951); Barrington Moore, Jr., *Social Origins of Dictatorship and Democracy* (Boston, Mass.: Beacon Press, 1966), chap. iv.

[7] James R. Townsend, *Political Participation in Communist China* (Berkeley: University of California Press, 1967), chap. i.

the Great Leap Forward and the Cultural Revolution. Rather than the promise of some new "route" to a "better" form of "modernization," these vast stirrings may be the first major steps in the direction of state and nation building. How institutions of popular participation will fit into these efforts at penetration and integration, and how much popular welfare can be distributed in the course of these efforts at resource mobilization, are questions of the most problematic sort. In considering the prospects of this vast undertaking, one has to attach as much probability to the prospect of breakdown and disintegration, as one does to creative and innovative solutions to the problems of Chinese political development.

# *Index*

Agriculture: development, 159-61; farmers, number of, 195; grain production, 160-61, 163-64, 170, 174-76, 177; grain supplies, 127; gross national product, 199; National Development Program, 88; peanut crop, 127; production, effects on policy, 85
—Producers Cooperatives: administration, 206-7; Chekiang Province, disbanding, 140; development, process of, 141-44; percentage of, 167-68; reorganized into communes, 53; size and number, 203-4; work reports, 118
Albania, 54
*Anhui chiao-yü,* 271
Arendt, Hannah, 48, 49
Associations: clan, 7; *Landsmann* halls, 7, 11; membership, determination, 10-11; neighborhood, 11; orientations, total, 9; secret societies, 7, 11; voluntary and involuntary, 7, 13
August 1 School, 277
Authority: acceptance of, 45-46; belief system, 46; characteristics in 1949, 47; obedience, bases of, 48; phenomenon of, 44; revolutionary, 36, 38, 46-47; role and occupant, distinction, 45; sources, theories about, 49; traditional, 38. *See also* Government

Bandwagon psychology, 20
Bank of China, People's, 198, 328
Barghoorn, Frederick, 378

Barnett, A. Doak, 4, 305
Blau, Peter M., 44, 50
Burki, Shahid Javed, 218

Canton work conference, 89
Capability Cultivating School, 277
Capitalism, revival, 26-27
Chang, Parris H., 130
Chang An Ta Chieh avenue, 3
Chang Chung-liang, 132
Chang Fei, 96
Chang Han-fu, 308, 311, 313, 337
Chang K'ai-fan, 131
Chang T'ung, 321
Chang Wen-t'ien, 97, 337
Chang Yen, 331
Chao Chien-min, 128, 131
Chao I-min, 335
Ch'en Chia-k'ang, 308
Cheng Chu-yüan, 285-86
Chengtu conference, 85, 91
Ch'en I, 330, 331, 336, 337
Ch'en Po-ta, 90, 98, 108, 110
Ch'en Shao-yü, 308
Ch'en Tseng-ku, 280
Ch'en Yi, 93
Ch'en Yü, 134
Ch'en Yün, 60
Chiang Ch'ing, 84, 249
Chiang Hua, 128
Chiang Kai-shek, 58, 136, 306
Chiang Nan-hsiang, 288
Chiang Wei-ch'ing, 97

# CONTRIBUTORS

JOHN M. H. LINDBECK. Born in China. Until his death in January, 1971, member of the Department of Political Science and director of the East Asian Institute, Columbia University. Chairman of the Joint Committee on Contemporary China of the American Council of Learned Societies and the Social Science Research Council, 1964–70; vice president of the National Committee on United States–China Relations, 1968–70; member of the Pacific Science Board, National Academy of Sciences, 1968–70; and many other activities related to the furtherance of scholarship on China.

GABRIEL A. ALMOND. Born in the United States. Professor of Political Science, Stanford University. Author of *The American People and Foreign Policy* (1950), *The Appeals of Communism* (1965), *The Politics of Developing Areas* (1960), *Comparative Politics: A Developmental Approach* (1966), and *Political Development* (1970). President of the American Political Science Association, 1965–66.

ELLIS JOFFE. Born in China. Member of the Departments of Chinese Studies and International Relations at the Hebrew University of Jerusalem. Author of *Party and Army: Professionalism and Political Control in the Chinese Officer Corps, 1949–64* (1965).

CHALMERS JOHNSON. Born in the United States. Professor of Political Science and chairman of the Center for Chinese Studies at the University of California, Berkeley. His works include *Peasant Nationalism and Communist Power* (1962); *An Instance of Treason* (1964); *Revolutionary Change* (1966); and, as editor, *Change in Communist Systems* (1970).

DONALD W. KLEIN. Born in the United States. Research associate in the East Asian Institute, Columbia University. Coauthor of *Biographic Dictionary of Chinese Communism, 1921–1965* (1971).

VICTOR H. LI. Born in China. On the faculty of the School of Law, Columbia University. Field research in Hong Kong in 1965–66 and 1968.

DONALD J. MUNRO. Born in the United States. Member of the Department of Philosophy and associate of the Center for Chinese Studies, University of Michigan. Author of *The Concept of Man in Early China* (1969).

MICHEL C. OKSENBERG. Born in Belgium. Member of the Department of Political Science and research associate of the East Asian Institute, Columbia University. Author of *Policy Formulation in Communist China: The Case of the 1957–58 Mass Irrigation Campaign* (1969) and *China: The Convulsive Society* (1970).

LUCIAN W. PYE. Born in China. Professor of Political Science and senior staff member of the Center for International Studies, Massachusetts Institute of Technology. Author of *The Spirit of Chinese Politics* (1968), *Politics, Personality, and Nation-Building* (1962), and *Guerrilla Communism in Malaya* (1956).

PETER SCHRAN. Born in Germany. Professor of Economics and Asian Studies, University of Illinois, Urbana-Champaign. Author of *The Development of Chinese Agriculture, 1950–1959* (1969).

FREDERICK C. TEIWES. Born in the United States. Member of the Department of Government, Cornell University. Author of *Provincial Party Personnel in Mainland China, 1956–1966* (1967); and coauthor of *Ssu-ch'ing: The Socialist Education Movement of 1962–1966* (1968).